PILLARS OF MONARCHY

AN OUTLINE OF THE POLITICAL AND SOCIAL HISTORY OF ROYAL GUARDS 1400–1984

PILLARS OF MONARCHY

AN OUTLINE OF THE POLITICAL AND SOCIAL HISTORY OF ROYAL GUARDS 1400–1984

PHILIP MANSEL

QUARTET BOOKS
LONDON MELBOURNE NEW YORK

First published by Quartet Books Limited 1984
A member of the Namara Group
27/29 Goodge Street, London W1P 1FD

Copyright © 1984 by Philip Mansel

British Library Cataloguing in Publication Data
Mansel, Philip
  Pillars of monarchy.
  1. Great Britain. *Army. Household Division—History*
  I. Title
  335.3'1'0941   UA649.5

ISBN 0-7043-2424-5

Typeset by M.C. Typeset, Chatham
Printed and bound in Great Britain

CONTENTS

ACKNOWLEDGEMENTS

First I would like to thank all those who were kind and patient enough to give me interviews, whose names are listed on page 198. I would also like to thank Terence Benton, Antonia Burrows, John Cambridge, Caroline Davidson, the late Gerald de Gaury, Ghislain de Diesbach, J. Dolinski, Captain N.S. Egelien, Charles Esdaile, the late F. Frearson, Godfrey Goodwin, Donna Hole, Bill Johnson, Deniz Kiliçer, Dr C. Kuçuk, Professor Y.T. Kurat, Nicholas Lynn, Colonel Meakin, Colonel Minkiewicz, Boris Mollo, Gail Mooney, Tim Oldroyd, the staff of the Soviet Studies Research Centre, Sandhurst, and Mrs Storey for their help in the research and writing of this book. I am particularly grateful to Major Peter Hunter for his help with research. I would like to thank the British Academy for the grant which enabled me to continue the research for this book. Lastly I would like to thank the staff of the British Library, London Library, Bibliothèque Nationale and Archives Nationales, without whom this book could not have been written.

LIST OF ILLUSTRATIONS

PREFACE

GUARDS ARE A key to history. Until this century monarchies were a vital force in the lives of their subjects, and royal guards were a decisive aspect of that force. For royal guards, often regarded simply as a decorative appendage to the lives of their monarchs, were in fact the largest military force in the capitals of the monarchies of Europe and the Middle East (as they still are in London). Therefore, it was they who, in moments of crisis, often decided the fate of the monarchy.

Guards were on duty when history was being made, and they often made it themselves. According to the future Louis XI of France, who tried to bribe the Gardes Ecossais to kill his father the King, they 'kept the Kingdom of France in subjection'. Catherine II of Russia, who had the sensible habit of choosing her lovers from the guards, owed the throne of Russia to their intervention in 1762. Her son Paul I, who disliked the guards regiments, was deposed and murdered by guards officers in 1801. In 1789 the desertion of the Gardes Françaises supplied the leadership and weapons which were essential for the success of the crowd's attack on the Bastille. In 1802, on the other hand, the Garde Consulaire was described as having a great effect in Paris where its mere presence 'maintains public tranquillity and upholds the usurped throne of Bonaparte'.

Guards were also monarchs' last resort, used on some of the most dramatic occasions in history to remove over-mighty subjects or princes: it was royal guards who imprisoned Thomas Cromwell in 1540, seized Don Carlos in 1568, murdered the Duc de Guise in 1588 and arrested the Cardinal de Rohan in 1785.

Thus the history of guards, their formation, strength and loyalty, although it rarely appears on the surface of conventional political history, nevertheless forms an underlying military reality which explains many otherwise surprising events. Only the slow build-up of their guards by Henri III in the 1580s and by Charles II in the 1670s, for example, enabled them to withstand the crises of 1588 and 1679–81. The apparently irrational preoccupation of monarchs such as Louis XIV, Peter the Great and Frederick William I of Prussia with the discipline, appearance and wellbeing of their guards was due to their belief that a reliable guard was the ultimate basis of their power.

Guards are not only a key to history. They are also confirmation of the unity of European history, and of its affinities with the history of the Middle East. The fact that every monarch, including the Ottoman Sultan and the Shah of Persia, had a guard, presented them all with similar problems: how to control the guard; how to keep it loyal; and how to prevent it from alienating the rest of the army or the country. Different monarchies adopted different solutions. But all guards operated within the same framework of the throne, the capital and military force.

INTRODUCTION

PILLARS OF MONARCHY is an outline of that aspect of the social and political history of monarchies which is revealed in their relationship with their guards. It is not a work of military history and does not deal with guards' performance on the battlefield or, except in passing, with their military function as a model for the rest of the army. *Pillars of Monarchy* is written in the belief that Louis XIV's remark, that there was 'an almost infinite contrast between the rest of my troops and those of my household', is also applicable to the guards of other monarchies, and that royal guards differ in purpose, function and composition from other troops. Guards are defined as troops with the word 'guard', or its equivalent, in their formal title, and having the function of guarding their monarch.

The similarities of formation, composition, situation, function and aspiration between different royal guards seem greater than the differences of geography and time. This is suggested by the fact that, in European monarchies, and in nineteenth- and twentieth-century Persia, the same word – *garde, guardia, guard, gwarde* – from the same French or Italian origin, was used to describe the force guarding the monarch: an etymological correspondence with few parallels in the case of other social or political institutions.

The first four chapters of *Pillars of Monarchy* describe the organizational history and distinguishing characteristics of the royal guards of the major monarchies of Europe and the Middle East: France, Austria, Spain, England, Sweden, Denmark, Russia, Brandenburg-Prussia, Piedmont, Naples, the Ottoman Empire, Persia and Morocco, and of those smaller monarchies which they influenced. The monarchies of the Middle East are included because, as many travellers since the sixteenth century have noticed, they reflected the same needs and forces, although often with different results, as those of Europe. In addition they frequently influenced, or were influenced by, the royal guards of Europe.

The date chosen to start is 1400, since, from that date, after the institutional confusion of the Dark and Middle Ages, royal guards have a continuous subseqent history. To describe the royal guards of the ancient world, the Gibbonim of King David or the Immortals of the Persian Emperors, would be to enter too many worlds for one book. Chapter 5 describes the royal guards' further distinguishing characteristic of unusual social and racial composition. Chapters 6 and 7 describe the political role, Chapter 8 the way of life, and Chapter 9 the form of appearance which resulted from royal guards' particular duties and purpose.

'The better he was guarded the more his Enemies would fear him and his Friends love him' LORD HAWLEY TO CHARLES II IN 1661

'My sailors — my own sailors — I can't believe it! They are all our personal friends!' TSARINA ALEXANDRA FEODOROVNA, ON THE DESERTION OF THE GARDE EQUIPAGE IN 1917

1
THE RISE OF ROYAL GUARDS, TO 1730

A T CHINON NEAR the Loire, one day in April 1446, the Dauphin was looking at the Scottish Guard of his father, King Charles VII of France. 'There go those who keep the Kingdom of France in subjection,' he said, wishing he could set them against the King. His companion, Antoine de Chabannes, replied: 'But this guard is a fine thing, and I admire it more than anything the King has done. It is certainly very honourable for a prince, like the King, when he rides through cities or in the country, and it is also a great security for his person. If it were not for his guard, many things would have been done which no one has dared to undertake.'[1]

This remarkable and revealing conversation between a prince (the future Louis XI) and a courtier shows the presence, from the beginning of the history of modern royal guards, of those factors which were to determine the course of the guards' existence: a royal guard could be used not only to guard the king (sometimes with foreigners), but also to increase his prestige, to dazzle his subjects and to assert or defend his authority, even against his own family.

Indeed, it was the number and the vigour of the attacks on his authority which led Charles VII to raise a guard. For, as Chabannes implied, the King of France had not always had a Scottish guard. Like most medieval monarchs he had been guarded by ill-defined groups of household knights and esquires.[2] If there were organized royal guards – the Arab Guard of Frederick II of Hohenstaufen, the uniformed Noble Guard of the Duke of Milan in 1369, the twenty-four Archiers de la Garde of Charles VI of France in 1398, or Richard II's 'select bodyguard' of 311 Cheshire archers in 1397–99 – they were usually fairly short-lived experiments.[3] Defined and organized European royal guards, with a continuous subsequent history, developed after 1400. The first was founded in the valley of the Loire where the future Charles VII, at that time Regent for his mad father, had taken refuge from the English and the Burgundians. Threatened by internal, as well as external enemies the Regent appealed to Scotland for soldiers. As early as 8 June 1419 a document signed by Thomas de Seton refers to the twenty-seven mounted soldiers and 100 mounted archers 'designed as well to accompany Monseigneur le Régent for the safety of his person as to serve the King and the Regent against the English'. The document probably refers to the Scottish Archiers de la Garde and Archiers du Corps, under a Capitaine de la Garde du Corps du Roi (Captain of the Guard of the King's Person), who in 1425 were a clearly defined body of 108 soldiers.[4]

On 12 November 1437 they preceded the King *en grand habillement* when he re-entered his disloyal capital of Paris. Royal guards were now, as they had not been before, an indispensable part of the King of France's entry into a French, or foreign, city.[5] They preceded Charles VII into Rouen in 1449 'all clad in jackets without sleeves, of the colour of red, white and green, covered with gold embroidery, with plumes on their helmets of the same colours and leg armour richly coated with silver',[6] (see illustration I). The splendour guards added to royal entourages was often almost as important a reason for their existence as the protection they provided for royal persons.

In addition to his Scottish company of Gardes du Corps, Charles VII had a French company by 1428. Louis XI, a distrustful King, added another company in July 1473 'to serve henceforth for the Guard of our Person' and Francis I added a fourth in 1515, from those who had guarded him before he ascended the throne.[7] His Gardes du Corps followed the King wherever he went, on foot or on horse, at court or in the battlefield; they probably saved the life of Charles VII at the Battle of Montlhéry in 1465, and of Louis XI at the siege of Liège in 1468. As well as guarding him during the day, Gardes du Corps slept on straw outside his room at night, as the Papal Master of Ceremonies noted with astonishment during Charles VIII's invasion of Italy. This was known as being *de paillasse* ('on straw duty').[8]

In addition, perhaps by as early as 1481, the King of France had 100 Swiss Guards, referred to in a document of 27 February 1496 as being 'Around Us for the Guard of Our Person'. They may derive from the twenty-four German Guards of Charles VII in the 1450s: they were often called the Cent-Allemands as well as the Cent-Suisses. They were the first of the Swiss Guards, who were to seem so reassuring to monarchs afraid of their own subjects. Other guards of the King of France, formally organized in the fifteenth century, were the Gardes de la Porte who, as their name implies, guarded the entrances to his residences, and 100 Gardes de la Prévôté, responsible for enforcing the law and keeping the peace at, and around, the court, who were reorganized in the 1450s.[9] In addition, in 1471 and 1498 two companies of 100 gentlemen each, known as the Cent-Gentilshommes, were established, as an *ordonnance* of 10 June 1475 put it, 'for the guard of our person'. In the late sixteenth century ten were on duty every day in the King's antechamber, and they accompanied him with their axes (the other guards had halbards) 'when he goes out in public'.[10]

This enormous royal guard, which was to remain one of the distinguishing features of the French monarchy, had no rival in size and splendour among other Christian monarchies. At the same time, however, other monarchies were also beginning to feel the need for an organized guard. The creation of permanent royal guards, distinct from the royal household, in the fifteenth century, was a result not only of monarchs' need for security and splendour, and of the influence of the French royal guard, but also of the creation of standing armies and the increasing complexity of warfare. Since France, Burgundy and most Italian states had acquired standing armies by 1450, it was natural for their monarchs to acquire permanent guards at the same time. In 1444 James II of Scotland, who had such close ties with his ally the King of France, established a royal guard of about 100 soldiers.[11] By 1473 the Duke of Burgundy, the cousin and rival of the King of France who ruled most of the Low Countries, had '126 men of his guard for the security of his person, all nobles, and he calls them the esquires of the guard' (*escuyers de la garde*). They were quite distinct from the equerries (*escuyers d'escurie*), although, as in other monarchies, the royal household still acted as a military unit in time of war. The Duke of Burgundy's guard, which also included 126 archers and 126 men-at-arms, was so large that it was organized into eight squadrons, with fifteen guards always on duty in the palace *devant le prince*.[12] By 1473 the Duke of Savoy had sixty, and the Duke of Lorraine twenty-four Archers of the Guard.[13]

East of the Rhine most courts were protected by guards called Trabants, a word derived either from the German *traben*, to trot, the Czech *drab*, a foot soldier, or the Persian/Turkish *dêrbân*, a door-guard. The Leibtrabanten of the Elector of Brandenburg, for example, were first referred to in 1477. They dressed in black, grey and white and existed 'for the protection of the life and person of his princely grace and of his wife and issue, day and night at the castle' in Berlin.[14] The introduction, by the early sixteenth century, of Trabants at the courts of Poland, Sweden, Denmark, Austria, Bavaria, Saxony and Brandenburg is a sign of the international nature and common purpose of royal guards.

In England, Edward IV had twenty-four Archers of the Guard *pur gard corps du Roy*. But it was not until 1485, after his victory at Bosworth, that, in one of the first acts of his reign,

Henry VII set up, perhaps on the French model, a permanent royal guard of 150–300 Yeomen of the Guard. Although, as in France and Burgundy, the royal household remained a real and decisive military force, the Yeomen of the Guard played an important part in Henry VII's victory over Yorkist rebels at Stoke in 1486. The Yeomen of the Guard wore the white and green Tudor livery until the 1520s when it was replaced by the red which is still the dominant colour of their uniform.[15] They were the main guard of the court, about 600 strong in 1513 when the King was at war, and about 200 strong in 1547.[16]

In 1509 the French court, in this case its Cent-Gentilshommes, was also possibly the inspiration behind Henry VIII's foundation of the Spears of Honour, a royal bodyguard designed to train those 'extracte of noble blod' in the art of war. It had disappeared by January 1516, no doubt on account of its cost, but in December 1539 a similar royal guard of fifty-five Gentlemen Pensioners was set up by the King 'that his Chamber oft be furnished of gentlemen' and 'to escort him to Messe'. More immediate reasons for its foundation were the familiar royal need for security – because of the challenge presented to Henry VIII's authority by the Pilgrimage of Grace in 1536 – and splendour – since his court had to make a fine show at the King's marriage with Anne of Cleves the following year. They remained on duty, with axes, in the Chamber, and later the Presence Chamber, until the nineteenth century. In 1544 about forty Gentlemen-at-Arms were added to this unit but by 1558 there were only twelve, and by 1591 they had ceased to exist.[17]

The Pope felt the need for a permanent guard at the same time as the King of England. From 1485 Innocent VIII had a noble guard and in 1505 Julius II decided to have a Swiss Guard (there had also been a Swiss Guard for a time before 1484) which arrived in Rome on 22 January 1506. By the reign of Leo X they numbered 300 and impressed the Venetian Ambassador with their green and yellow uniforms *di una estrema bellezza*. The establishment of permanent diplomatic representatives, such as the Venetian Ambassador, at most European courts by 1530, like the creation of royal guards by the same date, was a sign of the increasing complexity of political life; and henceforth diplomats' despatches are among the most useful sources of information about royal guards. Thus another Venetian Ambassador was deeply impressed by the 'silver breast-plates' and 'very rich display' of the Yeomen of the Guard of Henry VIII at the Feast of Saint George in 1515.[18]

The Swiss Guards defended the Castel Sant' Angelo heroically in 1527 during the sack of Rome. But, like the Noble Guard, they had to be disbanded after the Pope's defeat, and the two guards were not reorganized until 1548 and 1555 respectively. Thereafter the Swiss Guard of 232 (140 by 1643) and the Noble Guard (known as the Lanze Spezzate) of 100, continued to guard respectively the entrances and the interior of the papal palaces and to provide the Pope with armed escorts.[19]

Spain and Austria (as the hereditary lands of the House of Habsburg will henceforth be known) were the last of the great European monarchies to acquire permanent royal guards. According to tradition, the kings of Castile had been guarded at night by the Monteros de Espinosa ever since a courtier from this village near Bilbao had saved the monarch's life in 1009. The Monteros de la Camera y Guardia de S.M., all from Espinosa, numbered forty-eight in 1522, as they did in 1828. They continued to perform their duties, interrupted only by invasion (1808–14) and revolution (1868–74), until the fall of the monarchy in 1931. It is a sign of the exceptional force of the past in the life of royal guards that not only do the Yeomen of the Guard of England and the Swiss Guard of the Pope still guard their sovereigns today, but a unit of the Guardia Real of King Juan Carlos I of Spain is called the Monteros de Espinosa.[20]

A proper military royal guard was not formed in Castile, however, until the creation of the Guardias Viejas, composed of 2500 veteran soldiers in 1493. Although they were stationed all over Castile, one company of 100 soldiers, soon known as La Lancilla, or La Vieja, was always, in theory, on duty at the palace. In 1504 the Duke of Burgundy, Philip the Handsome, became King of Castile by marriage with the daughter and heiress of Isabella the Catholic; his guard of 104 noble Archiers du Corps became part of the royal guard of Castile. After his death in 1507 they returned to the Netherlands. Thereafter they guarded Philip's son Charles, Duke of Burgundy, who also became King of Spain after the death of his grandfather Ferdinand in 1516, and Holy Roman Emperor after the death of his other grandfather Maximilian in 1519. After his abdication in 1555 they guarded his successors as kings of Spain and rulers of the Netherlands until 1707. All nobles or distinguished soldiers, all with a fine presence and 'without evil in their hearts' – as an ordinance of Philip II put it – and all subjects of the King of Spain from the Netherlands or Franche Comté, they were the most distinguished unit of his guard and accompanied the King 'whenever he went out'. They were a visible sign of the enduring strength of the dynastic connection between the Netherlands and Spain, and they soon acquired, in addition to their Burgundian name, the Spanish name of La Cuchilla from the *cuchilla*, or slash, in the sleeve of their yellow costumes.[21]

In 1504, after the death of Isabella, perhaps to counterbalance his son-in-law's Burgundian guard, Ferdinand founded a guard of 200 halbardiers, from the esquires of the gentlemen of his court. The guard became an established part of the Spanish court after Ferdinand's return from Italy in 1507, and was known as La Amarilla, the yellow, from the colour of its costume. To La Lancilla, La Cuchilla and La Amarilla, Charles V added, after he became Holy Roman Emperor, La Alemana, a German guard of 100 halbardiers, which was always commanded by a German. Consequently, Philip II at Brussels in 1556, like subsequent kings of Spain until 1700, was guarded by Burgundian, German and Spanish companies of 100 guards each, under Count Hornes, Count Schwarzburg and Count Feria respectively. He also had a guard of 100 English archers, under Sir John Huddlestone, as husband of Mary I, and king consort of England, from 1554 to 1558.

1.   R. Peril. *Cortège of Charles and Clement VII at the Coronation of Charles V in Bologna*. 1530. BRITISH MUSEUM.

Charles V was the first Holy Roman Emperor to have a permanent, organized and international bodyguard. His guards cried 'Vivat Carolus! Vivat Imperator!' as they escorted the Emperor to his coronation. Their halbards were intended for protection against 'the crowd and popular tumult', according to the picture's printed description.

CLEMENS VII PONT MAX IM

Charles V's younger brother Ferdinand, founder of the line of Austrian Habsburgs established from 1521 at Vienna, also had a guard of forty Archers (later called Hartschieren) and forty-three Trabanten. The Archeros, in black and yellow livery, had come with Ferdinand I from the Netherlands at the beginning of his reign and escorted him whenever he left his palace.[22]

These royal guards, all established between 1400 and 1530, were a new and international element in the life of the courts of Europe. This is shown not only by Antoine de Chabannes's praise of the Scottish guard of the King of France in 1446, but also by English chroniclers' comments on the Yeomen of the Guard. According to Hall they were 'to give daily attendance on his person, which precedent men thought that he learned of the French king when he was in France, for men remember not any King of England before that time which used such a furniture of daily soldiers'. According to Polydore Vergil, Henry VII was 'the first English king to appoint retainers, to the number of about two hundred, to be a bodyguard . . . in this he imitated the French king so that he might thereafter be better protected from treachery'.

The example of Spain, as well as those of England and Burgundy, shows that France was the supreme model for European royal guards. When Louis XII met Ferdinand of Aragon at Savona in 1507 he naturally brought with him French, Swiss and Scottish guards. When the King's guard was being posted for the night, 'the King of Aragon and the Spanish lords watched with pleasure and stood at the castle windows every evening to see the guard [*guet*] being set; it was a fine sight, for as they said no one in all Christendom had such a guard, nor one which was so well ordered'. During that visit Ferdinand was guarded by Gardes du Corps of the King of France; but when he returned to Spain he brought with him his own guards 'dressed like the Swiss' who were now, for the first time, 'constantly on duty in the palace and went out with the King wherever he wished'.[23]

At first seen as an absurd novelty, this guard was also soon accepted as a natural adjunct of the monarchy. Royal guards were not only new; they were also foreign. The

SVPF AVG   HENRICCOMESANASSAV ARCHIEPSBARREN EPSCAVRIEN EPVSBRIXIEN NIC PERNOT MICHAELMAIVS   IVNVMERICANONVM LEGVMQVE DOCTORES   VIRI CONS

creation of the Scottish Gardes du Corps of the King of France, the influence of the French Guard on England, Burgundy and Spain, the installation of Burgundian Archiers at the courts of Madrid and Vienna, the presence of Swiss Guards around the King of France and the Pope, and the prevalence of Trabants in central Europe and Scandinavia shows that, at least where their guards were concerned, the monarchies of Europe found foreign influences and servants as natural and useful as their own traditions and subjects.

Although, in 1507, the Guard of the King of France had no equal 'in all Christendom', that of the Ottoman Sultan was at least its equal in size, splendour, variety and antiquity. Indeed the Janissaries, the finest fighting force in Europe, and the first to be permanently uniformed and organized, by 1438, had originally begun as the Sultan's bodyguard. By the early sixteenth century, however, their immense expansion and the growth in a taste for splendour at the Ottoman court, had led to the selection of four of the 196 *ortas* or chambers, numbers sixty to sixty-three, to be the Sultan's bodyguard. Known as Solaks, they were described in 1567 by the Imperial Ambassador as 'archers keeping always neere unto the person of the Great Turke', on the battlefield as well as in the palace. There were about 400 of them, selected from the Janissaries for their 'fine appearance and valour'. They were better paid and more lavishly dressed; their helmets were surmounted by a vast fan-shaped crest of white feathers.[24]

In addition to the Solaks, the Sultan's guard included Peiks, from the Persian word for messenger, founded after an attempt to assassinate the Sultan in 1492. There were about 100 Peiks who were on duty in the palace every day and formed part of the Sultan's escort in processions. A Peik was sent to Mecca every year to ascertain the pilgrims' safe arrival. The most important unit of the Imperial Guard was the Bostangis or Gardeners, between 2000–3000 strong. 'Literally the gardiners [sic] but in reality the bodyguard of the Sultan', their duties were 'to form the first guard of the Seraglio [the Sultan's palace in Istanbul], to have the care of all the delicious places of the Grand Signor and those of his court and to give the torture to malefactors'. Three hundred of them, known as *khassekis* or bodyguards, always followed the Sultan and provided the oarsmen for his personal boat. This guard was intimately connected with the life of the Sultan and his court; its commander, the Bostangi Pasha, was the only adult man beside the Sultan to live at the heart of the palace and was often chosen to replace, or execute, the Grand Vizier.[25]

Whereas all these guard units were recruited from the Janissaries, and so from the annual contingent of slaves from Christian subjects or captives of the Sultan, the Müteferrikas, about 200, later 500, strong, were usually, like the Archiers du Corps of Burgundy or the Gentlemen Pensioners of England, what one French traveller called *gens de qualité*. The Müteferrikas were sons of eminent pashas or generals, or of tributary rulers such as the King of Bosnia and the Princes of Wallachia and Moldavia, or were favoured artists, craftsmen and doctors of the Sultan. They were probably the same as the 'Sultan's bodyguard. . . mounted on horses which were not only very fine and tall but splendidly groomed and caparisoned', described by Busbecq, the Imperial Ambassador, in 1555.

Busbecq was profoundly impressed by the stillness, the cleanliness, the 'silence and good discipline' of the Ottoman army, in contrast to the 'cries and murmurs' and 'quarrelling and acts of violence' so common in Western armies. The Ottoman army was so impressive, and so good at winning battles, that it is probable that the elite force of *streltsi* or musketeers, set up by Ivan the Terrible in 1550 – some of whom were a royal guard known as *streltsi* of the stirrup – was 'created on the model of the Turkish Janissaries'.[26]

The growth of royal guards meant that, by 1530, the royal apartments in every palace were preceded by one or two rooms full of armed guards (the Guard Chamber, the Salle des Gardes, the Hartschieren Saal), just as monarchs were usually surrounded by their guards when they left their palaces. In the second half of the sixteenth century royal guards further increased in size and variety. In 1559 the restoration of the Duke of Savoy to his dominions automatically meant the restoration of his Archer Guard, of about sixty nobles, and of a company of *archibugieri* or gunmen, who, after 1566, acted as halbardiers guarding the entrance of the ducal apartments. In 1579 the Duke of Savoy also acquired a Swiss Guard of about sixty; and a year later the Duke of Lorraine, whose dynasty was constantly trying to rival the power and prestige of the House of Savoy, acquired a guard of thirty Swiss 'to follow him habitually and be near his person'.

There were now four European monarchs who had Swiss Guards: the King of France, the Pope, the Duke of Savoy and the Duke of Lorraine. Soldiers from the Alps played, in the history of European royal guards, a role almost as important as did soldiers from the Caucasus (birthplace of many Janissaries) and the Elburz mountains south of the Caspian, in the history of the royal guards of the Ottoman Empire and Iran. Monarchs evidently found that soldiers from mountain regions were, as the Ottoman Ambassador to France wrote of the Swiss in 1721, 'strong and courageous people and with that very exact and very faithful in carrying out the orders they are given, [so] they have been chosen for the guard'. A similar preference for 'steadiness' and 'obedience' had led the first Medici Duke of Tuscany to choose 200 Germans, rather than Spaniards or Italians, to form his Trabant Guard in 1541.[27]

Almost all monarchs felt the need to augment their guards, at a time when their courts were becoming increasingly splendid. From 1572 to 1576 the Elector of Brandenburg had a

2.   P. Coeck van Aelst. *Procession of Suleiman the Magnificent through Constantinople*. 1533. SEARIGHT COLLECTION.

Like his enemy Charles V, Suleiman the Magnificent took care to be surrounded by guards. The soldiers in front of him are Solaks, whose helmets were later even more magnificent.

mounted guard of thirty knights 'to wait on Our person immediately, to increase the splendour of the Court and to act as messengers'. The experiment was repeated in 1590–98, but again abandoned for reasons of economy, leaving the Elector with twenty-four Trabants as his sole guard (the number was increased in time of war or for special ceremonies).

In 1580 the Duke of Bavaria created a guard of fifty mounted noble carabineers (the Korbinergarde). Expanded and given experienced officers in 1602, it distinguished itself at the Battle of the White Mountain in 1620, and throughout the Thirty Years War. It was reorganized and renamed the Hartschierengarde in 1668, and as such continued to guard the rulers of Bavaria, and increase the splendour of their court, until 1918.[28]

But it was in France, in the sixteenth as in the fifteenth century, that the most important developments in the history of royal guards took place. On 1 August 1563, at a time when, as after 1418, the French monarchy was threatened both by internal disorder – the Wars of Religion – and external attack – the English occupation of Le Havre – the Gardes Françaises was set up. This was an infantry regiment of about 1000 soldiers, rather than a small elite force like the Gardes du Corps or Yeomen of the Guard, and thus represented a new departure in the history of European royal guards. But, as attacks on the authority of the French monarchy multiplied, such a large, military royal guard seemed necessary. Moreover, regular armies were now bigger and better organized than in the fifteenth century: the French army, for example, numbered about 50,000 in 1550. Therefore, a larger royal guard seemed appropriate. Although it was twice disbanded, due to opposition from the enemies of the monarchy and lack of money, from October 1574 onwards the Gardes Françaises were a permanent part of the guard of the King of France.

In the turmoil of the Wars of Religion it became increasingly difficult to guard the King, as Charles IX complained in a letter of 27 August 1572. Nevertheless, these guards remained in existence, helping in the Massacre of Saint Bartholomew's Eve in 1572, or guarding the King's enemies such as his cousin the King of Navarre (the future Henri IV) and his brother the Duc d'Alençon in 1574.

The guards were the first to recognize Navarre when he succeeded to the throne on 30 July 1589, and the Gardes Françaises, as well as the Gardes du Corps, escorted him when he finally entered his rebellious capital on 22 March 1594. Another unit which escorted Henri IV into his capital was the Chevau-Légers de la Garde, a small force of about 200 mounted gentlemen who formed part of his guard when King of Navarre. By an edict of 25 December 1593 they received the same privileges as the Cent-Gentilshommes, whose role they gradually took over. The Duke of Savoy had created a similar guard of mounted gentlemen in 1590, who functioned as a royal escort outside, rather than a guard within, the palace, namely the forty-seven Corazze-Guardie di Sua Altezza (Cuirassier Guards of His Highness).[29]

The reign of Louis XIII saw a further expansion of the French royal guard. Louis XIII was indeed the first of the long line of European military monarchs for whom nothing was more important or more congenial than drilling, maneouvring, reorganizing and redesigning the uniforms of, as well as fighting with, their guards. When he was only four years old his father wrote that he had 'a mind more inclined to arms than to anything else'. When he was Dauphin he organized and drilled a company formed from the children of the Cent Suisses, and took turn as a guard with the Gardes Françaises on duty. Soon after he became King the company of Gendarmes which had guarded him when he was Dauphin was renamed the Gendarmes de la Garde; the King became their captain and also captain of the Chevau-Légers de la Garde, on 11 July 1611.[30] As these developments show, royal guards were now increasingly distinguished from other troops by the personal connections between them and the monarchs they guarded, as well as by their duties, privileges and appearance.

In March 1616, when the court was at Tours trying to suppress a rebellion, the Swiss Régiment de Gallaty of about 3000 soldiers became the Régiment des Gardes-Suisses. Other Swiss regiments had been employed to guard the French court since 1567, but none had received the formal designation of a guard regiment. In 1622 Louis XIII renamed a unit of fifty carabineers the Mousquetaires de la Garde. They were 'children of the best families of France, equipped with a blue casaque and distinguished by silver crosses'. As early as 1623 a Parisian noted in his diary that they were a unit 'of which the King is extremely fond and which he puts on guard duty in front of his residence in the places where he goes'.[31] They need no introduction to readers of *The Three Musketeers*.

Thus by 1625 the guard of the King of France was an enormous body of 6000 or 7000 soldiers: the Gardes Françaises and Gardes Suisses guarded the outside of the palace; the Chevau-Légers, Gendarmes and Mousquetaires de la Garde escorted the King when he went on a journey; the Gardes de la Prévôté had the *police extérieure* of the court; the Cent-Suisses and the Gardes de la Porte guarded the entrances of the palace. The Cent-Gentilshommes now appeared at court only on days of great ceremony (and were abolished, on the death of their last captains, in 1687 and 1721). But the Gardes du Corps were always with the King. In the *Règlement* of August 1598, which was still being followed in the 1720s (although numbers had increased and weapons been improved); their duty was defined as to keep order at court and to control access to the King: twelve were on duty every night still *couchant aux paillasses*. The captain of the guards in waiting followed the King as closely as possible, on foot or on horse, whenever he left his appartments.[32]

There were four captains of the guard, all French, since the last Scottish captain of the Scottish company, Jacques de Montgomery, had lost his job for accidentally killing King Henri II in a tournament in 1559. That a captain of the guard should be crossing lances with the King shows how closely connected with the life of a royal family its guard could be. Similarly, two of the greatest favourites of Elizabeth I had been Christopher Hatton, captain of her Gentlemen Pensioners, and Sir Walter Raleigh, captain of her Yeomen of the Guard. By the early seventeenth century, due to the Protestantism of most Scots, and the accession in 1603 of the King of Scots to the throne of England, places in what was still known as the Compagnie Ecossaise were 'for the most part filled with French'. But as late as the 1780s, no doubt helped by the Jacobite emigration after 1688, there were still a few Scottish Gardes du Corps du Roi. Indeed, after 1642, there had been a momentary revival of the Scottish connection with the guard of the King of France, since on 27 February 1642 the Earl of Irvine, son of the Earl of Argyll, signed an agreement with the French Ambassador to raise a regiment of Gardes Ecossaises, to rank after the Gardes Françaises and the Gardes Suisses and, like them, to have the privilege of a detachment of its soldiers always being on guard around the King. This regiment disappeared after the restoration of the Stuarts in 1660, when its colonel, Lord Rutherford, returned to England.[33]

The King of France's enormous guard not only protected his person and his palaces. It also fought his enemies, who were, until 1629, rebellious nobles and Huguenots inside France, from 1629 to 1648 the forces of the Habsburgs and their allies, and after 1648 the rebellious Frondeurs in France. On 28 July 1652, for example, the fourteen-year-old captain of the Chevau-Légers de la Garde, Mazarin's nephew Paul Mancini, died in the battle to recapture Paris for Louis XIV, at the end of the civil wars of the Fronde.

The military uses of a royal guard, as the elite of the regular army which most monarchies, in addition to Spain and France, were beginning to acquire in the early seventeenth century, as well as the traditional royal desire for security and splendour, led to the expansion of other royal guards beside that of France. In 1615 the Elector John Sigismund of Brandenburg set up a Leibguardy-compagnie, which was 'the root of the old army' and by 1657 had developed into a Leibregiment of 1200. Also in 1615 King Gustavus Adolphus of Sweden founded the Hovregementet or Court Regiment, known as the Yellow Brigade from the colour of its uniform. It performed brilliantly in many of the battles of the Thirty Years War and in 1649, after many changes, it was renamed the Royal Guard or Life Regiment.[34] From 1620 the Electors of Saxony, whose rivalry with the Electors of Brandenburg showed itself in the development of their guards, had an infantry Hoffahne or Court Banner, by 1663 known as the Leibregiment. From 1631 the Electors of Saxony also had a horse Life Guard.

Not only the rulers of France, Brandenburg, Sweden and Saxony but also the King of Spain felt the need to add a regular, professional regiment to his guard. In 1634, just before the outbreak of war with France, a regiment of 2500–3000 infantry guards was founded in Spain, perhaps on the model of the Gardes Françaises (known to contemporaries as 'the best regiment of all Christendom'). Olivares, the King's chief minister, was its colonel. It was expanded into two regiments in 1639, but the second was disbanded in 1641 because of its lack of discipline and high rate of desertions, while in 1661 the first lost all its privileges – guarding the King, proximity to the court and the capital, higher pay and rank and more splendid uniforms – due to the hostility of the King's illegitimate son, Don Juan of Austria.[35]

A major reason for the creation of these guard regiments was the warfare endemic on the continent between 1618 and 1659. In England, which had been at peace for so long under Elizabeth 1 and James 1, there had been little change to the guard of Gentlemen Pensioners and Yeomen of the Guard before 1639, although when he was King of Scots the future James I, had, by 1594, recruited 400 Foot Guards and two troops of Horse Guards. In 1639, his son, facing armed rebellion from the Scots, raised four infantry companies of Life Guards under Lord Willoughby d'Eresby, as part of the army assembled to invade Scotland. After the disbandment of this army in 1640 Charles I again had no organized guard apart from the Gentlemen Pensioners and Yeomen of the Guard. Therefore, faced with an unprecedented challenge to his authority, he intended, as he told Parliament on 8 April 1642, to raise 'a Guard for his own Person'. By the outbreak of the Civil War in September 1642 he had a 'Life Guard of Horse' of two troops of about 300 each, many of whom were gentlemen, under his cousin Lord Bernard Stuart; Lord Willoughby d'Eresby again commanded the 'Life Guard of Foot' of about 670, many of whom were Derbyshire miners: infantry has nearly always had less social prestige than cavalry.

Both units performed bravely, perhaps too bravely, at Edgehill (where the Gentlemen Pensioners guarded the Prince of Wales and the Duke of York), as they did in the subsequent course of the Civil War, during which the 'Life Guard of Horse' rose from two to four troops. But the King's Life Guards, which were still with him at Chester in September 1645, disappeared with the collapse of the Royalist cause in the following six months. In Scotland in 1650 Charles II recruited 'his Majestie's footte regiment of his Lyffe guards' and two troops of horse Life Guards from 'the choicest men of the army'. They disintegrated, like the rest of his army, after Cromwell's victory at Worcester on 3 September 1651.[36]

More firmly established monarchies were able to found more permanent guards. On 2 June 1652, although Brandenburg had been at peace since the end of the Thirty Years War, the Elector wrote to his Privy Councillors that it was 'absolutely necessary that the Elector should have a Life Guard'. The result was that his Trabants were converted into a fifty-man horse Life Guard, later expanded, which was paid for by the estates. The next year, in a magnificent blue, silver and gold livery, it escorted him to Prague.

France, Brandenburg, Sweden, Saxony and Spain already had foot guard regiments. Such a pillar of their authority was beginning to seem a necessity to most, although not all, European monarchs, and on 30 June 1658 the Danish regiment of Foot Guards was formed to help combat the Swedish invasion of that year. In 1659 the Royal Life Company of the regiment was placed on permanent guard duty in the royal castle, a duty it shared with the

Trabants and, after 1661, with the regiment of Horse Guards formed that year. A third regiment was added to the Danish royal guards in 1701 with the creation of the Grenadier Guards regiment, which alternated with the Foot Guards in guarding the King's palace.

On 18 April 1659 the Duke of Savoy also created a regiment of Foot Guards, the Reggimento delle Guardie, almost certainly modelled on the Gardes Françaises: the Venetian Ambassador wrote that it was organized *ad uso di Francia*.[37] But it was in England that the royal guard acquired the greatest importance. After his treaty with Philip IV of Spain in 1656, the exiled Charles II began to organize a Royalist army in the Spanish Netherlands, in which, as in 1642 and 1650, there were a certain number of royal guards. (Charles II also needed an armed guard for protection from Cromwell's government.) By 1659 he had at least eighty Life Guards under Lord Gerard of Brandon, the last commander of his father's 'Life Guard of Horse', and 400 Foot Guards under Lord Wentworth, whose father was captain of the Gentlemen Pensioners.

When Charles II returned to England he may have had as many as 600 Life Guards, who were 'always next to the King's person' when he entered London in triumph on 29 May 1660. By January 1661 the Life Guards had been organized into three troops: the King's troop under Lord Gerard; the Duke of York's troop under Sir Charles Berkeley, a close friend of both Charles II and James Duke of York; and the Lord General's Troop under Sir Philip Howard, who had been in Cromwell's ephemeral Life Guard. The Life Guards, all of whose troopers were gentlemen, performed the function not, as is the case today, of a mounted escort outside the royal palaces, but of a permanent bodyguard for the monarch wherever he went. One hundred were always on duty in the palace of Whitehall. From 1678, when fears for Charles II's life were beginning to grow, an order was issued that an officer of the Life Guards 'is always to attend and follow next our person, indoors and out, excepting always our bed chamber'. The captain of the Life Guard on duty, known from 1678 as Gold Stick in waiting, from the symbol of his office, soon came to be (as he still is on state occasions) the military officer nearest the person of the monarch. In 1685, for the first time, the captain of the Life Guard on duty was directly behind the King during the coronation. The new importance of

3. Dirck Stoop. *Charles II's State Entry into London*. 22 April 1661. MUSEUM OF LONDON.

The Duke of York's Troop of Life Guards leads the procession, the King's Troop brings up the rear. Around Charles II are the Gentlemen Pensioners. General Monck, the first Colonel of the Coldstream Guards and author of Charles II's restoration, follows him on horseback. As this picture shows, Charles II followed Lord Hawley's advice and, unlike his predecessors, took care to be 'well guarded' from the moment (indeed even before) he ascended the throne.

the Life Guards diminished the role of the Gentlemen Pensioners, who were reduced to forty in 1668, and by the reign of George I were on duty in the Presence Chamber only on Sundays and feast-days. The Yeomen of the Guard, however, although reduced to 100 in 1670, were still on duty every day at court.[38]

In addition to the Life Guards the Royal Regiment of Horse Guards, known as the Oxford Blues from the name of their commander the Earl of Oxford, and the colour of their uniform, were also by November 1661 officially a guard regiment, although not so closely connected to the King's person as the Life Guards. The Oxford Blues numbered about 500.

Because Lord Wentworth's Foot Guards were left behind in the Spanish Netherlands (and acted as the garrison of Dunkirk until October 1662), on 23 November 1660 Charles II issued a commission to raise a regiment of Foot Guards to a devoted Royalist soldier, Colonel John Russell. By January 1663 it contained 1200 soldiers in twelve companies, five of whose captains had fought in the Royalist cause during the Civil War. In 1665, on Wentworth's death, it absorbed his regiment of 1200 Foot Guards. In addition, on 14 February 1661 on Tower Hill, General Monck's regiment of 1440 foot was reconstituted as the Lord General's Regiment of Foot Guards (soon known as the Coldstream Guards from the name of the river dividing England and Scotland which this regiment was the first to cross on its way south to restore Charles II). On 2 April 1661 a Scottish troop of Life Guards was formed in Edinburgh under Lord Newburgh, who had commanded a troop of Life Guards for Charles II in 1650; by 1 May 1662 a regiment of Foot Guards had also been formed in Scotland, as had, by 23 April, 'our regiment of guards in our Kingdom of Ireland'. On 27 September 1662, when there was a review of the guards in London, the *Kingdome's Intelligencer* wrote, 'The horse and foot was in such exquisite order that 'tis not easie to imagine any thing more exact.'[39]

The reason for this extraordinary and rapid expansion of royal guards – in England alone they numbered 3574 in 1661 – was not only Charles II's conviction that, if Charles I had had a proper guard or army, he would have kept his throne. It was also due to the English distrust of standing armies, learnt by bitter experience during the Civil War and the Protectorate. It was easier to justify the army, which Charles II had always intended to maintain, if it was called a guard, for the Act disbanding the old Cromwellian army allowed Charles II a guard 'such as His Majesty shall think fit to dispose of and maintain at his own charge'.

Some Members of Parliament soon regretted this favour. In 1674, for example, Charles II's guards were attacked in the House of Commons as 'a school and nursery for men of debauched and arbitrary principles, and favourers of the French Government'. They were not even English: 'Guards or standing armies are only in use where Princes govern by fear, rather than by love, as in France.' For, as this speech implies, in Europe in the second half of the seventeenth century, royal guards were inevitably associated with the person and policies of Louis XIV.

Louis XIV loved and honoured his guards as much as his father had done. When he met his cousin Marguerite de Savoie, a possible future wife, in 1658, he talked to her 'about his Mousquetaires, his Gendarmes, his Chevau-Légers, the Regiment of Guards, the number of his troops, their commanders, their service, their manner of marching'. 'I judged from that,' added his cousin la grande Mademoiselle, 'that he took pleasure in talking to her, for these are agreeable topics for him, as he is very keen on such matters.' He himself wrote in his *Memoirs:*

> I had often noticed the almost infinite contrast between the rest of my troops and those of my household, whom the honour of being more particularly mine, the most exact discipline, the more certain hope of rewards, the examples of the past, the spirit which had always reigned among them, rendered absolutely incapable of a bad action. Therefore

it seemed useful to me to increase rather than diminish their number, a policy which I also thought to be one of dignity and grandeur.

This classic royal affirmation of personal monarchy, elitism and military discipline, not without a note of realism (the emphasis on rewards), was, despite Colbert's constant opposition, translated into action. In January 1657 the Mousquetaires de la Garde, disbanded in 1646 by Mazarin, an enemy of their commander de Tréville, were restored. In 1660 Mazarin gave his own company of Mousquetaires to the King, and in January 1665 it became officially part of the Maison Militaire, the royal household troops, as the Gardes du Corps, Chevau-Légers, Gendarmes and Mousquetaires de la Garde were now usually called. Thenceforth there were two companies of Mousquetaires of 250 officers each, 'mainly composed of young lords and gentlemen, the first school where they learn the profession of war'. Known as the Mousquetaires Gris and Noirs, from the colour of their horses, they were the most admired units of the French royal guards.[40]

On 30 September 1664 Louis XIV reorganized the Gardes du Corps, limiting the powers of the captains of the guard, abolishing purchase and giving himself, rather than the captains, the right to choose the Gardes du Corps from amongst men who had given 'proof of their courage and of their experience in war'. They were even more explictly the elite of the army between 1701 and 1715 when they were chosen by the King in person from three soldiers sent by every regiment in the army. In December 1676 he added to his Maison Militaire the Grenadiers à Cheval de la Maison du Roi, another elite troop of 154 soldiers. In 1678 the King of England, and in 1687 the Elector of Brandenburg, raised similar troops of horse Grenadier Guards.

During Louis XIV's wars the Gardes Françaises and the Gardes Suisses, with the units of the Maison du Roi, for the first time acted as un corps séparé, the spearhead of his army. At court they were even more in evidence than before, for Louis XIV loved to be surrounded by guards. For example 'not finding himself accompanied enough when hunting deer', he ordered four Gardes du Corps to follow his carriage whenever he went hunting. In 1683 the Venetian Ambassador was struck by how heavily guarded the King was, and saw it as a sign of the same fear of la populace de Paris which had led him to move to Versailles:

The tragic examples of the Kings his ancestors have increased his natural suspiciousness; perhaps the ministers have kept it alive so that the appearance of force around the royal person should increase veneration for the King's authority, on which they rely and of which they are the instruments. It is certain that no sovereign has ever been more protected with a more complete vigilance. The large numbers of Gardes Françaises and Gardes Suisses guarding the Louvre, the Gardes du Corps in the different rooms are not enough. His Majesty never goes from one apartment to another without guards being placed in the corridors, on the stairs, and in the communicating passages.[41]

Such a large, visible and, at this stage, victorious royal guard, deeply impressed foreign monarchs, perhaps even more than Louis XIV's court and palaces. The Grenadiers à Cheval were not the only unit to find imitators. In 1665 the Elector of Saxony created a company of 125 Swiss Guards, like the Cent-Suisses, commanded by a former officer of the Gardes Suisses of France, who in 1679 also became commander of the Elector's regiment of Foot Guards. The model of Louis XIV's guard was even followed by his political or religious opponents. In 1672, during the French invasion of the Netherlands, after William of Orange had been made captain-general of the Dutch forces, certain Dutch regiments become guard regiments. The former guards of the states of Zeeland and Holland became, respectively, the Gardes du Corps of His Highness, about 200 strong, and the Horse Guards of His Highness, about 500 strong. They continued to be paid by the states; but, as early as 3 March 1672, they wore the Prince's coat-of-arms on their helmets and coats of Nassau blue, and soon received

4.   R.D. Hooge. *The Entry of William of Orange into London.* 18 December 1688. BRITISH MUSEUM.

The Prince of Orange was surrounded by his Dutch Guards, ready for a fight, when he entered London to deliver it from the tyranny of James II. William III was as proud of, and attached to, his guards as were his enemies James II and Louis XIV.

privileges of rank like those of the Maison Militaire: a cornet had the rank of lieutenant; a major that of colonel; a colonel that of general-major. On 12 June 1674 two Dutch foot regiments became the Foot Guards of 2500 soldiers, which in 1684 also received the same privileges of rank as the Horse Guards. In 1678 another regiment became the Guards Dragonder regiment, whose officers in 1682 received the privilege of one rank in the army being added to their rank in their regiment.[42]

These privileges of rank were an important element distinguishing royal guards from other military units; at the end of the seventeenth century, in most European monarchies, they were codified and extended. In 1664 the regiment of Foot Guards of Savoy received double-rank privileges, as did, in 1684, the Dutch and Danish Foot Guards. From 1666 every captain in the English Life Guards had the rank of colonel. In 1687 captains in the English Foot Guards were given the rank of lieutenant-colonel, and, in 1691, lieutenants the rank of captain. In 1691 sous-lieutenants and enseignes in the Gardes Françaises were given the rank of lieutenant-colonel and captains the rank of colonel.[43]

Royal Guards were now so important that there were few historical events which they did not influence, or reflect, as is shown by the example of the British Isles in 1687–90. James II's attempts to strengthen the position of Catholics, and his own authority, are shown by his decision to raise a fourth troop of Life Guards under Lord Dover, from Catholic gentlemen, in May 1686, and his plan in November 1687 to raise a force of 'Musketeers du Roi' like those of Louis XIV. The collapse of his authority became apparent when, on the night of 16–17 December 1688, the Foot Guards of his son-in-law William of Orange, known as Blue Guards from the colour of their uniform, took up sentry duty at Whitehall, 'and the King's Guards dismissed and treated like a pack of rogues', as Lord Ailesbury wrote. Thereafter the Dutch Foot Guards were often in England; and the Gardes du Corps under William's cousin, Henry of Nassau-Auverquerque, replaced Lord Dover's troop as the fourth troop of Life Guards until, in March 1699, the xenophobia of the House of Commons forced William III, to his

5.   F. Colosoni. *The Duke of Gloucester Drilling his Company of Child Guards.* C. 1698, BRITISH MUSEUM.

Behind the Duke of Gloucester are his parents, the future Queen Anne and Prince George of Denmark. Monarchs' and princes' obsession with their guards could begin at an early age. Like Louis XIII and Peter the Great when children, the Duke of Gloucester (who died in 1700 at the age of eleven) commanded and drilled guards of his own age recruited from the children of his parents' courtiers and servants.

rage, to send them back to the Netherlands. He was so angry that he threatened to abdicate. For his guards meant as much to Protestant, constitutional William III as to his Catholic, autocratic rival Louis XIV. William III's famous comment, 'By God, if I had a son they should stay,' reveals how closely the fate of a guard is connected to the state of the dynasty it is guarding. For, if he had had a son, and the politicians knew that England would be ruled in the future, as well as in the present, by the House of Orange, they would have treated what the King most cared about, that is to say his guards, with more respect and William III would have felt strong enough to resist their demands.

The only royal guards which, in the end, fought for James II were the Irish Foot Guards. In addition, during his campaign in Ireland in 1690, he had two troops of Life Guards or Gardes du Corps, 200 strong under Lord Dover and the Duke of Berwick, and a troop of Horse Grenadiers. After his defeat by William III, whose army included Dutch, English and Danish Guards, James II's Life Guards and Foot Guards fought for Louis XIV in the French army until they were disbanded, in February 1698, after the end of the war.[44]

The example of Louis XIV continued to dominate the royal guards of Europe, even when his armies ceased to be consistently victorious. On 4 August 1685 the different companies of *arcieri*, *archibugieri* and *corrazzi* of the Duke of Savoy were reorganized as four companies of Guardie del Corpo, and one company of Guardie della Porta 'as in France'.

After the revocation of the Edict of Nantes in 1685, the influence of Louis XIV was even carried by refugees from his religious persecutions. From 1687 to 1707 the Elector of Brandenburg had two squadrons of Grands Mousquetaires, numbering 182 officers. Not only were their name and idea French, but most of the Mousquetaires, like many officers in the Dutch guards, were French Huguenots, and their uniforms were based on models of the Mousquetaires' uniform ordered from Paris. From 1692 to 1718 the Elector of Saxony also had Grands Mousquetaires. The commander of the Grands Mousquetaires of Brandenburg, the Maréchal de Schomberg, was a classic example of royal guards' ability to ignore frontiers. A German Protestant, for many years an officer in the Gardes Ecossais of France, he commanded a Brandenburg guard unit in 1687, and was second in command of William of Orange's invasion of England in 1688.

After the funeral, in 1688, of the Elector Frederick William of Brandenburg, his Trabantenleibgarde was dismissed. Instead his successor, the Elector Frederick, had, from 1692, a Garde du Corps of 240 officers. From 1701 the Elector of Saxony, who on 15 September 1697 had been elected King Augustus II of Poland, also converted his Trabants, and small units of Grenadiers à Cheval and carabiniers, into a Garde du Corps of 333 officers. These years saw an expansion of the Saxon Guard in keeping with the Elector's elevation to the rank of King: in 1699 his Foot Life Guard was divided into two regiments, the First or Polish, and the Second or Saxon, Guard Regiment; in 1699, after the end of the war between Poland and the Ottoman Empire, he acquired a Janissary Corps of 180 (see illustration 6). In 1703 he added to what was now known, in Saxony as in France, as the Maison du Roi, a unit of Chevaliers-Gardes.

In 1717 the guard of the King of Poland, which had grown greatly in the seventeenth century, was reorganized into a Foot and a Horse Guard regiment for the kingdom of Poland, stationed in Warsaw, and a Foot and a Horse Guard regiment for the Grand Duchy of Lithuania, stationed in Grodno; they disappeared at the final partition of Poland in 1795. The Saxon Guards of Augustus II and Augustus III (1733–63), like the Dutch Guards of William III, caused great jealousy when they were used, in preference to indigenous guards, for guard duty in the capital of their master's new kingdom.[45]

In addition to the units of Gardes du Corps now guarding the rulers of England (in all but name), Savoy, Brandenburg and Saxony, as well as the King of France, the small, splendidly uniformed units of Swiss Guards at the entrance to royal apartments in many of the palaces of Europe were another sign of French influence. In the 1690's not only the King of France and the Pope, but also the Duke of Savoy and, until 1697, the Elector of Saxony, had Swiss Guards. (The Elector of Saxony lost his, which had been recruited from the Protestant cantons, when he became a Catholic in order to obtain the throne of Poland.) On 14 August 1696 the Elector of Brandenburg ordered a guard of 127 Swiss soldiers from the Protestant cantons, which arrived in Berlin on 31 March 1697. When the Elector was crowned the first King in Prussia on 18 January 1701 – thus recovering equality of rank with his rival of Saxony – his Swiss Guards were 'dressed almost exactly like those in France at the coronation' and performed similar functions, according to the official account. Many of their officers, like those of the Swiss Guard of Saxony, had served in the Cent-Suisses or Gardes-Suisses of France.

In 1698, when the Duke of Lorraine recovered the duchies from which his dynasty had been expelled by Louis XIV, he ordered a Swiss Guard from the Catholic cantons 'as soon as it will be possible'. For him, as for many other sovereigns, a Swiss Guard was an indispensable attribute of sovereignty. In addition to this company of Cent-Suisses, he had two companies of Gardes du Corps of sixty-three each (many of whom came from James II's recently disbanded Life Guards), two companies of Chevau-Légers de la Garde of sixty-four each and, unlike previous Dukes of Lorraine, a regiment of Foot Guards, the Gardes

6. Le Prince. *Le Janissaire Polonais.*
SEARIGHT COLLECTION.

From the late seventeenth century the
King of Poland, and senior officials of
the Kingdom of Poland and the Grand
Duchy of Lithuania, had guards dressed
and armed like those of the Ottoman
Sultan. Like the figure in Turkish dress
in the foreground of illustration 3, this
is a tribute to Europe's fascination with
the splendour of the Ottoman Empire,
epitomized by the contemporary
proverb: 'If you seek wealth, go to
India. If you seek learning and knowledge go to Europe. But if you seek
palatial splendour come to the Ottoman
Empire.'

Lorraines. Many of the uniforms for these guards came from Paris.

An astonishing example of the cosmopolitan nature of royal guards, and of the
monarchs they guarded, occurred after Francis I's exchange of the Duchy of Lorraine for the
Grand Duchy of Tuscany in 1736, on his marriage to Maria-Theresa, the heiress of Austria.
Although his other units of guards were disbanded, the Swiss Guards followed their Duke to
Florence, where they replaced the Trabants. In 1745 they were summoned to attend Francis
I's coronation as Holy Roman Emperor in Frankfurt and before the service they had a violent
quarrel over precedence with the Swiss Guard of the Elector of Saxony (which had been
reformed in 1725). From 1745 to 1767 they served in Vienna, commanded by Pfyffer
d'Altishofen, whose brother was commander of the Pope's Swiss Guard.[46] Clearly the
purpose and duties of a royal guard were much the same whether they were on guard in the
palaces of Nancy, Florence or Vienna.

The most explicit case of French influence on other royal guards occurred in Spain
after the accession of Louis XIV's grandson Philip V in 1700. The Spanish Habsburgs had

already tried to expand their guard. Between 27 April 1669 and 22 January 1677 there had been a regiment of 3000 Guardias del Rey to guard the palace and serve as a model for the rest of the army. Called La Chamberga from the foreign uniforms they wore, which resembled those which had been seen on the army of the Maréchal de Schomberg, the future captain of the Brandenburg Grands Mousquetaires, they were reduced to the status of a line regiment, as Philip IV's guard regiment had been, due to the opposition of Don Juan of Austria. On 27 December 1697 a regiment of Horse Guards under the command of a Prince of Hesse-Darmstadt was raised to protect the court. It too was reduced to the status of a line regiment by Philip V, who was determined to eliminate German influence and openly based his guard on that of 'the most Christian King my lord and grandfather', as he called Louis XIV.

On 17 October 1702 it was decided to raise a regiment of Gardes Wallonnes from what was still the Spanish Netherlands; it arrived in Spain in late December 1703. A regiment of Gardes Espagnoles had been formed by 1 December 1703, and not only did both regiments have the same organization, disciplinary regulations (those of 1691) and uniforms as the Gardes Françaises, but in December 1703 a detachment of Gardes Françaises under an aide-major, Monsieur de Luzançy, arrived in Spain to serve as their instructors.[47]

Four companies of Guardias de Corps were formed on 12 June 1704, enjoying, as the Ordinance of Formation put it, 'distinctions and privileges appropriate to the service of the palace', and destined for service on the battlefield, as well as at court. There were two Spanish companies, one Italian and one Flemish, formed from the Mousquetaires de la Garde de la Personne, organized by Louis XIV for his grandson, who had arrived in Milan in December 1702. On 6 May 1707 the three remaining traditional royal guards (La Alemana had been disbanded), were reduced and re-formed as a company of halbardiers (Alabarderos) for internal palace duty. The Alabarderos were recruited from NCOs but the other guards were as elitist and privileged as in France (all Guardias de Corps had the rank of lieutenant and a captain in the Foot Guard ranked as a colonel in the army), and as resented by the rest of the army.

This enormous – there were about 600 Guardias de Corps and 8000 Foot Guards – and cosmopolitan royal guard continued relatively unchanged during the eighteenth century. Although the southern Netherlands ceased to be Spanish after 1713, the Gardes Wallonnes continued to be overwhelmingly Walloon in composition, and were commanded by men with names like Carondelet de Baudignies, Bryas de Malenghien and Flodorp de Clabbecq; in December 1795 only twenty-one officers were not Walloon. Their composition, like that of the Flemish company of the Guardias de Corps, was a sign of the inhabitants' continued love for the Spanish monarchy, which had defended their faith and helped create their identity, in the southern, now Austrian, Netherlands. Despite intermittent efforts, the Austrian authorities found it impossible to stop men from the southern Netherlands enlisting in the Spanish royal guard.[48]

The Spanish monarchy did not, however, have any mounted guards for escort duty. In 1730 four squadrons of 168 veteran NCOs each were formed, called Carabineros Reales, which in 1742 became Tropas da Casa Real (household troops). In 1731 the Granaderos a Caballo del Rey were formed on the model of the Grenadiers à Cheval du Roi. Before they were disbanded in 1749, they served as a guard for the younger son of Philip V when he conquered the kingdom of Naples from Austria in 1734. One of his first acts as King of Naples was to form a privileged royal guard of his own, based on that of his father: two regiments of Foot Guards, of which one was foreign, the Reali Guardie Italiani and the Reali Guardie Svizzeri; a company of halbardiers, and three companies of Guardie del Corpo. In 1749, when another son of Philip V, the Infante Philip, became Duke of Parma, his guard of Guardie del Corpo, Alabardieri and one Foot Guard regiment was organized for him by the

7.   J.H. Wedekind. *Charles XII of Sweden*. 1701. ROYAL ARMY MUSEUM, STOCKHOLM.

Charles XII of Sweden, the greatest warrior king of his age (and first cousin of the Duke of Gloucester), unlike most other monarchs, often led his guard in battle. He also used it as a training-school for officers and a model for the rest of the army. He was so attached to his Drabants, shown in the background of this portrait, that he chose them himself; and the first letter he wrote after his catastrophic defeat by Peter the Great at Poltava contained instructions for their recruitment.

Marques de Bondad-Real, a first lieutenant in the Spanish Guardias de Corps. Not only at Madrid, but also at Naples and Parma, the sight of the royal guard was reminiscent of Versailles.[49]

The royal guards of Sweden and Russia, however, reflected not the bewitching influence of Versailles but the particular needs of the two monarchies. In Sweden, the King's Guard or Life Regiment was complemented in November 1667 by a Horse Life Regiment (Livre-gimentet till Hast). Both regiments performed magnificently during the wars of Charles XI (1660–97) and Charles XII (1697–1718). Charles XII made one of the most original uses of royal guards by making the 200 armed Drabants, also called Gardes du Corps, whom he had inherited from his father, into 'a senior officers' school as well as a superb fighting arm'. By September 1700 they were a separate unit of 200 officers, with double-rank privileges and having the King as their captain. The Drabants followed their King everywhere, in the thick of battle as well as into exile in the Ottoman Empire after his defeat at Poltava (where the Foot Guards were 'almost annihilated') in 1709. By 1716 only thirty-eight Drabants were left, and in 1718 the King created a new unit, called the Household Squadron, which included soldiers as well as officers. In 1721, after his death in battle against the Danes, the Swedish parliament, jealous of all manifestations of royal authority, abolished the Household Squadron, and the Drabants were reduced to the status of Standdrabanter, whose only function was to guard the interior of the royal palaces.[50] The regiments of Foot and Horse Guards, however, remained.

The army which defeated Charles XII at Poltava was that of Peter the Great. One of the most important elements in it – indeed one of the most important creations of Peter's reign – was the Imperial Guard. The Imperial Guard began in 1683 in the villages of Preobrazhens-koe and Semenovskoe outside Moscow, where Peter was living during the regency of his

8.   Section of a Gobelins Tapestry.
Peter the Great at the Battle of Poltava.
1709. NOVOSTI.

Peter the Great is wearing the uniform
of the Preobrazhensky Guards, which
he commanded and in which he served
from his youth. From his reign until the
Revolution the Tsar was always Colonel of the Preobrazhensky Regiment,
the most prestigious and, usually, the
most politically active regiment of the
guard.

sister Sophia. As fond of everything military as the young Louis XIII, he began to drill and
manoeuvre his playmates, sons of court officials, grooms and nobles. The first volunteer was
Serge Boukvostov, an equerry; by 1684 there were 300 and, by 1685, 1000 volunteers.
Although these forces did not play a significant part in Peter's seizure of power from his
sister in 1689, they became more important thereafter. In 1692 they were finally organized
into the Preobrazhensky and Semonovsky Guards regiments, and Peter received the rank of
sergeant in the former. In 1695 they received their baptism of fire at the siege of Azov and in
1698 they helped crush the revolt of the Streltsi. When some of the Streltsi were executed on
10 October 1698 'the whole regiment of guards was drawn up in array under arms'. The
Streltsi (whom Peter called 'in truth nothing but begetters of evil and not soldiers'),
including the 'elite palace guard' set up after the revolt of 1648, were abolished in June 1699.

By September 1699 the Preobrazhensky Guards numbered 1698 and the Semenovsky
1238. It was symbolic of the change in the character of the Russian monarchy that, at the first
Epiphany procession of the new century on 15 January 1700, the Tsar was for the first time
not sitting on a throne beside the Patriarch of Moscow, but leading the Preobrazhensky
Guards regiment who were dressed 'in handsome new green uniforms' (the Semenovosky
wore light blue).[51] On 3 October 1700, having served in every rank from drummer-boy up, he
became a captain in the Preobrazhensky Guards. Subsequently the Guard greatly distinguished itself in Peter's wars. By the end of his reign a foreign observer could write that the
'Guard broke the back of that veteran corps [the Streltsi], established the Czar's throne,
procured him safety at home and reputation abroad. For which Reason he caresses and
maintains this Guard, which now consists of ten thousand men, as the support of his

Government, above any other of his Forces'.

Foreign influence was not completely absent from the creation of the Russian Imperial Guard. Many of the officers of the two guards regiments were German, while General Le Fort, who helped to train the regiments, was a former officer of the Gardes Suisses of France, and is said to have modelled the guards' uniforms on those of Denmark. 'To aggrandize the coronation' of his wife, the future Catherine I, in 1724, Peter created a unit of Chevaliers Gardes, possibly modelled on those of Augustus II: the troopers were captains, the corporals lieutenant-colonels, and the uniforms were of the utmost magnificence (it was disbanded in 1731). On 17 April 1730, just after her accession, the Empress Anna created the Ismailovsky Guard regiment, named after another imperial residence outside Moscow, and on 31 December 1730 the regiment of Garde à Cheval, 'on the foot of the late King of Sweden's trabans', to replace the Chevaliers Gardes. Many of the officers were foreign, many of the Ismailovsky soldiers came from the Ukraine. These two regiments had been raised partly, an officer wrote, 'to counterbalance the old ones and prevent any uprising by the people'.[52] Tsars of Russia could be as afraid of their guard as they were of their subjects.

The two Muslim monarchies of Persia and Morocco had also developed elaborate bodyguards by 1700, the only guards to contain an explicitly religious element. Since they set up their state in 1501, the Safavid Shahs of Persia had had a religious bodyguard of a few hundred Sufis, who guarded the interior of their palace. In addition they had a guard of a few hundred *ghulams* or slaves from the Caucasus. In 1654 Shah Abbas II added to what one French traveller called his Maison du Roy 4000 Gardes du Corps called Ziezairis or Kechikchis: their uniform was decorated with silver plaques and they were called *l'honneur des troupes de Perse*.[53] In 1679 in Morocco the great Sultan Moulay Ismail, after a campaign in the south of his empire, raised a guard of black slaves called the Abeed al-Bukhari, from the book by the great theologian al-Bukhari on which they swore their oath of unfailing loyalty to the Sultan.[54]

2
ROYAL GUARDS UNDER ATTACK, 1730–89

ROYAL GUARDS NOW provided a protective and decorative barrier around every European monarch. On 13 July 1698, when an Austrian ambassador went to pay his respects to Peter the Great, 'Guards were everywhere', and 'filled the court of the castle as far as the vestibule of the first apartment'. Nine hundred Gardes Françaises and Gardes Suisses, and 240 Gardes du Corps, were stationed at Versailles under Louis XV. The King was always surrounded by guards, at Mass, out hunting, at court and when going from one palace or *pavillon* to another. In and around London there were even more royal guards after the arrival, in February 1709, of the Scottish troops of Life Guards and Horse Grenadier Guards, and in February 1712 of the Scottish Foot Guards: their presence in London symbolized Scotland's loss of independence after the Union of 1707 with England.

The Yeomen of the Guard continued to follow the monarch even when, like William III or George II, he was on campaign abroad; forty-one were on duty in Saint James's Palace every day, and the Yeomen of the Guard escorting George III saved him from assassination attempts in 1786 and 1800. Two hundred and ten Foot Guards, more than the total of her courtiers and servants, accompanied Queen Anne to Windsor in 1704; 400 (excluding officers and NCOs) attended the Prince of Wales to Parliament on 23 July 1716. In Piedmont, 212 soldiers of the Reggimento delle Guardie were usually on duty in Turin during the eighteenth century; about 200 royal guards were on duty in and around the royal palace of Naples in the 1740s.

When Charles III, having changed the throne of Naples for that of Spain, arrived in Madrid on 13 July 1760, he was preceded by Alabarderos and Guardias de Corps, his carriage was surrounded by footmen, pages, and 'all the officers of the Lifeguard that were not otherwise stationed', and the route was lined with, and the enormous procession closed by, soldiers of the Spanish and Walloon guards.[1] The number of guards surrounding European monarchs ensured that, at least when they were making a public appearance, there was now almost always a military aspect to the presence of royalty.

The capitals of the different monarchies of Europe – London, Copenhagen, Stockholm, Versailles, Madrid, Naples, Turin, Potsdam and St Petersburg – were now cities of guards, depending on royal guards for the enforcement of law and order and the maintenance of royal authority. There were so many guards guarding the monarch and his court that most palaces, in addition to guard rooms at the entrance to the royal apartments, had barracks at the entrance to, or just beyond, the palace courtyard. The Horse Guards in Whitehall, for example (rebuilt in its present form in 1750–59), was originally the guard house at the entrance to the palace of Whitehall, as it is now, in theory, the guard house at the official entrance to Buckingham and St James's Palaces.

In the eighteenth century royal guards not only almost always protected the monarch and his palaces, they also symbolized his possession of sovereign power. When, on 12 September 1737, British guards' commanders received instructions that 'it is His Majesty's command that none of the three regiments of Foot Guards take notice of the Prince and Princess of Wales, or any of their family, until further notice', it was a sign that, like Princess

Anne between 1692 and 1694, and George II himself when Prince of Wales between 1717 and 1720, the Prince and Princess of Wales were in opposition to the King's government and so no longer entitled to share in the most obvious outward symbol of his sovereignty. Royal guards even symbolized the sovereignty of exiled monarchs: James II at Saint-Germain, and his son in Rome, were guarded by detachments of, respectively, the Gardes Françaises and the Lanzze Spezzate, as a sign of their hosts' respect for their claims to sovereignty as much as for their own protection; the former King Stanislas of Poland, when he was Duke of Lorraine (1737-66), had his own Gardes du Corps and, from 1740, a regiment of Gardes Lorraines, with a more splendid uniform and better pay than other regiments.[2]

One reason why royal guards were such a potent symbol of royal sovereignty was that guards were increasingly restricted to sovereigns and their families. The days when great lords and generals had had their own guards were over by the last quarter of the seventeenth century, although in eastern Europe they never completely died out: Prince Esterhazy still had his own company of 200 guards in Hungary in the 1770s. It had needed the exceptional danger and the exceptional royal favour enjoyed by Cardinals Richelieu and Mazarin for them to be allowed their own guards, which died with them. Now guards were allowed only for monarchs' personal representatives, such as viceroys and, in France, governors of provinces. Exceptions were the Princes of Orange, captains-general of the United Provinces' armed forces, who continued to have foot guards (although the Gardes du Corps and Garde à Cheval had been dissolved); indeed from 1748 to 1795 the Princes of Orange had a regiment of Swiss Guards, as well as their regiment of Dutch Guards.[3]

Guards were restricted to sovereigns in another sense, in that they were usually under the direct control of the monarch rather than of a commander-in-chief or a minister of war. In France, for example, the commander of every unit of the guard, and every company of the Gardes du Corps, worked directly with the King on matters concerning his command. Only afterwards would he communicate the result to an often irritated minister of war. A similar pattern prevailed in the other Bourbon monarchies of Spain and Naples. In England, although the Foot Guards were often under the control of the commander-in-chief, the Household Cavalry remained directly under the control of the King, or its colonels, until 1830.

A sign of monarchs' control of, and interest in, their guards is the fact that, by 1730, most monarchs were colonels or captains of at least some of the regiments of their guard. This was the case with the Kings of France after 1611, the Kings of Sweden after 1700, the Kings of Denmark after 1701, the Kings of Prussia after 1713 and the Tsars of Russia after the reign of Peter the Great. Some monarchs were almost as proud of such titles as they were of being kings.

Although such universal protectors of monarchs and symbols of their sovereignty, royal guards were neither very large nor, usually, constituted a large proportion of the regular army: 8971 of 172,760 (5 per cent) in France in 1753; 7369 of 98,525 (7.5 per cent) in Spain in 1760; 2881 of 31,852 (9 per cent) in Naples in the 1740s; 9647 of 267,368 (3.6 per cent) in Russia in 1732. But whereas line regiments were often under-strength, badly paid and ill-trained, so that their numbers on paper rarely represented a military reality, guards regiments usually remained what they were meant to be: full strength, well-drilled, splendidly uniformed and highly privileged corps.[4]

In the middle of the eighteenth century the prestige of royal guards and the power of their monarchs might have seemed bound to guarantee them generations of power and privileges. But, for a variety of reasons, military, ideological and financial, some royal guards now came under attack. The supreme royal guard of the seventeenth century, that of the King of France, had not particularly distinguished itself in the Wars of the Spanish (1702–14) and Austrian (1740–48) Successions. The Gardes Françaises in particular, 'whom their continual residence in Paris has turned into cowards', fought badly at Malplaquet in 1709, Dettingen in 1743 and Fontenoy in 1745. The speed with which they swam back across the river Main during the Battle of Dettingen earned them the name, 'the ducks of the Main', and inspired a terrible letter from Louis XV to their colonel, the Duc de Gramont: 'May it be God's will that in the future they can wipe out the memory of the waters of the Main.' Even the brilliant performance of the Maison du Roi at Fontenoy in 1745 did not entirely restore the military reputation of the French royal guard. Count Kaunitz, the Austrian Ambassador, was deeply impressed by its size and splendour when he came to Versailles in 1751, but he was less impressed by its training, discipline and fighting potential.

For a new star was rising in the east, and was rapidly replacing France as a model for other European monarchies. In 1739 the Prussian army, from now on one of the most important and harmful forces shaping the history of Europe, was, in the opinion of Count Algarotti, composed of 'the most brilliant troops it is possible to see'. This opinion was soon accepted by most educated people in Europe. The great tactician the Comte de Guibert wrote, in his admiring account of the Prussian army, *Observations sur la Constitution Politique et Militaire des Armées de Sa Majesté Prussienne* (1774), that they were 'the finest and the best disciplined in Europe'[5] and Mirabeau, in 1788, that they were 'the first in Europe'. And one of the distinctive features of the eighteenth-century Prussian army was the relative lack of importance and independence of its guard.

This peculiarity was largely due to the influence of one of the most remarkable Kings of Prussia, Frederick William I (1713–40), for whom, his daughter wrote, the army was 'his dominating passion', and who 'acquired eternal glory by the marvellous discipline he introduced in it, thereby laying the foundations of the greatness of his dynasty'.[6] He had a new vision of the role of the monarch, which was to have an immense influence in Europe. He saw himself not as a godlike figure ruling his subjects from on high, but as the first servant of the state: he called himself the 'Finance Minister and Commander-in-Chief of the King of Prussia'. He was opposed to most forms of outward splendour and one of his first acts, on his accession in 1713, was to abolish his father's Swiss Guard and Gardes du Corps; the Grands Mousquetaires had already been abolished in 1707. Thus, in his reign, the only guard of the King of Prussia was the Foot Guard regiment (infantry regiment number fifteen) into which, in 1717, the King incorporated his beloved giant grenadiers (see Chapter 9).

In 1740, when his son Frederick II ascended the throne, he revived the Gardes du Corps as a cavalry regiment like the others, except that it did guard duty at the King's residence. It had an excellent battle record, was expanded in 1756, and thereafter remained one of the most aristocratic regiments in the extremely aristocratic Prussian army, officered by nobles with names like von Münchhausen, von Schulenberg, von Posadowski. The Foot Guards regiment had privileges of pay and rank over the rest of the army, as did its first battalion over the other two. Both regiments, which played decisive roles in some of Frederick's most famous victories, such as Zorndorf and Kolin, remained part of the line; they did not act as *un corps séparé*.[7]

The modesty and success of the King of Prussia's guard and army soon affected other royal guards. In 1730 the King of Prussia sent officers and NCOs to introduce 'Prussian drill' in the newly created Garde à Cheval of Russia. On 3 May 1750, at a review by Louis XV on the Plaine des Sablons, the Gardes Françaises and Gardes Suisses, for the first time, performed *exercice à la Prussienne*; the Foot Guards did 'the Manual Exercise of the Prussians', also for the first time, in St James's Park on 24 April 1756.[8] Prussian influence was not, however, confined to drill.

Not only the example of Prussia, but also the spirit of the age, tending to question traditional beliefs and received ideas, led some of the officials and officers in monarchs' service to question the usefulness of large, independent and expensive royal guards. In the

9. Chodwiecki. *Frederick II Reviewing the Foot Guard Regiment.* 1777. MANSELL COLLECTION.

Reviews and parades were a way in which monarchs could check on the number and discipline of their guards, at the same time as impressing their subjects and foreign observers with the power of their monarchy. Frederick II not only frequently reviewed his guards, he also drilled the First Battalion of his Foot Guards every morning at eleven, 'let the business be never so important', and always wore its uniform.

second half of the eighteenth century, usefulness and reason were beginning to seem more important than tradition and privilege. Yet tradition was one of the *raisons d'être* of royal guards. They based their existence – as some still do – on precedents, as is shown by the fact that the Gardes du Corps *Règlement* of August 1598 was still in use in the eighteenth century. Some idea of the attitudes governing royal guards is conveyed in the *Histoire de la Milice Française*, in which Père Daniel examines precedents and early references to the royal guards with the zeal and earnestness of a Biblical scholar analysing early texts of the Gospels.

A new generation was beginning to question not only the validity of basing military organization on tradition but also the validity of privilege itself. The performance of the Prussian army showed what could be achieved by an army which was not hampered by an excessively privileged and independent royal guard. Moreover, monarchy itself, especially if ineffective, was beginning to be regarded with a little more scepticism. The days when 'the honour of being more particularly mine' or 'the service of the palace' could automatically justify the privileges given to royal guards were passing. Lord Chesterfield showed his customary perception, as well as an aristocratic delight in the prospect of difficulties for monarchs, when he wrote, on 13 April 1752, that, even in France, 'reason and good sense' were beginning to question 'the divine right of the Lord's anointed. . . this I foresee, that before the end of the century the Trade of both King and Priest will not be half so good a one as it has been'.

A spirit of reform had already shown itself in England in December 1746 when, for reasons of economy, the Life Guards were reduced from four to two troops. An attempt to abolish them in November 1751 was defeated by Thomas Pelham because of the danger of insurrection and the need to protect the royal family. Correspondingly in Denmark in 1763 the Minister of War, the Comte de Saint-Germain, a passionate admirer of the Prussian army, and formerly an officer in the Austrian and Bavarian services, abolished the Drabants and the Grenadier Guards, and for six years merged the Horse Guards with the Foot Guards.[9]

When on 27 October 1775, to the delight of Frederick II, Saint-Germain became

Secretary of State for War in France, he led an attack on the privileges and numbers of the largest and most famous royal guard of all. In 1775 the royal guard of France, with its glorious history and twelve independent units, all commanded by officers directly responsible to the King, rather than the Ministry of War, was a living image of the *ancien régime*. Like many other institutions of the *ancien régime* it had become more rigidly traditional, as is shown by the choice of its commanders. Thus the Sourches family had been Grands Prévôts since 1643, the Noailles captains of what was still called the Compagnie Ecossaise of Gardes du Corps since 1651, the Rohan-Soubise captain-lieutenants of the Gendarmes de la Garde since 1673, the Louvois captains of the Cent-Suisses since 1688, and the Villeroy captains of another company of Gardes du Corps since 1695.

In a report prepared for the Council of Ministers in 1775, the Baron de Wimpffen, a dedicated professional soldier, wrote that 'Distinguished units with their own privileges are always very expensive and can only be kept up at the expense and to the disadvantage of the rest of the army. They fight less than line troops, are usually badly disciplined and badly trained and are always very embarrassing on campaign.'[10] This sentiment, stressing the military disadvantages of, rather than the political, social, historical and ceremonial reasons for a royal guard, has been shared by many professional soldiers before and since. And Louis XVI and the Comte de Saint-Germain put it into practice. By ordinances of 15 December 1775 the King proclaimed his desire to sacrifice 'part of the splendour which surrounds him', in accordance with his 'views of economy and order', so as to be able to afford to increase the line cavalry and infantry: the two companies of Mousquetaires and the Grenadiers à Cheval were abolished; the Gendarmes and Chevau-Légers de la Garde were reduced from 230 to seventy-four officers each; the Gardes du Corps were reduced from 1468 to 1272 and had to provide certificates of 200, or for senior officers, 300 years of nobility – a stiffer requirement than before. Curiously, although the military record of the Gardes Françaises was much less distinguished than that of the Mousquetaires, who had just helped to maintain order during the serious bread riots of 1775 in Paris, they were increased on 17 July 1776 from 4000 to 4878.[11]

This was not the only revolution in the organization of the royal guard under Louis XVI. In March 1778 the Gardes de la Prévôté were made more military and slightly expanded. In 1787-88 another reformer, the Comte de Guibert, was in power, as Président du Conseil de la Guerre, at a time of severe financial retrenchment. No feeling of fear that Versailles might be threatened by the expanding and increasingly improverished population of Paris, or by the increasingly discontented aristocracy, impeded the work of reform. The Gardes Françaises and Gardes Suisses, the two largest military units of the guard, were relied on; after the annual royal review on 3 May 1786 the Marquis de Bombelles could not decide 'which is the finest of these corps, the better at marching and the better disciplined'.

Guibert was irritated not only by the expense and privileges of the Maison Militaire but also by its beneficial effect on its officers' careers. Although very small in size, its officers' wealth and easy access to the court and the Ministry of War ensured them a disproportionate share of senior positions. Guibert attacked the Gendarmes and Chevau-Légers de la Garde for being 'one of the unjustifiable openings leading to the rank of general officer', and revealed the inspiration behind his reforms when he complained that 140 of the 225 lieutenant-generals and 538 Maréchaux de Camp came from the Maison du Roi, 'which is more than the number of general officers in the entire Prussian army'. Therefore on 30 September 1787 the Chevau-Légers, Gendarmes de la Garde and the Gardes de la Porte were abolished. Guibert even criticized the cost of the Gardes Françaises and Gardes Suisses, claiming that the 2200 Gardes Suisses and 3800 Gardes Françaises cost the equivalent of 2919 regular Swiss and 9728 regular French infantry. On 2 March 1788 the Gardes du Corps who, in January 1759, had been stationed in Beauvais, Châlons sur Marne, Troyes and Amiens instead of all over the Ile de France, were, as a further economy, concentrated in Versailles and their number, having risen again, was slightly reduced to 1288. A former officer of the Chevau-Légers, de Belleval, was not the only person who, at the time, felt 'people may repent and regret it in the future'.[12]

The French and Danish were not the only monarchies to reform their guards in the second half of the eighteenth century. The Guardia Nobile of the Grand Duke of Tuscany, founded in 1746 after the Swiss Guard had left for Vienna, was abolished in 1776 by the Grand Duke Peter Leopold, who thereafter contented himself with a few armed escorts. In November 1787, just after Guibert's reforms in France, the Baron de Salis, a disciple of Saint-Germain who had formerly served in the French Ministry of War, persuaded Ferdinand IV of Naples to abolish the Reali Guardie Italiani e Svizzeri, despite the furious opposition of the Queen and the nobility. In England the Life Guards, who were still part of the King's daily guard and escort, had lost much of their former prestige. The Duke of York, son of George III and a dedicated professional soldier, wrote that they were 'the most useless and unmilitary troops that ever were seen' and 'nothing but a collection of London tradespeople'. Therefore when Pitt's government embarked on an economy drive, there were few people to defend them. Like Louis XVI, George III was prepared, as his Secretary at War told the Commons on 10 December 1787, 'to sacrifice ornament to service'. On 31 March 1788 the four troops of Life Guards and Horse Grenadier Guards were amalgamated into two regiments of about 230 soldiers each. Most of the men came from the Horse Grenadier Guards, which enjoyed a much greater military reputation than the Life Guards. This represents 'the first attempt by the Government to encroach upon the privileged position of these units'.[13]

10.   Moreau le Jeune. *Review of the Gardes Françaises and the Gardes Suisses on the Plaine des Sablons.* C. 1780. BIBLIOTHÈQUE NATIONALE.

Louis XIV had reviewed his guard and his army so often that he was called *le roi des revues*. His successors, who did not inherit his military mentality, reviewed their guard only once a year in May on the Plaine des Sablons, watched by 'all Paris'. Under Louis XVI, who is on the left of this print, the Gardes Françaises and Gardes Suisses were believed to be particularly well-disciplined and reliable.

Whereas in Prussia, Denmark, England, France and Naples reform was the order of the day, Piedmont and Spain remained unaffected, while Austria, Russia and Sweden, which continued to evolve at their own pace, according to the particular needs of their monarchies, did not reform but expanded their royal guards. Austria, like Bavaria, had continued with its traditional guard of Hartschieren and Trabanten with very few changes since the sixteenth century. Whether this was due to an especially trusting and relaxed relationship between the Habsburgs and their subjects, to the lack of a Habsburg sovereign with a personal interest in his army and guards, or simply to dynastic tradition, it is impossible to say. The War of the Austrian Succession (1740–48) and the weaknesses it had revealed, however, were traumatic enough to inspire in the Austrian government a zeal for change like that of the governments of Louis XIV, Charles II and Peter the Great a century before. Maria-Theresa was grateful to the Hungarians for the help they had given her apparently desperate cause in 1741. Her son and heir, the Archduke Joseph, was about to marry a princess of Parma – the first of the series of Bourbon/Habsburg marriages which were intended to heal their ancient dynastic feud and strengthen the alliance of the two monarchies against Prussia.

The result was the formation of the Hungarian Noble Guard in September 1760. Chosen from eighteen- to twenty-year-old nobles recommended by the counties of Hungary, there were at first 120 and, after 1769, ninety guards who went into the army or the civil service after three or four years' service. The incomparable splendour of their uniforms could be admired at the entry of Isabella of Parma into Vienna on 6 October 1760 (see illustration VI). But as well as adding to the splendour of the court, they served as messengers carrying the Emperor's and Empress's letters – including their secret correspondence with Marie-Antoinette at Versailles urging her to dominate her husband and his ministers.[14] They remained a living symbol of the connection between the Habsburgs and the Hungarian

11.   U.F. Pasch. *Count Armfelt.* 1777.
SVENSKA PORTRÄTTARKIVET.

Armfelt was one of the many royal favourites who owed their opportunity to win royal favour to service in the guard. He came to the court of Gustavus III of Sweden as an officer in the Light Dragoons of the Life Guard, whose uniform he is wearing in this portrait. By 1780 he was 'first in the King's favour', and his apartment was connected to the King's 'by a secret communication'. Until his death in 1814 *l'Alcibiade du Nord*, as Armfelt was known for his dangerous charm, was an important figure in Swedish and European politics.

nobility, and from 1762 to 1787, 1791 to 1833 and 1902 to 1915 their captain was, suitably, Prince Esterhazy, the head of the greatest of Hungarian noble families.

By the same process which had taken place with the Cent-Gentilshommes in France and the Life Guards in Great Britain, the Hartschierengarden gradually became too inferior in status to fulfil their functions satisfactorily. Their furious complaints at the privileges of the Hungarian Noble Guard at court ceremonies were met with the reply that they were 'no longer fit for duty'. In December 1763, for the coronation of the Archduke Joseph as King of the Romans, the royal, noble Roman Arcieren Leibgarde (soon called Arcierengarde) was formed from fifty, later eighty, young nobles, with similar functions and purpose to the Hungarian Noble Guard, and it soon replaced the old Hartschierengarde.

In 1767 the Swiss Guard, which had come over the Alps from Tuscany, and the Trabants, were disbanded and, despite Kaunitz's suggestion of a Tyrolean guard, were replaced on 1 June by an Imperial Royal Life Guard of Foot of seventy-two soldiers. By 1790, by the fairly common process by which a newly organized guard adopted an old name (as the Arcierengarde had done), this guard had been renamed the Trabantenleibgarde, and as such continued to guard the Habsburgs' palaces until 1918. Also in 1767 the army invalids and *gardes-bosquets*, guarding the exterior of the palaces, were reorganized as a *schlossgarde* or palace guard which, after an interruption subsequent to 1781, was renamed the Hofburg-wache or Hofburg Guard in 1802.[15] It was the nearest the Austrian Habsburgs got to a regiment of foot guards.

On 16 November 1782, just before the visit of Pope Pius VI to Vienna, Joseph II erected a Galician Noble Guard, on the model of the Hungarian Noble Guard. There were to be sixty guards with access to the court, the possibility of promotion into the army or the civil service after six years' guard duty, and other 'considerable advantages'. The guards were nobles because 'noble families especially merit our particular consideration'; before the second half of the eighteenth century such a justification of a basic principle of European monarchies would not have been necessary. The dynasty, however, did not have the same position in the life of the Galician, as it did in that of the Hungarian, nobility. There were few candidates for the Galician Noble Guard. In 1790 it was reduced to the Galician section of the Arcierengarde, but even this vestige was abolished in 1809.

The reorganization of the Habsburgs' guard after 1760 was not only designed to associate wider sections of the high nobility with the monarchy. It also represented the Austrian equivalent of the militarization and modernization of the royal guard which had taken place in France under Louis XIV, in Spain under Philip V and in Russia under Peter the Great. Unlike the old Hartschierengarde, the Noble Guards were military units, destined to prepare young nobles for service in the army. The Trabantenleibgarde and the Hofburgwache were also military units now, composed of NCOs and soldiers with particularly good records of service in the army. That the Austrian Guards had become fully military symbolized the emergence of the Habsburg monarchy as a great military power under Maria-Theresa.[16]

In Russia the guard also increased in this period. In 1764 Catherine II replaced the privileged Life Company, formed by the Empress Elizabeth in 1741 from the grenadiers of the Preobrazhensky regiment who had helped her to seize the throne, with a company of Chevaliers-Gardes. There were sixty Chevaliers-Gardes, all nobles, with the rank of lieutenant. Twelve were on duty every day in splendid uniforms in the throne room. The commander of the Chevaliers-Gardes was, usually, Catherine's lover of the moment. In 1775 Catherine added small squadrons of Cossacks and Hussars to act as mounted escorts during a visit to the Ukraine to celebrate victory over the Ottoman Empire. Thereafter they formed part of the guard based in St Petersburg.

The Swedish royal guard was expanded for more directly political reasons. In 1772, as a reward for their part in the coup d'état which had restored royal authority after fifty years of aristocratic domination, Gustavus III, to the disgust of the existing Life Guards, created the Light Dragoons of the Life Guard under Count Sprengtporten, from the Finnish Light Dragoon corps and two squadrons of the Crown Prince's Hussars. In the same year Hamilton's regiment was given the title of the Queen Dowager's Life Regiment and stationed in Stockholm. In 1780 the Drabants or Gardes du Corps were reorganized into four companies – Svea, Göta, Vendes and Finska (the King's title was King of the Swedes, the Goths and the Wends, and Grand Duke of Finland) – each under a captain-lieutenant.[17] The captain of the Finnish company was Axel von Fersen, who was as popular with Gustavus III as he was with Marie-Antoinette. In 1789, however, he was serving not at the Court of Sweden but in France, as colonel of the Royal Suédois regiment. So he was able to witness the events, precipitated by the desertion of the Gardes Françaises on 12 and 13 July, which were to transform the existence, and confirm the necessity, of royal guards.

3

THE GOLDEN AGE OF ROYAL GUARDS, 1789–1830

THE FRENCH REVOLUTION, the initial success of which was made possible by the attitude of the French royal guards, nevertheless ended, or rather interrupted, their existence. The Gardes Françaises who helped to storm the Bastille on 14 July were disbanded by Louis XVI on 31 August 1789; only one soldier, Sergeant Julien, had remained loyal. Many former Gardes Françaises now joined the Garde Nationale de Paris, the revolutionary armed force responsible for the maintenance of law and order in Paris. At the same time the Garde Nationale, like much of the population of Paris, was becoming increasingly radical, and opposed to the moderation of the King. The Garde Nationale joined a Paris mob in marching on Versailles on 5 October. The Gardes du Corps, a few of whom resisted the mob at Versailles, were sent to their old provincial garrisons in the same month, after the court moved to Paris. Thereafter the King was guarded in the Tuileries palace by the soldiers of the Garde Nationale de Paris, under the orders of La Fayette. Therefore he was, as he complained when he fled from Paris on 20 June 1791 'prisoner in his own kingdom, for what other name can be given to the state of a king who only gives orders to his guard on matters of form, who does not appoint any of its officers and who is even forced to see himself surrounded by several individuals whom he knows to be filled with evil intentions for himself and his family?'

This proclamation not only reveals the vital role which the state of his guard can play in a monarch's decisions, but also provides an essential clue to an understanding of French politics from October 1789 to September 1791: La Fayette's physical control of the King. The Gardes du Corps were disbanded on 27 June 1791, after the recapture of the King and of the three Gardes du Corps who assisted his flight, at Varennes. The Gardes de la Prévôté, most of whom had preferred to guard the National Assembly rather than the King, were abolished on 10 May 1791 and the Cent-Suisses on 16 February 1792.

The humiliation and imprisonment of Louis XVI naturally made other monarchs pay attention to their guards. It was widely believed that, as the Portuguese Ambassador in France wrote to his government on 14 February 1791, when urging the creation of a new royal guard in Portugal, 'if the King of France had kept his military household, composed of ten thousand men, it is without doubt that he would not have seen this frightful revolution in his kingdom'.[1] Few monarchs' ministers would be prepared to propose the reform or abolition of royal guards now. The cousin and ally of the King of France, the King of Spain, was the first monarch to learn from the lesson of Louis XVI. Moreover, his favourite minister, Godoy (who may also have been his wife's lover), had won his favour by expert use of his position as a Guardia de Corps. It was due to Godoy's influence, as well as to the fears of King Charles IV, that, on 7 April 1790, a decree confirmed the privileges and facilitated the promotion prospects of the Guardias de Corps. In 1791 their pay was doubled and on 7 April 1793 a fourth, American company was added to the Spanish, Italian and Flemish companies.

12.   Anon. print. *Godoy in the Uniform of the Guardias de Corps.* C. 1790. REAL ACCADEMIA DE BELLAS ARTES DE SAN FERNANDO.

Like Armfelt, Godoy owed his chance to win royal favour to service in the guard. He rose so high that from 1792 to 1798, and 1800 to 1808, he dominated the Spanish government. In 1797 he even married a cousin of the King.

Although European royal guards have received many contingents from Africa and Asia, this is the only example of an American equivalent; it was a sign of the Spanish monarchy's desire to strengthen ties with its American colonies, on whom it feared the influence of the United States and the designs of Great Britain. In 1795 a company of light-horse artillery was added to the Guardias de Corps, and in 1802 336 carabineros were added to the Carabineros Reales as a special escort for Godoy, now Generalissimo of the Spanish army.

Warned by the fate of Louis XVI, Piedmont also strengthened its guard in this period. On 15 June 1790 the ruler issued a proclamation increasing the pay and privileges of his Guardie del Corps, and calling them 'the first [unit] in his armies and the most distinguished by its functions'. In 1791 Gustavus III of Sweden further increased his Hustrupper or Household Troops. The Horse Guard regiment was expanded and divided into the cuirassier, dragoon and infantry units of the Livregimentets Brigaden. The Queen Dowager's Life Regiment became the Second Foot Life Guard Regiment, whose officers were intended to counterbalance the exclusively aristocratic and therefore, to Gustavus III, threatening officers of the First (after 1791 Svea or Swedish) Life Guard Regiment. In 1791, as a reward for their fine performance in the war of 1788–90 with Russia, the Ostgöta infantry and cavalry regiments became the Livgrenadjar Regimentet and so part of the Hustrupper.[2]

In 1791, for a short time, a royal guard of four companies, composed of 'the flower of the nobility of the time' was created in Portugal, whose monarchs had previously contented themselves with one hundred halbardiers and a guard from whichever line regiment was stationed in Lisbon. Even revolutionary France, in a moment of moderation, allowed the King a guard of 1200 infantry and 600 cavalry by the Constitution of September 1791. Known as the Garde Constitutionelle du Roi, it was chosen from soldiers of the line with good records and *bonne tournure*, from members of the Garde Nationale and from volunteers; to their rage, former soldiers of the Gardes Françaises were excluded. It was a remarkable body and included in its ranks a Rohan-Chabot and a Brancas, two future marshals of the Empire, Murat and Bessières, Tocqueville's father (who, like Brancas, served as a soldier) and, as its commander, the *ci-devant* Duc de Brissac, former commander of the Cent-Suisses, chosen for the 'loyalty and special affection' which he, unlike so many others, showed for his King. Having fulfilled all the regulations and sworn all the oaths required by the Constitution, the guard was formally installed by Louis XVI on 16 March 1792. The guard, however, had already been denounced by revolutionaries and their newspapers as full of *aristocrates enragés*; 210 soldiers left for a variety of reasons, some political. By May there were frequent scenes in the street between soldiers of the guard and revolutionaries. On 29 May the Garde Constitutionelle was denounced in the Assemblée Législative and Brissac sent for trial in Orléans; on 30 May Louis XVI disbanded it in a vain attempt to reassure public opinion and preserve its officers' lives.[3]

At the same time as the Revolution, in its moderate phase, was creating the Garde Constitutionelle, the counter-revolution was reviving the traditional royal guard of France in its entirety. Its supporters believed that, as a former Mousquetaire wrote to the Comtes de Provence and d'Artois at Coblenz on 10 September 1791, if Louis XVI had kept his guard the Revolution would not have succeeded, and furthermore, that a large royal guard would be 'so advantageous for all the young and loyal nobles who have come to offer their Royal Highnesses their courage and their lives'. By June 1792, at the start of the campaign which was intended to crush the Revolution, the princes' army included 1600 Gardes du Corps, 360 Gardes du Corps of Provence and Artois, thirty Cent-Suisses, 259 Gardes de la Porte, 208 Gardes Françaises, and 1200 soldiers of the Compagnies Nobles d'Ordonnance, the name given to the former Mousquetaires, Chevau-Légers and Gendarmes de la Garde – a quarter of their entire army. This enormous royal guard was a monument to the alliance being forged during the emigration between the French monarchy and its nobility; it was disbanded with the rest of the emigré army, after their defeat by the revolutionaries, at Liège on 28 November 1792.

The princes' royal guard was not only a monument to their alliance with the nobility but was also one of the main accusations levelled against their brother at his trial, after the fall of the Tuileries and the disbandment of the Gardes Suisses, in December 1792. For Louis XVI, as would have been the case for most other monarchs, it was unthinkable that because events had led to the disbandment of his Gardes du Corps they should therefore lose their livelihoods. So, in accordance with their decree of disbandment by the National Assembly, he had continued, as was public knowledge, to pay their salaries (and those of the Gardes Françaises who had not been re-employed). When they began to be reassembled at Coblenz, Louis XVI gave the order, transmitted by the intendant of his household on 24 November 1791, that only Gardes du Corps with certificates of residence in France should be paid; in fact, so few presented themselves that they were a very small charge on the civil list. Nevertheless, given the importance of royal guards as a symbol of sovereignty, their re-creation in Louis XVI's name at Coblenz greatly increased popular distrust of him in

France. Could the King be sincere in his support of the Constitution when his own Gardes du Corps were being assembled in order to destroy it? The Gardes du Corps were right to fear 'the misfortunes which could occur to the King and the Queen through our fault',[4] as the Comte d'Agoult, one of their aide-majors-généraux, wrote to the Duc de Guiche, one of the two captains of the guard at Coblenz (three remained in France) on 31 January 1792. The King was found guilty and guillotined on 21 January 1793.

Louis XVI was not the only king to suffer misfortunes in this period. In November 1795, Ferdinand IV of Naples was forced to reform his Guardie del Corpo as the Corpo Reale dei Guardie, composed of 248 officers from the army, rather than of members of the nobility. The reason was a conspiracy among the Guardie del Corpo who had, in the words of the Queen, been 'entirely corrupted' by revolutionary ideas. The guards of the Prince of Orange were disbanded in 1795, and those of the King of Sardinia, ruler of Piedmont, in 1798, when it became evident that resistance to the armies of the French Republic was useless.

In other monarchies, however, the increasingly monarchical and anti-revolutionary spirit of the age, added to the personal influence of the monarchs, led to an increase in the size, splendour and independence of their guards. Even more than the age of Louis XIV, this was the golden age of royal guards. Paul I of Russia, after his accession in 1796, incorporated most of his 2400 'Gatchina troops', named after his palace outside St Petersburg, and drilled and uniformed 'in every respect like Prussian soldiers', into the Imperial Guard. He ensured that between October 1797 and January 1801 the exiled Louis XVIII was guarded by over 100 Gardes du Corps in his palace at Mittau. By 1800, after many changes, he had developed the Chevaliers-Gardes and the Cossack and Hussar squadrons of Catherine II into three full guard regiments.[5]

13.   Gabriel Lory. *View of the Grand Parade in front of the Winter Palace.* 1799. PHOTO THOMAS AGNEW AND SONS.

In the reign of Paul I these daily parades, which took place whatever the temperature, were 'at once an endurance test for officers, the chief ceremony of state and a means by which Paul could exercise direct personal control of the Empire'. Guards were so closely connected with monarchies that an impressive proportion of their activities took place in front of, or inside a palace, as is shown by the illustrations in this book.

But the most important guard of the golden age, a guard which became a legend and a model in its brief lifetime, was the Garde Impériale of Napoleon I. The Directory had already endorsed the principle of a privileged guard by creating guards recruited from soldiers over 1m 70cm tall with good service records for itself and the Corps Législatif in 1795. After Bonaparte's coup d'état of 10 November 1799, they formed the nucleus of the Garde des Consuls, which numbered 2089 by 3 January 1800, under the command of Murat. Continuity with previous French guards was shown by the fact that many soldiers of the Garde des Consuls, such as General Hulin, who led the attack on the Bastille, had served in the Gardes Françaises, while Murat, their commander, had been in the Garde Constitutionelle. From the beginning, soldiers in the Garde had more splendid uniforms, higher pay (240 francs for a grenadier of the Garde, 128 francs 10 centimes for a grenadier of the line) and higher rank than soldiers of the line, and there was a height requirement of 1m 78cm. Bonaparte intended, as he wrote in January 1800, that 'the guard shall be a model for the army'. His guard was not only a model but also a pillar of his ever-increasing authority. For, already the most successful and admired general of his age, he was rapidly becoming the absolute master of France. In the years between 1800 and 1804 he used the regular reviews of his guard in the courtyard of the Tuileries (see illustration 14), so recently the scene of the battle between the Gardes Suisses and the Paris mob, as an opportunity to display his power. Most French people were now so exhausted with politics, and so intoxicated with military glory, that they did not mind having Bonaparte as their master. Therefore, these reviews, in the words of an English visitor, 'excite a very strong sensation at Paris, where their presence alone maintains public tranquility and upholds the usurped throne of Bonaparte.

On 10 May 1804 the guard was renamed the Garde Impériale and received a new eagle-strewn uniform, as Bonaparte had become Emperor of the French: four marshals, Bessières, Soult, Mortier and Davout were the four colonels-general of the guard. By January 1805 it numbered 52,224 soldiers, a small army in itself, and included representatives of every division of the armed forces, even the navy (the Marins de la Garde).[6]

One of the essential features of the Garde Impériale was that, even more than most royal guards, it ignored national frontiers in its composition as well as in its movements. On 1 October 1802 a squadron of 172 Mameloukes de la Garde, recruited during Bonaparte's invasion of Egypt, was added to the Garde des Consuls. Although a majority of Mamelukes was always from the Middle East (for example, Abu Salmoud, born in Cairo in 1780, who served as a Mameluke of Napoleon until 1806, or Abdallah Mansour, born in Jaffa in 1774, who served until 1804), many of them were French or West Indian. The main purpose of the Mamelukes de la Garde was to dramatize the figure of Napoleon and to impress the inhabitants of whichever country he happened to be in.

14.   Isabey. *Review by General Bonaparte, First Consul.* 1800. PHOTO ROGER VIOLLET.

These brilliant parades left a profound impression both on contemporaries and on posterity. Watching one, a resigned Deputy of the Corps Législatif exclaimed, 'Behold the Master of the earth'. Nicholas I of Russia (1825–55) said that he kept a picture of a parade of the Garde Impériale in his study 'always in front of me, because it was able to beat us'.

After April 1807 Napoleon I had two, and after July 1812 three, companies of Chevau-Légers Polonais in his guard, although he was not sovereign of any portion of Polish territory. They were some of the most devoted and intrepid soldiers of his guard. In 1809 the Garde Impériale absorbed 1075 Italian Velites, raised to guard Napoleon's viceroys, Prince Borghese in Turin and Elisa Bonaparte in Florence. In August 1810 the Garde Impériale also absorbed the Dutch Royal Guard, just as the French Empire absorbed the Kingdom of Holland, after the abdication of its King, Louis Bonaparte. On 8 October 1812 the Garde Impériale received another Oriental contingent in the form of a company of Lithuanian Tartars (relics of the enormous medieval Grand Duchy of Lithuania, which had included many Muslims) commanded by an officer whose name, like his functions, is a symbol of the connections between Europe and the Middle East: Mustapha Musa Achmatowicz. The uniform of the Lithuanian Tartars – yellow turbans, green jackets, crimson sashes and wide green trousers – was even more exotic than that of the Mamelukes.[7]

As King of Italy Napoleon I also had a large Italian Royal Guard. It paraded in the courtyard of the Tuileries on 20 January 1805 when a deputation came to offer him the crown of Italy, but it was normally stationed in Milan. Other members of his family in addition to Louis Bonaparte also had large, privileged royal guards. Jerome and Joseph Bonaparte had their own guards as Kings of Westphalia (1807–13) and Spain (1808–13). The Royal Guard of Naples, created during Joseph's brief reign in 1806, reached its apogee under Murat (1808–15): in 1815 it numbered 14,197 or 17.5 per cent of the army. These guards were so cosmopolitan that an enormous proportion of their officers was French. Napoleon complained on 4 May 1807, and again on 10 January 1809, that so many officers were being recruited from the French army for the Royal Guards of Naples and Holland, as well as for 'my guard', that its 'spirit' was bound to suffer. A third of all French officers serving in the Neapolitan army were serving in the Royal Guard of Murat. Even their uniforms, particularly those of the Royal Guards of Spain and Italy, were almost exactly the same as those of the Garde Impériale. Another factor that these satellite royal guards had in common was an aristocratic unit called Guardie d'Onore in the kingdoms of Italy, Naples and Spain, and Gardes du Corps in the kingdoms of Holland and Westphalia; most were, as an officer of the Dutch Royal Guard recalled, 'young people of good family having the rank of sub-lieutenant in the line'.[8]

Although, as King of Italy, Napoleon I had, from 20 June 1805, four companies of one hundred Guardie d'Onore each, as Emperor of the French he had no aristocratic guard units. His Garde Impériale was splendid, privileged and victorious, but not especially aristocratic. Yet to the Emperor and many of his subjects an aristocratic guard unit still seemed as essential in his guard, as it had always been in other monarchs'.

On 3 March 1806, Senator Dubois-Dubais, who had been an officer of the Garde du Corps from 1763 to 9 October 1789 (he had probably resigned out of fright at the attack on Versailles three days before), sent a circular to his former comrades in the Gardes du Corps suggesting that as 'the partisans of the throne', which 'Napoleon had just restored with splendour', they should volunteer to be Gardes du Corps of the Emperor. Two hundred and sixty-nine former Gardes du Corps, including Varicourt and Miomandre who had defended Marie-Antoinette's apartment against the mob on 6 October 1789, 108 sons or nephews of former Gardes du Corps and 289 former officers of the army of Louis XVI were among the 795 volunteers. The same Comte d'Agoult who had preferred to serve Louis XVI rather than his brothers in 1792, wrote a long and fascinating Mémoire describing the functions of the different guards at Versailles and urging Napoleon I to have 3356 Gardes du Corps (Louis XVI had had only 1500) with more privileges than in the past. Some of the cost was to be borne by the cities of Paris and Versailles precisely because they 'destroyed the corps by attacking the monarch'.

This remarkable document shows how strong the monarchical instinct now was among the French aristocracy. But Napoleon did not dare re-create the Gardes du Corps, although he was jealous when his brothers did, and wrote, as if his family had been royal for hundreds of years, 'Ce n'est pas l'étiquette de notre famille.' He contented himself with sending 140 former Gardes du Corps to serve Joseph in Naples. Instead, on 1 October 1806, two companies of aristocratic Gendarmes d'Ordannance were formed under the command of the Comtes de Mortemart and d'Arberg. Despite performing well in the campaign of 1807, they were bitterly resented by the Garde Impériale, with whom they shared the duty of escorting the Emperor, and on 12 July 1807, probably for that reason, they were disbanded; Napoleon I was always a little frightened of his guard.[9]

On 22 October 1812, the almost successful coup d'état of General Malet, a former Mousquetaire, was foiled by the detachment of the Garde Impériale left in Paris under General Hulin, a former sergeant in the Gardes Françaises. It revealed the fragility of Napoleon's regime and made the Emperor, when he returned to Paris, think of strengthening his guard. On 30 December 1812 he dictated the following note, very revealing of a monarch's attitude to his guard.

It is thought that the Garde Impériale is not splendid enough, and that its uniforms and decorations do not make a sufficient contribution to the splendour and majesty which should surround the sovereigns. It is thought that the entrances to the palace and the doors to the apartments are not sufficiently guarded. . . A project for the formation of companies of Gardes du Corps could be studied: at the same time as being a real guard they would be a nursery of officers for the army. A plan could also be drawn up for the formation of one or more companies of Gardes des Portes, on the model of the Hungarian Noble Guard in Vienna or the Cent-Suisses in Saxony. They would be given a splendid uniform. As for the Gardes du Corps they could wear breast-plates.

Several such projects were drawn up, some based on Louis XVI's ordinance of 15 December 1775. But in the end, on 3 April 1813, a decree was published announcing the Emperor's decision to raise 10,000 Gardes d'Honneur, from the families of the highest taxpayers of his Empire. By September, there were 6837 French, 1232 Italian, 1165 Belgian, 524 Dutch, and 302 German Gardes d'Honneur. Although, by a decision of 29 July 1813, they were part of the Garde Impériale, they never had any guard duties and in fact only demonstrated the hostility of much of the aristocracy to the Emperor. In August 1813 there was a royalist conspiracy among some of the French Gardes d'Honneur; by the autumn all the foreign Gardes d'Honneur, except the Belgians, had turned against the regime. In January 1814 the Emperor decided that they no longer formed part of his Garde Impériale.[10]

Napoleon loved his guard, was always surrounded by it, in his palaces or on the battlefield, and jealously preserved its innumerable privileges and independence. On 15 January 1809 he even wrote to his Chief of Staff, Berthier, 'The guard is not part of the army.' Another Emperor who loved and expanded his guard (so much that it doubled in his reign) and ensured that, as an Austrian observer wrote, a 'difference and separation' was 'kept up between the guard and the rest of the army', was Alexander I of Russia. During his reign the Russian Imperial Guard acquired, often as a reward for distinction in battle, a regiment of chasseurs in 1806, regiments of lancers and dragoons in 1809, Lithuanian and Finnish regiments, and an escort of Black Sea Cossacks in 1811; regiments of cuirassiers and grenadiers, and the Pavlovski Regiment named after Paul I's favourite palace, in 1813; the Moscow Guard regiment in 1817; regiments of lancers and cuirassiers, and the Volhynian Guard regiment from western Ukraine in 1818; and the regiment of Grodno Hussars, named after a city in Lithuania, in 1824. The guard also had its own artillery and sappers and, from 1814, a separate staff and divisional organization. This dramatic expansion showed that not only Napoleon I, who owed his throne to the Revolution, but also his rival, Alexander I, who owed his throne to heredity, felt the need for a large, independent guard as a support for his authority and an inspiration for his army. The Russian Imperial Guard was one of the most impressive forces in Europe. The English general, Sir Robert Wilson, wrote, 'There cannot be a nobler corps or one of more warlike disposition than the Russian Imperial Guard.' At Tilsit in 1807 it displayed 'a combination of . . . manly expression and warlike simplicity, of martial character and beauty which was not only unrivalled but elevated above all comparison'.[11]

The meeting between Alexander I and Napoleon I at Tilsit witnessed one of the first of the joint reviews or banquets, treating royal guards as forces with the same purpose and character, which marked and symbolized their golden age. On 27 June, Alexander I reviewed the French Garde Impériale. Napoleon I was determined 'that his guard should justify the high reputation it had acquired' and 'he urged us on and encouraged us with his voice, his gestures, and his look', according to one of its officers. The next day the Gendarmes d'Ordonnance entertained the Chevalier-Gardes and the Garde Impériale entertained 800 soldiers of the Russian and Prussian Guards, to banquets: the Garde Impériale on the whole preferred the Prussians because they did not get so hopelessly drunk. It is said that Alexander I was so impressed by the efficiency of the Marins de la Garde in ferrying Napoleon I to the raft in the Niemen where the two Emperors met, that he decided to create his own naval guard, the origin of the famous Garde Equipage of the Romanovs formed in 1810. In 1812–15 royal guards were so important both for their performance on the battlefield, and as reflections of the state of their monarchies, that French and even European history can be viewed in terms of their evolution and actions. Of the 30–35,000 soldiers of the Garde Impériale who crossed the Niemen to invade Russia on 24 June 1812, only 3000 remained by 20 December. During his retreat from Moscow, Napoleon travelled so quickly that he outshot his own guard; on 30 October he had to be guarded by the delighted soldiers of the Grand Ducal Guards of Hesse-Darmstadt, who at this time formed part of the Garde Impériale.

The 'French' Imperial Guard – which now contained many Italians and Germans – in the campaign of 1813 was more than ever the elite and reserve of the army. At the same time, probably under the influence of Frederick William III's friend and ally, Alexander I, the Prussian Guard greatly increased in size and independence, as part of the expansion and reorganization of the Prussian army in preparation for the final onslaught on Napoleon. On 19 June 1813 a Second Foot Guard Regiment was created; on 1 July the First Foot Guard Regiment was withdrawn from the line; squadrons of Uhlans and – a clear sign of Russian influence – Cossacks of the guard were raised that summer. By 10 August, 7091 of the 161,764 troops in the Prussian army belonged to the guard, which now had a 'separate organization'.[12]

The Prussian and Russian Guards acted in the main allied army of 200,000 as a separate reserve of 37,000 troops around their monarchs during the campaigns of 1813–14 – another sign that guards were thought to have a common, particularly monarchical character and a different purpose from line troops. The Emperor Francis I of Austria was so impressed by the heroism of the Russian Guard at the Battle of Kulm, that he erected a monument, *A l'Honneur des Gardes Russes*, on the battlefield. But it did not make him want to change the nature or size of his own guard. On 4 August 1813, because the Arcieren Garde and the Hungarian Noble Guard were overstretched by the demands of guarding the Emperor in the field and the court at Vienna, a Bohemian Noble Guard of 120 (including servants) was created. The Austrian Habsburgs' extraordinary indifference to guards, and to provincial enthusiasm, is shown by the fact that this guard, a living and, in part, spontaneous symbol of Bohemian nobles' loyalty to the monarchy, was allowed to lapse after the Emperor's return to Vienna on 16 June 1814. Its members were dismissed with a commemorative medal.

As the allied troops drew nearer to France the symbolic and military role of the guards grew more prominent. After crossing the Rhine, there was a joint parade of the Prussian and Russian Guards before the three allied monarchs, where 'shouts of joy rang up to the heavens': they knew they were on the way to Paris and to victory. By 5 March 1814, 27,307 of Napoleon I's tiny army of 39,304 were soldiers of the Garde Impériale, and this campaign, one of his most brilliant, was known as 'the campaign of the Imperial Guard'. After his inevitable defeat, the Prussian Horse Guards led the allied entry into Paris on 31 March; the Comte de Rochechouart, an emigré officer in the Russian Garde à Cheval, commanded the garrison of Paris – now composed not of French but of Prussian and Russian Guards – until 3 June.[13]

Back at Fontainebleau, the remnants of the Garde Impériale, still guarding their Emperor, were more admired than ever. At allied headquarters 'everyone spoke of the Emperor and his Guards as if there was something in them more than human to be dreaded'. When the Emperor set out from Fontainebleau for Elba on 20 April, his farewell to his guard acknowledged and immortalized their glory.

> Soldiers of the Old Guard! I bid you farewell! I am satisfied with you. For twenty years I have found you loyal and brave! . . . Serve with loyalty the sovereign whom the nation has chosen. I could have died but I want to live on for you! I want to write; the finest occupation of my life will now be to record your achievements for posterity . . . I cannot embrace you all, but I will embrace your general and the eagles which have guarded you in the days of danger and glory. Adieu!

Over 830 soldiers of the Garde Impériale, including 120 Chevau-Légers Polonais and six Mamelukes, followed the Emperor to Elba.

Napoleon I had thought it unwise for Louis XVIII to keep the Garde Impériale as his own guard. Indeed, the King could have heard for himself their cries of 'Vive l'Empereur'! when he entered Paris on 3 May. It was hardly surprising that, at the first meeting of his Council on 5 May, the first measure which the King proposed was the restoration of the Maison Militaire as it was before 1775; Artois, always frank, 'links the preservation of the monarchy to the creation of these corps'. It was not only 'the preservation of the monarchy', however, which made Louis XVIII and his family desire the re-creation of these ancient corps. It was intended to use the Maison Militaire to rally both the royalist and the Napoleonic aristocracy to the monarchy. Thus, two new companies of Gardes du Corps, under the Napoleonic marshals, Berthier and Marmont, were added to the four traditional ones in order, as Louis XVIII said, to 'prove to the army that his confidence is equal in all Frenchmen'. In addition, the ordinance of 15 June re-establishing the Chevau-Légers de la Garde referred to 'the Throne needing to be surrounded by all the splendour appropriate, and the King finding the means to reward useful services by re-establishing his Household as it was in the past (but for the changes necessitated by the passage of time)'. For the royal guard was also to be used to increase the splendour of the throne – a more popular concept now than in the 1770s and 1780s – and to provide employment for those royalists disappointed by the King's policy of leaving most of the Napoleonic personnel of the army, the administration and the law in place. The number of the new Maison Militaire was to be 4859, including 2686 Gardes du Corps, a thousand more than in the eighteenth century.[14]

Although, as Louis XVIII intended, the Maison Militaire contained many former soldiers of the Empire – five of the fourteen commanders, most of the Grenadiers à Cheval, seventy-two of the 358 Mousquetaires Gris for example – it was bitterly resented by most of their comrades. The surviving regiments of the Garde Impériale were furious that, although they kept their privileges of pay and rank, they were no longer the guards of the monarch,

15.   Montfort. *The Adieux of Fontainebleau*. 20 April 1814. PHOTO RÉUNION DES MUSÉES NATIONAUX.

One of the most famous of all pictures of a historical event, *The Adieux of Fontainebleau* is also the supreme representation of a guard's personal bond with its monarch. In the courtyard of his palace, the fallen Emperor bids farewell to his weeping, devoted guard. He is wearing the uniform which they have led to victory across Europe. After the adieux those guards who stayed with their Emperor provided him with a nucleus of loyal followers without which he could not have reached Elba or recovered France.

stationed in Paris where they belonged, but line regiments stationed in the provinces. And, as one officer wrote, their 'former *esprit de corps* was not dead'. In Paris the Maison Militaire was also unpopular with the Garde Nationale, which had briefly guarded the Tuileries palace, and with some of the people of Paris: on 11 November 1814 the Directeur-Général du Ministère de la Police reported to the King that 'the Gardes du Corps are not popular in Paris precisely because they are a privileged body'. The revival of the Maison Militaire was one of the most important factors in alienating sections of public opinion from Louis XVIII. Moreover, events would show that it was not even a useful fighting force.

When Bonaparte landed near Antibes on 1 March 1815, he was accompanied by most of his guard from Elba and published a proclamation, 'The Garde Impériale to the Generals, Officers and Soldiers of the Army', which stated: 'We have landed on the sacred soil of the fatherland with the national cockade and the imperial eagle. . . We have kept your Emperor

16.   Anon. print. *Chacun son Tour, ou la Fin du Roman.* 1815. MUSÉE CARNAVALET.

Guards were now so important that they could be used to symbolize the monarchies they served, as is shown by this print depicting Napoleon's return from Elba. Two soldiers of the Garde Impériale are extinguishing a Mousquetaire on the left and a Garde du Corps on the right, who symbolize the unpopular ancien régime aspect of the government of Louis XVIII. Above, the imperial eagle is flying in triumph to Notre Dame.

for you. They [the Bourbons] have forgotten nothing and learnt nothing.' The Emperor's guard, laughing and cheerful as it swept on to Paris, provided the indispensable nucleus of armed force without which he would never have dared to land in France and but for which, it is possible, French troops would not have hesitated to obey orders and shoot.[15]

Back in Paris, the guard round the Tuileries was tripled, on 11 March. By 13 March there were more than 300 volunteers, from what one officer called 'the scum of the city of Paris', in the Cent-Suisses. By 16 March there were more than 1000 volunteers in the Gardes de la Porte. But any attempt by the King to make a stand in Paris with his guard was doomed to founder on the fact that, in January 1815, the King, Artois and Maréchal Soult, the Minister of War, had decided, for reasons which have never been explained, not to revive the military core of the old royal guard, the Gardes Françaises and the Gardes Suisses. Thus there were no large infantry units of the guard to oppose the Bonapartist forces advancing on Paris. The King was alarmed that there might be Bonapartists even in the Gardes du Corps. And the feeble attempts made, too late, to win over the former Garde Impériale – such as the

Duc de Berri's letter of 13 March to Maréchal Oudinot offering it the title of Garde du Roi –
had no effect.[16]

On the night of 19 March, Louis XVIII left the Tuileries, accompanied by a few courtiers
and Gardes du Corps. Louis XVIII had told Maréchal Marmont, who was in command of the
Maison Militaire, to retire to Lille. But the King, using post-horses, rushed on ahead of his
guards. They were left to retreat north, in appalling conditions, at the pace of their exhausted
horses; one Gendarme de la Garde writes of 'waves of mud' everywhere, and of the horses
being 'up to their stomachs in mud'. The soldiers were exhausted, frightened and without
news of the King. By the time they reached the frontier there had been many desertions; only
450 chose to cross into Belgium with Artois on 27 March.[17]

In Paris, the Emperor, who had abolished the Maison Militaire on 13 March, rapidly
re-formed his Garde Impériale. It soon had enough *esprit de corps* to resent the inscription,
Séjour des Braves, which the guard from Elba erected outside the Hôtel opposite the
Tuileries palace where they had replaced the Cent-Suisses. The end of the Empire and, as
John Keegan has written, 'the reversal of the most powerful current in recent European
history', was signalled by the defeat (but not, contrary to legend, decimation) of the Garde
Impériale at Waterloo by British troops including the First or, as they were henceforth called
in commemoration of their rout of the Grenadiers de la Garde Impériale, Grenadier Guards.
The Cuirassiers de la Garde also disintegrated before a celebrated charge by the Life Guards.
An indictment of Napoleon I's use of his guard as a tactical reserve, rarely thrown into battle
– it was also held in reserve at Jena, Friedland, Wagram and Borodino – is that at Waterloo,
when the guard was used, and retreated, the agonized, incredulous cry, '*La Garde recule!*'
led to the disintegration and flight of the rest of the French army. The Garde Impériale was
dissolved at Orléans on 3 August.

Louis XVIII returned to Paris escorted by ever increasing numbers of his Maison
Militaire. To one former Garde d'Honneur, now a Chevau-Léger de la Garde, Heriot de Vroil,
their triumphant re-entry into Paris on 8 July to ecstatic cries of '*Vive le Roi!*' was 'the finest
day of our life'. The inadequacy of the old Maison Militaire, however, had been clearly
shown by the débâcle of March 1815. Already the Duc d'Orléans had, on 25 April, suggested
to the King that it was better to be in the Tuileries surrounded by a guard 'organized on the
principles of modern tactics', despite the danger that it might be a 'praetorian guard', than 'in
Ghent surrounded by the debris of his Maison Militaire'. In July 1815 there was a deluge of
projects suggesting ways of, as Maréchal Marmont put it, 'protecting the Throne from new
insults'. A plan of 8 July even suggested that the entire army should be called the Garde du
Roi (Napoleon I had made a similar suggestion to the King of Prussia, for financial reasons, in
1810): 'Another glory, that of guarding the monarch, must be put in the place of military
glory, which will always recall Napoleon.'[18]

At first, however, neither the liberal Minister of War, Maréchal Gouvion Saint-Cyr, nor
the President of the Council, the Prince de Talleyrand, wanted a large royal guard. Gouvion
Saint-Cyr, who often said that 'the Emperor of Austria seemed to him the best guarded
monarch in Europe, precisely because he did not have a special guard', which might have
pretentions of its own and alienate or weaken the army, wanted a royal guard of at most
12,000 troops. His project was refused by Louis XVIII who, on the advice of Alexander I, and
without consulting his ministers, decided to increase his guard's size and privileges. At a
council where 'the King discussed briefly but very positively, from the military and political
point of view, the advantages of such an increase', it was decided to create a Garde Royale of
26,678 soldiers, of whom 3700 were to be Swiss. On 25 September, the Gardes du Corps were
reorganized, reduced to about 1500, placed under the authority of the Minister of War rather
than of the Maison du Roi, and their passage into, and from, the line army facilitated.[19]

Except in the royalist south and west of France, it was more difficult than had been expected to find recruits for the Garde Royale, as the Prefects' correspondence shows: they had to be not only more than 1m 78cm high and between nineteen and twenty-seven years old, but also produce a certificate signed by three notables of their 'good conduct' and 'devotion to the King'. The English and Prussian Guards, however, who had been performing 'public duties' in Paris since October, were able to make way for the Garde Royale in January 1816. As before, Swiss units guarded the left, and French units the right, of the outside of the King's palace. Many of the officers of the Garde Royale came from the old units of the Maison Militaire, to whom the King said adieu on 31 December 1815. For example, the Comte de Lauriston, a Napoleonic officer who had been captain-lieutenant of the Mousquetaires Noirs, commanded the First Infantry Division of the Garde Royale.

The loyalty and splendour of the Garde Royale was seen as a test of the Restoration's ability to survive. When Louis XVIII received such an important political figure as Princess Lieven, in October 1817, he talked only about his health and his guard: 'He told me "there are people who claim the guard was finer in the time of Bonaparte, but as for me, I do not think so".' Many other people agreed with the King. For example, in 1823, during the French invasion of Spain, a French officer, M. de Bussy, also judged the Empire and the Restoration by their guards, and found the Garde Royale at least the equal of the Garde Impériale. He wrote that the Garde Royale, 'cited in Paris for its discipline and fine appearance, has displayed all the military virtues in Spain, and has raised itself brilliantly to the height of the Garde Impériale'.[20]

In the golden age of royal guards, Prussia was another monarchy which continued to increase the size of its guard. On 19 May 1814 the Guard Fusilier battalion recruited from Neuchâtel, and formerly in the service of Maréchal Berthier, Prince de Neuchâtel (now a captain of the guard of Louis XVIII) became part of the Prussian Guard, thereby reviving – although not in name – a Swiss Guard. On 14 and 19 October 1814, the two Garde Grenadier regiments, Kaiser Alexander and Kaiser Franz, named after their colonels the Emperors of Russia and Austria, were added to the Prussian Guard. The creation of two Prussian Guard regiments whose colonels were, until 1914, foreign monarchs, like the expansion of the Garde Royale of France in 1815 on the advice of Alexander I of Russia, was a sign that royal guards tended to exist in a separate, royal and cosmopolitan sphere, which was different from the more normal, and more national, world of line regiments. On 21 February 1815, the Guard Dragoon and Uhlan, and on 2 March the Guard Hussar regiments were created, the second from the existing guard squadrons of Uhlans and Cossacks (it was renamed Guard Cuirassier regiment on 25 September 1821). On 14 April 1819 the First, and on 3 April 1821, the Second, Landwehr Guard cavalry regiments – part of the liberal citizen army which was so distrusted by conservatives – were formed. The Prussian Guard was now a separate brigade, stationed in Berlin, under its own *Brigadechef*, the King's brother-in-law, Duke Charles of Mecklenburg. An admirer of Napoleon I, he made the guard 'the focal point of all the reactionary trends in the army', denounced the Landwehr to the King and blocked Clausewitz's career.[21]

The Prussian Guard was not only politically influential, it was also very impressive to look at. On 3 April 1813 an officer of the Russian Guard wrote that the Prussian Guard 'impressed us enormously with the simplicity of their uniforms and their splendid bearing'. After a review of 12,000 Prussian Guards in Paris on 24 July 1815 – never has a city seen so many reviews of so many different guards, Russian, Prussian, English, French Imperial, traditional French Royal, modern French Royal, as Paris in 1814–16 – Lady Shelley wrote that 'I never beheld such troops and the Duke [of Wellington] thinks them finer than any he has ever seen.' At this review the Emperors of Russia and Austria, in the uniform of Prussian Guards officers, led regiments of the Prussian Guard past the King of Prussia, also in the uniform of a Prussian Guards officer. Indeed these years were such a cosmopolitan period in the history of royal guards that, in Paris in 1815, 'the duty of mounting guard upon the persons of the monarchs is performed by the troops of each nation in succession'. The Prussian Guard remained closely linked with the Russian and, on 30 March 1829, Frederick William III created a company of seventy NCOs 'to guard the Royal Palace and gardens', on the model of the Palace Grenadiers created by Nicholas I on 2 October 1827. One of the Tsar's ADCs, Prince Wolkonsky, came to Berlin to supervise the details.[22]

A large independent royal guard 'organized according to the principles of modern tactics' was thought to be such an essential aspect of monarchy in this period that, for the only time in its history, the Bavarian monarchy also had one. Proposed in January 1811, on the model of the Garde Impériale, 'to increase the glory of the Royal Crown', the guard of one regiment of Gardes du Corps (commanded by Prince Constantin von Löwenstein-Wertheim-Rosenberg), and one of Grenadier Guards, was finally set up on 16 July 1814. Field Marshal von Wrede, the hero of the Bavarian army, favoured the creation of the guard because of the military advantage of 'exemplary troops'; the money for the new regiments, which had extremely lavish uniforms, came from the profits of the war with France. On 30 November 1825, however, both regiments were reduced to the status of line regiments by the new King Ludwig I, who had opposed their creation in the first place, and wished to devote his

17.   Carle Vernet. *Parade in Paris.* 1815. SCHLOSS CHARLOTTENBURG.

Frederick William III, Alexander I and Wellington are reviewing the Prussian Guard in front of the Ecole Militaire. Palmerston, and many others, found the Prussian Guard an extremely impressive spectacle, its soldiers 'particularly tall and well-sized'.

18. Brücke. *The Changing of the Guard.* 1854. SCHLOSS CHARLOTTENBURG.

In Berlin, as in most other capitals of Europe, the changing of the guard was a very popular spectacle.

revenues to making Munich an artistic, rather than a military, centre.

The kingdom of the Two Sicilies also expanded its royal guard, after the restoration of Ferdinand IV, on 8 December 1815. It now included, in addition to Gardes du Corps and Alabardieri, six regiments and six companies of regular soldiers. This enormous royal guard constituted 11,342 soldiers or 12 per cent of the army in 1855. On 30 May 1833 Guardie d'Onore, 'unique in all Europe, born out of his subjects' spontaneous love for their sovereign', were created in the different provinces. The guard disappeared with the kingdom of the Two Sicilies in 1860. In 1815, a year when royal guards were being created or expanded all over Europe, Alexander I of Russia, as King of Poland, created a Polish royal guard, including some of Napoleon's Polish Guards, of about 6000. Officers of the Polish and Russian Guards had celebratory banquets together in June 1815. It was disbanded in 1831, as a result of the Polish revolt against Alexander's brother, Nicholas I.

Nicholas I, who, in 1826, remarked that 'the guard is everything now for a monarchy', added to his Russian Guard in 1827 by creating the Palace Grenadiers and the Escort of His Majesty – squadrons of horsemen from the recently conquered provinces of the Caucasus, who escorted the Tsar on his journeys. An English traveller was very impressed by their 'scarlet kaftans' and 'chain-armour' when he saw them exercising before the Emperor, with the Chevaliers-Gardes, in the summer of 1829. That year Nicholas also added a second Cossack regiment, the Atamanskii, to the guard.

19.   *Uniform of the Schlossgarde,*
drawn by Frederick William III of
Prussia, 1829, from Leo von
Pfannenberg, *Geschichte der
Schlossgarde-Kompagnie Seiner
Majestät des Kaisers und Königs.* Berlin
1909.

This uniform was modelled on that of
the Palace Grenadiers of Frederick William III's son-in-law, Nicholas I of
Russia, founded two years earlier,
which in its turn was modelled on that
of the Garde Impériale of Napoleon I.
Monarchs were particularly concerned
with their guards' appearance in the
early nineteenth century. George IV, for
example, was said to spend more time
with his tailors than with his ministers.

Piedmont not only recovered its traditional royal guard, as well as its legitimate rulers,
in 1814, but added a fourth, Genoese, company to the Gardes du Corps on 18 July 1815,
which was intended to symbolize the attachment of the newly acquired province to its new
rulers. On 1 April 1816 the regiment of Sardinia became the regiment of Cacciatori
Guardie.[23]

In Sweden, under the critical eye of Maréchal Bernadotte, who became King Charles
XIV Johan, in 1818, the guard also became more disciplined and larger; the Life Grenadier
Regiment was expanded into two regiments in 1816; and the Life Regiment brigade became
three separate units, the Life Regiment Dragoon, Hussar and Grenadier corps. In all, in 1833,
there were nine regiments of Swedish Hustrupper, 7017 soldiers or 17 per cent of the army.

In the United Kingdom, royal guards also increased in size and status. After Waterloo,
'as a mark of our royal favour for the distinguished gallantry of the brigade of Foot Guards',
its ensigns received the rank of lieutenant in the army. Since it had been stationed at

Windsor instead of the provinces in 1804, the regiment of Horse Guards known as the Blues had become a great favourite of George III and in reality, as well as in name, a royal guard. On 1 March 1820, its distinguished military record and the 'partiality' of George III, led to it being granted 'the same honours and privileges in every respect as are possessed by the two regiments of Life Guards'. In 1822, the petition of the Company of Archers, a Scottish nobles' sporting club, to become a royal guard in Scotland as a means of 'testifying their loyalty to the Crown and Constitution, and their attachment to His Majesty's person' was granted. Henceforth, in a more casual episodic way, the Company of Archers had a similar function to the Hungarian Noble Guard in that it symbolized the attachment of a distant and hitherto partly hostile aristocracy to a slightly alien monarchy. The captain-general of the company acts as 'Gold Stick for Scotland' when the monarch is in Edinburgh.[24]

Spain provided one of the most dramatic examples of the expansion of royal guards in the later part of this period. In 1814 the traditional royal guard, sections of which had continued to fight the French during the Peninsular War, was restored with the Bourbon dynasty. The principal changes were that the Gardes Wallonnes became increasingly Spanish in composition until, on 1 June 1818, they were renamed the Second Regiment of Royal Guards of Infantry. The Guardias de Corps were renamed Guardias de la Persona del Rey on 3 May 1815, and on 28 October 1816 a Brigade of Flanquadores or light cavalry was added to the royal guard. The entire guard was disbanded in July 1822 after it had attempted to rescue the King from the control of the revolutionaries in Madrid (see Chapter 6). When the King was finally rescued by the French army, he was guarded for a year, from July 1823 to June 1824, by French Gardes du Corps and Gardes Royaux; his minister, Ofalia, wrote to say 'how satisfied He was with the excellent conduct of the French Gardes du Corps'.[25]

Meanwhile, an enormous Spanish royal guard directly modelled on that of France (the commander of the guard infantry was a Frenchman, the Comte d'Espagne), was being organized: it was the fourth time, after the guards of Charles V, Philip V and Joseph Bonaparte, that a new royal guard had been created in Spain on a foreign model. Six companies of Guardias de la Persona del Rey were created on 9 August 1824, including two foreign companies, one of which was known as la Sajona, or the Saxon, from the nationality of Ferdinand VII's current wife. On 1 May 1824 a large modern Guardia Real was created, as the royal decree stated, 'to sustain the rights of the Throne, to maintain order in the Monarchy, to go wherever is necessary with the other troops in offensive and defensive wars, and to serve as a model and stimulus for the rest of the army'. Soldiers were chosen from conscripts 'who are not vicious' or line soldiers of 'robust complexion' and 'irreproachable conduct'. Officers had to prove 'adherence to the person of the King Our Lord'; clearly, as in France after 1815, the authorities were not leaving the political reliability of the Guardia Real to chance. On 9 August 1824, four regiments of provincial militia, known as the Guardia Real Provincial, were added to the guard.

The Guardia Real was always stationed near the court, never in the dreaded provincial garrisons, and had its own staff and headquarters, quite separate from the command structure of the rest of the army. It had the characteristic privileges of pay (30 per cent higher than in the army) and rank and, as in France, the King was, though slightly against his will, colonel-general. It was 'the most effective portion of the army', used as 'a training centre to produce a higher standard of discipline and officer'. By 1830 it numbered about 20,000, perhaps half the army.[26]

Another indication of the importance of guards in this period is the role of the Ottoman guard in one of the most important events in Ottoman history: the modernization and westernization of the army. From 1794 to 1807, at the instigation of Sultan Selim III, a new military corps under French instructors had been disguised as part of the guard of Bostangis in an unsuccessful attempt to make it acceptable to the Janissaries. The Janissaries, now

20.   Anon. *Illustration from a Roll of Names of Hassa Officers.* C. 1828/9. TOPKAPI SARAY MÜZESI.

This picture shows the modernized Ottoman Imperial Guard, which Sultan Mahmud II helped drill and train himself.

largely 'composed of the tradesmen, boatmen and workmen of the capital', had risen in number from 54,458 in 1794 to the incredible total of 109,971 in 1809: a sign of the number of civilians who succeeded in being entered on the payroll rather than of the number of genuine soldiers in the force. The Janissaries revolted against Selim III, deposed him and finally killed him and put an end to his new army in 1808. It took long preparation and brilliant organization for the great reforming Sultan Mahmud II, in what was officially called 'the Blessed Affair', but was in reality a ruthless bloodbath, to suppress the Janissaries on 10 June 1826.

Almost immediately a new army, organized, in the words of the Grand Vizier, according to 'modern Muslim' (not European) methods came into existence. It was reviewed by the Sultan on 29 June. An important part of it, which was, in the words of Avigdor Levy, 'modelled on Europe's Royal Guards and attached to the Imperial Household', was the Muallem Bostaniyan-i-Hassa, 'Trained Imperial Gardeners', or the guard. As in 1794, their traditional Ottoman name was intended to make them appear less modern and controversial. But in fact they were a 'completely independent unit', distinct from the Bostangis, who now ceased to be a military guard. They were disciplined, drilled and reviewed by the Sultan himself, rather as Peter the Great had organized the Preobrazhensky and Semenovsky Guards regiments himself after 1683 – a comparison familiar to some of Mahmud II's contemporaries. By November 1827 there were 29,500 'new troops' of whom 2500 were in the guard. The Sultan now rode to mosque on Friday surrounded by a military escort 'entirely composed of the new troops and the Bostangi corps organized à la franque'. There were still some Solaks and Peiks in their amazing helmets, but they had been reorganized as two infantry corps, reduced to 220, and called Servants of the Imperial Stirrup; many of them became officers of the new guard.[27] The Müteferrika were abolished in 1839.

An important element of the new guard was the band. From September 1828 it was directed by Donizetti Pasha, formerly one of Napoleon's guards on Elba, who, instead of composing operas like his brother, wrote the first Western military music, such as the 'March of the Sultan', to be used by Muslim armies. That year an English visitor was 'reminded of guards in England by one such air', played by the band of the Ottoman Imperial Guard. The Imperial Guard also controlled its own medical school and officers' school and the battalion of the Agas of the Inner Service or Court Battalion. Founded in 1826 to train household slaves – many, as usual, from the Caucasus – and sons of Muslim grandees for military service, the Court Battalion had a richer uniform than the guard and was instructed by Calosso, a former Napoleonic soldier from Piedmont who was known in Constantinople as Rustum Pasha. In 1827, 400 corporals transferred from it to the regular army with the rank of major. It was abolished in May 1830, perhaps because of disloyalty within its ranks.

By 1831, 9000 of the 41,000 infantry of the new army were in the guard. The guard cavalry took longer to organize, although in 1828 it was described as 'the favourite corps of the Sultan' who, when drilling it on horseback, 'sits firm and erect and might really pass muster among a regiment of our fine horse guards'; evidently this was regarded as one of the finest compliments that could be bestowed on a foreign horseman. Foreign observers differed in their judgement of the new Imperial Guard. Although MacFarlane, writing in 1828, thought it as good as European guards, other writers disagreed. Maréchal Marmont, for example, a former captain of the guard and major-général de la Garde Royale of Louis XVIII, although impressed by the guard school, barracks and hospital, wrote of a review, 'it is difficult to imagine anything less good or less impressive'. But the new Ottoman guard, nevertheless, represents a successful attempt at modernization of the drill, weaponry, uniforms and organization of a Middle Eastern armed force on a Western model. It also showed that a guard, trained under the eye of, or by, its sovereign, could, as in France under Louis XIII and Louis XIV, or in Russia under Peter the Great, be used as a model and an officers' training school for the rest of the army. After 1839 it was less independent of the rest of the army and after 1841 it was simply one of the seven divisions of the Ottoman army.[28]

The other great Middle Eastern monarchy, that of the Qajar Shahs of Persia who had seized the throne in 1796, had also begun to modernize its guard before 1830. Their guard consisted of a bodyguard of 12,000 soldiers drawn 'principally from the Mazanderun [the area south of the Caspian] and the tribes connected with the King's own race', which was of Turkish origin. Three thousand of these guards, or Kechekchees, were on duty at a time and 'distributed in all parts of the palace'. In addition, there was a bodyguard of three thousand Goulam-i Shah, or Slaves of the Shah, a term 'used to express their devotion to the King's service for they are not in reality entered into a state of servitude by actual purchase'. Some authorities, however, disagree and state that many, like some Ottoman guards and some of Napoleon's Mamelukes, were slaves from the Caucasus; others were 'the sons of the first nobles of Persia', so great was the honour attached to the position and so urgent the Shah's need to have hostages for his nobles' good behaviour in his guard. Whatever their origins all Goulam-i Shah were said to be 'distinguished by the excessive richness of their dress and the insolence of their manner'. What had been proposed for Prussia in 1810 and for France in

1815 was a reality in Persia: the Shah's guard was the only regular armed force in his monarchy; they were also the first Persian troops to be 'disciplined in the European manner', as a result of a French military mission which arrived in December 1807. When Sir Harford Brydges, the English minister, went to see the Shah on 17 February 1808, he found in 'the different courts [of the palace] the troops dressed in a very poor imitation of European uniforms . . . going through such exercise as the French had taught them'.[29] Again the guard had been used, as in France, Spain and the Ottoman Empire, as a model and training school for the rest of the army.

In their golden age, royal guards were, naturally, extremely important politically. Not only did they decide the fate of Louis XVIII and Napoleon I in 1814–15; they also overthrew such monarchs as Paul I of Russia in 1801, Charles IV of Spain in 1808, and Gustavus IV of Sweden in 1809 (see Chapter 6). In July 1830, however, the Garde Royale failed to save the throne of Charles X of France. It fought bravely, but briefly and unsuccessfully, against the revolutionaries in Paris. Charles X had to bid farewell to his Garde Royale and Cent-Suisses at Maintenon on 5 August and to his Gardes du Corps at Cherbourg on 16 August. These ceremonies were as moving, to the participants, as the adieux of Napoleon I to his guard sixteen years before: at Maintenon, Charles X, in tears, declared to his Garde Royale 'that he will always remember their fine conduct, their devotion in enduring the fatigues and hardships which they have suffered during these unfortunate events'. At Cherbourg he told his weeping Gardes du Corps (one of whom, Cleret, had followed the Emperor to Elba with the same devotion that he followed the King to Cherbourg) 'that he receives our flags without stain, and that he hopes the Duc de Bordeaux [his grandson] will return them to us in the same state'.[30] Back in Paris, however, the success of the July Revolution had opened a new and more threatening era for monarchies and their guards.

4
THE SURVIVAL OF ROYAL GUARDS, 1830–1984

THE FOLLIES AND bloodbaths which followed the Revolution of 1789 had seemed, even to its most enthusiastic supporters, to confirm the necessity of strong monarchy. Thus the Gardes Françaises who had stormed the Bastille were proud, fifteen years later, to serve in the Garde Impériale of Napoleon I. After the Revolution of 1830 in France, however, the preservation of the fabric of society, at the same time as the installation of a revolutionary but pacific monarchy under King Louis-Philippe I, proved the dispensability of many traditional aspects of monarchy. Louis-Philippe I did without a court and abolished the Garde Royale on 10 August 1830. Splendour and privilege, the essence of royal guards, were as unfashionable in western Europe as they had been in the 1770s and 1780s.

The realization that, if not monarchy itself, at least its traditional buttresses, could be dispensed with, without unleashing a social revolution, posed a great threat to the existence of royal guards. Moreover, by 1830, in most capitals, police forces had begun to do the work of law enforcement which had hitherto usually been, in part, the responsibility of royal guards. Instead of patrolling the capital they were increasingly confined to guarding royal palaces. In some monarchies even this role seemed dispensable.

After France, the first monarchy to begin dismantling its guard was Piedmont. King Charles-Albert (1831–49) was a professional soldier who, despite having served with the French Garde Royale in Spain in 1823, had no especial liking for traditional royal guards. Moreover, there had been a conspiracy among several Guardie del Corpo to force Charles-Albert's predecessor, King Charles Felix, to sign a constitution on his deathbed. Therefore, by a decree of 5 November 1831, despite the protest of the four captains of the guard in the name of 'this ancient and wholly monarchical Institution which has known well how to defend the Thrones of France and Spain in every Revolution', the four companies of Guardie del Corpe were reduced to one. Their recruitment was now elitist in a military, rather than a social, sense: they were chosen not from the flower of the nobility but from army sergeants with over fifteen years' good service. On 17 December the Swiss Guard was abolished because, in the opinion of the King, 'it was useless'; and on 1 January 1832 the two companies of Guardie della Porta were replaced by a company of Guardie de Real Palazzo, recruited from old soldiers below the rank of sergeant.

King Charles-Albert had maintained the privileges of the militarily most important part of the guard, the regiments of Granatieri and Cacciatori Guardie. But on 20 April 1850, despite their brave performance in the recent war against Austria, they lost the name and functions of guards because of his son, Victor Emmanuel II's decision 'to suppress every kind of ancient privileges and prerogatives in accordance with the principle that there should no longer be distinctions between units of the same arm'. The Piedmontese monarchy, which had granted a constitution in 1848, was clearly embarked on a radical and utilitarian course. In 1859–60 it was sufficiently radical, and successful, to conquer almost the whole of Italy, with the help of France, from other monarchies. On 1 September 1867, although they had been expanded to cope with the increase in their duties after the multiplication of Victor Emmanuel II's residences and journeys following the unification of Italy, the Guardie del Corpo were abolished in the interests of economy, as were the Guardie del Real Palazzo in 1870.[1]

Spain was another monarchy which dispensed with a royal guard. The Guardia Real had not been particularly obedient since the death of Ferdinand VII in 1833. In 1841 it was suspected of favouring moderate policies, perhaps even a coup in favour of the exiled Queen Mother Maria Christina, by the radical Regent Espartero. On 3 August he reduced it to two infantry and two cavalry regiments, a quarter of its previous size, and in November it was abolished altogether. The guard of the Spanish monarchy now consisted solely of the Monteros de Espinosa and about 300 Alabarderos. The lack of prestige of the Spanish monarchy among its subjects for much of the nineteenth century may be related to its lack of a strong, devoted, conservative royal guard.[2]

While other monarchies were reducing theirs, the Austrian monarchy, still living in a world of its own, increased its guard. On 6 September 1838, in an attempt to win over the discontented nobles of his Italian provinces, the Emperor Ferdinand I, who had just been crowned King of Lombardy-Venetia in Milan, created a Lombard-Venetian Noble Guard of sixty officers, 'to increase the brilliance of our Court and finally to make accessible to nobles of Lombardy-Venetia a military career in the most favourable form'. Guards had to be between seventeen and twenty, strong and of proven morality. After four years they went into the army or the civil service. The revolt of the Habsburgs' Italian subjects in 1848, however, made this guard, which had been regarded with suspicion in Lombardy-Venetia, an embarrassment. After May 1850 it no longer served at court and it was finally abolished on 1 June 1856, three years before the annexation of Lombardy to Piedmont.

The Revolution of 1848 and the campaign of repression which followed led to the creation of the Garde Gendarmerie in 1849, to serve as an escort for the Emperor when he was on campaign. On 21 April 1867, at the time of the creation of the Austro-Hungarian dual monarchy, the Hungarian Noble Guard, which had been in abeyance since the revolt of 1848, was revived 'for the protection of My Person and the members of My Imperial House as much as for the increase of the splendour of My Court' – a concept which other monarchies were no longer daring to advocate publicly. In 1904 a Hungarian Trabant Life Guard, of sixty-three German-speaking Hungarians, was created, so that royal guards as well as other institutions should be parallel in both halves of the dual monarchy. The Life Guard Horse Squadron and Infantry Company, as the Garde Gendarmerie and Hofburgwache were known after 1869 and 1884 respectively, were open to NCOs from either half of the monarchy.[3]

In other monarchies, royal guards were now regarded as controversial. In 1852 Louis-Napoleon did not re-establish the Garde Impériale when he was proclaimed Emperor of the French, although he already had an elaborate court. He waited until 1 May 1854, when the prospect of war with Russia gave him a sure means, 'of assuring the new guard of a station in the French army'.

The new Garde Impériale of eight regiments had privileges of pay and rank and 'the pick of all the tallest and most powerful young fellows'. After it had distinguished itself in the Crimea it was increased, by 1856, to seventeen regiments (34,000 men). Like many European monarchs' guards, it had a Middle Eastern element. It included a regiment of Zouaves de la Garde, in 'Algerian' uniforms and, after 1863, a battalion of Algerian cavalry – the equivalent for Napoleon III of his uncle's Mamelukes de la Garde. But the unit which most impressed Queen Victoria on her visit in 1855 – she called them 'very like our Life Guards, magnificent men of six feet and upward . . . and their dress very handsome' – was the Cent Gardes. Founded on 24 March 1854 as a corps of 148 cavalry NCOs 'for the guard of the Emperor and the service of the imperial palaces', they accompanied the Emperor everywhere and guarded the inside of his palaces; until 1858 one even slept outside his bedroom. Having escorted the Prince Impérial to the frontier on 26 August 1870 they were, like the Garde Impériale, suppressed in October, a month after the fall of the Empire; their horses were used for food during the siege of Paris. To one foreign visitor Paris without the Cent Gardes was 'no longer a capital'.[4]

In Russia and Prussia, however, where the monarchy was so strong and the monarchs so devoted to their guards, the guards, far from contracting or disappearing, like those of France, Spain and Piedmont, continued to increase in size and splendour. In Russia the Escort was increased to the strength of four squadrons in 1856: it now included Circassians, Georgians, Lezghians, Tartars and Cossacks. This magnificent, exotic and partly Muslim unit showed, like the Persian Goulam-i Shah, or the Lombard-Venetian Noble Guard, that guards served not only to guard the monarch but also, in certain monarchies with particularly discontented aristocracies, as a means to guard the guards themselves. Two of the Escort of Alexander II were sons of Shamyl, the greatest enemy of Russia in the Caucasus. Clearly, they were less of a threat to the Tsar as guards in St Petersburg than as potential troublemakers in their recently conquered homeland. By 1877 the guard numbered 75,179 out of a total of 942,030 in the regular army (8 per cent). It was thus the largest, as it was one of the most splendid, guards in the history of the monarchies of Europe and the Middle East.[5]

In Prussia, William I (1860–88) was devoted to his guard. He had served in it since 1814, had commanded the guard corps from 1838 to 1848 and, when he was King, inspected not only every regiment, but also every company and battalion of his guard every year, with an attention to detail which impressed all observers. By the reorganization of the army on 7 May 1860, and the abolition, despite opposition, of the Landwehr, five new guards regiments, including the Third Foot Guard Regiment, the Third Uhlan and Second Dragoon

21.   A. Ladurner. *Parade before the Winter Palace*. 1855. NOVOSTI.

The Romanovs frequently held parades of their enormous guard, and spent several weeks with it every summer at the guards camp at Krasnoe Seloe.

22. *Guards of the Shah of Persia.*
1862. PHOTO BIBLIOTECA MARCIANA.
VENICE.

The Shah of Persia had had guards
trained and uniformed on Western
lines since 1807. But he did not have an
effective Western-style guard until the
creation of the Cossack Brigade after
1878.

Regiments of the Guard, were created. There were now nine infantry and eight cavalry
regiments of the Guard. It was 8.5 per cent of the army (which numbered 278,223) and one of
its nine corps. The guard achieved an immense reputation in the war of 1866 against Austria
and was praised by the great Prussian writer, Fontane, for its victory at Chliem.

The same willingness to die 'for God, King, and Fatherland' (as a history of the Gardes
du Corps put it) was shown in the Franco-Prussian War. The prestige of the Prussian Guard
was symbolized by the fact that William I wore the uniform of the First Foot Guards at his
proclamation as German Emperor, in the Galerie des Glaces at Versailles, on 18 January
1871.[6]

Even in Prussia, however, royal guards had occasionally to face the challenge of that
frame of mind, so powerful in Europe, especially in France, Spain and Piedmont, to which
privileges of pay, rank and function were indefensible and old-fashioned. Such views were
also frequently expressed in the parliament of the United Kingdom, when the electorate was
in a radical mood. In 1868, Cardwell, Secretary of State for War, even wondered whether the
distinction between the guards and the line should be dropped altogether. In a wave of
reforms which again shows that guards in different monarchies were often subject to the
same forces at the same time, royal guards lost their privileges of pay and rank in Denmark in
1866, in Sweden in 1870, and in Denmark the regiment of Horse Guards was abolished. On

31 October 1871, despite the opposition of the Commander-in-Chief, the Duke of Cambridge and other members of the royal family, always eager to protect their guards, the old privilege of double rank (which had meant that to reach the rank of captain, for example, an officer in the guards took four years and five months while an officer in the line took seven years and five months), was abolished. Even in Russia the Imperial Guard was reduced from double- to single-rank privileges in 1884.[7]

Another sign of an increasing feeling that royal guards were anachronisms had been the abolition of such traditional palace guards as the Trabants of Bavaria in 1807, the Swiss Guard of Saxony in 1814, and the Drabants of Sweden in 1821. Their English equivalents survived, however, by becoming more military. From 1835 the Yeomen of the Guard, and from 1862 the Gentlemen at Arms (as the Gentlemen Pensioners were called after 1835), were restricted, as they still are, to, respectively, former NCOs and former officers with 'long or meritorious service'. As one historian of the Gentlemen at Arms writes, it was therefore again 'as it was at its institution a purely military body'. After 1837, and the monarch's departure from St James's, these units, which continue to adorn great ceremonial occasions, no longer had any real guard duties. The installation of a guard room at the entrance to the State Apartments in Buckingham Palace, the first major alteration undertaken when Queen Victoria moved in, was a symbolic rather than a practical act, a sign that royal guards were still an indispensable symbol of sovereignty. The only guards on duty every day, then as now, were forty-five Foot Guards guarding the exterior of the palace.[8]

The abolition or transformation of the least defensible privileges and units of royal guards, by the 1870s, was followed by another flowering of royal guards in the period preceding 1914. Monarchies which had thought they could do without guards rediscovered their uses; a self-conscious taste for tradition fuelled monarchs' desire to increase the size and splendour of their guards. On 7 February 1868, less than a year after the abolition of the Gardie del Corpo, eighty Carabinieri Reali were summoned to Florence to act as guards during the wedding of Crown Prince Umberto. The Carabinieri Reali had been intended for 'the accompaniment of the Royal Persons' since their foundation on 13 July 1814; from May 1836 they had joined in guard duties; by 1870 the Squadrone Carabinieri-Guardie del Re of 105 Carabinieri, endowed with 'special physical qualities of height and strength', had been created. For ceremonial occasions, such as the entry of King Victor Emmanuel II into his new capital of Rome in 1870, they wore helmets and cuirasses left over from a tournament held in Turin in 1842 – a clear sign of the role of fashionable antiquarianism in the survival of royal guards. The Carabinieri-Guardie del Re continued to guard and escort the King of Italy in war and peace until 1946.

Spain, the development of whose royal guard so often reflected the same needs and pressures as that of the House of Savoy, also felt the need of a more elaborate guard, after the restoration of the monarchy in 1874. In 1875, not only were the Alabarderos and Monteros de Espinosa restored, but on 19 April the Escolta Real of 108 soldiers with rank of sergeant and above was created, partly on the model of the ephemeral Guardias de la Reina of 1852–53, and solely to add splendour to royal ceremonies. All three units disappeared with the fall of the monarchy: the last time Alfonso XIII heard the cry 'Viva el Rey!' was from his Alabarderos as he descended the great staircase of the Palacio Real on his way into exile on 14 April 1931.[9]

Persia and the Ottoman Empire also expanded their royal guards in the second half of the nineteenth century. By the 1850s, the Goulam-i Shah, whom one English traveller thought 'resemble Louis XI's Scottish archers', were the main guard of the Shah. According to this traveller, there were 400; according to another, more probable account, there were 2500 'well mounted and armed, and excellent horsemen'. The kechiks who now had 'accoutrements of silver' on their uniforms and horses, were also fewer in number than

23. *Frederick William III, Frederick William IV and William I of Prussia,* from von Bruehl, *Übersicht der Geschichte des Königlichen Regiments der Garde du Corps von 1740 bis 1810.* Berlin 1890.

A guard's view of itself as a support for its monarchs, who were themselves its commanders and wore its uniform, is expressed in this illustration from one of the innumerable histories of Prussian guards regiments published in the reign of William II. In the nineteenth century the Prussian guard was the most admired and effective of European royal guards.

before. The only units to have bands in the Persian army, they continued to guard the Shah and his palaces until the First World War when they were suppressed for 'budgetary reasons'.[10]

The guards could look impressive at a review, but that was 'only the gilded surface', as a Tuscan officer in the Persian army wrote in 1875: 'in reality it is all superficial and the army remains as it was before, lacking in everything', a situation which hardly changed before 1921. 'By far the best unit' in the army, according to a British Guards officer, was the Cossack Brigade, raised after 1878 by Russian officers at the request of the Shah, who had been greatly impressed by the Cossacks he had seen on a visit to Russia. Recruited, like so many Middle Eastern royal guards, from the region of the Caucasus (Turki, the language of the area, not Persian, was the language of command), they were 'smart looking and of excellent physique' and 'trained and drilled after the Russian type'. At first about 600, later as many as 10,000, they were 'regarded as specially attached to the person of the Shah' and helped to guard him and his palaces. One of the Shahs' favourite occupations was to review their Cossack Brigade. By the First World War it was the most important armed force in and around Tehran.[11]

The Ottoman Imperial Guard, after a bad period in the middle of the century, when foreigners found it 'ragged and dirty', reached a peak of splendour and efficiency under Abdul Hamid II (1876–1909), when it was one of eleven army corps. Among its most famous units were the Ertoghrul Lancers, named after the founder of the Empire; the Zouaves à Fez, a regiment of Albanian guards; the Zouaves à Turban, a regiment of Arab guards from Syria and Tripoli; and Cossack and Circassian regiments. Albanians were famous throughout the Levant for 'their courage and absolute fidelity' and Abdul Hamid also had, as internal palace guards, about 100 Albanian Tufekdjis.

When the Sultan went to mosque every Friday, a ceremony known as the Selamlik, his guards were much admired. An officer of the Grenadier Guards wrote of 'the smart and stately appearance of the troops at Yildiz' (the Sultan's palace), and was impressed by their 'heartfelt groan of respect and veneration' as the Sultan went past. This was the last example of a monarch's weekly religious attendance being used to display the splendour and discipline of his guard. Other monarchies had given up the custom in the first half of the century.[12]

In Russia a relentless terrorist campaign had culminated in the assassination of Alexander II in 1882: he had been an easy target since he returned from watching the changing of his guard at the same time every day. Although his successor, Alexander III, reduced the Escort to two squadrons of 200 Kuban and 200 Terek Cossacks in 1882, like Abdul Hamid, he had to take unprecedented security precautions. Therefore the Combined Battalion was raised, from the best men in the different guards infantry regiments, to act as an interior palace guard. With the Escort and the different police forces in and around the palace (so numerous that the Tsar's palaces seemed like prisons), it was under the orders of the Commander of the Palace, a very important figure, who, in the words of one police officer, was 'effective head of the entire personal security service of the Tsar'. In 1907 Nicholas II converted the Combined Battalion into the Personal Infantry Regiment of His Majesty, composed of representatives of the different units of the army and the navy, in the hope that it would give him a clearer idea, as he said, 'of the state of the units from which they come'.

Nicholas II was encouraged to take an interest in his guard by his cousin the German Emperor William II. For, even more than his grandfather William I, William II loved and

24. *William II Installs Prince Oskar of Prussia in the First Foot Guards.* 1898. PHOTO ULLSTEIN BILDERDIENST.

One sign of the militarism of the House of Hohenzollern was the tradition that all its princes enter the First Foot Guards at the age of ten – despite the difficulty they had in keeping up with the long legs of the guardsmen at parades. When Prince Oskar's eldest brother first put on his First Foot Guards uniform, he exclaimed, 'now at last I have something decent to wear'.

cherished his guard – so much indeed that the rest of the army felt resentful. As a prince he had served in four different guard regiments and it was there, rather than at home with his liberal parents, that, as he recorded in his memoirs, he found 'my family, my friends, my interests, everything I had previously missed'. In his memoirs he also defended his own, and his ancestors', cult of drill and parades:

> The parades recall not only what that great soldier Frederick William I finally made out of the ridiculed mounting of the guard, which his successors had still further developed, but also very much more. For they constitute a test of discipline, of the skill of the individual man, of his capacity to control his nerve and muscle, of his ability, of the submerging of the single will in that of the majority.

After he ascended the throne he stationed all the Gardes du Corps at Potsdam (where he lived), had more of the Schlossgarde on duty for more of the time than before, and in 1889 created a second company of Leibgendarmerie for the Empress. On 1 April 1897 the Fifth Foot Guard Regiment was created from the Third and Fourth Guard Grenadier Regiments and the Guard Fusilier Regiment. The Prussian Guard under William II was the supreme model for other royal guards.[13]

The United Kingdom also increased its guard at this time. Partly at the suggestion of the Commander-in-Chief, Sir Garnet Wolseley, a plan which had been rejected in 1855 was now adopted, and on 1 April 1900 it was announced that 'Her Majesty the Queen, having deemed it desirable to commemorate the bravery shown by the Irish regiments during the operations in South Africa in the years 1899–1900, has been graciously pleased that an Irish Regiment of Foot Guards be formed, to be designated the Irish Guards'. The first commanding officer, many other officers and the first regimental sergeant-major were from the Grenadier Guards, and the new regiment soon formed an integral part of the Brigade of Guards.

During the First World War the British, Russian and Prussian Guards fought as separate divisions or, in the case of Russia, one, and, in 1916, two Guards corps, despite the fear, in the United Kingdom, of 'envy and jealousy in the troops of the line'. No monarch tried to keep back his guard to protect his throne at home. Like their cousin George V, William II and Nicholas II seem to have felt that their thrones did not need protection; and perhaps, in 1914, they were right. The Kaiser said farewell to his guards at Potsdam on 18 August 1914 with the words: 'I expect of my First Guard Regiment on Foot and my Guards that they will add a new leaf of fame to their glorious history.' Thereafter, he was guarded only by a few 'ersatz battalions'. George V refused to have a guard battalion to guard himself in London, so only one guard battalion stayed in London for 'public duties'. A large number of guards stayed in and around St Petersburg. But they were mainly reserve troops and invalids. The crack troops of the guard were fighting at the front. In July 1915, for example, the Prussian and Russian guards, which had so often in the past manoeuvred together, paraded together and imitated each other's uniforms, met for the first time in battle near Krasnostav. It was the Russian Guard, whose officers were often incompetent, which, after crippling losses, retreated.

After retraining in 1916 the losses of the Russian Guard were still enormous.[14] Its heroism was shown by the fact that the proportion of prisoners to dead and wounded was nine to ninety-one in the guard, twenty-one to seventy-nine in the cavalry and thirty-five to sixty-five in the infantry. The Tsaritsa wrote to her husband on 4 September 1915, 'our losses are colossal, the guard has dwindled away', and on 15 September 1916, 'One must save and spare the guard.' But the needs of the war were put before those of the monarchy.

In 1917 almost all units of the guard supported the Revolution and the provisional government, and continued to fight until the Bolshevik takeover in November and abolition of the old army on 29 December 1917. Thereafter, although the Garde à Cheval did have an

25.   *Nicholas II and His Children at the Fête de l'Escorte.* September 1916. PHOTO ROGER VIOLLET.

Nicholas II, like all his male predecessors and most grand dukes, served in the guard, where he was 'happier than I can say', before he ascended the throne. He loved his guard and put his faith in the round of reviews, parades, dinners and fêtes, such as the one illustrated here, which connected it to his dynasty.

ephemeral resurrection as the guard of the great counter-revolutionary, and former guards officer, General Wrangel, the guard survived only in the regimental reunions, magazines, and museums scattered throughout the non-Communist world.[15]

Almost all the Austrian guards had melted away even before the fall of the Habsburg monarchy on 11 November 1918. Most regiments of the Prussian Guard were still at the front on 9 November 1918 when the Kaiser, convinced that his troops would not fight for him, abdicated. Soon after the guards regiments returned to Berlin and Potsdam in December 1918, they were disbanded.

In contrast to the fate of the defeated Russian, Prussian and Austrian guards, the triumphant return of the victorious British Guards to London on 22 March 1919 was 'a sight that no one will forget'. Not only were the British Guards victorious and acclaimed, they were also larger than ever. A regiment of Welsh Guards had been formed in February 1915, largely at the instigation of Lord Kitchener.

The Ottoman Guard was the last of the great imperial guards to disappear. The old Ottoman army had disintegrated after defeat in the First World War and in the civil war with the nationalists under Mustafa Kemal. When the nationalists took Constantinople on 14 October 1922, the first action of their commander, Refet Pasha, was to place his soldiers on guard around the Sultan's palace. That the Sultan's own guard had melted away was evident at the last, funereal imperial visit to a mosque on Friday 10 November. On 16 November, 'considering my life in danger in Constantinople', the Sultan wrote to the English commander (allied troops had been in Constantinople since 1918) to ask for help. On 17 November soldiers of the Grenadier Guards drilling near his palace at Dolmabahce took him by ambulance to a waiting British ship, which then sailed for Malta. That was the end of the Ottoman Empire.[16]

While thrones were falling and guards disappearing in Petrograd, Vienna, Berlin and Constantinople, in Tehran a new monarchy was emerging. The immense power of Britain after 1918 is shown by the decisive part it played in the rise of the Pahlavis as well as in the fall of the Ottomans. From 1918 Britain paid for the Cossack Brigade, and in February 1921 General Ironside put Colonel Reza Khan, who had joined the Cossack Brigade as a simple soldier, 'definitely in charge of the Persian Cossacks'. On 21 February 1921, with British encouragement, he entered Tehran at the head of about 2500–3000 soldiers of the Cossack Brigade. Soon after he became the first Shah of the Pahlavi dynasty in 1925, a guard division of cavalry and infantry regiments was formed. In 1942, after the humiliating collapse of Reza Shah's authority and the allied occupation of the country, a special Imperial Guard of 700 volunteer soldiers was raised. Between 8 and 20 August 1953, Mossadegh's brief triumph and the Shah's absence from the country were symbolized by the removal of the Imperial Guard from the gates of the Saadabad Palace, and its replacement by ordinary infantry soldiers: royal guards were still a potent symbol of sovereignty.[17]

After the Shah's return, the Imperial Guard, then less than a brigade, was expanded and modernized. It soon formed a division and included, in addition to conscript units, a special unit of Javedan or Immortals – the same word which had been given 2000 years before to the guard of the Achaemenid Emperors of Persia: once again royal guards show an astonishing ability to ignore the passage of time (the Byzantine Emperors had also had a guard of Athanatoi or Immortals). Recruited from volunteers and the elite of the NCOs of the army, the Javedan, in the words of a former officer of the Imperial Guard, 'would give their life for the Shah', and 'were always closest to the Shah'. They were distinguished from the rest of the army by their height, their blue stocks and the position of their officers' aiguillettes (on the right, as in the British royal household) as well as by their training, dedication, prestige and rewards. By 1978 they formed a brigade of about 4000–5000, including one battalion armed with Chieftain tanks. The Javedan guarded the interior and exterior of the Shah's palaces; a special plain-clothes unit selected from the Javedan, called Mahmounin Makhsouz, provided even closer security for the Shah and his family.

After 1972, a division of ordinary conscript soldiers, called the Lashkari Guard Division, was attached to the Imperial Guard, in addition to the Javedan and the Conscript Brigade. The entire Imperial Guard, on the eve of the Revolution, numbered about 18,000 soldiers, 6 per cent of the army, the only units stationed in and around Tehran. Its commander reported directly to the Shah, not to Ground Forces Command. The increase in size, splendour (a unit of Household Cavalry, in cuirasses, was formed after 1968 in the Javedan), independence and protectiveness of the Imperial Guard, particularly marked after the riots of 1963 and the assassination attempt at the Marble Palace on 10 April 1965, was thought by many to symbolize, and perhaps to deepen, the divide between the Shah and his people. The Imperial Guard was disbanded after the fall of the monarchy in 1979.[18]

The expansion of the Iranian Imperial Guard is a sign that, in the twentieth century, where monarchy survives, and often even where it does not, royal guards continue to flourish. The need for security is probably greater than ever; the other great driving force in the development of royal guards, the desire for splendour, is, contrary to a common assumption, as characteristic of twentieth-century governments as of their predecessors.

As in the past, important ceremonies – which still tend to be national festivals, state visits, and the arrival and departure of an ambassador – are celebrated with a splendour to which royal guards can make a decisive contribution. Even republican governments feel a need for splendour. This is shown by the fact that, after the fall of the Italian, Tunisian and Greek monarchies, in 1946, 1957 and 1974 respectively, the royal guards of Carabinieri, Gardes Beylicales, and Evzones, have continued to guard the President of the Republic and adorn the capital in Rome, Tunis and Athens. These royal guards had become such a useful and popular adjunct of sovereignty that they were able to survive under republics.

Even in the Soviet Union, in the words of the *Soviet Military Review*, 'units whose personnel have displayed unusual courage in the face of the enemy' have been give the title of guards unit and special guards' insignia, rewards introduced by Stalin in the desperate days of September 1941 when he turned to traditional Russian patriotism as a weapon against the German invader. By 1945, when the practice of awarding this distinction·ceased, about a quarter of the Soviet armed forces had been called guards units, a name they still keep today, in order to preserve what the *Soviet Military Encyclopaedia* calls 'the military traditions of the Guards'. In other republics, the desire for splendour and security has also led to the expansion of republican guards, often, like previous royal guards, trained or inspired by foreigners (for example Israelis in Zaire, Cubans in Libya and South Yemen, Americans in Egypt).

But republican guards are too vast and too distinct a subject to be included in a book on royal guards. Of the surviving royal guards, the Swedes have lost five regiments by amalgamation or abolition since 1900, and the new Constitution of 1974 has weakened its connection with the monarchy. But the five remaining guards regiments (Svea Livgarde, Livgrenadjar and Livregementets Grenadjar, Dragoon and Hussar corps), numbering in all about 4300 men, survive and, with regiments of the Swedish army, still guard the King at the royal palace in Stockholm. The Danish Life Guard of about 1500, larger and more popular than ever, also continues to guard its monarch and to attract crowds when changing the guard. Its traditions are so strong that 'the 1682 regulations concerning the saluting of the Royal House, high-ranking Government officials, officers and others, are almost the same as the present guard regulations'.[19]

The Norwegian Royal Guard, one battalion strong, is a direct continuation of the Norwegian guard which was stationed in Stockholm to guard the King of Sweden and Norway from 1856 to 1888 (it was withdrawn in 1888, since its presence in Stockholm was seen as a sign of Norwegian subordination to Sweden). Since the creation of the independent kingdom of Norway in 1905, it has expanded to four companies and a ski reconnaissance platoon. In the words of an official handbook, a soldier of 'His Majesty the King's Guard stands out from the other units not only because of his uniform [created by a King of Sweden on a Piedmontese model in 1854] but because of his special devotion to his job to guard the King and his family and to be a member of this representation unit'. Detachments of the Swedish, Danish and Norwegian royal guards spend a week with each other every year.

Another sign of the appeal of splendour in the twentieth century is that Belgium and the Netherlands created royal guards in 1938 and 1948 respectively. The Escorte Royale Belge of over 100 mounted grenadiers was founded on 6 April 1938 in anticipation of the state visit of Queen Wilhelmina and is still primarily a ceremonial unit, used to escort the royal family, foreign heads of state and ambassadors; it enters the royal palaces only on ceremonial occasions. It considers itself a descendant of the Grenadiers à Cheval of the Garde Impériale of Napoleon I and wears a similar uniform. It so impressed President Mobutu of Zaire that, in 1970, with the help of some of its officers, he created a similar Congolese unit in time to escort him for the National Day celebrations that year.

In 1948, as a sign of the Netherlands' emergence from its provincial past, and in order to mark the accession of Queen Juliana, three guard regiments, the Garderegiment Grenadiers (which also considers itself a descendant of the Garde Impériale), the Garderegiment Jaegers and the Garderegiment Fusiliers Prinses Irene, were created. These regiments are used largely for ceremonial functions rather than for guard duties which, as in most European states, are the responsibility of special security units.[20]

In 1975, when the monarchy was restored in Spain, the Guard Regiment of His Excellency the Chief of State (which had included a special Moroccan cavalry unit before the independence of Morocco in 1956) became the Guardia Real of King Juan Carlos I. It is now about 2100 strong, larger than any royal guard in Spain since 1841. About 1400 are professionals known as 'permanent Royal Soldiers'. The rest are Royal Volunteers, an institution created in August 1979 for the Guardia Real and designed, in the words of its Colonel-in-Chief, to give 'Spanish youth the opportunity to do military service close to His Majesty the King'. After two years, the best forty or sixty remain in the Guardia Real; the others return to their original units. Through the Royal Volunteers, the Guardia Real includes representatives from every unit of the armed forces, cavalry, infantry, navy, air force and Guardia Civil.

The Guardia Real is a vital security unit which accompanies the King everywhere, even on the ski-slopes, and is totally devoted to him. Its colonel who, like all its officers is appointed by the King, not the Minister of War, is trying, in his own words, 'to adapt it to the traditions of the monarchy, taking into account modern necessities and security techniques'. In the last few years some units have been given traditional names such as Monteros de Espinosa and Alabarderos; the Alabarderos often wear the old Alabarderos uniform on ceremonial occasions in the King's presence.

In recent years the Papacy has been one of the few monarchies to cut back its guard. In 1970 the Palatine Guard and the Noble Guard, which was still recruited from nobles of the former Papal states (despite a public appeal in the 1920s by King Alfonso XIII that it should be open to all Catholic nobles), were abolished as part of a drastic reform of the Papal court. They were thought to be 'no longer appropriate'. The only remaining Papal guard, still recruited from Catholic Swiss bachelors who have done Swiss military service, are over 1m 74cm high and have certificates of health, morality and civic conduct, is the Pontifical Swiss Guard. Although there were more in the past, and although they are now the sole guard for both the interior and the exterior of the Vatican Palace, there are only 100 Swiss Guards. Most of them stay for only two years and so have limited opportunity to learn the indispensable security techniques.[21]

The largest surviving royal guard is the Household Division (as the Foot Guards and Household Cavalry have been called since 1951) of the United Kingdom, about 7000 soldiers in an army of 135,000 (5 per cent). Although the First and Second Life Guards Regiments were amalgamated in 1922, and the Blues were amalgamated with the Royal Dragoons to become The Blues and Royals in 1969, the twentieth century has otherwise treated the Household Division remarkably kindly. The Irish Guards have survived the independence of Ireland and the abolition of most other Irish regiments in July 1922, as well as the renewal of sectarian violence since 1969. All regiments of Foot Guards distinguished themselves in the Second World War, as well as in the First, earning from Field-Marshal Montgomery one of the most glowing tributes ever paid by a Commander-in-Chief to a guard: 'They maintain always the highest standards and give a lead to all others . . . we need your high standards, your great efficiency in all matters and your old tradition of duty and service.' In 1946, the King's Troop, Royal Horse Artillery became part of the Household Troops, at the suggestion of George VI. It performs the duties of the Queen's Life Guard at Horse Guards in Whitehall for a month every summer. The major-general commanding the Household Division, who is always from one of its regiments, still commands the military district of London as he has done since 1870.

The Guards Depot, feared by generations of guardsmen, still maintains its awesome standards of drill. Training there, a fortnight longer than in other depots because of the need to teach ceremonial drill, is one of the factors which distinguish the Household Division from the rest of the army, and it is so respected that the Guards Depot All Arms Drill Wing trains drill instructors from the rest of the armed forces and the police, as well as from abroad. Other factors distinguishing the Household Division, noticed by soldiers of the Royal Dragoons on amalgamation with the Blues, were an increase in parades and drill, a decrease in emphasis on operational ability, and a lack of coloured recruits: all factors except the last have, however, been resolved, and pay, recruitment, and morale are better now than they have been for a long time.[22]

Both the Foot Guards and a composite regiment from the Household Cavalry, called the Household Cavalry Regiment (Mounted), continue, despite Irish bombs, to perform public duties in London and to change the guard at Whitehall and at Buckingham Palace, as well as to carry out normal military duties. Thus the regiments of the Household Division have, like all British regiments, served in an extraordinary variety of overseas operations since 1945. They are also, with the other royal guards, still able to provide a magnificent royal and military display during a state visit to London. Foot Guards provide a guard of honour along the ceremonial route. A sovereign's escort of Household Cavalry guards the Queen's procession. The King's Troop, Royal Horse Artillery, having fired a salute in Hyde Park, form up at the Victoria Memorial. Gentlemen-at-Arms and Yeomen of the Guard are on duty at the Grand Entrance of Buckingham Palace. A detachment of Household Cavalry – a reminder of their original role as bodyguards – line the staircase to the state apartments.

The ceremonial role of the Household Division has indeed increased since 1945, another indication of the appeal of splendour in the twentieth century. The Household Cavalry has participated in the Lord Mayor's procession since 1946, and is now frequently used to add splendour to royal visits to the provinces. Such ceremonies are so appealing and impressive that when one journalist saw the Trooping of the Colour, 'one of the most beautiful pieces of formal design you could see', in 1980, he felt that he had 'an intuition of how the country works'. Not only its ceremonial role, but also the Household Division's recruitment and attachment to the monarchy have suffered little change. The fear of Winston Churchill, a great admirer of the Grenadier Guards – he served with them in 1915 and dedicated his life of Marlborough, who also served in the regiment, to them – that 'the army stands on a democratic basis and "the Guards" have been sacrificed to the spirit of the age' has proved groundless. The overwhelming majority of its officers come from public schools and are convinced that things should stay that way. The Duke of Edinburgh, Colonel of the Grenadier Guards and, as Senior Colonel of the Household Division, a very influential figure indeed, has written that the Household Division are 'the Sovereign's personal troops'; anyone who has talked to them knows how fervently they agree. They are also Elizabeth II's 'personal troops' by virtue of her personal interest and influence in the Household Division. Like her predecessors since 1901, she is Colonel-in-Chief of all the regiments of the Household Division, and she may have as much influence over the appointment of their colonels and of the major-general commanding the Household Division as the authorities responsible to Parliament. Appointments of officers of the Household Cavalry are sent to her for approval; and she knows the names of their horses as well. She visits, and presents new colours to, battalions of the Household Division more often than is the case with other units of the armed forces.

Although the guards continue to perform 'public duties' in London and to guard the exterior of Buckingham Palace, St James's Palace and Windsor Castle, and although they have 'gone tactical', i.e. patrolled the grounds with loaded guns at night since 1972, they do not, as they did during the Second World War, play a great part in the daily protection of the monarch. Nor, as recent intrusions in Buckingham Palace have shown, do they guard the interior of her palaces. The police have overall responsibility for the security of the monarch and her palaces. The absence of a security role could help those in the Ministry of Defence eager to diminish the independence, if not the size and splendour, of the Household Division, whose existence has been confirmed by the failure, despite royal suggestions, to reintroduce a separate guards brigade with its own staff and organization (as had existed before 1976) in the British Army of the Rhine since the reintroduction of brigades in 1980.[23] A guards brigade appeals to guards officers because 'everyone speaks the same language . . . it is like a large club'.

The Household Division of the United Kingdom has not only maintained its size, splendour and monarchical and social traditions. It has also assumed, since 1945, the role as model for other royal guards, previously held by France and Prussia. This is not only due to its own reputation but also to the continued military, cultural and sartorial influence of the United Kingdom, despite the evaporation of its Empire. The Governor-General's Horse Guards in Canada, and the President's bodyguard in Pakistan have been, in part, inspired by, respectively, The Blues and Royals and The Life Guards. The status and uniform of the Governor-General's Foot Guards, formed in 1872, are based on those of the Coldstream Guards. The Imperial Guard of Ethiopia and the Royal Guard of Thailand based some of their ceremonies and drill on those of the Household Division.

Its influence has been especially strong in the Arabian peninsula, the last region in the world where monarchies are still vitally important. In the twentieth century the Arabian peninsula has witnessed a transformation in monarchs' guards comparable to that which occurred in Europe in the fifteenth century. In 1930 most rulers in the region had an ill-defined bodyguard of tribal warriors called *mutarzieh* or *zkirt*, and black slaves. Since 1930 traditional Middle Eastern guards have been replaced by clearly defined royal or Emiri guards, trained and uniformed in a Western, usually British, style. Thus in 1948, the traditional Emiri guard of the Emir of Kuwait was replaced by a modern Emiri guard with a ceremonial uniform, in the words of its present commander, 'exactly the same as the Queen's Guard' (this uniform was changed in 1972 for one more suited to the local climate).

In 1951, soon after the state had become an independent kingdom and had acquired the left bank, Jordan created a ceremonial guard of police cavalry whose scarlet tunic, adopted on 'His Majesty's wishes', was also based on a British model. The King of Jordan also has an Honour Guard of twelve Circassians, the last survivor of those guards of Caucasian warriors which once protected the Ottoman Sultan, the Shah of Persia and the Tsar of Russia. Founded in 1922 by the Emir Abdullah, who liked splendour and had known the Ottoman court, they were, in the words of one of them, 'a sign of his sympathy towards, and trust in, the Circassians who were isolated in such an Arab milieu': indeed his choice of Amman as his capital may have been partly due to the fact that it was, at one time, a Circassian settlement. In their Circassian costume, almost the same as that of the Escort of Nicholas II (see illustrations 25 and 33), they still guard the inside of the King's offical residence, Basman Palace, in the daytime. More important is the Royal Guard Battalion, formerly a brigade, founded in about 1964. A highly professional unit of about 800 soldiers of proven loyalty, it guards the royal family wherever it is, in its palaces or on journeys, on land or under water, at home or abroad. Its reputation is so great that it has helped train guards from Kuwait, Bahrain, Qatar, Abu Dhabi and Oman.[24]

One of the factors which has increased the influence of the Household Division of the United Kingdom has been the professional prestige of the SAS. Founded by two officers of the Scots and Welsh Guards, David Stirling and Jock Lewes, it has retained a close connection with the Foot Guards through its G squadron of guardsmen: of the fifty-three guardsmen who died in the Falklands in 1982, five were serving in the SAS. This unit, whose knowledge of security techniques is legendary (Stirling set up his own 'protection' company, Watchguard, in 1967), has been used to provide instant bodyguards for, among

26.   *The Oman Royal Guard at the National Day Celebrations.* 1978. PHOTO MINISTRY OF INFORMATION, OMAN.

The Household Troop is followed by the Royal Guard Mounted Troop; the Royal Guard Mounted Band is in the background. The Royal Guard of Oman, in which the Sultan takes a keen personal interest, although only created in 1972, is now one of the largest and most splendid royal guards in the world.

others, the rulers of Abu Dhabi and Oman. In 1972–75 an officer in the SAS helped to train and modernize the Harass al-Khass or bodyguard ('Khass' from the same word as the Khasseki Bostangi guard of the Ottoman Sultans) of the Emir of Dubai. The traditional Arab dress and, at first, personnel of his Mutarzieh were retained, but it is now a modern professional security force of about 100. As in other monarchies, a desire for a more modern and effective guard has been combined with a desire to maintain the appearance of an unbroken national tradition. In 1974, an Emiri guard of about 600 was set up as part of the Dubai army; its drill and ceremonial uniform, modelled directly on those of the Foot Guards by an officer of the Irish Guards, were first seen on the occasion of a visit by Elizabeth II. A similar transformation took place at the same time in Abu Dhabi and Sharjah.[25]

In Oman the Sultan was, until 1970, guarded by four or five hundred black slaves and armed retainers, askaris from his province of Dhofar. However, in 1973, after the deposition of Sultan Said bin Taymur in the coup of 1970, a modern royal guard regiment was formed 'by order of His Majesty the Sultan as an independent self-contained unit'. In the words of an official handbook, it 'has the distinction of coming directly under the command of His Majesty', and prepares its own budget independently of the Ministry of Defence. It now numbers about 3000, 20 per cent of the army, and on 1 March 1981 became the Royal Guard Brigade. British influence has been strong on both its security and its ceremonial roles. Like

27. *Two Saudi Royal Guards.* 1940.
COLL. GERALD DE GAURY.

This photograph shows a guard in the recently introduced Western-style uniform next to one in traditional costume.

the guard of the Emir of Abu Dhabi, it has a British commander and, from 1975 to 1979, an officer of the Blues helped to set up 'a Household Cavalry like London' which is known as the Household Troop. Although the Dhofari Askaris have not been incorporated in the royal guard, the other component of the traditional guard, still of different legal status and colour from the other soldiers, provides a link with the past by serving in the Household Troop. The Oman royal guard is one of the most splendid, independent and efficient royal guards in the world today.[26]

Two other Arab monarchies, Morocco and Saudi Arabia, also have large and independent royal guards. Like the Sultans of Morocco and Oman and his own ancestors, Abdul Aziz ibn Sa'ud, first King of Saudi Arabia (1930–53), had been guarded by a 'bodyguard of coal black negro slaves who never left him'. In addition, he was guarded by fifty or sixty soldiers 'from the most intelligent, trustworthy and physically fit young men of the Nejd' – his dynasty's traditional power base. During the Second World War this guard was modernized and sections of it given Western uniforms, training and equipment. Although there were still black guards up to 1964 (see illustration 58), and there is still a section in traditional dress as in Dubai and Abu Dhabi, the Saudi royal guard is now a well trained, modern ceremonial and security force of about 2000–3000. They constantly surround the King and his palaces, and played an important part in the transfer of power from King Sa'ud to King Faisal in 1964.[27]

In Morocco the Garde Royale today is a direct continuation of the guard of black slaves, the Abeed al-Bukhari, founded three hundred years ago by Sultan Moulay Ismail. Only in 1956, after the French withdrawal, did his descendant Sultan Mohammed V decide to alter its composition and open it to the best Moroccan soldiers; there are few blacks in the Garde Royale today. Composed of infantry, cavalry and artillery, it has important security and ceremonial roles, and has helped train guards from other Arab monarchies such as Saudi Arabia and Abu Dhabi. Like many other royal guards, it is directly controlled by the King, and is completely independent of the Ministry of War.[28]

28. *Sultan Mohammed V Reviewing the Moroccan Royal Guard.* 1957. PHOTO ROGER VIOLLET.

The Moroccan Royal Guard ceased to be black for the first time in three centuries in the years after this picture was taken.

5

THE COMPOSITION OF ROYAL GUARDS

MOST ROYAL GUARDS have, therefore, been distinguished from other troops by their independence, and by the attention paid to them by the monarchs they have guarded, as well as by their names, the nature and location of their duties, their privileges and the degree of foreign influence on their organization. They have also been distinguished by their social and racial composition. Most monarchies have had guard units composed of, or officered by, members of the aristocracy of birth or power (aristocracy is used here to mean the ruling class of the monarchy, whether noble or not). For example, the Gentlemen Pensioners of Henry VIII were created 'that his Chamber oft be furnished of gentlemen'. The Gardes du Corps of France, Spain and Piedmont, the Archer Guards of Austria and Bavaria, the Noble Guard of the Papacy and the Hungarian Noble Guard (still restricted to nobles when revived in 1867) were all, at least in theory, composed of guards who had proven that they were of noble birth. Even in the Ottoman Empire and Persia, whose monarchies were notorious, in European eyes, for their lack of a supporting cast of hereditary aristocracies, there were guards composed on similar principles, namely the Müteferrika and the Goulam-i Shah. The Müteferrika were often sons of vassal princes. The Goulam-i Shah included sons of the most powerful lords and chieftains of the monarchy. In addition to such aristocratic guard units there were also guards, such as the Alabarderos of Spain after 1707, the Hofburgwache of Austria after 1767, the Grenadiers du Palais and Schlossgarde of Russia and Prussia after 1827 and 1829 and the Yeomen of the Guard after 1835, which were based on a different form of elitism, since they were composed of NCOs with particularly good service records.

Even in the guard regiments created after the foundation of the Gardes Françaises in 1563, the composition of the officers, by the late seventeenth century, was unusual in that it was at least as aristocratic as in the small aristocratic units, and often more so. Ideas of what constitutes aristocracy have varied in the monarchies of Europe since 1400. In the French monarchy, for example, noble birth was not always more important than wealth, distinguished service or useful connections. But what has been constant is that, whether they were chosen for their birth, wealth or services, the members of the small aristocratic guards units, and the officers of the guard regiments, have nearly always represented the composition, and aspirations, of the ruling class. Thus, in the relatively fluid world of the sixteenth and early seventeenth centuries, before social divisions within the elite of power and wealth had hardened, many of the officers of the royal guard of France were scarcely noble – as is shown by the fact that letters of nobility could be obtained *after* twenty years' service as a Chevau-Léger de la Garde.

Many officers of the Gardes Françaises, for example the future Maréchal Fabert, were not noble, while the future Marshals Vauban and Catinat came from very obscure noble families. In the Mousquetaires in the 1630s, D'Artagnan, Athos (Armand de Sillègue d'Athos d'Antelle), Porthos (Isaac de Portau) and their commander Tréville all came from families of successful merchants of Béarn who had recently acquired noble status. Only Aramis (Henri d'Aramitz) was from an old noble family. Louis XIII, however, clearly wanted the officers, or even the soldiers, of his guard to be nobles. Proudly pointing out a soldier in the Gardes Françaises to his brother-in-law, the Duke of Savoy, in 1629, he said: 'Do you see that soldier on sentry duty? He is called de Bréauté; he has more than 30,000 livres income from government stocks. In my regiment of guards I have more than 400 gentlemen from just as good families.'[1]

The desire to have 'gentlemen from good families' in his guard was felt even more strongly by Louis XIV. In 1666 he wrote that 'the particular care which I took of the troops which served about my person ensured that the majority of young gentlemen in France passionately desired to come and learn their *métier* there'. He even had the pleasure of being able to complain about the number of requests he had to turn down from gentlemen wanting to serve in his Gardes du Corps. From the reform of 1664 more nobles served in the Gardes du Corps which, like the Mousquetaires, had been infiltrated by non- or semi-nobles. Regulations of 1676 and 1674 stipulated that recruits to the Maison Militaire were to be 'gentlemen so far as possible'. The Mousquetaires, in which the flower of the French nobility, as well as the King's grandsons, served, were now more exclusive than before. Saint-Simon, who was one himself, wrote that Louis XIV insisted that all *jeunes gens distingués* wanting to serve in the army spend a year in the Mousquetaires.

During the wars of the end of his reign the immense French losses forced Louis XIV to relax his standards a little, and in the first half of the reign of Louis XV wealth was as notable a characteristic of the Gardes du Corps and the Maison Militaire as noble birth. Of the 476 patents of nobility registered in the Cour des Aides of Paris between 1712 and 1787, forty-six went to officers of the Gardes du Corps and thirty to officers of the Maison Militaire, which shows what an important means of securing social ascension, as well as royal favour, service in a royal guard could be.[2] But one of the most important features of the eighteenth century was the increasingly aggressive and exclusive attitude towards non-nobles adopted by the nobles, and many monarchs of Europe, despite a steep decline in noble numbers after 1750. Certified nobility began to be required more rigorously than before and the French royal guard's role as a means of training and employing the nobility expanded. In 1728 thirty-three positions were created in the Gardes Françaises, 'to serve for the instruction of young nobles'. In 1740 the regiment of Gardes Lorraines was revived not only to guard King Stanislas but also 'to give employment to the nobility of the area'. In 1741 the rules for admission to the Chevau-Légers de la Garde were tightened up, probably at the insistence of Louis XV, and 140 years of proven nobility on the father's side, and an income of 600 livres, demanded. Of 656 Chevau-Légers whose certificates of nobility have been found, 363 (55 per cent), a very large proportion indeed, came from families which had been known to be noble for so long that they did not need to produce proofs.

On 22 December 1758 entry to the Gardes du Corps was restricted to 'gentlemen or men of families *vivant noblement*', the phrase which implied so much in eighteenth-century France. From 15 December 1775 candidates had to prove, by a certificate signed by four gentlemen, including one Garde du Corps, that their family had been noble for at least 200 years. In 1789, on the eve of the outburst of revolutionary egalitarianism, the government was planning to demand nobility dating back to 1400.[3]

The noble birth of so many officers of the French royal guard did not mean they all belonged to the world of the court. On the contrary, except for the magic circle of Rohan, Noailles, Brissac, Beauvau and Montmorency, who commanded the different units of the guard, most of the guards seem to have come from families of the provincial nobility; 76 per cent of officers of the Gardes Françaises from 1752 to 1789 were from outside Paris. On a late-eighteenth-century list of 267 Chevau-Légers de la Garde, 232 (87 per cent) were domiciled in such towns as Rodez, Périgueux or Grenoble, away from Paris and Versailles, while few came from the families which had been presented at court. On a list of over 500

Gardes du Corps' addresses in the 1780s only two lived in Paris; others came from Bordeaux, Figeac or, like the philosopher Maine de Biran who served with five cousins in the Compagnie de Noailles, from Bergerac in the heart of France. Thus, the enormous royal guard, far from acting as a barrier, connected the French monarchy with its provincial nobility. In contrast to Napoleon I's Gendarmes d'Ordonnance and Gardes d'Honneur, the social composition of the officers of the Garde Impériale was not particularly aristocratic. But the revival and expansion of the traditional royal guard at Coblentz in 1791–92, and in France in 1814–15, was in part designed to provide employment for the royalist aristocracy.[4]

Another monarchy whose royal guard was designedly aristocratic was the Spanish monarchy under the Bourbons. In 1701 Louis XIV wrote: 'If distinguished people can be obtained as officers, the guard will be on a better footing, that will perhaps persuade the nobility to serve in the armies.' Thereby he makes explicit what he implied in his boast of 1666 about the nobility flocking to his guard to learn their *métier*: namely, that one of the principal reasons for the existence of large royal guards, for their privileges of pay and rank, and for their distinguishing features of royal interest and sartorial splendour, was to use the guard as a bait to lure the nobility into the army. For, after a few years in the guard, nobles could be promoted to senior positions in the army.

Indeed, until 1808, and even to a certain extent afterwards, all officers of the Spanish royal guard had to prove that they were nobles with private incomes. The list of the officers

29. *The Noble Guard of the Papacy.*
c. 1950. COLL. GERALD DE GAURY.

Founded in 1801 – on the model of the Guardias de Corps of Spain – to replace the Lanzze Spezzate, this was one of the many small aristocratic units to which the monarchs of Europe and the Middle East entrusted the guard of their persons.

of the Gardes Wallonnes, according to their historian, is the golden book of the Belgian aristocracy. Aristocratic recruitment was also a feature of the royal guard of Naples, even under Murat. In 1813 the originally non-aristocratic Guardie del Corpo had to be transferred to another regiment because 'the nobles and landowners did not want to be part of it so as not to be mixed with the soldiers'. After 1815 it was still necessary to prove that all four grandparents had been noble to be admitted to the Guardie del Corpo. In 1791, and for many years afterwards, all officers of the guards – and of the cavalry – of Piedmont were noble.[5]

That a monarchy needed to create a privileged guard in order to induce its nobles to serve in its armies is suggested by the example of Austria, which had the smallest guard of any great European monarchy. It is likely that this was one reason why, as Maria-Theresa and Metternich complained, the Austrian nobility was so unwilling to serve in the army. The situation in its successful rival, the Prussian monarchy, was quite different. In the early eighteenth century, it is true, as in France, there were non-noble guards officers, who were expressly assured, by a cabinet order of 11 March 1704, of the same treatment in matters of promotion as their noble comrades.

But Frederick II was, in the words of Jean Meyer, the European monarch 'probably the most favourable' to the nobility. In 1748, in a famous pronouncement, he declared of the Prussian nobility, which his predecessors had regarded with distrust, 'the breed is so good that it merits to be preserved by every means'. One means he chose, like Louis XIV and Philip V, was service in his army, and particularly in his guard. This was the most appealing solution for the monarchs of Europe to one of their fundamental problems and principal ambitions in the seventeenth and eighteenth centuries, namely, as Jean Meyer says, 'to integrate the nobility in the modern state'. Thus, between 1789 and 1853, and 1808 and 1853 respectively, all the officers of the Garde du Corps and the First Foot Guards were nobles who bore some of the most famous names of the Prussian nobility: von Maltzahn, von Arnim, von Alvensleben, Finck von Finckenstein, von Bismarck-Schönhausen. Other newer guards regiments were not always so exclusively noble, but throughout the nineteenth century the guard remained a bastion of the nobility.[6]

This was partly true of the Prussian army as a whole, 50 per cent of whose officers were still noble in 1867. But the difference between the guard and the army became more pronounced in the last quarter of the nineteenth century. In 1890, whereas the officers of the line infantry and cavalry were 41 per cent and 79 per cent noble respectively, officers of the guard infantry and cavalry were 97 per cent and 98 per cent noble; they were perhaps more noble than in 1815. The situation had changed very little by 1914, although by then only 30 per cent of the officers of the army were noble, and although the government, perhaps at the Kaiser's instigation, tried to introduce rich bourgeois officers into the guard after 1908.

In Russia the nobility had a unique incentive to serve in the guard after its creation by Peter the Great. In 1714 he issued a *ukase*, in force until the creation of the cadet schools in 1731, forbidding noblemen who had not served in the guard from becoming officers. Therefore, in the words of Brenda Meehan-Waters, 'Since service was compulsory for the nobility from 1722 to 1762 and since the guards regiments were a training ground for all officers and the surest path to promotion, nobles vied for places in these regiments despite the necessity to serve in the ranks.' For under Peter and his immediate successors, nobles really did, like the Tsar and his son, serve in the ranks, living in the same barracks, receiving the same rations and doing the same duties as the other soldiers of the guard. By 1725 48 per cent of privates in the guard were nobles.

Voltaire's comment: 'Nothing was more extraordinary nor more useful' shows the immense importance he, like most of the monarchs and aristocrats of Europe, attached to the services of the nobility. Indeed one reason why the Tsar and his son and, in the nineteenth century, so many grand dukes and princes in other monarchies (seven Hohenzollerns in the

THE COMPOSITION OF ROYAL GUARDS

Gardes du Corps of Prussia between 1789 and 1853) served in their guards was not only to bind them to the monarchy but also to encourage nobles to serve in them. By 1724 there was so much competition to serve in the guard that the Tsar could restrict access to 'distinguished nobles according to fitness', thereby introducing the concept of merit. In 1730 the British Minister described the Preobrazhensky and Semenovsky Guards as 'two formidable regiments consisting of seven thousand men in which are persons of the greatest families of this country'.[7]

Under Catherine II, so favourable to the nobility, guards officers were, in the words of the Prussian Ambassador, 'mostly young men from the leading families of the country who are enrolled here to obtain the quickest possible advancement'. There was no necessity now to serve in the ranks. Indeed, many nobles were enrolled when still children, like the hero of Pushkin's *The Captain's Daughter*, in order to have the rank of second lieutenant in the army by the time they were sixteen. A Prince Galitsyn joined the Preobrazhensky Guards at three, and the future General Borozdin at five. In this way the guard provided most of the officers of Catherine II.[8]

Paul I reformed the worst abuses of service in the guard. No longer could nobles be enrolled when unable to handle a gun or stand to attention. But throughout the nineteenth century, and as late as 1912, guards officers continued to be from what an English traveller called 'perfectly well-known', in other words, noble, families. Even during the First World War, guards regiments refused to admit non-noble officers.

Guards regiments maintained their noble character by the tradition that, in contrast to regiments of the line, 'Not even the Emperor's influence could get an officer accepted if the regiment itself did not want him.' Regiments even vetted their officers' choice of wives. When in 1908 there had been some rather mild criticism of the social composition and recruitment of officers of the guard in the Duma, the War Minister replied that 'the government had no right to interfere in the social life of officers'. In 1915, Nicholas II had to obtain the agreement of the officers of his regiment of Guard Cossacks before Prince Stanislas Radziwill was accepted as an officer. Guards officers had to be rich as well as noble since they had to have enough money to face the expenses of life in St Petersburg and to pay regimental dues. As in Prussia the exclusively noble character of the guards meant that it was becoming more and more different from the army, which following the reforms of 1874 and even before, was far from being an aristocratic preserve. The social tension between guards and line officers was perceptible even in Denikin's counter-revolutionary army of 1919.[9]

In Sweden, from the reign of Gustavus III until 1940, the officers of the regiments of Hustrupper, in particular the Svea Livgarde and the Livregiment till Hast, were almost entirely nobles; and in the Svea Livgarde the older officers were responsible for choosing new officers. This remained the case even under Socialist Ministers of War. Even after the opening of the gates to the middle classes one officer in the 1940s was forced to change his surname because it was thought to be too plebeian for the guards, and a non-noble officer of the Svea Livgarde found 'a certain limit to the heartiness of some of the older officers'.

A brief exception to this noble domination was provided by the Drabants of Charles XII. In this unique royal guard sons of peasants fought beside representatives of Sweden's most famous noble families, a Horn, a Wrangel, the last of the Oxenstiernas. For Charles XII believed that 'Nobility in itself, be it old or new, adds nothing to the qualities of a man. So long as a trooper is a good soldier, it can be of no consequence whether or not he is a man of family.' Few of his fellow-monarchs or of his, or their, successors, except perhaps Peter the Great, shared his point of view.[10]

Certainly in Great Britain such an attitude has found few imitators; and, even today, the Household Division remains, unlike other surviving royal guards, if not aristocratic, certainly idiosyncratic in composition. At first this was not the case and there were many complaints, in the 1660s, about the 'robbers and hackney coachmen' in the Life Guards. From 1660 to 1699 only forty peers or peers' sons served in the guards regiments and troops. But between 1700 and 1749 there were 107, and between 1750 and 1799, despite the drastic decline in the aristocratic composition of the Life Guards and Horse Grenadier Guards (from forty-three to seventeen) there were 180 (see Table I).

Table I. Peers and peers' sons who have served in troops and regiments of Household Cavalry and Guards

	1660–99	1700–49	1750–99	1800–49	1850–99	1900–49
Life Guards and Horse Grenadier Guards	36	43	17	60	77	57
Royal Regiment of Horse Guards (The Blues)	5	14	5	38	39	35
First Foot Guards (after 1815 Grenadiers)	1	20	60	69	59	X
Coldstream Guards	3	37	56	X	X	X
Scots Guards	18	37	42	61	59	X

X = no figures available

Sons of great Whig peers such as the Dukes of Devonshire, Bedford and Portland, were not too proud to serve the King in his guards in the eighteenth century. To serve the King in his guards was also the dearest ambition of such Protestant aristocrats as the Duke of Richmond in 1770, Lord Herbert in 1785, and the Duke of Buckingham and Lord Londonderry in 1830.[11] The importance of such aristocrats' service in the guards is shown by the fact that, in 1787 when the reform of the Life Guards was being discussed, George III felt 'more reluctance on account of the difficulties which were to be apprehended in satisfying these Noblemen [their commanders] than on any other Account'.

There was a peak of aristocratic service in the guards during their golden age in the reign of George IV. In 1813, for example, when Wellington offered his brother the right to appoint a cornet in his regiment, the Blues, he stipulated: 'But he must be a *Gentleman*, and he ought to have something to live on besides his Pay.' Thereafter, as Table I suggests, the tradition has hardly changed. Ten Cokes, of the family of the Earls of Leicester, served in the Scots Guards between 1843 and 1934. Five dukes or future dukes served in the Blues in the first half of the twentieth century. The character of the composition of the Household Division, and the way in which its exclusive and equestrian aspects feed and strengthen each other, is suggested by, for example, this obituary of the Earl of Halifax in 1980: 'In 1933 he joined the Blues at the same time as his life-long friends Bobo Roxburghe and Toby Murray Smith. He followed the usual Knightsbridge-Windsor routine and he married in 1936 Ruth Primrose – the happiest of marriages, which also had the effect of encouraging a joint love of the turf.'

In addition to the aristocratic element in the composition of the officers of the Foot and Horse Guards, the element of wealth, often new wealth, which had penetrated the Maison Militaire in France and the Life Guards in the second half of the eighteenth century, was also important and is by no means extinct today. Five Astors served in The Life Guards in the first half of the twentieth century. Many applicants to serve as officers in the Household Cavalry today have 'private incomes or access to family inheritances in time of trouble'. A sign of their wealth is that the overwhelming majority of officers in the Household Division has been to public schools which, while no guarantee of aristocratic origin, makes elitist attitudes more likely and certainly sets them apart from officers who have not been to public schools. Therefore, as in the Prussian and Russian armies before 1914, the difference in social origin between the guards and the line, an increasing number of whose officers have not been to public schools, is becoming apparent. It is felt by both officers and soldiers of the Household Division, however, that officers who have not been to public schools are 'generally a mistake'.[12]

Thus, in most periods of the history of most royal guards, their officers and sometimes their soldiers have been deliberately chosen from the ruling elite, and usually from the nobility. The principal reason for this remarkable noble dominance and for the use of royal guards as baits to lure nobles into monarchs' armies, was the military and moral reputation of the nobility. Nobles were thought to be particularly good material for officers and soldiers. Brantôme wrote that 'to carry arms is the mark of the nobility'. Louis XIV thought that warfare was nobles' métier. Cromwell compared parliamentarian and royalist troops to the advantage of the latter, because of the composition of their officers: 'Think ye, that the mean spirits of such base and low fellows as ours will ever be able to cope with Gentlemen, who have honour and resolution in them.'

It was honour that was the key to the reputation of the nobility as supremely suitable for officers' commissions. The Comte de Bonneval, who began his military career in the Gardes Françaises but became Bonneval Pasha in the service of the Ottoman Empire, explained to the Sultan in the 1740s that, for noble officers in European armies, 'honour is their great criterion and none of them would not prefer death to a dishonourable action or the least sign of fear or weakness'. He believed that their bravery and sense of honour commanded the respect and obedience of their soldiers and of the rest of the nation.[13] Frederick the Great wrote: 'I always choose my officers from the nobility, for nobility nearly always has a sense of honour. It can be found among bourgeois of merit but it is rarer . . . If a noble loses his honour he is ostracized by his family; whereas a commoner who has committed fraud can continue to run his father's business.' Most of his contemporaries agreed with him.

Nobles' sense of honour meant that not only were nobles likely to be better officers, in the opinion of most educated Europeans, but they were also felt to be better and more reliable people than non-nobles. They were, therefore, the perfect material to serve in royal guards. 'Officers of birth and from illustrious families . . . feel more perfectly the honour of having served about the royal person of your Majesty,' wrote the Colonel of the Gardes Wallonnes to Philip V in 1718. Nobles' sense of honour, he believed, meant that they were more likely to feel loyalty to their monarch. In addition, since most nobles were fairly rich, at least in comparison to the great majority of the population, belief in their reliability was strengthened by that fear and distrust of the poor which haunted the ruling classes of most monarchies until, at the earliest, the second half of the twentieth century. The Venetian Ambassador in France in 1561 felt that the military prominence of the nobility was due to 'the fear of giving arms to the plebeians who, once they were armed, would rise against the nobles and the upper class to avenge themselves for the oppression they are enduring'. The author of Considérations sur les Gardes du Corps et sur leur Mode de Recrutement (1821) felt that guards should be nobles, or at least rich, because 'among men who have received no education, who hold no rank in society, who do not have to take their families into account, in one word, who only have their fortune and their career to make . . . one finds most bad characters, because their criminal passions are restrained by less powerful bonds'. Since 'criminal passions' were so widespread, it was best to choose as officers, and especially as guards, those believed most likely to uphold and respond to the honour of guarding a monarch, namely nobles.[14]

Another unusual factor in the composition of royal guards, in addition to aristocratic dominance, was the presence in many of them of foreigners or of guards from particular parts of a monarch's dominions. The Janissaries, and therefore the Sultan's guard of Solaks, Peiks and Bostangis, were, until the late sixteenth century, recruited exclusively and thereafter at least partly, from captured slaves (usually Caucasian) and the Christian population of the Empire, in a deliberate attempt to keep them distinct from the majority of the Sultan's subjects. By the 1860s, however, the Sultan had adopted the principle of forming his guard from soldiers from particular parts of his Empire: Arabs, Albanians and Circassians, as well as Turks. In addition, he had a guard unit which combined the two principles of aristocracy and geography, since it was 'composed of the scions of various families of rank representing the various races under the Ottoman dominion [Turks, Persians, Albanians, Bedouin, Bulgars . . .], two from each race, in the peculiar costume of their respective nationalities'. From the 1670s until after 1956 the guard of the Sultan of Morocco, like that of many other Muslim rulers since the ninth century, was composed of black slaves, whom the Sultan married to other blacks as part of a deliberate policy to keep them racially homogeneous and distinct from his Arab and Berber subjects (see illustration 28).

In Europe the King of France had a Swiss and, until the late sixteenth century, a Scottish Guard, while Napoleon I had Mamelukes, Poles, Dutch, Italians and Lithuanians in his guard. The King of Spain, when a Habsburg, was guarded by Burgundians and Germans, and when a Bourbon, by Walloons and Italians, as well as by Spaniards. The King of Naples, the Pope, and the Dukes of Savoy and Lorraine had Swiss Guards as well as guards recruited from their own subjects. The Austrian Emperor had Hungarian and, briefly, Polish and Lombard-Venetian guards. The Tsar of Russia balanced his Russian guard regiments by recruiting guards from the Baltic provinces or the Ukraine into the Ismailovsky Guard regiment founded in 1730, and by raising guard regiments from Finland and the former Grand Duchy of Lithuania in the early nineteenth century. An abnormally large proportion of officers of the guard, as of all senior officials and officers, was always of German origin. After 1775 there were Cossack Guards and, after 1827, a Caucasian Escort.

The King of Great Britain had Scots Guards from 1709, Irish Guards from 1900 and Welsh Guards from 1915 on guard in London (in addition, the Yeomen of the Guard in the reigns of Henry VII and Henry VIII had been strongly Welsh in composition). Only the monarchies of Denmark, Sweden and Prussia seem to have relied almost always on their own subjects from all areas of their dominions.

The great variety of guards' geographical origins is partly due to monarchs' natural desire to associate every region of their dominions with the supreme honour of guarding the monarch – as was clearly the case with, for example, the guards of the Spanish and Austrian Habsburgs. Other examples were provided by the Swedish Drabants after 1780, and the Piedmontese Guardie del Corpo, which were divided into companies representing different regions of their monarchs' dominions. Moreover, by recruiting different units of their guard from different regions, monarchies encouraged feelings not only of association but also of emulation. As an eleventh-century Persian book of *Rules for Kings* put it, if you had different races in your guard 'each race strove to preserve their name and honour . . . thus all races endeavoured to surpass one another'. This is, surely, one reason why the maintenance of the particular ethnic character of, for example, the Scots, Irish and Welsh Guards has been felt to be so important and, in 1920, in the case of the last two, was made a condition of their continued existence.[15]

But an even stronger reason for guards' unusual racial and geographical composition was fear. Just as fear of the unrestrained 'criminal passions' of the poor led most monarchs to entrust their persons to units composed of, or commanded by, aristrocrats, so fear of their subjects in general led many monarchs (and some modern dictators) to entrust their persons

30. *The Ottoman Imperial Guard at a Selamlik.* C. 1900. YILDIZ PALACE LIBRARY, ISTANBUL.

The Ottoman Imperial Guard also served to connect the different races of the monarchy to the person of the monarch. Here Arab guards in turbans are waiting next to Turkish guards in fezzes for the arrival of their Sultan and Caliph, Abdul Hamid II, for Friday prayers at the mosque he had built outside his palace of Yildiz.

31. *Review of the Circassian Escort in St Petersburg,* from Paul Vassili, *La Sainte Russie,* 1890. BRITISH LIBRARY.

The escort included Cossacks, Tartars, Lezghians, Circassians, and Georgians, in a variety of dazzling uniforms. It served both to connect the Tsar with the recently conquered provinces of the Caucasus and to surround him with guards unlikely to be affected by a movement such as the Decembrist Revolt of 1825.

32. *Review of His Majesty's Guard Cossacks at Tsarskoe Seloe.* 31 December 1905. MUSÉE DES COSSAQUES DE LA GARDE, PARIS.

This review was used by Nicholas II to thank the regiment for its loyalty during what he called 'the troubled days that God has inflicted on Russia' – the Revolution of 1905: 'In your persons I thank all the Cossacks of the Don dear to me. Thank you from all my heart for your services.' He also announced that the commander of the regiment had been attached to his suite, and that the captain of the Tsar's Squadron (every guard regiment had a company or squadron, of which the Tsar was technically head) had become one of his ADCs. This is a clear example not only of Nicholas II's belief that the reinforcement and multiplication of personal ties between the dynasty and the guard was an effective defence against revolution, but also of the usefulness of a guard from a particular race.

to more reliable foreigners. In theory, for example, as Francis I proclaimed in an edict of 1523, between the King of France and his subjects, 'there has always been a greater bond and connection of true love, open devotion . . . and intimate affection than between any other Christian monarchy and nation'. In reality, the Kings of France, quite rightly, doubted their subjects' 'true love' and preferred to rely on the loyalty of their Scots and Swiss Guards (who were usually very unpopular in Paris and among other units of the guard) or of their nobles. Similar doubt about their subjects' 'true love' was probably one reason for the Spanish Habsburgs' use of Burgundian and German Guards and Ottoman Sultans' and Persian Shahs' preference for guards from the Caucasus. The Bourbons, in particular, made it a principle of government to have a partly foreign guard, as their creation of the Gardes Suisses in France, the Gardes Wallonnes in Spain and the Guardie Svizzeri in Naples shows. In 1701 Louis XIV wrote that Philip V must have foreign regiments in his guard.

A similar fear of their own subjects was the main reason why until 1960 rulers of the Arabian peninsula and Morocco used black slaves without potentially dangerous local connections as guards, and chose their other guards from a tribal roster, rather than from a single tribe, 'so there [was] little danger of disaffection or of combinations against their employer'.[16] But might not a royal guard, composed in such an unusual way, and, indeed, created in the first place as a result of monarchs' fear and distrust of their subjects, itself become a cause for fear?

33. *Circassian Guards of the King of Jordan.* c. 1980. PHOTO ROYAL PALACE AMMAN.

Because of their reputation as fighters, Circassians have long been valued as guards by monarchies in the Middle East. Even today Circassians believe that if the King of Jordan's cousin, the King of Iraq, had also had a Circassian guard, he and his family would not have been butchered in 1958. The costume of the Circassian Guard of the King of Jordan is almost exactly the same as that of the Circassian Guard of the Ottoman Sultan and the Escort of the Tsar.

6
INSTRUMENTS OF POWER

THE REASON FOR the unusual social and racial composition of royal guards, and for the ardent personal interest they aroused in the monarchs they guarded, was that they were not simply a means to protect a monarch and increase the splendour of his court. Nor was their main purpose to try out new military techniques or to lure the aristocracy into the army. Royal guards were primarily instruments of power and, at least in intention, pillars of royal authority.

For in most monarchies, for much of the period between the fifteenth and nineteenth centuries, monarchs' authority was continually under challenge, either directly through armed rebellion or assassination, indirectly through attempts to seize control of the levers of power, or simply in the imagination, in the hopes of ambitious subjects and the fears of their monarchs: it is not difficult to detect a rather hunted look in the portraits of most European or Middle Eastern monarchs. These challenges usually came from the monarch's most powerful subjects, the members of the aristocracy.

To take only a few examples, P.M. Holt writes of the Mameluke Sultans of Egypt: 'Between the Sultan and the oligarchy of magnates there was almost constant tension . . . In spite of the splendour and luxury that surrounded him, the strict and formal nature of his public appearances, and the pompous ritual of his accession, the Sultan occupied a precarious position' – unless he had an unusually strong character or was fighting an external enemy. The Kings of France were also often in a precarious position. One reason why Louis XI increased his guard so much in the 1470s, according to Commynes, was his fear that 'one lord or several might attempt to take his palace by night either in league with those inside or by force, and that they would take away his authority and make him live like a man without a mind of his own and unfit to govern'.

Such a fear, however unlikely it might seem, haunted his successors and many other European monarchs. James II of England, for example, knew that the interests of 'the nobility and the gentry' and of 'the monarchy' were different and might be so opposed, in England or France, as to lead to rebellion or assassination. In 1788 one French courtier feared not the popular revolution which was imminent but 'an aristocracy which will only allow the monarchy to keep the appearance of power'.[1] In 1801 Alexander I of Russia went to his coronation preceded by the murderers of his father, followed by those of his grandfather, and surrounded by aristocrats equally ready to murder him. For, to take only the most obvious form of challenge to monarchical authority, an extraordinary number of the monarchs who ruled in Europe and the Middle East between 1400 and 1900 died violent deaths at the hands of their subjects.

The reason why monarchs' authority was under such constant challenge from the aristocracy, as Louis XI and James II experienced, was that monarchy is an irrational form of government. It is hard to justify hereditary royal power, even when effectively exercised, since it concentrates power in the hands of one man. Moreover, the workings of heredity inevitably gave royal authority to people manifestly unfit to exercise it – such as Charles II of Spain, a physical degenerate, or Peter III and Paul I of Russia, both eccentric to say the least.

Under such monarchs, outraged or ambitious subjects found little difficulty in ignoring hereditary monarchical right and the prestige of the Lord's anointed.

But challenges to royal authority did not arise simply because of the failings of the monarchs. Within the ruling class or aristocracy, the desire to challenge monarchs' abuses of their authority was often strengthened by a genuine desire to limit that authority in the interests of more liberty and representative institutions. Ambition was another motive for challenging royal authority. Most aristocrats were content to spend their lives in the service of the monarch, loyal to his authority and convinced that he was the best guarantee of the social order which protected their own rank and position. But another common aristocratic attitude was to prefer to weaken the authority of monarchs, who were from families believed to be no older and certainly no abler than those of, for example, Talleyrand, Guise, Condé, Percy, Grenville, Dolgoruky, Fersen, Infantado, Bismarck.

Many aristocrats wanted to enjoy the fruits of power and the responsibility of maintaining the social order as a right rather than as a favour, by an assured position in a representative assembly or a council (a few dared hope for the throne), rather than by attendance in a royal antechamber or service in a royal guard. Hence the frequent aristocratic leadership of, or participation in, attacks on royal authority.

One of the solutions most monarchies had adopted, by the seventeenth century, to these repeated challenges to their authority, namely a large royal guard, had two principal drawbacks. The first was expressed by Juvenal's famous question about the Praetorian Guard: 'Quis custodiet ipsos custodes?' (Who is to guard the guards themselves?) Every educated European was saturated in Roman history and was aware that the Praetorian Guard had been so powerful, for a time, that in 68, for example, it was able to auction the Roman Empire to the highest bidder. An awareness that modern royal guards might want to behave like the Praetorian Guard can only have been increased by the habit of, for example, Louis XIV and Maria-Theresa calling their guards, in official Latin documents, equites praetorienses or turba praetoriensis.

Every educated Muslim knew that, after the murder of the Caliph Mutawakkil by his guards in 802, the Caliphs' guard began to be a decisive force in politics. In other monarchies of the Middle East, such as that of the Ghaznavids in eastern Iran (962–1186) or the Mamelukes in Egypt (1250–1517), royal guards were so powerful that they not only dominated the monarchy but created it, by deposing the previous monarch and setting up a monarch from their own ranks. How could such an occurrence be prevented in other monarchies? One reason why so many European and Middle Eastern monarchs had guards from different nationalities was not only, as has been already pointed out, to encourage emulation within the guard and to protect monarchs from their own subjects, but also to diminish the threat posed to monarchs by their own guards. As A Mirror of Princes put it, with customary frankness·

> If a prince's bodyguard is all from one race, he is ever the prisoner of his bodyguard and tamely submissive, for the reason that the members of one race will be in alliance together, rendering it impossible to use them in holding each other in check. If they are of all races, one is held in check by another and no single group, through apprehension of the other, is able to be disaffected.[2]

Royal guards often acted not only to further their own ends but also, for example in Baghdad, as an instrument used by outside interests to further their ambitions. That the Praetorian Guard had also been used in this way is suggested by Claudius's decree in 41, forbidding Praetorian Guards from paying court to senators in the morning. Indeed, the second principal drawback to royal guards was the possible connection between Praetorians and senators, between the guard and the aristocracy. For, given the aristocratic composition of many royal guards, or guards officers, the existence of a royal guard might place the monarch in the power of just those people most likely to challenge his authority. Which would be the stronger, aristocrats' legendary sense of honour, which made monarchs entrust them with the safety of their persons, or aristocrats' love of power, independence and liberty which led to so many challenges to royal authority coming from the aristocracy? Would guards officers observe their oath of loyalty to the monarch they were guarding or follow the instincts and interests of their class?

Therefore, because they guarded monarchs and were composed of, or officered by, aristocrats, royal guards were often the cutting edge by which conflicts between monarchs and aristocrats were, sometimes bloodily, resolved. To study whether royal guards were pillars or manipulators (or both) of monarchies, it is proposed to discuss their role first in the absolute monarchies of the Middle East, Russia, Denmark and Spain, and then in the monarchies tempered by representative institutions of France, England, Sweden and Persia (after the grant of the Constitution in 1906). This division has been adopted because the political importance of royal guards seems to have been related to the power of representative institutions. As Napoleon I said on St Helena, 'Palace troops are terrifying, and become more dangerous as the sovereign becomes more autocratic.' An eighteenth-century traveller, Joseph Marshall (using a different definition of absolutism), wrote:

> in a free government or even in an absolute monarchy, provided there is some shew of liberty, as in the kingdoms of France, Spain, etc. we do not see the guards daring to act in this manner [as Praetorian Guards]; but in countries of pure despotism, like Russia, Turkey, Persia etc. a prince, in order to be safe, should have no guards in particular but all the regiments of his army guard in turn ... the Roman history is full of instances of emperors being deposed and others set up by the Praetorian cohorts.[3]

How many later emperors and kings suffered such a fate?

THE MIDDLE EAST
Such was the power and glamour of the Ottoman Empire that European contemporaries were well aware of one of the most notorious cases of a royal guard disposing of political power as did the Praetorians, namely, the Janissaries. Although only sections of them (the Peiks, Solaks, and Bostangis) were, strictly speaking, a guard, their political role deserves some attention since it shows what could have happened in the monarchies of Europe: the Janissaries were often described by European observers as 'their footguards', or 'the equivalent to our Foot Guards'.[4]

As early as 1444 the Janissaries mutinied to demand an increase in pay. They were so hostile to the new Sultan Mehmet (soon to conquer Constantinople) on his accession in 1451, and their support was so necessary, that he gave them money, a practice continued by his successors. The Janissaries were quick to defend their own interests. They disliked arduous campaigns away from the capital and in 1514 forced Sultan Selim I to abandon his winter campaign against the first Safavid Shah of Persia. In 1620 they refused to go on campaign in Egypt and sabotaged the Sultan's plan to raise an Arab army which might have shared some of their duties and privileges.

The Janissaries did not intervene simply to defend their own material interests, but also to impose Sultans of their choice or, more often, to eliminate those who had displeased them. In 1481 they helped to put Bayezit, not his brother Djem, on the throne; in 1512, crying 'Our Padishah is old and sick, we want Selim Shah in his place,' they replaced the ageing Bayezit not with his preferred successor Ahmet, but with another son, Selim. In 1622, crying 'In the name of the Law we want to have Sultan Mustafa Khan,' they overcame the Bostangis defending the reforming Sultan Osman II (who had already offended them by his plans for an Arab army) and replaced him by his idiot brother Mustafa I.[5] Divisions within the dynasty

34. *The Mutiny in the Ottoman Imperial Guard*. April 1909.
ILLUSTRATED LONDON NEWS.

The ringleaders of the mutiny in favour of Abdul Hamid II and reaction are in the middle of a square formed by constitutional troops. After being addressed by the constitutional general Mukhtar Pasha, they were led out and shot. Guards' interventions in politics could be dangerous for themselves as well as for their monarchs.

provided Janissaries with a favourable opportunity for intervention. An Ottoman Sultan lived in dread of the Janissaries' favoured cry, 'Long live the brother! God save the brother!', and so tended to lock brothers away in 'cages' in the palace or kill them.

Janissaries also helped to depose sultans in 1617, 1648, 1703, 1730 and 1807. In addition, acting in the name of religion, 'the Law', or the true interests of the monarchy, but no doubt, as Lady Mary Wortley Montagu suspected, manipulated by outside factions, they often intervened against ministers or royal favourites. In 1589–92, for example, they forced the replacement of three Grand Viziers; in 1631 they killed the Sultan's lover and in 1632 forced a change of Grand Vizier. In a similar way, in Morocco for fifty years after the death of Sultan Moulay Ismail in 1727, rivalries among his sons and grandsons and the absence of counterbalancing institutions allowed the Abeed al-Bukhari to depose sultans, on fourteen separate occasions, almost as they pleased. Only after their reduction to 6000 in the 1780s (at the same time as European royal guards were being reduced) by Sultan Muhammed III, the real founder of modern Morocco, did they become, as their successor the Garde Royale still is, a loyal pillar of the Sultan's authority.

The Janissaries show the degree to which, in an absolute monarchy without representative institutions, a royal guard can become politically important, often taking the place of a representative assembly as a means of expression for popular feelings; indeed, by the end of the eighteenth century so many civilians had become members of the Janissary corps, in order to take advantage of its privileges, that it did represent much of the adult male population of Constantinople. The Janissaries also show that divisions within the dynasty, unpopular royal favourites and challenges to the guard's status or privileges were the occasions most likely to provoke a political intervention by a royal guard.[6]

After the suppression of the Janissaries in 1826, the modern Ottoman Imperial Guard played little part in politics. After the Young Turk Revolution of 1908, however, they remained devoted to Sultan Abdul Hamid, for they were 'incapable of conceiving any loyalty except to the Sultan's person'. In October 1908 the Arab and Albanian Guards at Yildiz mutinied in horror at the prospect of leaving the capital to serve in the Yemen. Discontent was fuelled by the appointment of new officers who supported the Revolution, by the abolition of some religious observances in the barracks, and by the incorporation of Anatolians into Arab units. In April 1909, 2500 guards at Yildiz, with considerable popular backing, attempted a counter-revolutionary coup which was ruthlessly crushed, their commander Tahir Pasha, a former shepherd and favourite of the Sultan, murdered by constitutional troops. Abdul Hamid, who had been too broken to act, was forced to abdicate.[7]

In the absolute monarchies of the modern Middle East royal guards have been politically important. Indeed, one anthropologist sees the possession of a guard of slaves and mercenaries, free of tribal ties of kinship, as 'the initial nucleus and primary military strength used in establishing the superiority of the ruling house and protecting its continuity'. He is describing the now extinct monarchy of Hail in the 1830s but his remarks may reveal one of the reasons for the establishment of many of the longer-lasting monarchies of the Arabian peninsula. A loyal guard was certainly crucial in enforcing the ruler's orders.

A more recent example of the political role of a royal guard, again as a result of division within the ruling family, took place in Saudi Arabia. From 1956 King Sa'ud had been building up his royal guard as a crack regiment of 1500 uniformed men, commanded by his sons, the 'little kings', in addition to the traditional tribal and black bodyguards. He tried to use his guard as a weapon in his struggle for power with his brother Crown Prince Faisal in 1962–64. By December 1963 command of the royal guard was the only important attribute of sovereignty he had left. In the final showdown he threatened Faisal with its artillery but, having already secured its commander's support, Faisal smoothly replied in a letter of 26 March 1964 that henceforth the royal guard was under the authority of the Minister of Defence. Sa'ud left his kingdom early the next year.

In Oman in 1970 the action, or unexpected inaction, of the royal guard helped to facilitate the deposition of the Sultan in circumstances upon whose exact sequence no two accounts agree: reports differ as to whether, when the Sultan's palace was attacked, his slave guards defended him, deserted him, or had been locked up while at prayer in a mosque.[8]

RUSSIA

In its political role, the Russian Imperial Guard resembled the guards of the Middle East as well as those of Europe. Indeed, the Strelitz and their successors, the Russian Imperial Guard, were often compared by contemporaries, such as Voltaire, to Praetorians and Janissaries, so widespread was the belief in the similarities of character and purpose between royal guards. After its foundation by Peter the Great, the Russian Imperial Guard was a crucial force in the political life of the country until 1917, although it is an exaggeration to say, like Joseph Marshall, that the guards 'in fact are Praetorian cohorts giving away the Empire at their pleasure'.

Their importance was in part due to their aristocratic composition. For the Russian aristocracy was almost completely dependent on the monarchy. Unlike, for example, the Prussian or the French aristocracies, it did not have a sense of identity independent of the monarchy, nor were there institutions, such as provincial estates or aristocratically controlled law courts, likely to nurture it. With the exception of a few great families, such as the Dolgoruky, it tended to see itself only in relation to the Tsar and his service, rather than as an aristocracy based on birth or the possession of land. Therefore the Imperial Guard, a military force stationed near the seat of power in an absolute monarchy, was one of the few institutions through which the Russian aristocracy could express its desires and ambitions.

Under a strong Tsar the guard was a pillar of the monarchy. Peter the Great 'relied heavily on his guards officers, entrusting them with important diplomatic, political [such as fetching back the Tsarevitch Alexis from western Europe to his brutal execution in 1717] and administrative tasks . . . they were westernized, they were militarily proficient, they were predominantly noble and they were loyal to the new order'. In all, a third of the 179 officials in the top four ranks of officials in 1730 began their career in the guard, while 41 per cent had served in it at some stage of their career. The importance of the guard as a support of the monarchy in its struggle with discontented aristocrats is clearly shown not only by Peter's promotion of guards officers to key posts but also by his choice of them as judges of his aristocratic opponents. 'My brothers, having no one but you to whom I can better trust myself, I establish you as judges of those who have deceived me,' he declared in December 1717. From 1695 to 1729 the staff of the Preobrazhensky Guards acted as the first modern secret-police force in Russia.

After Peter's death in 1725, his guard immediately emerged as a crucial political force, decisive in eight of the eleven accessions of monarchs or changes of regents in the next hundred years. One reason for its political importance was, as in the Ottoman Empire, conflict within the ruling dynasty. For, from 1722 to 1797, succession to the Russian Empire was decided not by heredity but by designation by the reigning Tsar. Therefore, within the complex structure of the Romanov dynasty (see Table 2) there was always a large number of rival candidates for the throne. Such rivalry inevitably enhanced the importance of the guard. In 1725 a party of conservative magnates, led by Prince Repnin and Count Galitsyn, heads of two of Russia's oldest noble families, favoured the claims to the throne of Alexis's son the Grand Duke Peter, likely to be as conservative as his father. A meeting of the first four ranks of officials, the Senate, and the Synod was called in the palace on 28 January. There was a proposal to put the throne to the vote.

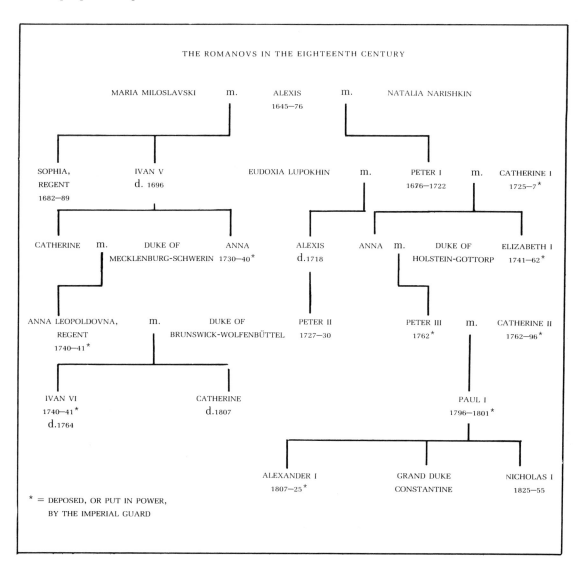

THE ROMANOVS IN THE EIGHTEENTH CENTURY

MARIA MILOSLAVSKI   m.   ALEXIS 1645—76   m.   NATALIA NARISHKIN

SOPHIA, REGENT 1682—89   IVAN V d. 1696   EUDOXIA LUPOKHIN   m.   PETER I 1676—1722   m.   CATHERINE I 1725—7*

CATHERINE   m.   DUKE OF MECKLENBURG-SCHWERIN   ANNA 1730—40*   ALEXIS d.1718   ANNA   m.   DUKE OF HOLSTEIN-GOTTORP   ELIZABETH I 1741—62*

ANNA LEOPOLDOVNA, REGENT 1740—41*   m.   DUKE OF BRUNSWICK-WOLFENBÜTTEL   PETER II 1727—30   PETER III 1762*   m.   CATHERINE II 1762—96*

IVAN VI 1740—41* d.1764   CATHERINE d.1807   PAUL I 1796—1801*

ALEXANDER I 1807—25*   GRAND DUKE CONSTANTINE   NICHOLAS I 1825—55

* = DEPOSED, OR PUT IN POWER,
    BY THE IMPERIAL GUARD

But Menshikov, Peter's favourite and lieutenant-colonel of his old regiment, the Preobrazhensky Guards, had already secured the support of the guard for Catherine, the Tsar's widow. He took a deputation of guards to the Tsarina. She promised payment of arrears and an increase in pay. They naturally cried, with that familiarity which was such a feature of the Russian Guard's relations with the Romanovs, 'We have lost our father but we have still our mother left!' When the aristocrats' proposal to put the throne to a vote was made, Tolstoy, one of the guards officers who had brought back Alexis to Russia, therefore frightened of his fate if Alexis's son should reign, made a speech in favour of Catherine which was applauded by the other guards officers present. General Buturlin ordered a roll of drums by the soldiers of the guard in the courtyard below. Catherine was proclaimed Empress that day. Clearly the drums of the guard were more important than the opinions of the senators in deciding who was to rule Russia.[9]

The guard saw its interests as linked to the westernizing autocracy created by Peter the Great. It was a bulwark against aristocratic power and conservative tendencies – although in 1727 it accepted the accession of the natural hereditary heir, Peter II, and Major Soltykov of the Preobrazhensky Guards arrested Menshikov.

In 1730 the guard's role as a pillar of westernizing monarchy against ambitious and conservative aristocrats was even more evident and decisive. On the death of Peter II (from a cold caught at a review of the guards) only fear of the guard's reaction had prevented the great aristocratic family of Dolgoruky from trying to seize the throne for the Tsar's fiancee Catherine Dolgoruky. Thereafter, the Council, dominated by the Dolgorukys and representatives of other aristocratic families, such as the Galitsyns, wanted, in the words of the French resident, 'either to abolish the monarchy or to diminish its powers drastically by a mixture of aristocracy', as in England, Sweden or Poland. The Dolgorukys and their allies wanted to establish the Council's control over war and peace, the guard and the army, taxation, official appointments and the monarch's choice of spouse and successor, and to abolish the monarch's powers over nobles' lives and property – a programme which reveals just how far aristocratic ambitions, even in a monarchy with such strong autocratic traditions, could go.

The reaction of the chosen heir, Anna, a niece of Peter the Great, again shows the use a monarch could make of her guard. Before she arrived in Moscow on 21 February for her coronation, she received the Preobrazhensky and Chevaliers Guards, declared herself their colonel and captain respectively, and 'gave every one of the officers and soldiers a glass of wine or brandy with her own hand, which has gained their hearts'. (Catherine I had done the same in 1725.)[10] From 21 February to 8 March Anna was kept almost a prisoner by the Council in the Kremlin but managed to communicate with the outside world through her ladies-in-waiting. Count Loewenwolde, formerly of the Swedish army, two guards officers, Major-General Soltykov and Prince Kantemir, Prince Tcherkaski of the Council and Prince Yussupov of the Preobrazhensky Guards, organized support for Anna and autocracy. On 23 February over 260 guards officers, and some nobles, signed a petition to the Tsarina in favour of autocracy. On 25 February 800 nobles and 150 guards officers came to the palace and begged her not to agree to the new aristocratic constitution, crying, 'that they did not want laws to be laid down for their sovereign, who should be as absolute as her predecessors . . . We cannot allow her to be tyrannized. Your Majesty only has to give the word and we will lay the heads of the tyrants at her feet.'[11] She ordered them to obey her loyal supporter Soltykov, now lieutenant-colonel of the Preobrazhensky Guards, and in effect the ambitions of the higher aristocracy were defeated by this demonstration of the lesser nobles and the guards. On this occasion, their resolve to support the autocracy which guarded their interests so well was strengthened by the hatred of the lesser nobility, from whom so many guards officers were recruited, for such great families as Dolgoruky and Galitsyn. They preferred the rule of one autocrat to the prospect of 'being tyrannized by great families'. The

Dolgorukys were executed in 1738–39 for trying again to limit Anna's power.[12]

After Anna's death in 1740 her favourite, Bühren, became Regent for her nephew, the infant Ivan VI. Bühren was detested in Russia as an upstart foreigner, and particularly detested in the guard which suspected him of planning to alter its aristocratic composition and privilege of being the sole troops garrisoned in St Petersburg. He relied on the less Russian regiments of the Garde à Cheval, whose lieutenant-colonel he was, and the Ismailovsky Guards. But at 3 a.m. on 9 November – his last chance, since it was the last day the Preobrazhensky Guards were on duty – their lieutenant-colonel, Marshal Münnich, took forty soldiers from his regiment and arrested Bühren in the Summer Palace. The guard and the people were delighted; Bühren and his family were sent to Siberia.[13]

The new Regent, Anna Leopoldovna, mother of Ivan VI, soon made herself unpopular, mainly by her use of foreign officers and officials, and again the guard was used by outside forces as a means of effecting political change. Her government had ordered the guards to leave for a winter campaign against Sweden – a prospect no more pleasing to them than the winter campaign against Persia had been to the Janissaries in 1512. The Grand Duchess Elizabeth, a daughter of Peter the Great, wanted power and may have been persuaded to act by sergeants of the guard, as well as by the French Ambassador, who disliked the government's pro-Austrian policy.

On the night of 25 November 1741 she went to the barracks of the Preobrazhensky Guards with seven devoted grenadiers who knew the password. She made a speech to the

35.   Groot. *The Empress Elizabeth on Horseback*. 1743. NOVOSTI.

The Empress is wearing the uniform of captain of the Life Company of the Preobrazhensky Guards, which she formed from the guards who helped her seize the throne in 1741. Uniforms, titles, the monarch's personal company or squadron in each guard regiment, and a common interest in power, were among the many links between Russian monarchs and their guards.

guards: 'Do you want to follow me, not only as brave soldiers but as my children? I swear on the cross to die for you; swear twice over to do the same for me.' They swore and, accompanied by 200 Preobrazhensky Guards, she swept on in her sledge to the Winter Palace. In the guard room she cried, 'Children, wake up! Our poor nation is groaning under the yoke of the Germans.' The soldiers, unlike their officers, did not hesitate. The Regent, Münnich (who had exchanged command of the Preobrazhensky regiment for that of the Garde à Cheval) and the Tsar were arrested and imprisoned. The new Tsarina left the palace for a triumphal drive through St Petersburg followed by the flags of the three guards regiments, for these were her real robes of state. The guards who had accompanied her the night she seized power became a special privileged Life Company, with the Empress as captain and her lover, Razumovski, as second captain. Like a guard in an Arabian monarchy they were lodged and fed at court, played cards with the Tsarina who called them 'my children', and even 'mingled with persons of the first rank', a rare, much resented breakdown in the normally rigid social hierarchy of a European monarchy.[14]

Like Peter II in 1727, Peter III, the obvious hereditary heir, succeeded his aunt (he was already Duke of Holstein through his father) without discussion in 1762. But his attacks on the property and privileges of the Orthodox Church and, in the words of the English Minister, Sir Robert Murray Keith, the 'severe discipline which the Emperor endeavoured to introduce among the troops, particularly the guards, who had been accustomed to great idleness and leisure', made his government increasingly unpopular. Moreover, he was

36.   Antrapov. *Peter III*. 1762. NOVOSTI.

Peter III is wearing the uniform of colonel of the Preobrazhensky Regiment. A few months later its soldiers helped depose and murder him. Before he ascended the throne, he had been lieutenant-colonel of the Preobrazhensky and Garde à Cheval regiments and received a report and gave the password every day.

thought to want to replace the guards, whom he called 'Janissaries', with his own Holstein troops, 5000 of whom were stationed in and around St Petersburg. The Life Company was indeed replaced by a Holstein unit called the Body Guard of the Imperial Household. Peter III also planned to send the guard away from St Petersburg to fight for his Duchy of Holstein. Yet again, fear of sharing its prerogatives, and of leaving the pleasures and privileges of the capital, helped to determine the guard's actions.

His wife Catherine had always been ambitious: the guard was to be the means by which she, like Catherine I and Elizabeth, realized her ambitions. Her agent in the guard was her friend Princess Dashkov, who spread 'right principles' among the officers of the Preobrazhensky and Ismailovsky regiments; in addition, Catherine's lover, Grigorii Orlov, and his brothers were, as she wrote, 'extremely determined people, much loved by the ordinary soldiers, having served in the guards'. Her coup is best told in her own words, as she recounted it a few days later in a letter to a former lover, Stanislas Augustus Poniatowski: 'The guards were all prepared and at the end there were thirty or forty officers in the secret and about ten thousand subalterns . . .' On the morning of 28 June the Empress and Princess Dashkov, in traditional Preobrazhensky uniforms, as opposed to the new Prussian-style uniforms introduced by Peter III, visited the Ismailovsky regiment with 'twelve men and a drum, who started to beat the alarm. The soldiers rushed to kiss my hands, my feet, the hem of my dress, calling me their saviour.' After oaths were sworn she 'went on to the Semenovsky regiment. They came to me shouting Vivat! . . . Then the Preobrazhensky

37. Rokotov. *Count G.G. Orlov.*
NOVOSTI.

Orlov, Catherine's lover, had served in the Semeonovosky Guards from 1744 to 1759, and used his influence in the guard to help her seize the throne from Peter III in 1762. He was so lavishly rewarded with titles, estates, serfs and money that other guards became jealous.

regiment arrived also shouting Vivat!' and then the Garde à Cheval 'in such a frenzy of joy as I have never seen before, weeping and shouting that the country was free at last' (among them was Potemkin, whom the Empress noticed and remembered). The Empress changed from Preobrazhensky to Semenovsky uniform at about ten in the morning, 'having had myself proclaimed colonel with great jubilations'. Although surrounded by his Holstein troops Peter abdicated the same day, as Frederick II said, just like a schoolboy being sent to bed. He was murdered, probably by Alexei Orlov, while under the guard of Preobrazhensky soldiers, on 18 July.[15]

Again the drums of the guard had decided the fate of the throne of Russia; indeed, for Catherine, the attitude of the different regiments of the guard was as important as the attitude of different political parties or factions to a prime minister in search of a power-base in an assembly. For, in eighteenth-century Russia, the guard fulfilled some of the functions of a representative assembly and in, for example, its hostility to Bühren, Anna Leopoldovna and Peter III, expressed the will of the ruling classes. This was thought to be a legitimate function of the guard. Even in the twentieth century, as an official regimental history of 1930 wrote, 'Guards officers were seen as the natural and decisive counsellors of the Emperors and Empresses of Russia.'

The emergence of the Imperial Guard as a pillar, or manipulator, of the Russian monarchy had two important results. First, it meant that the guard's particular interests, the maintenance of its privileges and its status as the sole guard, its dislike of arduous

38. Anon. *Potemkin*. NOVOSTI.

Potemkin was first noticed by Catherine II during the coup of 1762, when he was serving in the Garde à Cheval. He later became the most powerful of her favourites, an important general and minister, and commander of the Chevaliers Gardes.

campaigns away from the capital, were an important factor in Russian politics. Second, the political importance of the guard increased the importance of the personal factor in Russian politics. Soldiers and, perhaps especially, royal guards can be very emotional. Candidates for the throne of Russia had to be able to use the personal touch – pouring glasses of wine, calling their guards 'my children', wearing guards uniforms, relying on a lover's influence in the guard – to secure the throne. It is noticeable that both in 1741 and 1762 soldiers were more ready to risk themselves and flout their oaths than officers of the guards, a fact which served as confirmation that aristocrats were usually more reliable and less volatile than the poor.

The Russian Guard seems to have been happy with the status quo, as indeed, given its privileges, it had every reason to be. It may have been the indirect upholder of the status quo, as well as its direct protector against the changes planned by conservative aristocrats in 1725 and 1730, or by Peter III in 1762. It is possible that, in the 1760s, Catherine II was prevented from carrying out more radical reforms by fear of the reaction of the guard. There were frequent signs of discontent in the guards in the 1760s, partly caused by jealousy of their comrades, the Orlovs', rise to favour: in June 1763, for example, the Prussian Ambassador predicted that Catherine's reign would be as short as her husband's. In 1764 the former Ivan VI was killed by his guards for fear that he would be used by conspirators against Catherine II. In 1768 a captain of the Garde à Cheval, after a few, very limited, reforms complained, 'Now they are going to take away our estates completely. When they give freedom to the

39. Dumont. *The Future Paul I*. 1784.
PHOTO NICHOLAS LYNN.

At the time this portrait was printed, the future Paul I was training his own guards on the model of those of Prussia. His attempt to impose his obsessive standards of drill and discipline, and Prussian-style uniforms, helped to make him unpopular with the Imperial Guard after he ascended the throne. In 1813 his son Alexander I founded the Pavlovsky Guard Regiment, recruited from soldiers with snub noses like his father's, in his memory.

peasants what shall we live on?' In 1772–73, particularly, Catherine II was in a very exposed situation; this may be one reason for the rise of Potemkin, who knew the guard so well, to power and office at the time. She could not disband the guard because such a move would cause intense 'discontent among the nobility', according to the Prussian Ambassador. Similar fears may have impeded Alexander I's reforming intentions after 1801. A royal guard could be just as important by virtue of the fear it inspired by the mere fact of its existence as by its direct interventions in politics.[16]

In 1801 the guard intervened yet again to defend the status quo. Catherine's son, Paul I (1796–1801), was a reforming autocrat who often changed his mind about foreign and internal policy, as well as about the value of his senior officials. He was soon detested by many nobles who knew he was no respecter of their rank. Paul I was author of the famous remark to the Swedish Ambassador, which confirms the Russian aristocracy's dependence on the monarchy: '*Monsieur l'Ambassadeur*, you must realize there are no *grands seigneurs* in Russia except for the man I am talking to, and then only for so long as I am talking to him' – a classic exposition of a monarch's contempt for his aristocracy. On the other hand, Paul I was known and resented for the care he took of ordinary soldiers and the measures he was planning in favour of the serfs.

The aristocratic plot against Paul I was planned by Count von der Pahlen, a Baltic aristocrat who commanded the Garde à Cheval and was joint military governor of St Petersburg with the Grand Duke Alexander. Alexander was an accessory who approved of

40.   Anon. print. *Count von der Pahlen*. PHOTO ROGER VIOLLET.

Count von der Pahlen, one of the many Baltic German aristocrats who served the Russian monarch, entered the Garde à Cheval at the age of fifteen. While he was its commander he planned the coup by which, in March 1801, Paul I was murdered and replaced by Alexander I.

the plot and must have realized its inevitable consequences for his father. Other leaders in the plot were Zubov, last lover of Catherine II and a senior court official, Count Bennigsen, Count Tolstoy of the Semenovsky and Count Talysin of the Preobrazhensky Guards. Pahlen (who actually said, 'You cannot make an omelette without breaking eggs,') and Zubov were the main organizers of the murder.[17]

On the night of 11 March 1801 the conspirators met at Talysin's apartment in the Winter Palace where, to quote Bennigsen's account, 'wine had not been spared'. At about 11.30 detachments of the Preobrazhensky and Semenovsky Guards, led by Pahlen and Talysin, advanced on the Michael Palace, the stark fortress to which Paul I, who was aware of his own unpopularity, had moved for safety on 1 February. A separate group of eight or nine guards officers was led by Argamakov, an adjutant of the palace and an officer in the Preobrazhensky Guards, to Paul's apartment, bypassing the detachments of loyal Semenovsky and Preobrazhensky Guards of the Life Company at the entrance and on the ground floor, who in any case were neutralized by the guards led by Pahlen and Talysin (Paul I had dismissed the Garde à Cheval detachment normally on duty at the entrance to his apartment the day before). In Paul's bedroom Bennigsen said to him, 'You are arrested, Sire.' Another officer said, 'You should have been killed four years ago.' In the ensuing brawl it is possible that the actual murderer was Captain Boglovsky of the Ismailovsky Guards. It is a sign of the nightmare world of fear and suspicion in which a Tsar of Russia lived that Paul thought, from the red Garde à Cheval uniform of one of the conspirators, that his own son, the Grand Duke Constantine, Commander of the Garde à Cheval (who was in fact confined to his room that day for negligence) was among them. Alexander's first act as Tsar, which was to appear before detachments of the Preobrazhensky and Semenovsky Guards – only the latter, whose commander he was, were enthusiastic – confirmed their supreme importance in the Russian monarchy. Yet again the guard had removed an awkward monarch, although sections of the guard, particularly in the Preobrazhensky Regiment, where Paul I was 'much loved', had remained loyal.[18]

Throughout his reign Alexander I remained free from direct threats to his authority from his guard. Threats had become such a habit, however, that a guards coup, perhaps in favour of his sister the Grand Duchess Catherine, was talked about during the difficult period of peace with France in 1807–12. A mutiny in his beloved Semenovsky Guards in 1820 was a great shock and, since he was convinced it was a liberal plot, increased his reactionary tendencies. In 1825, however, a disputed succession gave the guard another opportunity to try to manipulate the Russian monarchy, this time without success.

Already in 1801 some guards officers had been in favour of a constitution. Their experience of the liberal Paris of Louis XVIII after 1814 convinced other guards officers, such as Bestuzhev of the Moskovsky and Pestel of the Litovsky Guards, of the necessity of change in Russia. In the words of Baron Rozen of the Finland Chasseurs Guards, 'The most zealous and active spirits of the Russian Guards enthusiastically imbibed the concepts of liberty, citizenship and constitutional right.' In 1822, the return of the guard from Lithuania, where it had been sent in preparation for an expedition to restore the monarchy in Naples, galvanized the conspirators into action.[19] Given the power structure of the Russian monarchy and their fear of the people, they naturally thought of a palace revolution in favour either of the Empress Elizabeth, wife of Alexander I, or his brother, the Grand Duke Constantine. Living in Warsaw he appeared less of a martinet than the designated heir, the Grand Duke Nicholas, from whose ruthless standards of discipline many officers and soldiers of the guards, as in the days of Paul I, had suffered. The death of Alexander I on 1 December 1825 triggered off the explosion.

While Constantine and Nicholas were both renouncing their right to the throne to each other in a futile attempt at self-abnegation, the conspirators in the guards, led by the

I. Jean Fouquet attr. *The Adoration of the Magi.* C. 1450. MUSÉE CONDÉ, CHANTILLY. PHOTO GIRAUDON.

Charles VII is shown as one of the Magi. His Gardes Ecossais are behind him. They were the first of the foreign guards which were intended to protect the monarchs of Europe from their own subjects. But, despite their reputation for loyalty, even the Gardes Ecossais sometimes plotted against the King.

II. Van der Meulen. *Passage of Louis XIV across the Pont Neuf*. 27 August 1660. MUSÉE DE GRENOBLE. PHOTO GIRAUDON.

The King's carriage is surrounded by Gardes du Corps, and preceded by Cent-Suisses. Gardes Français and Mousquetaires line his route. Louis XIV was devoted to his guards, frequently choosing, reviewing, and drilling them himself. The blue, silver, and red of their uniform, the colour of the livery of the King of France, was a sign of their connection with the household as well as the person of the King. Another sign that his guard was considered part of his household is that under Louis XIV the horse guards became known as the *Maison* Militaire du Roi, just as in other monarchies they were known as the Tropas da *Casa* Real, the *Hustrupper* or the *Household* Cavalry.

III. Danckerts. *Charles II Walking in Whitehall.* C. 1680. COLL. DUKE OF ROXBURGHE. PHOTO HECTOR INNES.

A company of Coldstream Guards – in red, one of the livery colours of the King of England – is being drilled on the left. The wooden building in front of the Banqueting Hall was the head-quarters of the guards, as its successor, on the same site, still is. The presence of guards surrounding the King's palaces and person was not only a novelty but also a source of strength for the Stuart monarchy under Charles II. But in 1688 they betrayed his successor.

IV.   Ghezzi. *The Lateran Council.* 1725. PHOTO CHRISTIE'S, ROME.

The Swiss Guard of the Pope, founded in 1506 and still in existence, is in the foreground. It still wears the same uniform on ceremonial occasions.

V.   Eriksen. *Catherine II on Horseback*. 1762. DAVIDS SAMLING, COPENHAGEN.

The Tsarina is in the Preobrazhensky uniform she wore on the day of the coup by which, with the help of the guard, she seized the throne of Russia from her husband. This portrait, whose original still hangs in the throne-room of the Palace of Peterhof in Russia, is a visible sign that the guard was acknowledged to be one of the principal sources of the Tsars' power.

VI.   Meytens and workshop. *The Entry of Isabella of Parma into Vienna* (detail). 6 October 1760.
KUNSTHISTORISCHES MUSEUM, VIENNA.

The princess's carriage is surrounded by soldiers of the Swiss Guard of the Dukes of Lorraine which, after serving in Lorraine and Tuscany, served in Vienna from 1745 to 1767. In the foreground are members of the Hungarian Noble Guard, on the first occasion they appeared in public. As in 1539 in England, or 1868 in Italy, a royal wedding was thought so important that it was an occasion for the creation as well as the display of royal guards. The Swiss Guards are wearing the yellow and black livery of the Habsburgs.

VII. Géricault. *An Officer of the Chasseurs à Cheval of the Garde Impériale.* C. 1810. MUSÉE DU LOUVRE.

The Garde Impériale was one of the most splendid, as well as one of the most victorious, guards in history. Géricault himself later served in the guard of Louis XVIII as a Mousquetaire.

VIII. J.F. Tayler. *Second Life Guards Band.* C. 1833. NATIONAL ARMY MUSEUM.

Music was almost as important a part of the pomp and circumstance with which royal guards surrounded their monarchs as uniforms. The Second Life Guards Regiment, founded in 1788, was disbanded in 1922.

IX. Ladurner. *Parade in Palace Square, St Petersburg, for the Unveiling of the Alexander I Column.* 1834. PHOTO NOVOSTI PRESS AGENCY.

Nicholas I, in the uniform of the Chevaliers-Gardes, is talking to their commander, his heir the future Alexander II. Behind them are some Grenadiers du Palais, an elite unit founded by Nicholas I in 1827. No other European guard was so large, so pampered, or so intimately connected to the reigning dynasty, as the Russian Imperial Guard.

X. *Trooping the Colour.* 1970. PHOTO COLOUR LIBRARY INTERNATIONAL.

The last of the great formal military rituals which used to dazzle the capitals of Europe, the Trooping, or its equivalent, has existed since 1729. In the words of one senior guards officer, it 'symbolizes what we have stood for over the centuries . . . [it is] not only the focal point of what we mean when we talk of ourselves, uniquely, as guardsmen, but also the outward sign of the Queen's Majesty.'

XI. *Queen Elizabeth the Queen Mother Presenting the Shamrock to the Irish Guards.* Saint Patrick's Day 1981. PHOTO IRISH GUARDS.

Like Queen Alexandra and the Princess Royal before her, the Queen Mother presents the shamrock to the Irish Guards every Saint Patrick's Day. Since the regiment's foundation in 1900, this ceremony has symbolized both the Irish Guards' connection with the British monarchy and their carefully maintained national identity. Even today about half their soldiers are born citizens of the Irish Republic, not of the United Kingdom. For the same reasons the Prince of Wales, as their colonel, also presents leeks to the Welsh Guards every Saint David's Day. The Scots Guards survive without a royal thistle.

XII. *HM the Queen Leaving Buckingham Palace.* 1981. PHOTO CAMERA PRESS.

Like almost every other European dynasty in the past, the House of Windsor maintains an impressive variety of personal connections with its guard. On her official birthday Elizabeth II, in guards uniform (with the badge of the regiment which is trooping the colour in her cap), is leaving her palace to review units of her Household Division, of which she is colonel-in-chief. She is followed by three royal colonels, the Duke of Edinburgh, Colonel of the Grenadier Guards, the Prince of Wales, Colonel of the Welsh Guards, and the Duke of Kent, Colonel of the Scots Guards, and by Gold and Silver Sticks in Waiting and the Field Officer in Brigade Waiting, officers through whom she can still, in theory, give orders directly to her Household Cavalry and Foot Guards.

Bestuzhev brothers and Prince Trubetskoy of the Preobrazhensky Guards, who had drafted a constitution, took action. They led about 2000 troops of the Moskovsky, Grenadier and Finlandsky Guards and the Garde Equipage on to Senate Square, and proclaimed Constantine as Tsar on 14 December. For the first time the people of St Petersburg appeared on the stage of Russian history, although only as onlookers, not actors: the crowd was 'ready and willing to co-operate' against Nicholas and often shouted, 'Long live Constantine!'[20]

But the conspirators had no definite plan or decisive leader: Trubetskoy was hopeless. Moreover, although they did hesitate, the Preobrazhensky, Pavlovsky, Ismailovsky and Garde à Cheval regiments remained basically loyal, despite the entreaties of some of their officers. Above all, in Nicholas, the Russian monarchy had an energetic and decisive military leader who, according to the Austrian Ambassador, in this terrifying and bewildering situation, 'displayed a sang-froid, a collectedness and a courage which inspired admiration in the crowd of onlookers'. As in 1730 or 1762 the monarch's personality was of decisive importance in dealing with the guard. According to Rozen, 'he continually rode up and down . . . now sharply ordering, now good-humouredly begging the people to disperse and hinder the troops' movements no longer'. Finally, he ordered the artillery of the guard,

41.   Kollman. *The Decembrist Revolt*. 14 December 1825. NOVOSTI.

Nicholas I and his staff are on the left. The Chevaliers Gardes, who remained loyal, are in the centre. As this picture shows, the people of St Petersburg were spectators while the different guards regiments decided whether to support Nicholas I or the Decembrist conspirators, who claimed to be defending the right to the throne of the Grand Duke Constantine. In 1825, as in 1762, 1801, 1905 and 1917, it was the guard which decided the fate of the Russian monarchy.

which had remained loyal, to fire on the rebels after three warnings. The resultant cannonade put an end to the rebellion at the cost of many lives; there were 'pools of blood in the snow and spattered up against the houses'.

Although some conspirators were not guards officers, the Decembrist revolt yet again shows the guard being used as the ultimate lever of power in the Russian monarchy. On 14 December Nicholas and the conspirators competed for the support of the different regiments of the guard like a prime minister and his rivals for the support of different parties or deputies in an assembly. Again, the guard had acted, in part, as the representative of aristocratic ambitions. The Decembrist revolt was described by one contemporary as 'a contest for power between the crown and the nobility [infuriated by increases in taxation and the length of military service] in a nation in which a third class does not exist'. This judgement, ignoring the insurgents' facade of constitutionalism, probably contains an element of truth.[21]

After the shock of the Decembrist revolt, 1333 guards were sent to serve in the Caucasus; in 1827 the creation of the Palace Grenadiers and the expansion of the Caucasian Escort, neither of which formed part of the command structure of the guard, were logical reactions by an Emperor who had been shown the dangers of trusting himself to a guard composed solely of Russians. However, the Preobrazhensky Guards, particularly the Life Company, to whom Nicholas had entrusted the guard of the Winter Palace and of his family on 14 December, had been outstandingly loyal. Nicholas called them 'my family' and thereafter, every 14 December, the Tsar and Tsarina went to the Preobrazhensky barracks, unaccompanied, 'for an inspection and a sort of family reunion' – again personal contact with the monarch and his family being used as a political weapon; in addition, many loyal guards officers became aides de camp to the Tsar.[22]

After 1825 there were no disputed successions and conflicts between the monarchy and the aristocracy were settled in the council chamber rather than on the street or in the guard room. There was one last manifestation of the guard's role as an expression of the will of the ruling class, in the final doomed year of the monarchy. By December 1916 the Tsar and, even more, his ministers, had lost the respect of the educated public. What she called 'the Preobrazhensky clique' hated the Tsarina. The absence of spectacular victories, and of a constitution more liberal than the half-hearted one granted in 1905, exasperated officers of the guard as much as other members of the Russian ruling class.

Few feared a popular revolution. Indeed, they were so out of touch with their own people that, in January 1917, some plotters, such as Guchkov, 'regard as unactionable their dream of seizing power under the pressure of the demonstration of the masses of the population, and all the more rest their hopes exclusively on the conviction of the inevitability in the near future of a palace coup, supported at least by one of the two army units sympathetic to the group', according to the head of the secret police.

Particularly in the Chevaliers-Gardes there was, according to the French Ambassador, talk of 'saving Tsarism by a change of sovereign', to be achieved either by a night march on Tsarskoe Seloe or by seizing the imperial train on one of its journeys to and from army headquarters. The Tsar would be forced to abdicate to his son and the popular and respected general, the Grand Duke Nicholas Nicholaievitch, would become Regent. The authorities in charge of the investigation concluded, however, with tragic accuracy, that it was all talk and no action.[23] Perhaps if the guard had acted, Russia and its neighbours would have been spared years of horror.

PRUSSIA

In Russia the guard often represented the interests or views of sections of the aristocracy, in conflict either with the monarch as in 1762 or 1801, with the high aristocracy as in 1730, or with the monarch's autocratic power as in 1825 or 1917. In other monarchies, because conflict was less acute or had other means of expression, the guard was less important politically. In Austria the guard was small and resistance to the Habsburgs' authority by aristocrats was slight or confined to particular provinces. Thus, there were, in the words of an eighteenth-century observer, 'no Mamelukes, no Praetorians, no Janissaries'.

In Prussia, after the compromise of 1654 whereby a regular army, whose nucleus was the Elector's guard, had been established in return for his protection of the privileges of the aristocracy, there were few points of conflict between the monarchy and the aristocracy; nor did a disputed succession give discontented aristocrats an opportunity for attack. The famous lines,

> *Und der König absolut*
> *Wenn er unsern Willen tut*

('Let the King be absolute so long as he does what we want') expressed the attitude of the Prussian aristocracy and monarchy, united by war and privilege.

On two occasions, however, conflict did appear possible. After 1806 the reforms and, in 1815, the relatively mild (by Prussian standards) peace demands of Frederick William III did provoke some hostility among his officers. In August and September 1815, in particular, Chancellor Hardenberg said he 'felt himself in the midst of Praetorian bands', while the Tsar, perhaps thinking of his own situation in Russia, remarked 'it is entirely possible that some day we may have to help the King of Prussia against his own army'.[24]

In March 1848 the army, and especially the guards, were hostile to Frederick William IV's policy of accommodation with the revolution which had broken out in Berlin. The officers of the Kaiser Alexander Garde Grenadiers discussed a march on Berlin from Potsdam to 'liberate' the King. As Prince Frederick Charles wrote, 'The officers are more royalist than the King when it comes to the point,' or rather not more royalist but, as in the Russian and many other monarchies, convinced that they, not the monarch, knew what was best for the monarchy. To officers in many royal guards their regiments were such an essential part of the monarchy they were guarding that a policy which went against their interests or opinions must, by definition, be wrong.

Thereafter, under conservative governments devoted to protecting the interests of both the monarchy and the aristocracy, there was little opportunity for conflict between the monarchy and its guards. Indeed, faced with the possibility of challenge from left-wing parliamentary parties, they drew even closer together, if that was possible. In 1887, for example, the future Kaiser William II wrote of the Reichstag: 'May the day come when the Grenadier Guards purge the place with bayonets and tambours.' Even as late as 1917 he saw his guard as his monarchy's ultimate weapon against democracy.[25]

DENMARK

Whereas in Prussia the guard was usually a loyal pillar of a monarchy whose authority was rarely challenged by the aristocracy, in the absolute monarchies of Denmark and Spain the guard, as in Russia, often acted as a force reflecting the views of sections of the aristocracy, or even the nation, in their conflict with an unpopular monarch or royal favourite. In Denmark the foundation of the regiment of Life Guards had preceded by a year, and no doubt facilitated, the establishment of the absolute monarchy in 1660. For the next hundred years the monarchy was the most absolute in Europe but was rarely challenged by an aristocracy which respected the monarchs and was satisfied by their policies.

In 1771, however, the monarchy came under increasing challenge owing to the reforming policies of the chief minister, Struensee, and Queen Caroline Matilda, all-powerful over her simple, easily led husband, Christian VII. Struensee was unpopular because he was not only a foreigner, a commoner and the lover of the Queen, but also a reformer. In accordance with the spirit of the age he wanted to attack the privileges of the nobility, to reduce the guard and improve the army. On 3 April 1771 the Horse Guards (already reduced by Saint-Germain) were abolished and replaced by 300 dragoons. On 24 December Struensee also decided to abolish the remaining battalion of Life Guards and divide it among line infantry regiments.

The guards were outraged and insisted either on remaining a distinct unit or on receiving their full discharge with compensation; anything rather than be confused with troops of the line. Reverdil, councillor of the King, recalled that 'the mutineers were encouraged by a population seething with discontent'. In other words, as in other absolute monarchies, the guard reflected the views of the majority of the population. Such encouragement was particularly easy because, with the approach of Christmas, immense quantities of alcohol were being drunk and few guards would refuse a free drink from a civilian. In the end, faced with the guards' refusal to go away, Struensee gave in and gave them their full discharge; some returned to Norway, some went to other regiments, others stayed in Copenhagen.[26] Meanwhile, popular discontent and what the English Minister called 'the opposition of the nobles', were increasing rapidly, and the Queen Mother, Juliana Maria, was prepared to lend her authority to the conspirators.

As in Russia and Spain conflict within the ruling family, added to aristocratic discontent, created a political role for the guard. On the night of 16 January 1772, with the aid of the grenadiers of Colonel Köller and the dragoons of Colonel Eichstadt, both on guard at the palace, the coup took place. Köller and Count Rantzau led soldiers of the grenadiers from the palace guard room and arrested Struensee and Caroline Matilda before they could get to the King. The fifth of nine points in the act of accusation against Struensee was his dismissal of the Life Guards. A few months after his execution, they were restored with great pomp. Clearly, the Danish Guards in 1772 were not only a crucial lever of power but also held to be, in some way, a component part of the Danish monarchy, and one which should not be tampered with.[27]

In 1784 the guard again acted as a decisive lever of power in the Danish monarchy. The son of Christian VII and Caroline Matilda, the Prince Royal, resented the domination of Juliana Maria. On 14 April, having secured the King's consent, he informed the Council, at the moment of the changing of the guard when double the normal number of guards were at the palace, that most of its members were dismissed. After the Council meeting, 'the Prince Royal next went to the guard of the palace, addressed the officers of the Foot and Horse Guards who were there to receive the password; he told them that from now on they should receive it from him alone, forbidding them at peril of their life to respect other people's, then he made them take the oath'. From then on, because he had secured the support of the guard, he was absolute ruler of Denmark as Regent and, after the death of his father in 1808, as King. Again, as in Russia in 1762 or 1825, the attitude of the guards was crucial in deciding the fate of the monarch or regent. The act of giving the password to the guard could be a sign not only of the regular operation of the military hierarchy, but also of where power really lay in a monarchy. And the moment of the changing of the guard could be the best occasion to seize power.[28]

SPAIN

In Spain the guard did not play a large part in the life of the monarchy under the Habsburgs. On one occasion when there was conflict in the royal family, however, it was crucial. In January 1568 Philip II's rebellious son, Don Carlos, was arrested by the King in the presence of the guards and, until his death, was guarded by the Monteros de Espinosa – probably the only time in their history they served during the day as well as by night. Philip II had been afraid of the power of grandees such as the Dukes of Alba, Braganza and Medina Sidonia. By the reign of his great-grandson, Charles II, royal authority had sunk so low that not only had the Braganzas refounded the kingdom of Portugal but the King was insulted in the streets of

42.   Goya. *Charles IV as Colonel of the Guardias de Corps.* C. 1799. ROYAL PALACE, MADRID.

In the eighteenth century neither the French nor the Spanish Bourbons had the same obsessive interest in their guards as the Hohenzollerns or the Romanovs. Nevertheless, Charles IV increased the privileges and wore the uniform of the Guardias de Corps. In 1808 they deposed and imprisoned him.

Madrid and the aristocracy was increasingly disrespectful of royal authority.

In 1669, one reason why a regiment of guards was founded (see page 18) was because as an adviser of the Regent wrote, it was believed to be 'the one and only means of maintaining all the tribunals, the grandees and the people in obedience and respect'. By this he did not mean that a regiment of guards was always physically necessary to enforce the will of the monarch, but that its existence would indirectly influence 'the tribunals, the grandees and the people' to accept the authority of the monarch more readily. No wonder it was abolished again in 1677.

One of the characteristics of the Bourbons was their reliance on guards. After he became the first Bourbon King of Spain, Philip V found that, like Charles II, he was not only insulted by the people of Madrid but was also thwarted by members of the aristocracy. On 18 May 1702 he wrote to Louis XIV that the Spaniards 'are opposed to all my wishes . . . I see clearly that so long as I do not have any troops of my own, and above all a regiment of guards on which I can rely, I will get nothing done'. The subsequent massive expansion of the royal guard of Spain was opposed above all by aristocrats – the members of the Council of Castile, the grandees and the Mayordomo Mayor (Lord High Steward of the Royal Household), whose right to give orders to the guard was now taken away. On Saint Louis's Day 1705 there was one of those disputes over precedence which, in the courts of Europe, were often an outward sign of a bitter political conflict. The grandees of Spain refused to attend services in the palace chapel because the Captain of the Guardias de Corps in waiting now stood between them and the King. A compromise was reached by inventing a tradition that the captains should always be grandees. But two captains were sacked for having sided with the grandees, and the size of the guard and its dependence on the King were maintained. Philip V's trusted adviser, the Princesse des Ursins, wrote to Madame de Maintenon a few days later, in a letter which Louis XIV surely saw and approved: 'The King of Spain cannot be the master unless he is able to make himself feared by the grandees: and if he does not have guards he will never succeed.'[29] Guards were the Spanish monarchy's answer to discontented aristocrats.

The eighteenth century was the golden age of Spanish absolutism, in part due to the existence of the royal guard, by which the King was always surrounded, when hunting or going from one palace to another, as well as when making a state entry into his capital. In 1766 when there were serious riots in Madrid, largely caused by opposition to the reforming policies of Charles III and probably encouraged by reactionary ecclesiastics and grandees, the guard was the firmest pillar of the monarchy. A well-known story describes Charles III's fears after he had fled to his country palace of Aranjuez and until he heard the sound of his guards' arrival: 'Take my boots off . . . I am safe; my guards are here; I am going to have a rest.'

As Tsars of Russia had found out, however, the great danger of a guard is that, by surrounding the monarch with soldiers commanded by aristocrats, it might put him in the power of aristocratic or dynastic factions opposed to his policies. Spain after 1800 was ruled by Charles IV, simple and well-meaning, with the help of his licentious favourite Godoy who had been given his own guard, of Carabineros Reales, in 1801. Godoy, who had been appalled at the guard's incompetence on campaign in 1801 ('not only useless but prejudicial', he wrote to the King and Queen), reduced both the Guardias Espanoles and the Gardes Wallonnes from six to three battalions each, in 1803. Thereby he dramatically worsened their officers' promotion prospects, since there were now more officers after fewer jobs.

By the autumn of 1807 the tensions within the royal family, and between the monarchy and sections of the aristocracy, had become explosive. On 27 October 1807, like Philip II in 1568, Charles IV arrested his treacherous elder son Ferdinand, who loathed Godoy, with the help of his guards. At this stage they were still loyal, although a few tried to prevent the removal of Ferdinand's papers.

43. Goya. *General José de Palafox*. 1814. MUSEO DEL PARDO.

Palafox was a leader of the guards conspiracy against Charles IV in 1808, before becoming a hero of the war of independence against the French.

By the spring of 1808 the situation had changed. In early 1808 Godoy further increased his unpopularity in the guard by merging the Flemish and Italian companies of the Guardias de Corps. Many aristocrats, such as the Conde de Montijo (whose niece Eugénie would marry Napoleon III) resented royal absolutism. He had been expelled from Madrid in 1795 for writing a pamphlet deploring the monarchy's 'oppression' of the nobility and nobles' lack of power: Charles IV, unlike his father, even sold patents of nobility. As in other monarchies, the guard was a means through which aristocratic resentments, exploiting divisions in the royal family, could express themselves. The Palafox brothers, cousins of Montijo, were particularly important: one, José, was an officer in the Guardias de Corps, another an officer in the Guardias Espanoles, a third Mayor-Domo Mayor of Prince Ferdinand, while their brother-in-law was also an officer in the Guardias de Corps. Another important plotter was the Marques de Castelar, Captain of the Alabarderos, who was particularly committed to an increased political role for the nobility.[30]

As French troops, including part of the Garde Impériale, poured into the country, and Napoleon's intention to take it over became obvious, the King began to think of imitating the Braganzas, who had fled to their dominions in South America in September 1807. In early March the court moved to Aranjuez, south of Madrid, on the way to the port of Cadiz. On 16 March the Council of Castile, which Montijo had recently visited, denounced the move and called for more consultation between the ministers and the Council – a clear sign of aristocratic resentment of royal absolutism. To hatred of Godoy and royal absolutism was now joined the guards' dislike of leaving their privileged routine and the pleasures of the capital. How would they cope with life in the colonies?

It is not known exactly how the riots or *motin* of Aranjuez began in the night of 17 March. The spark may have been a signal from Ferdinand's apartment in the palace, or his alleged remark to Jaureghin, an officer of the Guardias de Corps, on 17 March: 'Tonight is the journey, and I do not want to go.' It may have been a dispute between the Guardias de Corps and Godoy's Carabineros Reales, whom they had long hated and resented. A crowd of peasants and courtiers' servants, organized by Jaureghin and Montijo (whom they called Tio Pedro), stormed through Aranjuez threatening to kill Godoy who, when he came out of hiding on 19 March, was saved only by the Guardias de Corps. The entire guard mutinied in favour of Ferdinand, 'discipline broke down completely, the soldiers mingling with the mob'. On 18 March Charles IV dismissed Godoy. But the rioting continued. On 19 March the Minister of War and officers of the guard in waiting such as the Prince of Castel-Franco, Colonel of the Gardes Wallonnes, the Marques de Albudejte, an *exempt* in the Guardias de Corps, and the Conde de Villariejo, told the King that only Ferdinand could calm the mob. The King abdicated to his son who ascended the throne to immense popular acclaim as Ferdinand VII. The existence of a national conspiracy against Charles IV and Godoy, not confined to the guards, is shown by the fact that, at the same time, there were uprisings throughout Spain in favour of Ferdinand.[31] But pressure from the guard, and the opinions of its officers, were clearly decisive in 1808.

The intrigues which achieved this result are still a subject of discussion. Whether Montijo and the guards officers were used by Ferdinand or whether, as his mother claimed in an outraged letter of 6 April, 'It is the guards who do everything and make my son do what they want,' is not entirely clear, although at the time they had such a community of interests that the distinction is probably artificial. What is clear is Ferdinand's ability to calm and control the mob, and the ease with which guards could become jailers, manipulators rather than pillars of monarchy. Charles IV and Maria Luisa were so disgusted that in April they preferred to be guarded by the Garde Impériale rather than their own Guardias de Corps whom Maria Luisa decribed as 'all traitors and perfidious'.[32]

Thereafter, the Spanish monarchy disintegrated in a nightmarish mixture of foolish-

44. Anon. print. *The 19 March at Aranjuez*. 1808. PHOTO ROGER VIOLLET.

Probably deliberately, this print makes out the abdication of Charles IV to be the result of popular demonstrations and omits the crucial role of the guard in forcing the King's decision. The other country palaces of the King of Spain, the Pardo and La Granja, were also, like Aranjuez in 1808, scenes of coups by the guard, in 1822 and 1836 respectively – a sign of the danger of a large privileged guard in a monarchy with few counterbalancing institutions.

ness, incompetence and intrigue. By 9 April Charles IV, and by 16 April Ferdinand VII, were in the power of the French. On 5 May they abdicated at Bayonne, not even having taken the elementary precaution of surrounding themselves with loyal Guardias de Corps, although José Palafox, in waiting on Ferdinand VII, did escape to warn Spain what was happening. During May, Murat hoped that the guard would rally to Joseph Bonaparte, who arrived in Madrid as 'King of Spain' on 23 July. Some officers of the guard, for example Castel-Franco, briefly did. But after the Spanish victory over the French at Baylen in July many units of the guard fought on against the French until the return of Ferdinand VII in 1814.[33]

One result of 1808 was that intervention in the affairs of the monarchy became a habit with the guard and the rest of the army. On 7 March 1820, Ferdinand VII was persuaded, or compelled to adopt an extremely liberal constitution by the attitude of his guards. As the British Ambassador wrote, 'the Public Agitation fermented by the Military (Principally by the Gardes du Corps and the Foot Guard) had arrived at a Height which threatened a general Insurrection, when, in order to avoid its Consequences, the King determined to accept the Constitution'. If the guard had been loyal, such a capitulation would not have been necessary.

In fact, the constitution and the liberal ministries which enforced it were not particularly popular outside the towns or below the middle classes, and the guard soon began to change its opinion. Some Guardias de la Persona and Alabarderos published pamphlets affirming their support for the constitution. But they were more concerned with the reductions in their pay, promotion prospects, privileges and duties at court which took place in 1821 than with the fate of the monarchy or of the constitution. In 1822 they feared more attacks on their privileges, perhaps even on their existence.[34]

On 29 June and 2 July 1822 there were disputes between the guard and a revolutionary crowd: the guard crying, '*Viva el Rey netto*' ('Long live the absolute King'), the crowd shouting slogans in favour of the constitution. Some guards killed a constitutional officer of the Foot Guards, Lieutenant-Colonel Landabaru. On 2 July 1822, from the Pardo Palace just outside Madrid, the guard sent an address to Ferdinand, demanding 'that the Guard at last receive definite guarantees'. On 7 July, 2000 guards marched on Madrid and, in a very confused situation, came near to restoring the King's authority. Most of the population of

Madrid, by now thoroughly fed up, wanted the overthrow of the constitution. But line troops, the militia and a well-organized constitutional crowd, were stronger than the guard and the people. The latter were badly led by the Duke of Infantado and the Marques de Las Amarillas, who had 'raised and armed some hundreds of the lowest rabble', while Ferdinand VII showed no initiative and gave no encouragement. The guard was defeated and dissolved. Thereafter the King was guarded by, and, in effect, prisoner of, line regiments and the Alabarderos, many of whom were pro-constitutional, under his old friend and fellow-conspirator of 1808, José Palafox. Finally, the French invasion of 1823 and the subsequent reorganization and expansion of the royal guard (see page 50) gave the Spanish monarchy a firm power-base.[35]

The next decade showed how easy it was for a monarchy to pass from the risks of revolution resulting from a weak and unreliable guard to the perils of praetorianism caused by a large and self-confident guard. In 1832, because they openly supported the claims to the throne of the King's reactionary brother, Don Carlos, rather than of his legal heir, his daughter the future Isabella II, 400 Guardias de la Persona were dismissed and several hundred officers of the Guardia Real put on half-pay. The dismissed or suspended officers were to provide a nucleus of officers for the Carlist army in the Carlist War of 1833–37.

In August 1836, when Ferdinand's last wife, the Reina Gobernador Maria Christina (who had married a handsome sergeant in the guard, Munoz, a few months after the King's death), was in residence at the country palace of La Granja, the guard again intervened decisively in Spanish politics. The Carlist campaign was going badly: pay had recently been cut; discipline was more severe at court than on campaign; much of non-Carlist Spain had risen in favour of a constitution. On 10 August extremist agitators and newspapers from Madrid began to appear in the cafes of La Granja frequented by the guard. On the night of 12 August the officers of the guard were at the theatre. The Guardia Real Provincial (led by Sergeants Garcia and Gomez) began to mutiny; most of the Guardia Real deserted to them with only the Guardias de la Persona and the Grenadiers of the Guardia Real remaining loyal. Crying: 'Down with the chocolate drinkers! Death to the chocolate drinkers! Death to the little birds of the Queen!' (as the Guardias de la Persona were known) the Guardia Real Provincial invaded the palace. The Queen, who thought resistance useless, received twenty of them, led by their sergeants. After listening to their insults, she had to agree to sign the constitution of 1812, change seven ministers and the commander of the guard, the Marques de San Roman, and increase its pay and improve its food – a combination of demands very characteristic of a guard's intervention in politics. The guards then took her back to Madrid in triumph.[36]

Under the constitution imposed by the guard, Spanish politics became more left-wing. In 1840, under the radical Regent Espartero many officers of the Guardia Real who were 'well known to be of anti-liberal opinion', were dismissed or put on half-pay; Queen Maria Christina was sent into exile in Paris. A combination of the two forces decided to try to seize control of what was still the key to the political situation, the person of the monarch. Again, division within the royal family, and aristocratic discontent, created a political role for the royal guard. At about 7.30 on the night of 7 October 1841, soldiers from right-wing regiments led by former guards officers, tried to advance up the staircase of the Palacio Real in Madrid. The nineteen Alabarderos on duty – there should have been more, but they were 'at supper or various other engagements' – put up a stiff resistance from the top of the staircase, protected by the balustrade and a screen. Outside the palace most of the Guardia Real, with the exception of some of its officers, remained loyal to Espartero and hemmed in the insurgents, who had to surrender. As a result the Alabarderos were expanded and rewarded, the Guardia Real abolished. The experience of the Spanish monarchy showed again that a guard could be a threat, as well as a support, to a monarchy.[37]

45. Anon. print. *The Murder of the Duc de Guise*. 24 December 1588.
PHOTO ROGER VIOLLET.

Henry III was able to use his guard to kill or arrest his most dangerous opponents in the château of Blois in 1588. But he had reasserted his authority only in his palace, not throughout his kingdom.

FRANCE

In an absolute monarchy, such as the Ottoman Empire, Russia, Denmark or Spain, when there were so few alternative means of expression or institutional counterweights to military power, such as representative or aristocratic assemblies, or independent law courts, a royal guard could often behave like the Praetorian Guard or assume some of the importance of a representative assembly. But what was the political impact of a royal guard on the monarchies of France, England, Sweden, and (after 1906) Iran, when the power of the monarch was, to a varying extent, limited by the role of a representative assembly (although the Parlement de Paris was, in reality, a law court, it often claimed to be, and tried to behave as, a representative assembly)? Was it simply a matter of practical convenience that meetings of Estates were often held, and deputations of Parlements received, in the guard rooms of royal palaces?

In France the expansion of the royal guard took place at a time when the monarchy was under constant threat from its subjects, and the enemies of the King of France tried to use his guard, as they did every other available means, against him. In 1446 the Dauphin, the future Louis XI, did manage to corrupt some of his father's Gardes Ecossais. In June 1450 there was a conspiracy among some of them to introduce an English army into the King's camp. But for seventy years after 1490 there were few challenges to royal authority and the guard had little to do but patrol the palaces, line processions and watch over the King's money in the Tour de Nesle in the Louvre.

During the Wars of Religion from 1562 to 1598 the royal guard, with the help of Swiss mercenaries acting as guards although as yet without the formal title, did manage to prevent any of the aristocratic parties, using Protestantism, or Catholic extremism as a cover for their political ambitions, from seizing the King and making him reign, as Louis XI had feared, as 'a man without a mind of his own and unfit to govern'. Furthermore, the guard was one of the few reliable means of asserting his authority left to the King. Charles IX used it, and his brother's guard, to begin the massacres of the Huguenots in August 1572, which, he had been convinced, were necessary to restore his authority; his brother's captain of the guard had already killed one Huguenot leader, the Prince de Condé, a cousin of the King, in 1569.

When the final showdown between Henri III and the ultra-Catholic House of Guise, which was aiming for the throne, approached, the guard was also the King's ultimate weapon. On 9 May 1588 the King could briefly believe that, thanks to the recently expanded Gardes Françaises under *le brave* Crillon, and to his Swiss troops, he had recovered control of Paris. But he was soon closely besieged in the Louvre and had to withdraw, escorted by the Gardes Françaises, on 13 May. The combined forces of the Duc de Guise, the Catholic League and the Parisians had been too strong for this guard.[38]

That autumn, when the States General met at Blois, some deputies demanded the dismissal or reduction of the guard. Guise was so ambitious that he wanted to have a formal organized guard like that of a royal prince. To the many warnings he received about the King's likely reactions, Guise replied with the French proverb, '*Bien gardé que Dieu garde*' ('God's protection is the best guard'). He felt safe because he was so popular and was surrounded by hundreds of devoted armed followers of his own. But it had long been known that the act of paying court to the King in his cabinet, where even the Duc de Guise could not take armed retainers with him, was the moment of greatest danger.

On the morning of 23 December 1588 when he entered the cabinet, Guise found himself surrounded by eight of the Quarante-Cinq (a bodyguard of Gascon nobles raised by Henri III in 1584) who despatched him in a few minutes. The Gardes du Corps, evidently not trusted so much, had barred the approach routes. They later arrested and killed two other opponents of the King, the Cardinal de Guise and the Archbishop of Lyon, while the Gardes Françaises and the Prévôté arrested the most hostile of the deputies of the States General.[39]

But such an energetic assertion of royal authority by means of the guard did not prevent the Catholic League from rising in horror against the King and beginning a civil war. A royal guard can control the precincts of a palace, even a capital city, but not a nation in fury. The importance of being well guarded at all times was confirmed by the murder of Henri III on 1 August 1589 when he was besieging Paris, killed on his chamberpot by a fanatical monk; the Quarante-Cinq and the Gardes du Corps had been left waiting outside. A similar failure to be surrounded by his guards left Henri IV an easy target for Ravaillac's knife on 14 May 1610.

In the next fifty years, when the monarchy had to deal with a bewildering succession of civil wars, fomented by princes, great nobles, Parlements, and popular discontent, the guard played an important part in the monarchy's desperate efforts to maintain its authority. Throughout this period, when the King was often in the field against his subjects or under threat in Paris, the guard was a pillar of the monarchy in two ways. First, it kept the King physically safe and alive – something by no means to be taken for granted since, as James II recalled of the 1650s, 'everything was to be feared at a time when the ambition of a few great lords knew no bounds'. In other words, nobles were prepared to kill the King: had not the Guise encouraged the assassin of Henri III, and the Duc d'Epernon the assassin of Henri IV? In June 1610 the Regent Marie de Médicis, widow of Henri IV, was so alarmed by the ambitions of the Guise that she increased the guard around the Louvre to 4000.[40]

The second way in which the guard served the monarchy was by providing it with a devoted and reliable physical force with which to arrest its enemies when, like Guise in 1588, they came to pay court to the King in his palace; no French aristocrat could resist the lure of the court. Marie de Médicis would not have dared arrest the Prince de Condé and his supporters, the Ducs de Mayenne, Vendôme and Bouillon, in her bedroom on 1 September 1616 if the sight of the changing of the guard, when more guards were around the palace than usual, had not given her the idea. Today simply a spectacle, in the past the changing of the guard, in France in 1616 or in Denmark in 1784, could be the most favourable moment for a monarch to assert his authority.

On 24 April 1617 the Queen's all-powerful favourite, the Maréchal d'Ancre, was

46.   Anon. print. *The Murder of the Maréchal d'Ancre.* 24 April 1617.
PHOTO ROGER VIOLLET.

The Gardes du Corps killed the Maréchal d'Ancre, the detested Tuscan favourite of Queen Marie de Médicis, on the orders of her son Louis XIII. Louis XIII had so many enemies that his guard was particularly important to him. No other King of France, not even Louis XIV, devoted so much time and attention to his guard.

*Au Louure entrant il fut pour le bien de la France
Arresté, & tué, trop honnorablement:
Car il deuoit mourir au haut d'vne potence,
Et le ventre des loups eftre fon monument.*

arrested and killed on the orders, and to the delight, of Louis XIII by the captain of the guard in waiting, the Marquis de Vitry (who had arrested the Maréchal de Biron, an enemy of Henri IV, in 1602). After his murder, the Gardes du Corps ran through the streets of Paris crying, '*Vive le Roi! Le Roi est Roi!*' Other enemies of the King, arrested by his guard in this period, were La Vieuville, Superintendent of Finance, in 1624; Vendôme again in 1626; the Duc de Beaufort in 1643; Condé, Conti and Longueville in 1650; the Cardinal de Retz in 1652; and Fouquet, the all-powerful Superintendent of Finance, by d'Artagnan and his Mousquetaires in 1661 (Fouquet was so powerful that Louis XIV could not trust the Gardes du Corps to arrest him). If the arrest of the Président de Broussel had not been bungled by some Gardes du Corps on 26 August 1648, the subsequent uprising by the Parisians, which led to the disastrous civil war of the Fronde, might not have been so successful so soon.

Clearly, the royal guard was the ultimate resource and weapon of the King of France. It was a sign of Richelieu's unique authority over Louis XIII that in 1642 he managed to persuade the King to dismiss guards officers hostile to him, on the grounds that he was so frightened going past the guards at the entrance to the King's apartments that he would be forced to bring his own guards with him. The dismissed officers were reinstated after Richelieu's death in 1643.[41]

Louis XIV's glorious reign and constant wars – the surest way of strengthening a monarchy, or indeed any regime – removed most open challenges to the monarch's authority. But after his death the royal guard again emerged as a key factor in the power structure of the French monarchy. The regency of his nephew, the Duc d'Orléans was

47.   P.D. Martin. *The Departure of Louis XV after the Lit de Justice.* 17 December 1715. MUSÉE DE VERSAILLES.

The King, who is on the steps of the Parlement, has just forced it to change the terms of Louis XIV's will. His uncle the Regent had been careful to surround the Parlement with even more guards than usual in order to forestall any possible trouble. For the guard was the monarchy's ultimate weapon against the Parlement, as well as the people, of Paris.

contested by his bastard, the Duc du Maine, while the Parlement was eager to recover a degree of power. Orléans reacted by using the royal guard. Three thousand Gardes Françaises under their colonel, the Duc de Guiche, to whom, according to Saint-Simon, Orléans had just given 600,000 livres, surrounded the Parlement on 2 September 1715; Orléans broke the old King's will and assumed total control. On 29 September 1718 his rivals, the Maines, were arrested by Gardes du Corps. On 21 July 1720 Mousquetaires arrested leading Parlementaires, while Gardes du Corps, Gardes Françaises, and Gardes Suisses occupied the Parlement building to prevent a meeting hostile to the Regent's government. It is interesting that, according to a contemporary diarist, the officers of the guard, although carrying out their orders, 'speak out loud against the government; they only demand a movement to strike, and they say so frequently in the taverns'. But in 1720 the movement never came.[42]

Throughout the eighteenth century the guards were used to arrest the King's enemies and maintain his authority. Among those arrested were, yet again, a prince of the House of Condé, the Duc de Bourbon, in 1726 – 'Monseigneur, I have orders to arrest Your Most Serene Highness,' said the captain of the guard – and, rather less politely, the Cardinal de Rohan who had hoped to win Marie-Antoinette's favour by buying her a diamond necklace, in 1785. Since the reign of François I, the role of the guard as a pillar of the French monarchy had, surely deliberately, been stressed in the King's ceremonial visits to the Parlement. According to the official order-book of the major of the Gardes du Corps, the day before the King went there in state, accompanied by detachments of all eleven units of his guard, ninety-seven Gardes du Corps inspected the building and remained there overnight in order 'to receive the King the next day, to keep the crowd away from him and for the safety of his person'. The guard's role was not only ceremonial. During the periodic confrontations between the King and the Parlements in the eighteenth century, the guards (never the police or the line) were used to enforce the King's will. On 3 September 1787 and 5 May 1788, for example, it was officers of the Gardes Françaises who arrested, or took into exile, the most hostile members of the Parlement.[43]

One challenge which the French, unlike the Russian, monarchy did not have to face was that of a praetorian guard. This was not only due to the prestige of the King, or Regent, and to the force of the law and other civilian institutions, but also to the sophisticated and effective methods used to keep the guard dependent on the King and incapable of uniting against him. As a minister wrote to Louis XVI in the 1780s, 'In the constitution of the guard of the King it appears that the intention has been to make each of the units which compose it independent of each other,' and this had been explicitly proclaimed in an ordinance of 11 November 1724.

One sign of this policy was that all the commanders of the different guard units had the right to work alone with the King on matters concerning their commands. This was not only to maintain his personal control over his guard, but also to prevent them from forming a solid, potentially praetorian block of guards, and to keep the different units independent and jealous of each other. In addition, the *guet* of 257 Gardes du Corps sent every three months to guard the King were deliberately chosen from all four companies, never from the same one, so there was less chance of their uniting against him. The Comte d'Agoult wrote to Napoleon I in 1806 that the power of the captains of the guard was checked by that of the major and his staff, 'so that they should not use it in a sense contrary to the interests of His Majesty. In that way His Majesty divided authority in order to concentrate it in his person and attach his Guard to himself in a more particular manner.' Perhaps only a cataclysm like the French Revolution could have allowed an officer of the *ancien régime* to express the realities of its power structure in such unguarded language.

Under Napoleon I, however, the large, privileged and homogeneous Garde Impériale was the only force guarding the monarch. Napoleon wrote to Joseph in May 1806, 'Do not organize your guard so as to have to appoint a single commander. Nothing is more dangerous,' and he deliberately divided authority over his own guard between four marshals. But his guard was so devoted to its Emperor that it remained a pillar, not a manipulator, of his monarchy. In 1808 its presence deterred General Malet from trying to seize power, and in 1812 it defeated him when he did try. The soldiers of the Garde Impériale remained loyal until the end of the Empire, cheering the Emperor enthusiastically at the changing of the guard at Fontainebleau on 4 April, when Paris was already in enemy hands.

But on 5 and 6 April, not only his marshals but also, which was probably as important, the commanders of the guard such as General Friant, commander of the first infantry division of the Vieille Garde, refused to march on Paris as the Emperor ordered, and insisted on his abdication; as in Russia or Spain, officers of the guard found it easy in certain circumstances – military defeat, the encouragement of hostile or exhausted factions (the Senate and the government had turned against the Emperor) – to disobey the monarch. Only the Poles in his guard were wholly loyal – another indication of the advantages of a foreign guard.[45]

After the Emperor's decision to abdicate on 6 April, the guard played an important part as a reserve of support and supplier of agents for the Emperor and his wife, who had retreated to Orléans. On 8 April, declaring, in her words, that they were 'decided to be cut in pieces for you, your son and me', the Garde Impériale accompanying her helped her to resist

FIDÉLITÉ
HONNEUR
ET
PATRIE

HALTE LÀ, LA GARDE ROYALE EST LÀ.
Hommage aux Braves.

48.   Anon. print. *Halte-là! La Garde Royale est là!* 1816. MUSÉE CARNAVALET.

As this widely distributed, government-sponsored print makes clear, the government wanted the Garde Royale to be seen as a pillar of the authority of its Colonel-General, Louis XVIII. It proved its worth in the food riots of 1816 and in the political riots of 1820.

her brother-in-law's attempts to force her to join the allies. On 12 April, however, she finally left Orléans for Rambouillet to join her father, the Emperor of Austria. She exchanged her escort of the Garde Impériale for one of Guard Cossacks, and soon ceased to think and act as a Bonaparte. The same day a detachment of the Garde Impériale sent from Fontainebleau, although it failed to find the Empress, did seize several million francs at Orléans for the Emperor.[46]

On his way to Elba, and on the island, the Garde Impériale maintained the inhabitants' otherwise doubtful obedience. Individual officers or soldiers of the guard ran messages between the Emperor and his errant wife and subjects. The Garde Impériale, as has already been pointed out, also provided the Emperor with an indispensable nucleus of armed force which helped him to recover his throne in 1815. On his return from his defeat at Waterloo, on 21 and 22 June, the Emperor briefly thought of using his guard against the opposition in the Chambers. But the Chambers, and France, were determined to be rid of the Emperor from the moment he had lost a battle. Moreover Drouot, the commander of the Garde Impériale, was now prepared to obey the Chambers and the government they supported, led by Fouché, rather than the Emperor. As in 1814, only the soldiers remained loyal. On 25 June the Emperor abdicated in favour of his son. From 27 June, he was in effect a prisoner of his own guard at Malmaison. Under the escort of General Beker and a few guards he left Malmaison for the coast and, ultimately, exile, on 29 June. The weakness of the authority of even such an autocratic and awe-inspiring monarch as Napoleon I over his guard is shown by the ease with which, in certain circumstances, it could be turned against him and become his jailer.

After 1815 the debris of the Garde Impériale gave a certain unity and panache to Bonapartism. Former officers of the Garde Impériale such as Fabvier, Nantil and Dumoulin were among the most dedicated conspirators against Louis XVIII in the 1820s. The political statement of wearing the uniform of the Garde Impériale was made not only by the Emperor demanding asylum from the British on 14 July but also by Bonapartists visiting Lady

Holland in 1821 or trying to win over the army of Louis XVIII as it entered Spain in 1823. The Réunion des Officiers de l'ex-Garde Impériale helped to keep Bonapartist sentiment alive at banquets and funerals in the 1830s.[47]

One of the main reasons for the traditionally variegated form of the revived Maison Militaire in 1814 had been the King's fear of a praetorian guard. At first, after 1815, the new Garde Royale was obedient; its service was organized so that the King was never in the power of one commanding officer 'in conformity with the principles which should be followed in all Sovereigns' guards', according to Marmont, one of its major-generals. But political passions were so tense, and the prestige of guards was now so great, that the Garde Royale began to be used to try to manipulate the monarch. In 1818 there was a plan by some ultra right-wing officers to seize the King and his liberal ministers and force them to change their policy. Between 14–20 February 1820, after the assassination of the King's nephew, the Duc de Berri, some officers of the Gardes du Corps and the Garde Royale, believing they were acting in the best interests of the monarchy, but in reality manipulated by extreme politicians such as Vitrolles were, in the words of Louis XVIII, 'guilty' of threatening to kidnap or kill the King's favourite and liberal minister, Decazes. The threat of the King's niece on 18 February that, if Decazes did not resign, there would be 'another victim', is a further example of division within a reigning family leading to a heightened political role for the royal guard. The Gardes du Corps had to be confined to barracks. It is possible that the King, who had done so much to maintain the independence and privileges of his guard against his Ministers of War, was weakened in his resolve to keep Decazes in power by the hostility of his guard, as well as by the attitude of the Chambers, the press and the public.[48]

The unusual political importance of the French Garde Royale in 1820 was a sign of the immense power of royal guards in their golden age. They were now so important that, in 1820–21, they played a political role not only in France and, as has already been described, in Spain, but also in Naples and Piedmont. Inspired by the success of the Spanish Revolution of March 1820, Naples also had a revolution in July. Ferdinand IV, however, was fortunate in that his guard of about 4000 (known as the *archifideli*), the elite of the army and the larger part of the Naples garrison, remained a source of strength. Despite pressure from the revolutionaries, and the rest of the army, the Minister of War refused to disband it, citing the examples of France and England to prove that a royal guard was compatible with constitutional monarchy. Thus the safety of the royal family was never seriously in danger, and when the Austrian army invaded in March 1821 the guard sent a deputation of welcome and entered Naples in triumph with their allies on 21 March.[49]

In Piedmont during the revolution of March–June 1821, the Guardie del Corpo showed, as the King subsequently proclaimed when expanding their privileges, '*constante fedelta e perfetta devozione al trono*' ('unwavering loyalty and perfect devotion to the throne') in very difficult circumstances. The regiments of Granatieri and Cacciatori Guardie, although less unwavering in their devotion, were less sympathetic to the liberals than other regiments in the army.[50]

ENGLAND

In England in the sixteenth century, as in France in the seventeenth, the guard was a pillar of monarchy not only because it protected the safety of the monarch, but also because it was available to arrest his enemies; it was Yeomen of the Guard who arrested the Duke of Buckingham in 1521, Thomas Cromwell in 1540, the Earl of Surrey in 1546 and the Duke of Somerset in 1549. The Yeomen of the Guard and Gentlemen Pensioners also helped defend the palace against the attacks of Wyatt and Essex and their followers in 1554 and 1599. Essex's coup, one of the last examples of naked (as opposed to constitutionally disguised) aristocratic ambition in English history, might have succeeded. But instead of marching straight on the palace, seizing the Pensioners' halbards lying in the Presence Chamber, and entering the Queen's apartments, Essex made the fatal mistake of heading for the city, not the court, and his coup petered out. Nevertheless, both in 1554 and in 1599, the guard was so small (in 1598 Essex's followers outnumbered the Yeomen of the Guard commanded by his rival Raleigh), and the aristocracy so militarily powerful, that the monarch had to rely on troops raised by loyal aristocrats to defeat rebellions.

Thereafter there were no armed attacks to threaten the monarchy (although Charles I did use the Yeomen to arrest his wife's troublesome French attendants in 1626) until the growing confrontation between the King and his opponents in Parliament after 1640. One of the weak points in Charles's position was his lack of a large, devoted royal guard. His safety in Whitehall was often threatened by pro-parliamentary crowds. When he went to Parliament to arrest the Five Members on 7 January 1642, he was accompanied by 'all his guard and all his Pensioners and two or three hundred soldiers and gentlemen'. But the Members were safe in the city and the King did not have a large enough force to control his capital.[51]

His son made sure that he would not suffer the same humiliation. From 1660 he had a large, devoted royal guard, well able to suppress any riots in London. It is revealing that opposition to the new royal guard, on the grounds that it was an expensive innovation, came from great aristocrats like the Earls of Northumberland and Southampton as well as from Parliament and moderate opinion; in 1668 Pepys wrote that a proposed reduction of the guards was 'mighty acceptable to the world'. From 1674 to 1681 the guards were frequently attacked (although less than other regiments) in Parliament by enemies of the monarchy such as Lord Shaftesbury, who believed that 'little good is to be had of the King as long as he has his guards about him; if it were not for them we would quickly go down to Whitehall and obtain what terms we thought fit'.[52] In July 1679 and January 1680, when Charles wanted to conciliate Parliament (and save money), he dismissed units of his guard.

At the moment of crisis, when Parliament met at Oxford in February 1681, the guards were a key factor in the King's success. He took about 600 Foot and Horse Guards to Oxford, while the colonel of the Coldstream Guards, Lord Craven, was left in command in London. An adviser wrote, 'All arts possible are being used to bring discredit to His Majesty's affairs. The faction is deliberating at this time how to make the Guards an illegal institution.' But they failed and the guards ensured that there were no disturbances when the King suddenly dissolved Parliament on 26 March. Thereafter, the guards were seen by the Stuarts' Whig enemies (as they would be forty years later by the Hanoverians' Jacobite enemies) as the key force which had to be dealt with before the monarch could be overthrown. In 1683 the Rye House Plot to kill the King revolved around corrupting soldiers of the Life Guards escorting Charles II from Newmarket. The defence of Lord William Russell, son of the Earl of Bedford, was that it was not a crime, since guards were illegal. In 1685 some Whig conspirators believed they could seize London because they had 'above 500 men as well horsed and armed as the Guards in London and Westminster'.[53]

In the end, however, the real threat to the Stuarts came from James II and from within, rather than outside, the guard. Already, when Monmouth, captain of the Life Guards, was also commander-in-chief of all armed forces from 1674 to 1679, James had been alarmed and prevented him from being made colonel of the First Foot Guards as well, because it would so 'increase his power in military affairs'. As James's policies alienated the supporters of the monarchy in 1687 and 1688, more and more people turned to his nephew, the Prince of Orange, as the most likely saviour of the monarchy and the Protestant religion.

James reacted to the growing internal and external challenge by increasing his guard and army. In 1688 the Coldstream Guards and the four troops of Life Guards were increased. That autumn the Scottish troop and the Scottish regiment of Foot Guards were summoned to London and the Irish regiment of Foot Guards arrived in London on 24 October, 'well clothed, armed and disciplined'.[54] William landed at Torbay on 5 November, accompanied by an army of 11,212 of whom 197 were Gardes du Corps, 480 Horse Guards and 2522 Foot Guards.

When James arrived with his guard and army at Salisbury on 19 November it might have seemed that the King, a professional soldier who had often exercised and reviewed his guard in person, would have been able to rely on it to defend his throne. Indeed, on 19 November, some Life Guards and Dragoons did defeat Dutch troops in a skirmish.

But desertions had already begun, for a large section of the aristocracy, including many officers of the guard, had been permanently alienated by James's autocratic, pro-Catholic rule. Officers of the guard were the first to act. On 10 November the second-in-command of the Blues tried to lead his soldiers over to Orange. On 13 November Lord Colchester deserted with over sixty of the fourth troop of Life Guards; on 22 November some of the third troop of Life Guards deserted. But what Burnet, on the other side, called 'the last and most confounding stroke' was that, on 24 November, Lord Churchill, the future Duke of Marlborough who had come to court as an ensign in the First Guards and now commanded the Life Guards, the Duke of Grafton, colonel of the First Guards, the Duke of Ormonde, colonel of the Irish Guards and many other officers deserted to William (as Churchill had planned to do since August). Coupled with the wave of desertions and rebellion throughout the country, the evidence that he could not rely on his own guard fatally shook James's resolve to defend his throne.[55]

He could have chosen to rely on a rump of loyal guards, commanded by devoted officers, such as Lord Craven, colonel of the Coldstream Guards, the Duke of Berwick, colonel of the Blues and Feversham, now commander of the Life Guards. He knew that, as he wrote later, there was a 'greater honour and fidelity in the common men than in the generality of officers, who usually value themselves too much for those qualifications'. But the mental leap beyond the aristocratic assumptions on which his life had been based was too great for a King like James II. He returned to London, a broken man, on 26 November.[56]

The bulk of the guard was now either in, or around, London. Those to the west, for example the Scots Guards near Maidenhead, were going over to William. James was so frightened that, perhaps wrongly, he chose to entrust neither himself nor his wife and heir to those guards who remained loyal. On 6 December his wife and son fled from London with the help of foreigners. On the night of 10 December, having told the Duke of Northumberland who, as Gold Stick in waiting, slept outside his bedroom, to make sure the door was kept fast, James fled to Rochester. He was stopped by a furious and disloyal mob; without guards such a humiliation was always likely for a monarch. Finally, on the orders of the council of five aristocrats led by Lord Rochester which had assumed power in the King's absence, he returned to London, escorted by 240 faithful and overjoyed Life Guards under Feversham, on 16 December.[57]

Meanwhile, however, on 11 December, abandoned by their King, the guard and the entire army had, on Feversham's and Lord Rochester's orders, submitted by letter to the man now most likely to uphold the monarchy and social order, which seemed threatened by the London mob, the Prince of Orange. The remaining guards were recalled to London by the council. But William, who issued orders from 13 December, had different ideas. On 15 December William wrote to Lord Craven from Windsor, where he had arrived the day before, that he had ordered '3000 of my Guards of Foot to march thither . . . together with 800 of my Guards of Horse, you are to give such orders that they may be placed before my arrival in the quarters formerly taken up by the English guards'; in such a calm, royal way, backed by a large (but not as large as he claimed) and devoted guard, thrones are won. At first Craven, a dedicated supporter of the Stuarts, wanted to resist: 'while breath remained in his body no foreign force would make the King of England prisoner in his palace'. But James ordered him to obey, and anyway Craven's officers and the First Guards at Whitehall had already declared for William (a fact not always remembered in their regimental histories, or by Prince Albert when he declared, in 1860, that the First Guards had 'never failed in its duty to its Sovereign'). On the night of 16 December the Dutch Guards, the matches in their guns lighted as a sign that they were ready to meet resistance, occupied 'all the Royal posts at Whitehall, Somerset House, and Saint James's'. To Lord Ailesbury, a Lord of the Bedchamber in waiting, 'All this seemed to me so stupendous that I had good advice in my head to give to the King, but neither time nor circumstances permitted.'[58] Nor would his advice have been listened to, for James who, according to the Jacobite compiler of his memoirs, 'knew not whether those [the Dutch Guards] or his own were worse', had no more faith in guards.

Meanwhile, between 14 and 31 December, on William's orders, all English, Scottish and Irish Guards left London and its outskirts for towns in the Home Counties, such as Rochester, Lewes or Northampton. On 18 December, escorted by 100 Dutch Foot Guards under Sir Peter Lely's nephew, James left London for Rochester. The Coldstream Guards there were still loyal but only three officers resigned their commissions into his hands. On 23 December he sailed for France.[59]

That many of the guards were passively loyal to King James, who had done so much for them, is shown by William's insistence that they all leave London (they did not return until 18 August 1689), and by changes in their composition. By the end of 1689 all officers and all but fifteen of the Gentlemen Pensioners had been changed. There was considerable discontent in the First Guards and by the end of the year only six captains in the regiment were the same as in 1685. In 1693 and 1696 there was evidence of Jacobite sympathies among the Blues. That, until 1699, William maintained a large number of Dutch Guards – 2475 of a total of 7078 guards in November 1697 – in England may have been, as Burnet implied, due not only to personal pride but also, at the beginning, to fear.[60] He needed them for his own safety.

The experience of James II shows that, in England in 1688 as in Russia in 1762 and 1801, or Spain in 1808, a monarch who alienates a large proportion of his aristocracy is unlikely to be able to rely on a guard commanded by aristocratic officers. Although James was the principal author of his own downfall, the behaviour of his guards officers, such as Churchill, Grafton and Ormonde, was clearly very important. Thereafter such conflicts as existed between the monarchy and the aristocracy were usually mediated through the Houses of Parliament.

But the guard remained politically important as a pillar of the Hanoverian monarchy against the Jacobite threat (although some guards were hanged for drinking the Pretender's health in July 1716). There were so many guards at George I's coronation that, when the Archbishop asked for the people's consent, one peeress said, 'Does the old fool think that anybody here will say no to his question when there are so many drawn swords?' Guards were encamped in Hyde Park in July 1715 in order to overawe the largely Tory population and they patrolled London on 10 June 1716 to stop people wearing white roses for the Pretender's birthday.

Until 1745 what Lord Hervey called 'the disaffection of the nation to the present royal family' was so great that it is not surprising that George II and his son Cumberland, who 'always considered soldiers as the principal support both of their grandeur and of their power', paid so much attention to their guards. In the crisis of 1745 when the advance of the Young Pretender meant that, in London, 'the two great Passions, Hope and Fear . . . may be read in every man's face', the guards remained staunch. At a levée in St James's the officers affirmed their loyalty to George II. The guards left London to face the Jacobite army (see illustration 61) but were not needed. Thereafter, guards have been used to defend the social

49.   Hilleström. *Gustavus III in the Royal Palace of Stockholm*. 19 August 1772. STATENS KONSTMUSEER, STOCKHOLM.

Gustavus III is wearing the uniform of captain of the Drabants and is followed by guards officers whom he has just persuaded to support his coup against the aristocracy and the Senate. Gustavus III greatly increased the size of his guard, and in 1774 accepted the formal command of all its regiments which his successors enjoyed until 1974. Nevertheless it was three ex-guards officers who assassinated him at a masked ball in 1792 – a sign of how violent the conflict between the monarchy and the aristocracy in Sweden could be.

order but not to enforce or influence the will of the monarch, although Wellington claimed that, between 1828 and 1830, he was alarmed by the possibility that the Duke of Cumberland, colonel of the Blues and permanent Gold Stick in waiting, might use the guard, and mobs, to frighten George IV into supporting an ultra-Protestant policy.[61] Civilian institutions, especially the Houses of Parliament, were too important for it to be possible for conflict between the monarchy and sections of the aristocracy, or within the royal family – the usual causes of a political role for a guard – to be expressed through the guard.

SWEDEN
Sweden was another monarchy where the royal guard was an important, often crucial element in the power structure. After the death of Charles XII in 1719 the Swedish

aristocracy rapidly deprived the monarchy of much of its power. In the words of Claude Nordmann, 'the reality of power belonged to the Riksdag, itself dominated by the nobility'. For a time the monarchy was not even hereditary. In 1751, on the accession of King Adolph Frederick, the plan of Colonel von Lieven 'to use the Livgarde to wreck the Constitution' during a session of the Estates failed. In 1756 the King was finally persuaded to act by the Estates' decision to deprive him of command of his own guard except for the Life Company of the Svea Livgarde. The coup, led by officers of the Livgarde like Creutz and Stalsvard, was badly organized and begun too soon by a drunken officer trying to win over some soldiers. The conspirators were arrested. Stalsvard was executed so near a group of officer cadets that they were spattered with his blood – a deliberate warning by the aristocracy of the fate reserved for royalist guards officers. The King, who had not dared to act, was deprived even of his command of the Life Company which, with that of the regiment, was now assumed by the epitome of Swedish aristocratic power, Field-Marshal von Fersen. The Livgarde corporal who had revealed the drunken officer's approaches was ennobled.[62]

In 1772, however, the monarchy struck back in a coup which, as well as being a model of its kind, is a classic example of how a royal guard could be used against a representative assembly; the King revealed its essence when he wrote in triumph to his mother, 'After a speech to the guards, I had the Senate arrested.' The new young King Gustavus III, one of the most brilliant men ever to sit on a throne, was determined to recover some of the crown's power from the aristocracy. In 1772 the Senate had displayed its contempt for the crown by appointing a new captain of the Drabants, Count Dohna, before the King had had time to voice an opinion. If he was not even allowed control over his own Drabants, it was clearly time to act.

At first Gustavus planned to use troops from Finland under Colonel Sprengtporten. He did not trust the officers of the Svea Livgarde, whose colonel was so opposed to the power of the crown. But, in the summer, Fersen was out of Stockholm and another officer, von Salza, was convinced the Svea Livgarde could be used. Indeed, Major König was ready 'to dare everything for the sake of the King' and, on the morning of 19 August, summoned the officers and NCOs to the great Royal Palace overlooking the sea. At 11 a.m. when (as in Paris in 1616 or Copenhagen in 1784) the guard was being changed so there was double the number usually there, Gustavus III, in the uniform of captain of the Drabants, having inspected the parade, made a speech to the officers assembled in the palace guard room, 'with all that eloquence of which he is so perfect a master'. He gave them the choice between following him or executing him. After a few moments' silence a twenty-three-year-old Lieutenant von Lieven cried, 'We dare life and blood in the service of Your Majesty!' 'Yes, God save the King!' shouted all but three of the officers. The royal weapon of personal contact of the monarch with his guard had been used to good effect.

The NCOs and soldiers of the guard and the crowd outside the palace were royalist without exception or hesitation. Followed by guards, Drabants and grenadiers, Gustavus then moved from the guard room to the Senate chamber on the main floor of the palace. Normally his guards were not allowed into the Senate chamber. But that day they seized a senator who tried to close the door on them behind the King; and the Senators were arrested by Major-General Frederick Horn and Captain Arminoff of the Svea Livgarde. The King had won. The guards were rewarded with promotions, orders, medals and titles of nobility. Sprengtporten and his regiment arrived too late to influence events, but were rewarded by becoming the Light Dragoons of the Life Guards.[63]

During the reign of Gustavus III the Svea Livgarde were so indulged and privileged that their discipline suffered. In 1781 Lieutenant-General von Wrede wrote, 'The Guards could neither march nor stand still, they move neither with grace nor with precision. Disorder rules everywhere and disobedience is noticeable here as well as in the rest of the army.' As in

Russia, the guard's political power had led to a decrease in its military efficiency. The hostility between Gustavus III and the aristocracy had become so profound that, in 1789, he used a mob (the guard was on campaign) to overawe aristocratic opposition in the Senate – one of the rare occasions when a monarch has carried out such a manoeuvre with success. But in 1792 Gustavus III was assassinated by two aristocratic former guards officers, Ribbing and Anckarström. Another conspirator, an officer in the Svea Livgarde, warned the King but was not heeded.

For a time Gustavus IV was even more powerful than his father. The triumph of democratic principles in the French Revolution had transformed many former aristocratic opponents of royal power, such as Axel von Fersen, his French friends, and Whig contemporaries into, as his biographer has written, 'zealous defenders of royal power'. The senseless foreign policy of Gustavus IV, however, who by 1807 had managed to alienate both France and Russia, and his refusal to summon a parliament, appalled most of Sweden. After the loss of Finland he punished his Foot Guards by the *gardesdegradiring* of 12 October 1808, taking away their names, their flags, their double-rank privileges and their precedence over other regiments – an attack on the guard as unwise as that of Godoy in Spain in 1803 and 1808. Some noble guards officers thought of murdering the King.

In 1809 the overthrow of Gustavus IV was 'first and foremost the work of the nobility, as that Estate pointedly reminded the others at the Riksdag convened in May that year'. The instrument used by the nobility, as in Russia in 1762 and 1801 or Spain in 1808, was the guards, or their absence.[64] On 13 March 1809 Gustavus IV ordered the three ex-guards regiments out of the city to face a rebellious army marching from the west, and planned to leave himself. The guard of the palace, as in 1788–90 when his father was on campaign against Russia, was to be entrusted to the citizens' militia of Stockholm: the King had reason

50. Anon. print. *The Degradation of the Foot Guards by Gustavus IV*. 1808. LIFE GUARDS DRAGOONS COLLECTION, SWEDEN.

The degradation of the Foot Guards by Gustavus IV confirmed the alienation of the aristocracy which led to his deposition six months later, and to the replacement of the Vasas by the Bernadottes on the death of his uncle in 1818. He died in exile in Switzerland in 1835.

51.   Anon. drawing. *The Murder of Axel von Fersen.* 1810. NATIONAL MUSEUM OF FINLAND.

Guards and their officers looked on while Fersen, the leading defender of the claim of the son of Gustavus IV to the throne of Sweden, was beaten to death in front of the House of Nobility. Fersen's reputed mistress, Queen Marie-Antoinette, is waiting to receive him in the clouds. This incident is still remembered as 'the low point of Swedish dishonour'.

to fear aristocrats but not the middle class or the poor. But all orders issued that day have been 'lost', and an ordinary line regiment was on duty at the palace. Thirty officers led by General Adlercreutz went to receive orders from the King and, with six other nobles, arrested him. The King cried 'Save me! Save me!' and some Drabants and servants 'endeavoured to force open the door'. But Adlercreutz 'conjured them . . . not to attempt anything which might occasion bloodshed and endanger the life of the King'. They hesitated, some were arrested and that day the King was escorted to a palace outside Stockholm by the cuirassiers of the Life Guard. The next day the Foot Guards and their privileges were restored.[65] Such promptness shows one of the motives for the coup – the aristocracy's desire for revenge on a monarch who, among other blunders, had attacked one of the embodiments of its power and status, the guard.

In 1809 the guards helped to destroy Gustavus IV. In 1810 they helped destroy the party, represented by Axel von Fersen, which supported his son's claim to the throne. On 20 June 1810 the funeral procession of the Crown Prince (led by Axel von Fersen in his quality of Grand Marshal of Sweden) was escorted by the Livgarde till Hast and the Svea and Göta Livgarde. The guards had been ordered not to meet the expected – indeed planned – violence with violence; nor would they have been able to, since their guns were not loaded. King Charles XIII, the uncle and successor of Gustavus IV, and the large number of officers (such as Silfversparre who was in command of the capital) and officials who had compromised themselves in the dethronement of Gustavus IV, planned to remove the principal supporter of Gustavus's children's claims to the throne. Fersen was torn from his carriage, stabbed and stamped to death by a brutal, drunken, venal mob while the guard, on its commander's orders, looked on doing nothing. This horrifying event preceded by only four months Bernadotte's entry into Stockholm, escorted by the Svea Livgarde and the Livgarde till Hast. Thereafter, order was restored and the political role of the guards ended by a prince who, like his successors, knew how to make himself obeyed.[66]

PERSIA

The guard also played a political role in a monarchy's struggle with its parliament in Persia, after the grant of a constitution on 5 August 1906 (in part due to the success of the Russian Revolution of 1905 – the history of the Persian monarchy is, like the history of other monarchies, inextricable from that of its neighbours). Previously, the guard had been important only in the preservation or assassination of monarchs (for example, Nadir Shah, the conqueror of the Moghul Empire, was murdered by an Uzbek guard in 1747). After the grant of a constitution not only the person of the Shah but also the nature of his authority was a matter of dispute. In 1907 a British traveller thought that the Goulams and the Cossack brigade, if well paid and properly disciplined, 'should prove the strongest weapon in the hand of the Shah-in-Shah in his contest with the people', or those who claimed to represent the will of the people. Muhammed Ali Shah abandoned his first attempt to use his guards in a coup against the constitution and the Majlis (assembly), on the advice of the Russian, British and Ottoman Ambassadors, on 19 December 1907. But on 3 June 1908 he fled Tehran 'in a cloud of Cossacks', and again tried to use his guards against the Majlis and its supporters. Colonel Liakhoff, their tall and handsome commander, was appointed military governor of Tehran. He placed it under martial law, bombed the Majlis and arrested eight of the most hostile deputies. In the end, however, the Shah was defeated by the nationalist and Bakhtiari supporters of the Majlis. On 16 July 1909, having taken refuge in the Russian Embassy, he abdicated in favour of his son, Ahmad. Liakhoff was dismissed and thereafter the Cossack brigade was, in theory, under the control of the Minister of War, not the Ministers of Foreign Affairs or of the court.

But by 1911 the Cossack brigade was again acting as a separate force, partly under the orders of the Russian government; and right-wing forces (now including the Bakhtiaris, supported by Russian troops) soon controlled Tehran, despite a largely hostile population, in the interests of royal authority. On 24 December another guard unit, the Guarde Homayoun, took over the Majlis building and threatened the deputies with death. Thereafter Persia was controlled by a right-wing monarchist regency, unhampered by a Majlis, until late 1914.[67]

Reza Shah used the Cossack brigade to seize power from the Qajars, after years of confusion and civil war, in 1921–25. After his deposition in 1941 by the Russians and the British the authority of the monarchy was much weaker than before. But by 1953 a confrontation between Reza Shah's son, Mohammed Reza Shah, and the Prime Minister, Dr Mossadegh (formerly a supporter of the Qajars), who was supported by a majority of the Majlis and of the population, was inevitable. The guard again served as a pillar of the monarchy. On 12 August Colonel Nassiri, commander of the Imperial Guard, a close friend of the Shah, who compared him to the Three Musketeers, went to arrest Mossadegh. Instead, he himself was arrested, and the next day the Imperial Guard was confined to barracks, disarmed and on paper dissolved. It seemed as if Mossadegh had won. But between 17 and 19 August, American money and organization and a change in the attitude of the Communist Tudeh party, transformed the situation. On 19 August a monarchist crowd, led by Ayatollah Besbehani and recruited from the Houses of Strength (athletic clubs which had also been a source of royalist support in 1907–09), and from the poor with economic reasons to hate the bazaar merchants who supported Mossadegh, attacked government buildings. Nassiri and the rest of the Imperial Guard were released and acted as the spearhead of the attack on Mossadegh's house and pro-Mossadegh army units. The guard was, in the words of the Shah, 'invaluable as well as gallant'. The next day Mossadegh gave himself up. That year the guard was increased in size to a division. It had proved its worth.[68]

7
GUARDS AND REVOLUTIONS

R OYAL GUARDS WERE not only weapons in the struggles between monarchies and their aristocracies. They were also crucial weapons in the attempt to maintain the social order, and royal authority, against challenges from below. Guards' role as a barrier against popular disturbances was symbolized, on the most obvious level, by the fact that they kept crowds away from the monarch at public solemnities. This duty applied whether it was the Pope in Rome, the King of France going through the state apartments to Mass at Versailles, the Ottoman Sultan riding to mosque on Friday, or George I taking the air in his sedan-chair in the Mall. Order had to be maintained; the monarch's way had to be cleared; onlookers prevented from crowding around him. Even today, Gentlemen-at-Arms find it 'difficult to deal with thrusters' when guiding members of the British royal family through the crowd at a garden-party.[1]

It was less easy, however, to deal with crowds who wanted not only to thrust through the barriers surrounding the monarch, but to threaten or overthrow the monarchy itself. Because they were stationed in capital cities, and because they guarded monarchs, the behaviour of royal guards was likely to be crucial on such occasions. That royal guards were thought to be in some way the antithesis of popular feelings is suggested by the remark constantly made of monarchs lucky enough to be popular, such as Queen Anne, that 'the affections of her people were her surest Guard' – as if a guard was a symptom of unpopularity. Monarchs making a particular effort to court public opinion, such as Francis I of Austria entering Vienna in 1806, or Charles X entering Paris in 1824, or the Prince of Orange entering Brussels in 1830, boasted that they had 'no guards' or 'no halbards'.

Most monarchs, however, preferred to keep their guards with them. For, until the twentieth century, in most monarchies, the social order was so unstable that it was under constant threat from what one Müteferrika called, 'the unfortunate passion of cupidity, of avidity, and lust for other people's belongings, universal vices of humanity'. There was always the possibility of violence from the poor when pushed beyond endurance by their sufferings, or tantalized by signs of government weakness. In 1609, for example, Sir George Carew thought that Henri IV was as threatened by the common people, who were 'apt to mutinies and rebellion', as by the aristocracy. It has already been pointed out that, in England in 1688, the social order was threatened, and James II insulted and maltreated, by the poor, although in the end it was the aristocracy and gentry who deprived him of his throne.

Charles II and Philip V of Spain were often insulted by the Madrid mob. Paris in July 1789, Stockholm in June 1810, showed what could happen in capital cities when royal guards failed to do their duty. Russian guards officers in 1825 were convinced that the inhabitants of Moscow were 'ready to go for their knives and abandon themselves to every passion'.[2] The same fear of popular 'passions' was one reason for monarchs' choice of aristocrats to compose or officer their guards. There seems to have been an increase in popular violence after 1700. In England the Sacheverell riots in March 1709 (against the ministers, not the monarch) were so serious that the government had to summon the guards

52. Demachy. *Ceremony of the Laying of the Foundation-stone of the Church of Sainte-Geneviève.* Paris, 3 September 1764. MUSÉE CARNAVALET. PHOTO LAUROS-GIRAUDON.

There were few cheers for Louis XV, who is in the centre of this picture of one of his rare visits to his capital. As this picture shows, one of a guard's functions was to provide a protective barrier between a monarch and his subjects. The guards on this occasion were Gardes Françaises, who twenty-five years later led the attack on the Bastille.

53.   Francis Wheatley. *The Attack in Broad Street*. June 1780. BRITISH MUSEUM.

During the anti-Catholic and anti-government Gordon Riots in 1780 the guards just managed to maintain law and order in London. But some Foot Guards were reluctant to fire on the crowds.

from St James's; Queen Anne told Lord Sunderland 'to take both her Horse and Foot Guards, adding that God would be her guard'. Under the Hanoverians the guards protected the monarchy not only from Jacobite plots but also from popular discontent. Foot Guards suppressed riots by the Spitalfields weavers in 1719. They also protected Bedford House, that citadel of aristocratic power, in 1765 when 'the mob were so riotous that both Horse and Foot Guards had to parade the Square before the tumult was dispersed', and suppressed more riots in 1766 and, over Wilkes, in 1768.

The most dramatic intervention occurred in June 1780 during the Gordon Riots, when for a time it looked as if the London mob, in a fury of anti-Catholicism, would take over the city. The guards were hindered from suppressing the riots by the strange reluctance of the civil magistrates to call them out; but, even when they did, the Foot Guards sometimes refused to obey orders to fire on a crowd or to protect a peer's residence. It was the Horse

Guards, whose social origins were so different, who were relied upon to protect life and property, 'as the mob do not mind the foot'. Finally, line troops had to be summoned to London to bring the situation under control. Despite its desperate nature there were still aristocrats such as the Duke of Richmond, so distrustful of royal authority (or so annoyed that he had been refused command of the Blues in 1770) that he denounced 'military government' in the House of Lords.[3]

London was notoriously ill-policed and hard to control in the eighteenth century. But it was Paris which, in the end, fell prey to revolution. The abolition of the horse guards, despite the protest of the Lieutenant de Police, in 1775 and 1787 deprived the government of the sort of reliable and aristocratic repressive force whose usefulness was demonstrated in London in 1780. But the French government was not at the time frightened of the population of Paris. There is an unbelievable entry in the diary of a French diplomat in January 1786 describing the guards' security measures, and their closure of the palace railings, when 2000 starving workers marched on Versailles: 'The King made a joke of these preparations. The ball that evening at the palace was not affected by this absurd revolt; people danced with the greatest gaiety.'

With the approach of the meeting of the States General in May 1789, however, the time for jokes and balls was over. During riots in Paris in September 1788 and April 1789 the Gardes Françaises had controlled popular disorder without difficulty. As Jean Chagniot points out in a recent thesis, it was an excellent unit 'perfectly attuned to its duties as a police force'. But in May and June, as the confrontation between aristocrats and democrats in the National Assembly became more serious, and the monarchy appeared to be taking the side of the aristocrats, until recently its most determined enemies, the Gardes Françaises began to waver. It was not inevitable that they should side with the Parisians. Since the 1760s the Gardes Françaises lived in barracks rather than in Parisians' houses. They came from different backgrounds. Probably as a result of a deliberate policy, only 10.5 per cent of Gardes Françaises in the 1780s had been born in the Paris region, a far lower proportion than in the first two thirds of the century. Most came from the rural north or east of France. As so often in the history of royal guards, however, guards' sense of honour and the state of the regiment determined the conduct of the Gardes Françaises. Their role as the force destined, as the Lieutenant de Police wrote on 30 July 1772, 'to be the first to bring help when there is disorder', had been greatly increased since 1770, especially since the suppression of the Mousquetaires in 1775. The Gardes Françaises had not fought in a war since 1763. Therefore, they were particularly likely to be susceptible to appeals from public opinion to recover their honour and dignity, stop acting as policemen and support a national revolution. As early as June 1788 a *Lettre à un Officier aux Gardes Françaises sur le Devoir du Militaire Français* had appealed to their sense of honour to support the people against the King: 'But honour! What has become of it among you?'

Such propaganda increased in force and effectiveness in May and June 1789. Moreover, the regiment had particular cause for discontent. In the reforms of 1787 and 1788 some of its privileges – such as its sergeants' right to enter the Invalides with the status of officers – had been abolished by Guibert, who thought the regiment 'vicious and anti-military in many respects'. The Duc du Châtelet, who became colonel in late 1788, was another dogmatic reformer and admirer of the Prussian army, who (as is clear from his letters to his friend the Baron de Salis, the reformer of the Neapolitan army) was more interested in dismissing half the officers and teaching the soldiers to march at seventy-six steps a minute, than in the *esprit de corps* of the regiment. In June and July 1789 many officers were on leave or ignorant of the soldiers' state of mind. In the thirty days before the cataclysm of 14 July 1789, when the King was planning, finally, to resort to armed force, the history of the Gardes Françaises is a dramatic illustration of the unreliability of a royal guard in time of revolution.[4]

PRISE DE LA BASTILLE PAR LES BOURGEOIS ET LES BRAVES GARDES FRANCAISES DE LA BONNE VILLE DE PARIS , LE 14 JUILLET 1789 ,

Dédiée à la Nation .

54.   Anon. print. *The Taking of the Bastille by the Bourgeois and the Braves Gardes Françaises of the Good City of Paris.* 14 July 1789. PHOTO ROGER VIOLLET.

As the title of this print makes clear, in 1789 the Gardes Françaises took the side of the city of Paris against the French monarchy – a decision crucial for the history of France and Europe.

On 27 June five companies deserted. The Gardes Françaises were the first of the royal troops to mutiny and were so notoriously revolutionary that propaganda addressed to the army was now written as if it came from soldiers of the Gardes Françaises. On 12 July some Gardes Suisses also mutinied and there was a violent confrontation in the Palais Royal between Gardes Françaises and loyal troops from a German regiment. On 14 July Gardes Françaises such as Hoche, the future General of the Republic, and Lefebvre, the future Marshal of the Empire, played a decisive part in organizing and leading the Parisians' attack on the Bastille. Without their cannon it might not have fallen (see illustration 54).[5]

After 14 July the former Gardes Françaises provided at least a quarter of the paid troops of the Garde Nationale de Paris – the most effective part of the most important and revolutionary armed force in the kingdom. The Gardes Françaises still on duty at Versailles decided on 30 July that they preferred to guard the Revolution in Paris rather than the King in Versailles; it is true that, in the Garde Nationale, pay and promotion prospects for NCOs, such as Hoche and Lefebvre, were better. At the same time many Gardes Suisses were deserting (348 by 14 August) and some of them also joined the Garde Nationale de Paris. Even the aristocratic Gardes du Corps were caught by the fever of revolution; on 1 July, led by one of their captains, the Prince de Poix, a member of the Noailles family, some Gardes du Corps went to the National Assembly to swear 'to obey no order against the people, not being born French to act against the interests of France'. On 19 August they sent another deputation to the Assembly proclaiming their loyalty to the Revolution and asking for better pay, improved promotion prospects and an increase in numbers.[6]

Most guards in the Gardes du Corps and the Gardes Françaises, and even in the Cent-Suisses and Gardes Suisses, were sufficiently part of national life to feel, like French people of all classes in 1789, that they had entered a new era of freedom and happiness. Swept up by the fervour of revolution they found it easy to forget their regimental traditions and their personal connection with the monarchy, and to transfer their allegiance from the King they had sworn to defend to the Assembly where power and its rewards now clearly lay. As subsequent revolutions would also show, the needs and fears of the moment can easily sweep aside centuries of tradition and loyalty.

Moreover, the behaviour of a royal guard in such a moment of crisis depends not only on the revolutionary situation but also on the guard's personal relationship with its commanders and monarch. In France in 1789 Louis XVI had done nothing to endear himself to his guard. Nor were its commanders, the Baron de Besenval of the Gardes Suisses, or Du Châtelet, particularly respected.

Abandoned by those guards which he had not disbanded, Louis XVI, by September 1789, was in direct personal danger, largely due to his continued opposition to the Assembly's radical measures. In September 1789 the former Gardes Françaises in the Garde Nationale de Paris announced they wanted to resume their guard duties at Versailles as members of their new unit. On 23 September, in order to protect the palace and keep order at Versailles, a line regiment, the Régiment de Flandre, was summoned by the government with the agreement of the Versailles municipality. At the banquets held by the Gardes du Corps to welcome its arrival much wine and many loyal toasts were drunk; when they went around the tables the King and the royal family were cheered enthusiastically. In the revolutionary circumstances of 1789 it amounted to a provocation; and on 5 October an angry starving mob set out from Paris, followed by the Garde Nationale, some of whom were openly talking about the possibility of the Dauphin replacing the King.

The King cut short his hunt at 3.30 p.m., and raced back to the palace. To defend it there were only the Gardes du Corps, since the Régiment de Flandre and the Garde Nationale de Versailles were now militarily and politically unreliable. By eight in the evening, in consultation with La Fayette and d'Estaing, commander of the Garde Nationale de Versailles, Louis XVI decided not to use force against the Parisians and to allow the Garde Nationale de Paris, as it demanded, to take up the guard posts formerly occupied by the Gardes Françaises, which it did at 11 p.m. The main body of the Gardes du Corps, which had been under arms in very difficult circumstances in the square in front of the palace since 3.30 in the afternoon, withdrew to their hotel at 8.30 and then, as the King ordered, to the park of Versailles – away from any possible confrontation with the Garde Nationale or the mob. That evening the King finally gave his consent to the radical measures of the Assembly. In the words of the Duc de Guiche, one of the captains of the Gardes du Corps, 'Everyone was overwhelmed with sleep and lethargy, we thought it was all over.'[7]

The palace railings were opened at about five in the morning as usual, by the Garde Nationale, and soon after, a group of 300–500, or perhaps fewer, enraged men and women stormed in. They killed two Gardes du Corps on duty and swept on past the unresisting Cent-Suisses to the main staircase, the Escalier de la Reine, shouting, 'Where is the damned bitch? We want to eat her heart,' or 'We want to cut off her head and her heart, stew her liver and we won't stop there,' and other manifestations of the vigour of revolutionary appetites.

There were only five or six Gardes du Corps on duty at the entrance to the Queen's apartment. Unbelievably, the normal *guet* of sixty-one Gardes du Corps in the palace had not been increased since before the Revolution. But could it have been relied on if it had? Another unbelievable aspect of the October days is that the Gardes du Corps, who were subsequently worshipped in royalist legend as heroes to their duty, in reality turned and ran. In September and October, when the situation was visibly deteriorating, many letters arrived from Gardes du Corps in the provinces saying there were too ill – in other words too frightened – to serve. On the night of 5 October the Gardes du Corps in the park at Versailles, in the words of one of them, without having received orders from the King and entirely on their own initiative, 'retreated to the bottom of the Tapis Vert and having reached Trianon, took the road for Rambouillet' at 5.30 a.m. In other words, they fled. They reached Rambouillet safely at 11.30 a.m.[8]

Meanwhile, back in the palace, the few Gardes du Corps on duty slowly retreated through the antechambers to the Queen's bedroom; they had to wait outside while she dressed and fled to the King's apartment. In keeping with their orders they did not shoot. Finally, after some desperate moments, the doors being battered down by the baying mob, the grenadiers of the Garde Nationale – largely ex-Gardes Françaises – arrived and restored order. The Duc d'Ayen, a captain of the guard, found at 7 a.m. on 6 October 'the different rooms and posts normally occupied by the Gardes du Corps then occupied by the grenadiers of the Garde Nationale'; and this was, in terms not only of the organization of the guard of the King of France, but also of French history, the most important result of the October days. For the Gardes Françaises, metamorphosized into the Garde Nationale de Paris, now realized the old fears of the Kings of France and acted as a praetorian guard. They escorted Louis XVI in triumph to Paris on 6 October. They were the main force guarding his palace until 1791. Their commander, La Fayette, was the most powerful man in the kingdom and Louis XVI had to take account of his views.[9]

The débâcle of the French monarchy in 1789 shows how unreliable a royal guard can be in time of revolution. The Gardes Françaises deserted. The Cent-Suisses did nothing. The Gardes du Corps, with a few brave exceptions, bolted. Far from guarding the King, the Gardes du Corps were guarded by him. For it was Louis XVI who, by pleading with the Paris mob on the morning of 6 October, saved their lives.

The Gardes Suisses, who shared the duty of guarding the King with the Garde Nationale, continued to support the Revolution, no doubt because it was stronger than the King. Their lieutenant-colonel, the Comte d'Affry, sent a message of support to the Assembly the morning it discovered the flight of the King on 21 June 1791 to Varennes. On 20 June 1792, when the palace of the Tuileries was again invaded by a mob enraged by the King's refusal to sanction extreme measures, the Gardes Suisses, as on 5 October, did nothing. The King was left with a few courtiers and soldiers of the Garde Nationale during hours of insult and torment. Finally the mob withdrew. In the next few weeks the King's position briefly improved. But it soon deteriorated further, particularly after the declaration of the Duke of Brunswick, commander of the forces invading France, that Paris would be destroyed if any harm befell the royal family. Now, as an officer wrote of Louis XVI on 1 August: 'His only hope lies with the regiment of Gardes Suisses.' In a very fluid situation, which might suddenly change in favour of the King, perhaps a devoted royal guard could save the monarchy.

In July there were 2163 Gardes Suisses in all, of whom 300 were sent to Normandy to protect grain convoys on 5 August. On 7 August, as revolutionaries were obviously preparing an attack on the palace, about 1000 Gardes Suisses took up position at the Tuileries, with 200 royalist gentlemen; the other Gardes Suisses were in their barracks at

Courbevoie.[10] Although, as in 1789, many Gardes Suisses did not want to fight, they obeyed their officers', and the Paris municipal authorities', orders to meet force with force. This was the only time this policy, the opposite of the King's refusal to resist in October 1789 and June 1792, was practised by a royal guard during the Revolution; it ended in disaster.

After a discouraging last review of his guard at 5 a.m. on 10 August, the King with his family, escorted by about 200 Gardes Suisses, withdrew to the Assembly at 8.30. All but seventy of the Garde Nationale went over to the revolutionaries, with their cannon, during the night. The attack on the palace began at about 9.30 a.m. At ten the King ordered the Gardes Suisses in the palace and on the way from Courbevoie to return to their barracks, but it was too late. The fighting continued until the evening and ended (inevitably, given the difference in numbers) in the victory of the revolutionaries.

In all, on 10 August and in the massacres which took place in the next month, twenty-six officers and about 850 NCOs and men of the Gardes Suisses were killed, the biggest loss of life incurred in the defence of a monarchy in the history of royal guards. During the nineteenth century it was said that the trees in the Tuileries Gardens flowered early because of the fertilizing effect of the blood of the Gardes Suisses. On 13 August the King was imprisoned and on 22 September the monarchy abolished. Five of the thirty-three charges against him at the 'trial' which condemned him to death dealt with his use and payment of the Gardes du Corps in October 1789 and after June 1791, the composition of the Garde Constitutionelle in 1792, and his use of the Gardes Suisses on 10 August.[11]

In the early nineteenth century popular disorders gave the French monarchy few problems. In London, however, the Horse and Foot Guards had to be used so often to suppress popular disturbances that they were known as the 'Piccadilly Butchers'. Particularly unpleasant incidents took place in 1810, with the arrest of Sir Francis Burdett, and during riots in 1816 and 1817. The guards were so often used to protect the government that in 1819 the radical MP Hobhouse said that 'the real efficient anti-Reformers are to be found at the Horse Guards and the Knightsbridge Barracks', a remark thought so dangerous that he was sent to prison.

In 1820, the year their guards failed to save the Kings of Spain and Naples from granting constitutions, and the year the Semenovsky Guards mutinied, an almost revolutionary situation also emerged in England, provoked by divisions in the royal family (the trial of Queen Caroline, a popular heroine), although with deeper causes. The attitude of the guard was scarcely less important in London in 1820 than in Paris in 1789 because, as the Duke of Wellington, colonel of the Royal Horse Guards, wrote to the Prime Minister, in London 'the Government depend for their protection against insurrection and revolution, and individuals for their personal safety and property, upon the fidelity of 3000 Guards, all of the class of the people and even of the lowest of that class'.

On 23 February thirty Coldstream Guards under Lord Frederick Fitzclarence, an illegitimate nephew of the King, arrested the Cato Street conspirators who were planning to kill the cabinet. So far the guards had remained loyal. But later in the year there were alarming symptoms of discontent in the guards, particularly in the Coldstream and Scots Guards. Their quarters and conditions were bad, the soldiers were neglected by their officers, and guards now had such prestige that 'grievances whether real or supposed, are brought forward and urged in a more decided tone than before', according to Sir Herbert Taylor. Many people were seriously alarmed and feared, in the words of one member of the ruling class, that 'the extinguisher is taking fire'.

But in fact the guards maintained order and protected government buildings and the Houses of Parliament, where Queen Caroline was being tried, throughout the summer. After the end of Queen Caroline's trial in November, the situation grew calmer.[12] Thereafter, throughout the nineteenth century, in 1830 and 1848, during the Fenian scare of 1866–67,

55.   Lecomte. *The Battle in the Rue de Rohan.* 29 July 1830. MUSÉE CARNAVALET. PHOTO LAUROS GIRAUDON.

Swiss soldiers from the Garde Royale are firing from the first floor on crowds during the July Revolution. However, in fact the Parisians controlled most of the upper floors and after three days of street fighting the Garde Royale had to withdraw from Paris.

the Trafalgar Square demonstration of 1887, and in the 1826 suppression of disturbances among Lancashire workmen, the guards acted as a particularly reliable and impressive repressive force loyal to the existing government. In the twentieth century, the Duke of Edinburgh has written, 'their guard duties, although demanding, have fortunately never been vital'. But if there is a serious strike in London, Foot and Horse Guards still help to provide emergency services for the government.[13]

In France, the Garde Royale of the Bourbons was crucial in suppressing popular disturbances in the Ile de France in 1816–17, and in Paris in 1820, when a left-wing crowd tried to attack the Tuileries and the Chamber of Deputies while it was voting laws to strengthen the government. Charles X thought that he could rely on his guard, which was extremely privileged, and was unpopular with the line and the Parisians, in any emergency. The authorities were always worried, however, about the possibility that the guards stationed in Paris, Rouen or Orléans would acquire, as the Minister of War wrote to the major-general, 'a hostile attitude attributable largely to their contact with the bourgeois'.

This was one of the principal problems of a royal guard, which the behaviour of the

French royal guard in 1789 – or of the English royal guard in 1780 and 1820 – had revealed. By the nature of their duties they were stationed in or around the capital of the monarchy. Even if they had been recruited from the countryside or abroad, they were therefore exposed to contact with the inhabitants of the capital. Yet, owing to their number, political awareness, and opportunities, the inhabitants of a capital are likely to be precisely that section of the population most prepared to challenge the authority of the government and the stability of the social order. Could constant attention, enormous privileges and elaborate schemes of rotation, so that no regiment stayed in Paris, or even a provincial city, for too long, preserve the Garde Royale as a pillar of the French monarchy?

When on 26 July 1830 Charles X's unpopular and extremist government published the ordinances which drastically reduced the franchise and the liberty of the press, popular reaction was swift and furious: printing presses were the biggest single employer of labour in Paris. On 25 July the government had taken the precaution, as in June 1820, of placing the line regiments in the Paris military district (6750 of a total of 11,550) under the command of the major-general of the Garde Royal in waiting, Maréchal Marmont, unpopular because he was believed to have betrayed Napoleon I.[14] As disturbances grew worse on 26 and 27 July 'the line by the attitude it took . . . separated itself from the guard', according to the account of one guards officer. Marmont's generalship was bad: instead of concentrating the loyal troops in and around the Tuileries and the Louvre, which were relatively easy to defend, he sent them in columns through the city, thereby dividing them and exposing them to attacks by Parisians on upper floors. The Garde Royale began to feel isolated, dispirited and hungry, although on 29 July Charles X granted them one and a half months' extra pay. By 30 July, when they withdrew to the royal palace of Saint-Cloud, the line had deserted and, even in the guard, 'discipline was slackening' and soldiers were beginning to refuse to obey orders.

On 1 August the court retreated to Rambouillet. There were now about 8800 soldiers, almost all from the guard or the Gardes du Corps, around the King.[15] But desertions were beginning in the guard, while by 29 July perhaps 360 had been killed or wounded. In the first infantry regiment of the guard, there were eighty-nine officers and 1634 soldiers in Paris on 27 July; in Rambouillet on 3 August there were thirty-nine and 427 respectively. Yet again, as in Paris in 1789, lack of decisive leadership and the appeal of a national revolution against an unpopular government, proved more important than a guard's emotional and material ties to the monarchy. The Gardes du Corps, however, were spectacularly faithful – a sign that the Bourbon monarchy was more popular with the aristocracy in 1830 than in 1789. They had wanted to seize Louis-Philippe on 27 July, but instead he seized the chance of a throne given him by the folly of Charles X's government and the defeat of the Garde Royale. By 1 August it was clear that he had won power. On 3 August Charles X abdicated in favour of his grandson, the Duc de Bordeaux; the Ordre du Jour stated that the Gardes du Corps should 'serve the new King with the devotion of which they have given so many examples'. But France had escaped the control of the Bourbons and their guard. There were plans to retreat to the royalist west, but no one's heart was in it. As has already been recounted, Charles X took leave of his weeping Garde Royale on 4 August and of his Gardes du Corps on 16 August.[16]

Although many of the Garde Royale served in Louis-Philippe's army, where their arrogance sometimes caused resentment, only 10 per cent of the Gardes du Corps were prepared to serve the usurper. In accounts of the role of the guard, published in the 1830s, even those who disapproved of the cause for which they had fought praised their loyalty. The account by an officer in one of the Swiss regiments of the Garde Royale (which had been terrified of a repetition of August 1792) reveals the essence of what was hoped of royal guards in time of revolution. He wrote that the guards were animated by 'Principles of honour' and that 'we should not, we could not, not fight . . . in such cases one does not reason, one feels'.[17] Instead of using their reason to think about the political issues at stake, or the danger they were in, they should remember their sense of honour – and the interests and privileges which tied them to the monarchy. To instil 'principles of honour' and to make feelings more important than reason was, and is, the dream of every commander of a royal guard. In the revolutionary year of 1848 it was successful in the guard of Naples which maintained the throne of Ferdinand II of the Two Sicilies and, even more important, in the Prussian Guard. During the crisis of March 1848, when Berlin seemed like a town conquered by revolution, the commander of the guard infantry, Lieutenant-General von Prittwitz, was given supreme command of the capital. The guard, which was detested by the Berliners, remained *Königstreu* (loyal to the King) even when forced to yield guard of the Schloss to a civic guard on 19 March and to withdraw to Potsdam on 20 March. The King followed his guards to Potsdam on 30 March. Thereafter, the guard provided an indispensable reserve of military force for the monarchy, which enabled it to survive the revolutionary onslaught of 1848. In September 1848 it finally re-entered Berlin and on 10 November closed the National Assembly.

In Austria the guard was too small to play an important part in the Revolution of 1848. The first break between the monarchy and the Revolution, however, was provoked by the decision that, as in Berlin, the revolutionary National Guard should share in guarding the palace. For a generation brought up on tales of the horrors of the French Revolution, it was too much, and the court fled Vienna for Innsbruck on 17 May.[18]

After 1848, the growing prosperity of much of Europe and the widening of the franchise in many monarchies meant that some of the feared and distrusted poor began to acquire a stake in the social order. The necessity for royal guards to intervene to protect the social order grew less urgent, particularly because, after 1830, large and efficient police forces were usually available to maintain law and order. It is revealing of the increase in social stability, and of the importance of police forces, that the last time the royal guard of Sweden intervened to repress a strike or riot was in 1909, while since 1881, having in the past guarded much of the centre of the city, they guard only the royal palaces.

In Russia, however, the guard continued to play an essential part in maintaining order in the capital. There were usually about 100,000 guards and other troops stationed in and around St Petersburg. In 1904 after Russia's catastrophic defeat by Japan, discontent began to mount. Although it had been sent to the front during the Russo-Turkish War of 1877–78, the guard had deliberately been kept at home during the Russo-Japanese War in order to defend the monarchy against any possible danger. When the revolutionary threat began to show itself in giant demonstrations, General Prince Vassilchikov, the extremely capable commander of the guard, assumed command in St Petersburg. On 9 January 1905, when a vast, orderly workers' demonstration headed for the Winter Palace to present petitions to the Tsar (who was not there), the guard on duty – from the Preobrazhensky, Semenovsky, Chevaliers Gardes, Grenadiers and Pavlovsky Regiments – numbered in all about 20,000 (there were also some line troops). After three warnings, they shot at the unarmed workers. Hundreds were killed. Yet again there was blood on the snow in Palace Square, blood which had an immense psychological effect on the popular image of the monarchy and Nicholas II. For 'shootings in front of the palace seemed inconceivable without the express order of the tsar'.[19]

Throughout that year and the next, the guards maintained government control of the capital. The Semenovsky Regiment was also particularly effective in October in restoring order in Moscow; Nicholas II held a special review on 18 July 1906 to express his thanks. Again, that a royal guard was felt to be in some way the antithesis of popular movements is clear from the Tsar's diary and correspondence. On 6 August 1905, for example, the day the creation of Russia's first parliament, the Duma (housed in the Palais Tauride because it was

56.   *Outside the Winter Palace.* 9 January 1905. NOVOSTI.

In the 1905 Revolution the Imperial Guard, shown here firing on demonstrators in Palace Square, hitherto the scene of reviews and parades, remained loyal. This was the most important single factor in preserving the Russian monarchy. In 1917 Nicholas II expected the guard would be equally loyal.

surrounded by guards barracks), was announced, Nicholas II wrote in his diary, 'superb parade of the Preobrazhensky Regiment', and described the presentation of the Tsarevich to the regiment, the appointment of two of its officers to be his ADCs and a dinner with the Guards Uhlans. He was consciously using, and expanding, the familiar array of personal connections between the Romanovs and their guard as the surest defence against revolution and a representative assembly. It was not necessary for William II to point out to him, on 14 June 1906, that 'the best way to relieve the cares and worries the situation at home causes you, is, as you do, to occupy yourself with your fine guard by inspecting them and speaking to them'.[20]

But would the guard always be, as William II said he hoped, 'a loyal, trustworthy and keen weapon in the hands of their sovereign'? In June 1906, at the annual Krasnoe Seloe manoeuvres, two battalions of the Preobrazhensky Regiment, to the amazement of their officers, mutinied. Both officers and soldiers of the guard listened to revolutionary speeches in 1905–06.

Perhaps the mutiny was a momentary aberration, however. By 1907, order was restored. In the First World War, the monarchy was sufficiently confident, or belligerent, or afraid of public opinion, to send a large proportion of the guard to the front, where it was decimated. Thus, in February 1917, the 99,000 guards (of a total of 180,000 troops) in Petrograd – there were many more in the vicinity – were reserve battalions, consisting of 'as yet uninstructed new recruits and recuperating veterans', in the words of Allan Wildman. The order of the Tsar, who was afraid of possible unrest, to reinforce them with two well-trained guards cavalry divisions, including the Garde à Cheval, in December 1916, had not been put into effect by the General Staff on the grounds of the unavailability of suitable accommodation in the capital.

Meanwhile, to the almost total alienation of the ruling class from the government, which led to so many rumours of a guards coup in January 1917, was added, by the winter, a severe food shortage brought about by inflation, transport difficulties and conflicts between rival authorities. On 5 February 1917 a secret police report recorded that 'the food crisis is getting more acute every day'.[21] Within the guard, relations between officers – over 90 per cent of whom had joined since 1914, and were thus relatively inexperienced – and men were bad. The men resented officers' use of them as servants and officers' control of the regimental economy. On 25 February, three days after Nicholas II had left Tsarskoe Seloe for headquarters, riots in the capital began to be serious. The cause was not only, as the Minister of the Interior later remembered, 'a delay in baking bread, a false rumour of the lack of flour in the city' (for the flour was in fact there), but also political. Demonstrators' flags carried the slogans: 'We want bread', 'Down with War', and 'Down with Autocracy'. That day the evening conference of commanders of guards regiments decided, in accordance with the Tsar's personal instructions, to begin shooting after the ritual three warnings. On 26 February the Semenovsky, Pavlovsky, and Volhynsky Regiments obeyed orders and fired on the crowd.[22]

But on 27 February part of the Volhynsky Regiment was the first to join the Revolution and they managed to persuade most, but not all, of the soldiers of the Preobrazhensky and Litovsky, and later the Semenovsky and Ismailovsky, Regiments to join them. They seized ammunition stores and artillery and used the latter to force the Moskovsky Regiment to join them. According to a Soviet historian, 66,700 soldiers had joined the Revolution by the end of 27 February. The guards were now, in the words of the British Military Attaché, 'in complete control of the situation'.[23]

The exact reasons for such a rapid and, for the monarchy, catastrophic desertion will always remain mysterious since we do not know what went on in the minds of the guards. They were still largely drawn from country districts, so there was nothing inevitable about their feelings of solidarity with Petrograd workers. One reason for the scale of the desertions was probably what Hasegawa, an American historian who has recently written the most thorough account of the February Revolution in English, calls 'the extreme ineptness of the security authorities', the most senior of whom, such as General Khabalov, commander of Petrograd military district, had cultivated Rasputin's patronage.

In addition, many officers of the guard, including the Grand Duke Paul, commander of the First Guards Corps, to whom, after it was all over, the Tsarina gave 'a terrible blowing-up for not having done anything with the guard', had constitutional leanings which may have weakened their resolve to defend the autocracy of Nicholas II. According to Hasegawa, 'many officers did not use force to keep the soldiers from joining the revolt, maintaining non-committal neutrality as if they were indifferent bystanders'. But, if the officers had used force, their men would have shot them, while there was too great a mental barrier between them for words alone to be effective.[24]

On the night of 27 February, there were still about 2000 loyal guards from the Preobrazhensky, Ismailovsky, Egersky, Pavlovsky and Rifle Regiments in and around the Winter Palace. But they were badly led and supplied. The Tsar's brother, the Grand Duke

Michael, insisted they leave the palace either because they were making it filthy, or because their presence was compromising its art treasures, or because they were compromising the future of the monarchy – a revealing sign of his lack of faith in a military solution. The next morning they returned to barracks as ordered, or deserted. Government resistance in the capital was over. Some guards at Tsarskoe Seloe, where the Tsarina was in residence, remained loyal until 4 March, but the majority had gone over to the Revolution by 1 March.[25]

At headquarters on 28 February the Tsar, who still thought of his guard as a dynastic reserve, wrote to the Tsarina, 'I wonder what Paul is doing? He ought to keep them in hand,' and ordered the Garde à Cheval to Petrograd. Finally, on 2 March, convinced by telegrams from his generals and by the evolution of the military and political situation, Nicholas II abdicated the throne of Russia, in the words of one witness, 'as if he was handing over a squadron to another commander'.[26]

Unbelievably, he had not decided whether his son or his brother was to succeed him. But would his guards have supported a successor? In March 1917, after the proclamation of a republic, they found it perfectly easy to stop being imperial guards (although they retained their rank privileges until the October Revolution) and become soldiers of a republic : one officer recalls that senior guards officers, most of whom continued to serve, were more disturbed by changes in the guard's control of Petrograd military district than by the abdication of the Tsar. On 9 March, when the Tsar returned to his family at Tsarskoe Seloe, not a single guard returned his salute. Thereafter, he was guarded first at Tsarskoe Seloe, then at Tobolsk and Ekaterinburg in Siberia, by soldiers of the First Guards Rifle Regiment who, in the words of the Marshal of the Court, were 'horrible even to look at'. Yet again, guards had become (often quite brutal) jailers with ease.

The daughter of the Tsar's doctor writes of the Cossacks of the Escort, who rallied to the Revolution like the rest: 'After the extreme confidence and the exceptional comfort which they enjoyed with the Tsar! How could they forget everything in one day?' But a revolution speeds up time, it gives people the sensation of having lived years in a day and of having entered a new era of freedom and hope. In such a moment of exaltation it is easy for guards to forget 'everything', their privileges, as well as the elaborate network of personal connections and regimental traditions binding them to the monarch.

In July 1917 the Preobrazhensky, Semenovsky and Ismailovsky Regiments supported Kerensky's government and helped to defeat a Bolshevik attempt to seize power. But by October, like the Grenadiersky, Egersky and Pavlovsky Regiments, they were supporters of the Bolsheviks. Their officers seemed to have little authority over the soldiers, and, in any case, were demoralized, indecisive and more hostile to Kerensky than afraid of the Bolsheviks.

The guard was disbanded, with the rest of the army, after the Bolshevik seizure of power, in December 1917. The weakness of Russian monarchism is shown by the fact that neither in 1917 nor later did the guard form a nucleus of supporters for the monarchy or even for the right-wing. Its officers and soldiers fought for the causes of their ethnic homelands – Mannerheim of the Chevaliers-Gardes in Finland, Skoropadsky of the same regiment in the Ukraine, the Cossacks of the Escort and of the guard on the Don. Or, like Wrangel, they supported the non-monarchist Whites in the Civil War.[27]

The Russian Revolution shows the low place of the monarch, and even the monarchy, in guards officers' order of priorities: what really mattered to them in 1917 was a government which they could respect, and the future of their regiments. In 1918 other monarchies, also blamed for military defeat and food shortages, found themselves deserted with little hesitation by their guards. The social order was now sufficiently secure, and broadly based, for monarchies to appear to be dispensable embarrassments rather than indispensable guarantees.

In Austria the line troops guarding the palace of Schönbrunn marched away on 2 November. The Life Guards and Garde Gendarmes rapidly dwindled in numbers, except for the Life Guard Infantry Company. According to the Empress Zita 'the whole palace was now open. There were not even sentries at the main gate.' Military cadets were more loyal than the guards and helped protect the palace until the Emperor left on 11 November. When he finally left Austria on 24 March 1919, like the Ottoman Sultan three years later, he had to have a British military escort.

In Prussia at the same time the situation was no better. Military defeat and growing class conflict had created a situation where nothing was stable. 'This is a truly ghastly state of affairs . . . as soon as there is a suspension of hostilities then the trustworthy part of the army and the Corps of Guards will be concentrated around Berlin,' wrote the Kaiser to his wife from headquarters at Spa on 7 November.[28] But was the Corps of Guards trustworthy? At the time the Kaiser believed so. But many of the finest guards regiments were at the front – the Garde du Corps, for example, were on the eastern front at Minsk and Shitomir – or protecting headquarters. There were few guards in Berlin.

On 9 November, at a council of thirty-nine officers, only one, a former commander of the Guards Corps, felt he could rely on his troops to guarantee the Emperor's safety. Even the Rohr battalion, which was guarding headquarters, was forming a soldiers' council and the Second Guards division, also near Spa, was unreliable. The Kaiser wrote to his son: 'As the Marshal (Hindenburg) can no longer guarantee my safety, and can no longer vouch for the troops, I have decided after severe internal struggle to leave the wreck of my army. Berlin is totally lost.' On 10 November he arrived in the Netherlands.[29]

Not only could the guards at headquarters at Spa no longer be relied on to defend the monarchy – although they still performed their other military duties – but on 9 November the Third Guards, the Garde Jaegers and the Kaiser Alexander Garde Grenadiers in Berlin went over to the Revolution. At 12.30 p.m. there was a message to the Minister of War: 'On the grounds of a message from Guards [GOC Guards Reserves] that the great majority of available troops will no longer shoot and have formed Workers' and Soldiers' Councils, General von Linsingen asks whether under the circumstances firearms are to be employed.' The answer could only be no. A republic was proclaimed from the balcony of the Berlin Schloss. Count Kessler, a liberal aristocrat who had served in the Guards Uhlans, wrote that he had witnessed 'in a few hours the downfall of the Hohenzollerns, the dissolution of the German army and the end of the old order of society'. Berlin life, however, continued its orderly course. On 14 November Kessler noticed that, at the changing of the guard, 'the standard of marching was slightly more sluggish than that of the guards before the war, but tidy and entirely soldierly', although they no longer wore Hohenzollern insignia.[30]

What is interesting about the Prussian Guard is that, although it was not prepared to defend the Kaiser or the monarchy – what Kessler called 'the Emperor's utter personal failure, especially during the war', had destroyed 'the monarchical idea' in Germany – it did, unlike the Russian Guard, act as a spearhead of the movement to defend the capitalist social order. For, in late November 1918 as the German armies returned home after their defeat, the guards regiments naturally returned to their posts in Berlin and Potsdam. Stationed in and around the capital, the guards inevitably played a decisive role in the struggle between the Social-Democratic government and the revolutionary Spartacists, which hinged, Kessler wrote, on the existence of 'serviceable and reliable troops'.

While most soldiers were demobilized, some, with the approval of the Supreme Command, were organized into Freikorps or volunteer units. The most important guard Freikorps were those commanded by Captain Erbgraf von Fugger of the Garde du Corps, Major von Stephani and Colonel Reinhard of the First Foot Guards, Captain Pabst of the Horse Guards and Sergeant-Major Suppe of the Second Guards.[31]

These forces of a few hundred dedicated soldiers were organized by mid-December. On 24 December the Horse Guards under Pabst led the attack on the Spartacist sailors who had seized the Berlin Schloss. Soon Kessler saw 'large pallid patches on the Palace walls, traces of the artillery bombardment. The windows of the facade were no more than dark cavities, no panes, the sills splintered.' But it was difficult to seize control of the castle, and the Horse Guards were defeated. Only by 12 January 1919, helped by the Guards Freikorps, did the government win back control of Berlin. On 11 January the Garde Jaeger stormed the offices of the famous Spartacist newspaper Vorwaerts. On 15 January officers of the Volunteer Division of the Horse Guards, in a particularly brutal way, killed the Spartacists' leaders, Rosa Luxemburg and Karl Liebknecht. In the accompanying repression, and again in March, the Guards Freikorps also killed hundreds of suspected Spartacist sympathizers.[32] The role of the Prussian Guard after the fall of the Prussian monarchy suggests that, for a republic to succeed or to remain radical, it should eliminate the guard as well as the monarchy.

In 1919 the old guards regiments were dissolved. Regimental reunions, associations and histories (often dedicated to the Kaiser) flourished, however, while some of the new regiments of the Reichswehr became 'tradition bearers' of the old Prussian regiments: Infantry Regiment 9 carried on the traditions of the First Foot Guard Regiment, for example. The history of *Das Erste Garderegiment zu Fuss im Weltkrieg*, Berlin 1934, with forewords by the Kaiser and Prince Eitel Friedrich, was written to 'preserve the Potsdamer Spirit like a rock against which the shame of the disintegration and humiliation of the Fatherland must break'.

The persistence of these traditions was important because many guards officers remained in positions of power, like General von Seeckt of the Kaiser Alexander Garde Grenadiers, who commanded the Reichswehr from 1919 to 1926. Both Hindenburg and his son Oskar had served in the Third Guards. Around Hindenburg, when he was President of the Republic from 1926 to 1934, arose what was known as the 'Dritte Garde Gruppe' of right-wing, perhaps pro-Nazi, councillors led by General von Schleicher, who was Chancellor for a short time in 1932–33. Schleicher was 'a Dritte Gardist . . . Therein lay his strength. He could get along with everyone. He had his friends in every political camp,' according to another officer. Another right-wing favourite of Hindenburg, Von Papen, had also, like five of his nine ministers when he was Chancellor for a few months in 1932, served in the guards. The intrigues which hastened the end of the Weimar Republic and the arrival of the extreme right, and then the Nazis, in power were facilitated by the mutual loyalties and personal connections of former guards officers.[33]

So far royal guards, have, with a few exceptions, been shown to be less interested in defending monarchies in time of revolution than in defending the social order or thinking of their own future. In Iran in 1978–79, however, the Imperial Guard had to defend a monarch who may have been feared or disliked, but was respected as neither Louis XVI, nor Nicholas II, nor William II, had been. Moreover, his monarchy could be seen as the sole guarantee of the existing social order against a revolution which clearly had little to offer the officers and soldiers of the Iranian armed forces.

In 1963 the then commander of the Imperial Guard, General Oveissi, suppressed serious disorder in Tehran in a few days. In 1972 the Lashkari Guard had been attached to the Imperial Guard, after prolonged discussion, partly in order to have an armed force available to repress disorder in the capital which was not too closely attached to the monarchy. According to General Oveissi, the Immortals, and to a lesser extent the other soldiers of the Imperial Guard, were deliberately chosen from rural and non-Persian areas of Iran, on the grounds that their inhabitants were more warlike, and above all more reliable, than other Iranians. Therefore, the possibility of disturbances in Tehran was, contrary to a widely held opinion, anticipated by the government.

57. *A Guard's Farewell to the Shah*. 16 January 1979. POPPERFOTO.

The guard is probably Lieutenant-Colonel Yusuf-i-nijad, commander of the Javedan 'Immortals', in which the Shah had always taken a close personal interest. Unlike the French in 1789 and 1830, or the Russian in 1905 and 1917, the Iranian Guard in 1978–79 was not trained to deal with popular disturbances. Nevertheless it remained loyal, during six months of revolutionary demonstrations, until after the departure of the Shah.

When in 1978 economic discontent, social resentment and religious outrage combined with government weakness to create disturbances in the capital, the guard maintained military control without great difficulty. On 8 September, however, the death of perhaps as many as 400 demonstrators in Jaleh Square in Tehran, shot by the Lashkari Guard, was 'very important for the people of Iran', in the words of a former officer of the Imperial Guard. That the Shah's guard, on Oveissi's orders, was killing the people helped to deepen their hostility to the monarchy.[34]

Thereafter, in the most difficult of circumstances, defending a government which could not decide whether to follow a policy of concession or repression against what seemed like an overwhelmingly popular revolution, perhaps more popular than any other in recent history, the guard remained staunch. Perhaps the fact that its officers were tied in every way, emotional, financial, and from the point of view of their careers, to the regime, that they received, in the words of a familiar of the palace, 'everything from the Shah', whereas in, for example, the French and Russian Revolutions, the officers were already in part alienated, explains the remarkable loyalty of the Iranian Guard.

But the guard's control of the military situation was less important than the fact, obvious even to the monarch, that the monarchy had been rejected by the people. Some monarchists still believe that even when the Shah finally left on the advice on his American ally, not because of military necessity, on 17 January, the guard could have ended the Revolution. General Badrai, former commander of the Imperial Guard, then commander of the ground forces, and General Ali Neshat, commander of the Imperial Guard, may have wanted to launch a coup against the new constitutional government of Bakhtiar. But already, in November 1978, there had been an incident when soldiers of the Lashkari Guard had opened fire on an officers' mess and killed thirteen officers. By December, according to John D. Stempel, the desertion rate was increasing rapidly. Could the guard be relied on?

On 21 January manoeuvres of the Immortals, who were ready 'to die for the Shah', were arranged to impress foreign reporters. But there were only a few thousand guards, while in the town there were hundreds of thousands of demonstrators prepared to die for the Revolution. On 9 February, eight days after Khomeini had returned to Tehran, there was an incident at Lavezan Barracks, between monarchist Lashkari Guards and Air Force Auxiliaries who supported Khomeini. It ended in the retreat of the guard. The next day his followers were ordered by Khomeini to march on the barracks and key buildings, which the soldiers were ordered by the Chief of Staff, General Gharabaghi, on the advice of other generals, to evacuate. In the next three days the guard gave up in tears. General Badrai was killed. Part of the guard was disbanded, part was sent to fight the Kurds. Some guards disappeared to their villages. Other are in exile, planning a restoration.[35]

8
LIFE IN THE GUARDS

To be on guard duty guard in or outside a royal palace was to enter a special world. Osbert Sitwell, a Grenadier Guard between 1912–19, wrote that 'the days spent on King's Guard were of so special a nature as perhaps to resemble a little those spent by Catholics during a Retreat . . . a separate small lifetime of a month or two months in all, but in their quality, completely unlike any other kind of existence the same individual has led'. As Osbert Sitwell points out, however, he spent only a small proportion of his years in the Grenadiers on King's Guard. In Europe few royal guards except members of some of the smaller units, such as the Papal Swiss Guard, or the Yeomen of the Guard in England before 1837, spent much of their time on guard duty.[1]

Even the members of the smaller units or senior officers who did spend most of their lives in the palace were prevented by court etiquette from spending it with the monarch to the same extent as their Middle Eastern equivalents. In the monarchies of the Arabian peninsula, however, the *mutarzi* and the Harass al Khass are 'continually on duty' and some of them are always with the ruler or in his palace and are treated as part of his family. The royal guard or *zkirt* of Saudi Arabia, according to Ameen Rihani, 'is of the Palace and for the Palace. He lives and loafs and grazes in the Palace when he is employed. He hovers around the Palace when he is not.' This is a continuation of an ancient tradition. The *hujarriya* guards of the Abbasids were named after the *hujar* or chambers of the palace, which they rarely left. The Khassikiya Guards of the Mameluke Sultans of Egypt differed from other soldiers by the splendour of their dress, the quality of their horsemanship and the privilege of being 'admitted into the Sultan's presence in his private moments without previous permission'.[2]

In European monarchies such easy access and intimacy was rendered almost impossible by the rigidity of court etiquette and class barriers. There were a few guards, however, who were able to use the opportunities their service provided to become royal intimates. For service in a royal guard has, with service in a royal household, provided one of the main avenues to royal favour, and its rewards, in history. For example, two of the lovers of the Empress Elizabeth of Russia, and seven of the thirteen identified lovers of Catherine II, first won their monarchs' favour when serving in the guard.

Some guards have even, like the guards of the Middle East, although in a different way, become 'part of the family' by marrying into the normally inaccessible world of European royalty. Among them have been Lauzun, a captain of the guard of Louis XIV, who married the King's cousin la grande Mademoiselle; his nephew, the Comte de Rions, who married Louis XV's aunt the Duchesse de Berri; Captain Koulikovsky of the Guard Cuirassiers who married the Grand Duchess Olga, a sister of Nicholas II (her brother the Grand Duke Michael married the wife of an officer of the same regiment); and, in Spain, Godoy and Munoz.

With these exceptions, however, few guards in Europe had much contact with monarchs. They spent most of their lives away from the palace. To describe the lives of so many individuals is obviously impossible. What can be done is to isolate some of the most unusual and distinctive features of some guards' lives, those features which were most remarked by contemporaries or by the guards themselves.

58.   *The Future King Faisal of Saudi Arabia with a Black Guard*. New York 1944. COLL. GERALD DE GAURY.

Although, or because, they are often slaves, guards in the Arabian peninsula have had much closer personal relations with their monarchs than guards in Europe. Faisal called his guard 'little brother', and insisted on eating with him even in this 'restricted' American hotel. Since 1960 slave guards have disappeared from almost all the monarchies of the Arabian peninsula, as well as from Morocco.

Many of the distinguishing features of guards' lives arose from the basic fact that service in a royal guard brought men chosen for their social background or looks (see page 163) to the capitals of Europe. And one characteristic of the life of the officers of guards regiments was their energetic contribution to the aristocratic social life of the capitals of Europe. In France the Gardes du Corps were famous for their 'amenity' and 'politeness'; 'nothing equals the politeness of a Garde du Corps of His Majesty', wrote Mercier in 1783, sentiments echoed by Scott in 1816, and they used their good manners to ensure an enjoyable social life. The Mousquetaires had the reputation of being fond of *les plaisirs*.

During the restoration they were so social that the uniform of the revived Mousquetaires was first displayed not at a parade but at a soirée on 19 September 1814: 'the ladies found us charming', wrote one, as if that was his uniform's *raison d'être*. At the same time the Gardes du Corps felt, rather exaggeratedly, that 'all doors were open to them' in Paris. The Duchesse de Berri would order officers who were good dancers for her balls from the Garde Royale just as she ordered chairs and tapestries from the Mobilier de la Couronne. During the Second Empire the social success of the Cent-Gardes was compared by contemporaries to that of the Mousquetaires of Louis XIII and Louis XIV.[3]

In France and in Prussia, the guard was a means to taste the social pleasures of the capital as well as to follow a military career. A soldier of the Garde Impériale wrote in his memoirs that 'you need to be, like me, leaving a small ugly provincial town, and the paternal roof, for the first time, and to have seen nothing truly fine, to understand and conceive all my joy, all my happiness' when serving in the Garde Impériale in Paris. In the same way an officer of the Prussian Guard, von Suckow, a 'simple country gentleman', wrote of his 'infinite pleasure' at spending his first winter in Berlin in the early nineteenth century, 'in a continual round of parties'. Guards officers' physical fitness, as well as their social graces, seems to have made them particularly in demand as dancing partners. The novel *A Winter in Berlin* (1883) shows how much young girls longed to dance with officers of the Foot Guards or, even better, the Garde du Corps. All the officers of the Garde Reiter of Saxony 'danced superbly'.[4]

59. *Mia Entrada en el Mundo* from F. Fernandez de Cordoba, *Mis Memorias Intimas*. 3 vols. 1886–89. BRITISH LIBRARY.

In Madrid in the 1820s, as in many other capitals before and since, salons and ballrooms were full of guards officers.

CAPITULO III.

Mi entrada en el mundo. — El sargento Ceruti. — Una procesión. — Mi primera salida á Alcalá de Henares. — Destacamento en la Granja. — Lo que me aconteció en Torrelodones. — Un lance de honor. — Composición de la Guardia Real. — Acantonamiento en Segovia. — Guarnición del regimiento en Madrid. — Fusilamiento de Bessières. — De servicio en la Granja. — Más desafíos.

In Russia the guard was even more socially important. As the Prussian minister wrote to Frederick II in 1772:

Being in the capital and always close to the court, the officers have more opportunity to be known and to make use of the protection and influence of their relations in high positions. If you add to this the enjoyment of living in high society, participating in all the pleasures and not being especially burdened by service . . .

The combination of 'living in high society' and 'not being especially burdened by service' continued until 1914. Young officers of the guards were known for being the leaders of fashion by the 1790s. Pushkin was introduced to the pleasures of 'wenching and gambling', and drinking, by the friends he made in the Guards Hussars while studying at the Lyceum in Tsarskoe Seloe. In *The Captain's Daughter* he describes a youthful noble for whom: 'The

60.   Gorbunov. *Lermontov*. 1838.
NOVOSTI.

Lermontov is wearing the uniform of
the Life Guards Hussars, service in
which enabled him to enjoy the social,
amorous, and cultural pleasures of St
Petersburg.

idea of military service was connected in my mind with thoughts of freedom and of the
pleasures of Petersburg life. I imagined myself as an officer of the Guards which, to my mind,
was the height of human bliss.'

When Lermontov was back in favour in 1838, and so had been transferred from the line
back to the guard, he attended

balls daily. I throw myself into high society . . . the most beautiful women beg verses from
me and boast about them as about a victory . . . I excite curiosity. I am being solicited, I am
invited everywhere, and I never give any indication that I desire this; ladies who must
without fail establish the most fashionable salon wish me to visit them because I also am a
society lion.

His literary fame was the reason for his social success in St Petersburg; but without his
commission in the guards he would not have been able to enjoy it.[5]

Other guards officers enjoyed social life without writing poems for their hostesses.
Indeed, it was a sort of tradition to show that, 'apart from the service and the enjoyment of
life, no other interest existed', in the words of an officer of the Guards Hussars. 'The interests

of all were concentrated either on drill or on the details of society gossip,' remembered an officer of the Cossack Guard. Marshal Mannerheim, 'delighted' to be stationed in St Petersburg, remembered that 'a young officer of a crack regiment seldom found himself disengaged in the afternoons and evenings', and too many other accounts agree for this to be an unrepresentative impression. The guards were so social and so important that the St Petersburg Yacht Club, the great centre where careers and reputations were made and broken, was 'ruled by the *esprit de corps* of the Guard'.[6]

The social life of a particular part of London still feels the impact of the guards, as it has done since the Restoration, when they were described by Lord Ailesbury to James II as 'a nursery for all sort of debauchery and vice'. His position as a Life Guard, and then an officer in the Coldstream Guards, in the 1690s helped introduce Richard Steele to the social life of the capital which he was to describe in the *Spectator*. Boswell told the Countess of Northumberland on 9 January 1763: 'Ay, the Guards, Madam, that is the thing . . . The thing is that I am anxious to live in London . . . in the Guards my duty would be quite a pleasure to me.' On 25 February he further noted that 'in that way I could enjoy all the elegant pleasures of the gay world, and by living in the Metropolis and having plenty of time could pursue what studies and follow what whims I pleased, get a variety of acquaintances of all kind, get a number of romantic adventures and thus have satisfaction of life'. That Boswell was right to believe that service in the guards could be primarily a means of enjoying an agreeable social life, rather than of following a military career or protecting the throne, can be confirmed from other sources. As late as 1921 Lieutenant-Colonel Studd of the Coldstream Guards recommended this regiment to parents partly on the grounds that it offered a 'less restricted choice of friends than line regiments', and that an officer in it 'meets people of the most varied interests and avocations and through them enlarges his own interests and his outlook on life'.[7]

The intimate relationship of the guards with what Boswell called 'the elegant pleasures of the gay world' is confirmed by innumerable novels and memoirs. In the early nineteenth century Lord Alvanley of the Coldstream Guards, a friend of the Duke of York, was 'the idol of the clubs and of society' and 'his dinners were considered perfect and the best in London'. Jack Hinton, the guardsman in Charles Lever's novel of that name (1857), set in the early nineteenth century, had to leave London for Ireland six months after he had joined the guards because he was exhausted by 'the extravagant profusion and the voluptuous abandonment of London Habits'.

General Higginson, when a young officer in the Grenadier Guards in the 1840s, wrote that 'balls, theatres, and country visits relieved the not over-arduous duties even of a subaltern'; when he returned to London in 1863 from Canada, the first person to stop him on his first stroll down Bond Street to the Guards Club was 'a very smartly dressed lady who said, "Forgive my stopping you, but could you get my niece invited to the Guards Ball?" ' (held to celebrate the marriage of the Prince of Wales). A Life Guard in the 1870s remembered that, although he had 'no military flair', 'Life in the guards in those days was extraordinarily pleasant . . . the social side was most pleasant.' He ended as Master of Ceremonies at Court.[8]

In 1885 the wife of the French Ambassador complained, 'There is no one to dance with, the Guards are gone' (to Egypt to fight the Mahdi). But the ballrooms of London could normally count on the guards. In 1912, the future Field-Marshal Alexander, then in the Irish Guards, would play cricket or polo every day, have a bath and then 'go out to dinner and then on to a dance: I feel awfully fit and well and am very keen on dancing'.

Such energy in the pursuit of pleasure as well as of the enemy, is not completely unknown today, although guards officers' military duties are far more demanding. 'Invitations flowed in,' remembered Humphrey Lyttelton, a guards officer in the 1940s, and a

61.   Anon. print. *Fraternization of the British Horse Guards and the French Cent-Gardes at Boulogne – Drinking Her Majesty's Health.* 1854. HOUSEHOLD CAVALRY MUSEUM.

Drink was one of the principal pleasures of guards. Similar scenes of alcoholic fraternization took place between the French and Russian guards at Tilsit in 1807.

62.   Hogarth. *The March on Finchley.* December 1745. BRITISH MUSEUM.

The guards left London in late November and early December 1745, despite fears of a popular uprising in their absence, in order to set up a camp at Finchley to resist the Young Pretender, who arrived at Derby on 6 December. The guard in the foreground is shown torn between a patriotic and a Jacobite woman. A Frenchman is whispering treason on the left. The drunken officers and weeping prostitutes confirm the association of the guard with drink and sex, as well as with the survival of the Hanoverian monarchy, in the popular mind in the eighteenth century. George II was not amused by this print – 'Does the mean fellow mean to laugh at my guards?' – so it was dedicated to Frederick II.

guards officer's mantelpiece can still be an impressive sight. The proximity of Annabel's to St James's is not ignored; a weekend in Hong Kong is not unthinkable; the Guards Polo Club and, in particular, the Household Division Saddle Club (used by the royal family as well as by guards officers and their richer friends) can occupy much of the week in addition to the weekend. Officers of what is known as 'HM the Queen's Guard', the detachment of a highland regiment which is on duty at Balmoral when the Queen is in residence in the summer, can go out every evening: 'Aberdeenshire is very, very exhausting from that point of view,' according to one of them.[9]

Drinking was not only an indispensable part of social life but also an important occupation in itself, enjoyed by soldiers as well as officers of royal guards. In the words of Euripides, 'Dionysus has some share in the work of Ares,' and Oswyn Murray has noted 'the connections between drinking ritual and style of warfare' – or regimental pride. It has already been pointed out how much guards drank before making interventions in politics in Russia in 1741 and 1801, in Sweden in 1756, in Denmark in 1771, in France in 1789. Would they have been so bold if they had been less liquid?

The old royal palace of Stockholm was burnt down in 1697 because of a fire which started in a guards' tavern in the attics. In England, during and after the restoration, guards were frequently, and sometimes murderously, drunk. In 1726 troopers of the Life Guards were drunk 'while actually attending His Royal Highness'. In the eighteenth and nineteenth centuries drunkenness was common both on and off the battlefield. Alvanley was said to have more claret than blood in his veins. Shaw, 'the slashing Lifeguardsman', one of the strongest men in England, was probably drunk when he cut French soldiers to pieces at Waterloo. Drink is still an important part of the lives of the soldiers, though probably less crucial for the officers of the guards. The *Guards Magazine* contains frequent references to 'fairly liquid' meals.[10]

Other guards were also famous for their consumption of alcohol. In the Gardes Françaises in the eighteenth century the *cabaret* was the normal place of recreation and debts caused by drink a common reason for desertion; 188 Gardes Françaises were expelled for drunkenness between 1766 and 1789. When the French entertained the Russian Guard to dinner at Tilsit in 1807, three-quarters of both guards were drunk. The great musician Mussorgsky became dependent on alcohol when enjoying social life in the Preobrazhensky Guards in the 1850s. Count Gleichen, an officer of the Grenadier Guards, received 'lavish hospitality, particularly in the way of drink', when he visited the Russian Garde à Cheval and the Prussian Kaiser Alexander Garde Grenadiers in the 1880s. Heavy drinking, a problem with the entire Russian army, seems to have been particularly acute among guards officers in the reign of Nicholas II. In the Horse Grenadiers 'a lieutenant celebrating his twenty-first birthday, murdered a soldier left temporarily in charge of the officers' mess because the soldier refused to give him a bottle of champagne on credit'. A Chevalier Garde had to be capable of downing ten goblets of champagne in the mess. Officers 'routinely drank to excess in restaurants' and, to the horror of the Tsarina, at the front.[11]

Even in Middle Eastern guards there has been a fondness for alcohol. The pleasures of the Persian Cossack brigade were 'Drinking, gambling, whoring, and listening to music and entertainers'. Joseph Nasi, a Müteferrika, owed his influence over Sultan Selim 'the Sot', in the late sixteenth century, partly to his ability to supply him with wine. In Constantinople the Janissaries were notorious by the seventeenth century for their fondness for wine and taverns, a fondness continued in the Imperial Guard after 1826.

But their main peculiarity was the Janissaries' elevation of cooking and eating into signs of military hierarchy and political power. Officers' ranks all had names connected with cooking: the commander of the Janissaries was known as the Head Soup-Distributor. Janissaries' meals were used as an occasion to display the power of the Empire to foreign ambassadors. Until 1826, on entering the second courtyard of the palace on their way to present their credentials, foreign emissaires observed that 'the janizarries all uttered a loud shout and began running as quick as they could . . . for their pilaw' (a similar ceremony was held in the courtyard of the palace in Dresden for Augustus II's Janissaries). If, on their Friday pay day, they overturned the cooking pot and their pilaw it was a sign of discontent or rebellion. Until the end of the Ottoman Empire the succulence of the guard's pilaw was legendary.[12]

Love was also one of the main occupations of royal guards. Uniforms are a well-known aphrodisiac; capital cities, as military authorities have often noted with alarm, are skilled in

63.   *The Mess of His Majesty's Guard Cossacks.* 1912. PHOTO MUSÉE DES COSSAQUES DE LA GARDE.

The picture of Nicholas II in Guards Cossack uniform in the corner, like the toast to Queen Victoria in illustration 62, shows how much monarchs dominated the regimental social life of their guards. This photograph comes from one of the albums removed, with the contents of the regimental museum of His Majesty's Guards Cossacks, from Petrograd in 1917, and now in Paris.

satisfying the pleasures of the flesh. Royal guards were therefore likely to enjoy many adventures, particularly since so many of them, either because of their youth or because of the vows of celibacy which some units demanded (the Pope's Swiss Guard still does), were unmarried.

From the seventeenth century the royal guards of France were such well-known sex symbols that this role was celebrated in popular songs, such as:

> Dans les gardes françaises
> J'avais un amoureux,
> Ardent, chaud comme braises
> Vaillant et vigoureux

of 1760, or:

> Aimables Mousquetaires
> Favoris des amours . . .
> A la requête des maris
> On vous exile de Paris

of 1775.

Most officers and soldiers of the guards had what a police report called *leurs établissements* with women of Paris or Versailles, whom they would force to contribute to the expenses of military life. In 1716 a petition of the inhabitants of Saint-Denis complained not only about the Gardes Suisses' tax exemptions but also that they were 'all tall well-made men who use their looks and their figure to please the girls of their district'. Seventy years later a similar petition from Amiens denounced the damage caused by the Gardes du Corps among 'the sex'. In the 1770s one in twelve soldiers in the Gardes Françaises was treated for venereal disease. In the same decade de Lestorière, an officer in the Gardes Françaises and 'the handsomest man in Paris' was a byword for the number of hearts he had broken and balls he had attended. Poor officers in the Gardes Françaises found it easy to marry Parisian heiresses. The ferocity of Parisians' treatment of the Gardes-Suisses in August 1792 may have been due to husbands' jealous rage, or female fury at having been spurned.[13]

The soldiers and officers of the guards of the Bonapartes, and particularly the Bourbons, continued this tradition in the nineteenth century, as many songs and prints, such as 'La Grisette Abandonnée' (1828) testify. 'Drinking, gambling, women, I enjoyed everything,' remembered a Vélite of the Garde Impériale. Lieutenant Chevalier of the Garde Impériale was full of praise for the *bonnes et fraiches Allemandes* and the *aimables et très aimantes Hollandaises*, whom he met while on campaign.[14]

In England, guards were also able to enjoy what Boswell called 'romantic adventures'. Churchill, the future Duke of Marlborough, was able to make his first step to financial fortune – the purchase of an annuity of £500 p.a. for £4500 on 30 April 1674 – by pleasing the Countess of Castlemaine, the King's mistress, when he was a penniless young officer in the First Guards. In *Mars Stript of His Armour or the Army described in all its true Colours* (1709) an admittedly prejudiced pamphleteer asserts that captaincies in the guards were obtained 'by giving some bodily consolation to an ancient lady'.

In the nineteenth century Cornet Tim Heald of the Life Guards married Lola Montez, the legendary adventuress who had been the cause of the abdication of Ludwig I of Bavaria, in 1849 (he then had to resign his commission). The Prince of Wales received his sexual initiation when serving with the Grenadier Guards at the Curragh Camp in 1861. George Cornwallis-West of the Scots Guards, who found 'the life of a young officer in the Foot Guards . . . very pleasant. Soldiering was not taken too seriously,' married Lady Randolph

Churchill in 1900 and Mrs Patrick Campbell in 1914. An account of a guardsman's life in the 1930s (basically drill, drink and sex) states as a well-known fact that 'the girls'll chase you all over London'. In two works, 'The Guardsman and Cupid's Daughter', a poem by Villiers David (1930) and *A Guardsman's Cup of Tea*, a play by Thomas Browne (1955), the guardsman is treated primarily as a sexual symbol, as he is in Molnar's play, *The Guardsman*, which revolves around a husband's decision to dress up as a Russian guardsman in order to win back the love of his wife: 'It's a Guardsman she wants. She wants a Guardsman. I know it! I know it!'[15]

Members of other royal guards enjoyed similar success. In Madrid, in the late eighteenth century, 'the cadets of the guards are generally employed in this agreeable office [that of lover of a married woman]. They are generally necessitous and are supplied by the fair with the means for their extravagance' – a reputation which they maintained until their abolition in 1841. Russian guards officers thought themselves irresistible, even to Polish women, and devoted much time and energy to amorous conquest. At court balls in the 1890s, for example, guards officers 'would criticize every joint of a woman as if she was a horse'. In Stockholm in the 1870s girls would pay ten thalers to be able to 'stroll' with a guard on Sunday afternoon. But they would pay twenty thalers in order to 'stroll' with Norwegian Guards, who were thought even more attractive than their Swedish comrades.[16]

Guards enjoyed a similar success among homosexuals, one which was even more closely connected with money. Since royal guards brought large numbers of young men, partly chosen for their appearance, to capital cities, and since, in the United Kingdom until the late 1970s, they were relatively badly paid, this was not surprising. Their involvement with homosexuality was well established by the eighteenth century. In 1810 two Foot Guards were hanged for sodomy. In the nineteenth and early twentieth centuries repeated scandals connected guards with bishops, MPs and writers. As at court balls in Berlin, Horse Guards appear to have been more popular, and expensive than Foot Guards.[17]

The Garde Royale in France, during the restoration, served a similar function. Among its most enthusiastic patrons were the ex-Director Barras, seen going home at 11 p.m. with a corporal of the Garde Royale in 1820, and the Marquis de Custine, beaten up by four soldiers of the Garde Royale in 1824. In Prussia, under Frederick the Great, although many guards used the military orphanage in Potsdam as a source of mistresses and a dump for children, others seem to have had other inclinations: a French observer wrote that 'insult and rape are frequent, and those who do not have their Master's taste are *peu fêtés*'. In 1908 two officers of the Garde du Corps, Counts von Hohenau and von Lynar, had to resign as a result of the Eulenburg scandal.[18]

Social, sexual and alcoholic pleasures were not, however, the only occupations of guards off duty. Since royal guards brought young and often well-educated members of the elite to capital cities, which were often great cultural centres, many of their occupations were likely to be cultural. The clearest case of a royal guard having a definite cultural influence occurred after the foundation of the Hungarian Noble Guard in 1760. By 1772 George Bessenyei 'was the head of a brilliant literary clique in Maria Theresa's noble Hungarian Guard which was usually stationed in Vienna'. Although he wrote in Magyar, he represented the 'French or cosmopolitan school, whose source of inspiration was usually Voltaire'. Other Hungarian Noble Guards who became famous writers were Abraham Barcsay, Alexander Baroczy, and Alexander Kisfahidy. It is unlikely that they would have been such cosmopolitan writers if they had not been able to serve in the Hungarian Noble Guard in Vienna.

In Russia, in the words of Mark Raeff,

Serving in the guards, the young provincial found himself close to the Court and provided he had acquired the proper forms of dress and manners, he could participate in the social and cultural life of Saint Petersburg (and, on occasions, Moscow). No wonder that many an uncouth provincial youth discovered himself and his hidden talent for art, literature or philosophy while serving in the Guards.

Derzhavin, the greatest lyric poet of the eighteenth century, began writing love-letters for fellow-officers, as well as poems, when serving in the Preobrazhensky Guards from 1762 to 1777. Novikov, an important publisher, and Davydov, a poet who celebrated the joys of drinking with his 'bottle comrades', also served in the guards in the late eighteenth century.[19]

Pushkin's father and uncle acquired 'literary acquaintances' when serving in the guards. Pushkin himself knew Peter Chander of the Hussar Guards, author of *Philosophic Letters*, and Katenin, a playwright in the Preobrazhensky Guards. Lermontov and Pushkin learnt many of the poems and legends of the Caucasus, which they used to such effect in their writings, from a former Mullah serving in the Tsar's Escort. Later, however, it became a boast of Russian guards officers that all they read were the newspaper and the stud-book.

In *ancien régime* France, their service in the guard seems to have had little effect on writers such as Beaumarchais, Maine de Biran, Dorat or Destutt de Tracy. During the restoration, however, some writers did derive inspiration from their service in the guard. De Vigny first began to write when serving as a sub-lieutenant in the Garde Royale (he had refused the opportunity to be a lieutenant in the line). His *Servitude et Grandeur Militaires* (1835) is largely about the Garde Royale, and is full of praise for its obsession with honour and for the guards' 'habit of devoting themselves body and soul to their duty'. His first play, *Othello*, was produced through the influence of a former comrade in the Garde Royale, an important early patron of the Romantics who retained the manners and bearing of a guards officer of the restoration until the end of his life, Baron Taylor. Baron Taylor's *Voyages Pittoresques et Romantiques de l'Ancienne France* (24 vols., 1820–64), dedicated to a commander of the Garde Royale, the Marquis de Lauriston, was immensely influential in popularizing Romantics' interest in the countryside and the past. He also wrote an account of Spain inspired by his presence there with the guard in the war of 1823. His service in the Gardes du Corps inspired some fine prose by Lamartine in his different books of memoirs.[20]

In England the Household Division has produced some good writers in a robust, masculine but often extremely elaborate style. Colonel Fred Burnaby of the Blues helped to found the magazine *Vanity Fair* in 1868 and wrote, among other works, *A Ride to Khiva* (1873) before dying in the Sudan in 1885. Of Osbert and Sacheverell Sitwell, who served in the Grenadier Guards for seven and three years respectively before 1919, Anthony Powell writes, 'The Brigade of Guards ambience, not at all conspicuous in either of them, was always there.'[21] It is certainly present in their many unrivalled descriptions of monarchs, palaces and guards uniforms.

If there is one quality which seems common, at least to those guards whose lives have been written about, it is energy. Burnaby, while fighting in the Sudan, was learning Arabic and planning to set off to Khiva. Seymour Vandeleur, an officer in the Scots Guards, had so much energy that he went off to serve in Uganda, Nigeria and the Egyptian army, before dying in the Boer War, 'an instance of the toll exacted by the Empire'. Indeed, one of the attractions of service in the Guards was the ease with which an officer could obtain appointments 'in any part of the Empire', according to the commanding officer of the Coldstream Guards in 1921.

Such energy was not particular to the British Empire at its apogee. Another sign of it was that, in addition to being used by governments to try out new tactics or weapons, guards were often themselves interested in reforms and improvements. In France the Gardes Françaises was the first regiment to be uniformed, and the first to have a band and a school for soldiers' children in the 1760s. In England in 1773 the Blues were the first regiment to have a riding school; in the early nineteenth century the Foot Guards were the first units to have hospitals, libraries and football teams. In Russian in 1855 the commander of the Corps of Guards and Grenadiers, Count von Rüdiger, was very critical of the quality of officers and generals in the army, and wrote to the Tsar to suggest the creation of regimental libraries and schools.[22]

The opportunities for pleasure, and initiative, provided by service in a royal guard meant that life in the guards could be very enjoyable. Many guards have recorded their fierce joy when they joined their regiment. The Duc de Lauzun loved his position as a captain of the guard of Louis XIV so much that he spent his last forty years, after he had fallen from favour for marrying La Grande Mademoiselle, trying to recover it. The Comte de Saint-Priest, a future ambassador and minister, found that his three months' guard duty passed 'the most agreeably in the world for me. The King noticed me a lot.'[23] Even in the ephemeral and dangerous Garde Constitutionelle of Louis XVI, in 1792, the Comte de Villeneuve-Bargement wrote that, because they were bound to be 'advantageously treated', it was 'the happiest time of my life'. In 1854 an officer in the Scots Guards was 'thrilled to be off to the war, and such a position! Lieutenant-Colonel in the Guards! There is not a more enviable one in Society!'

In 1915 Harold Macmillan of the Grenadier Guards, like many other officers and soldiers before and since, 'began to take genuine pleasure in the high standards of discipline, in contrast to the rather sloppy way in which I had lived in school and university'. All his life he has been grateful for the breadth of view and the sense 'that if a thing is done at all it ought to be well done' which he learnt in the guards. For Osbert Sitwell, who had hated his line regiment, his time in the Grenadier Guards was 'the first period of my life that I enjoyed with a full sweep'. The future Edward VIII noticed a similar energy in the pursuit of pleasure in G. Trotter, a guards officer, who taught him that 'life should be lived to the full'. Von Papen, the future Chancellor of the Weimar Republic, remembered his years in the Guard Uhlans at Potsdam as 'probably the happiest of my life'. If there were soldiers and officers of the guards who did not enjoy their service, they did not write their memoirs.[24] It was indeed natural for guards to enjoy their service since it combined so many pleasures and advantages: proximity to royalty, life in a capital and, before the twentieth century in the French, British, Danish, Ottoman, Prussian, Austrian and Russian royal guards, quicker promotion than officers of the line.[25]

The main drawback to the pride and pleasure so many guards took in their position is that it often induced a sense of superiority and self-importance. In Russia the Garde à Cheval thought they were 'superior beings, demi-gods'. Many guards officers would not even talk to officers of the line. 'What is superior in the world to a lieutenant in the Hussars of the Guards? Nothing . . . The regiment is the only important thing on earth,' – more important, as has already been pointed out, than the monarchy itself. In Sweden the Svea Livgarde was known, for its attitude of superiority and exclusiveness, as 'God's own regiment'. In Denmark in the eighteenth century the officers of the Life Guards, who were 'not very military', spoke 'with a tone of shocking self-importance'.[26]

In Prussia the First Foot Guard Regiment was 'usually charged with being rather conceited', according to the Kaiser's sister-in-law; it called itself 'the first regiment in Christendom'. A description of a Prussian guards officer called Georg von Rudolstadt by a former officer in the Russian Guard, in 1865, is particularly repellent: he was 'a big fool of a fellow, the typical Potsdam guardsman, with a red face, silly, conceited and affected, with waved hair, spurs larger than his feet, filled with pity for all the poor devils who do not serve in the Prussian Guard, yet imagine themselves to be soldiers'.

In France the arrogance of the guard was always much resented, particularly when, as in 1814–15, it was not combined with a distinguished military record. When a company of Gardes du Corps was stationed in Amiens from 1758 to 1788 its demands and behaviour caused endless trouble, leading to the dismissal of the Mayor. In Spain, some officers of the Gardes Wallonnes, which had existed for only thirteen years, wrote in 1716 that any change in the number of battalions in the regiment would have 'fatal consequences for Spain and the monarchy' and, when it took place, resigned. It is doubtful if such self-importance and disobedience (and a similar ability to do without pay) would have been possible in a line regiment.[27]

In England the guards often tried to draw a line between themselves and the rest of the army. In 1745 they had to be formally requested not to laugh at the militia. Gillray's cartoon, 'A March to the Bank' (1787), represents the guards marching though the city to the Bank of England as the epitome of thoughtless arrogance. Even today the belief 'we quite simply are the best in everything', similar to the belief of the commander of the present Guardia Real of Spain, that it 'combines the best of the natures and qualities that I have met throughout my military life', is common. What a recent historian has called the Household Division's 'tendency to self-satisfaction' is familiar to anyone who has talked to its officers and soldiers.[28]

Self-importance has been another characteristic of many royal guards and, indeed, often a cause of their interventions in politics. Many guards have believed that their existence and their privileges were crucial to the fate of the monarchy and so have not hesitated to get rid of monarchs who did not appreciate this. Many guards have put their regiments or their careers before everything else and so have deserted the monarchs they were meant to be guarding with astonishing promptness.

What has made these privileged and sometimes conceited regiments tolerable is their performance on the battlefield. Indeed, they were usually intended to be an example to the army of which they formed a part.[29] In the overwhelming majority of wars guards have justified themselves magnificently and, in the words of the Duke of Windsor, purchased their prestige in blood. For example, the performance of the Household Cavalry in the Sudan in 1882 was, in the opinion of its commander, Sir Garnet Wolseley, so impressive that they owed to it 'the continuance of their existence'. He also found the Foot Guards 'the best troops I have'. The Prussian Guard made the deepest inroads in the Allied lines in the great German offensive of spring 1918.[30]

But their record has not been as consistently impressive as some nationalistic and regimental historians pretend, and this was sometimes, as the reformers of the eighteenth century pointed out, related to their status as guards. The Gardes Françaises had become too soft and too Parisian to perform well in the wars of the eighteenth century. The Garde Impériale, although usually superb, and the only force to retain a semblance of discipline during the retreat from Moscow, was also so much a law to itself that it was the worst looter in the Grande Armée, in January 1813 looting the funds of the army itself.[31] The disastrous charge of the Prussian Guard at Saint Privat in 1870 was, in part, caused by a desire to prove itself, to pluck the laurels before other units. The Russian Guard was ill-trained for war in 1914 partly because its manoeuvres were shams, arranged to look splendid and impress the Tsar, rather than a serious preparation for battle. The separate organization and relative softness of the Iranian Imperial Guard caused it many problems during operations in Oman in the 1970s.[32]

9
SPLENDOUR

GUARDS HAVE SO far been described in an institutional, social or political context: as expressions of a monarchy's attitude to its subjects, and as a means to protect a monarch and maintain his authority. But they also had a visual and ceremonial role, as royal officials often proclaimed. For example, in 1572 one of the motives for the creation of a new guard in Brandenburg was officially proclaimed to be the desire 'to increase the splendour of the court'. In 1627 an ordinance of Charles I, whose words were repeated in 1688, declared that the existence of the Yeomen of the Guard 'importeth not only the safety of our Person, but the Honour of our Court', and insisted that only individuals 'of tall personage, strong, active and of manly presence' be enrolled. In 1771 a French official engaged in forming a guard for the younger grandson of Louis XV, wrote: 'The first object of the institution of the guards of kings is the safety of their persons, the second is to characterize the respect and honour due to them.'[1] In some cases, for example, the Peiks of the Ottoman Empire, the Gentlemen-at-Arms since the late seventeenth century, the Escorte Royale of Belgium and the guards regiments of the Netherlands today, the ceremonial function of guards has almost entirely superseded their security role.

Another sign of royal guards' role as providers of splendour or prestige, as well as of security, is the award of small units of guards to monarchs' relatives. This was intended either, in the case of the grandsons of the King of France, or the cousins or Viceroys of the Holy Roman Emperor, to add to their dignity or, in the case of Prince Henry of Prussia in 1762 and (in direct imitation) his nephew Prince Charles of Sweden in 1790, as a reward from their brothers for their performance in war.[2]

That splendour was a reason for, and criterion of, royal guards is confirmed by, for example, the sequence of words in the *London Post*'s observation on the Life Guards in 1698, that 'The new uniforms are extraordinarily grand and the Life Guards are generally thought to be the finest body of Horse in Europe,' or Sir Robert Wilson's criticism of the Garde Impériale in 1807, whose soldiers, 'whatever their military merits make but a very indifferent appearance', compared to the Russian Imperial Guard. From these comments, and those of Louis XVIII and de Bussy on the Garde Royale of the restoration (see page 46), it is clear that a guard's appearance could be thought to be at least as important as its military prowess. It is perhaps unnecessary to point out that guards' splendour was masculine in nature. There was no equivalent, in the royal guards of Europe and the Middle East, to the Amazon guards of fourth-century China, Mauryan India, or nineteenth-century Dahomey (except for the *cantinières* of the Garde Impériale of the Second Empire, who wore a version of uniform).

The reason for such an obsession with appearances and splendour was the almost universal belief that splendour was a necessity for a monarchy. Since monarchy is a system which relies on its appeal to emotions rather than to reason, it is likely to want to appeal to such a popular and widespread emotion as love of display. On 30 December 1812, Napoleon I put forward as one reason for having a new guard, 'the splendour and majesty which should surround the sovereigns'. Even Madame de Staël admitted that *éclat* was 'a

64.   Levni. *Ahmed III Surrounded by His Court.* C. 1720. TOPKAPI SARAY MÜZESI.

As this picture shows, the Solaks, with their extraordinary fan-shaped plumes, and the Peiks in crested gilded helmets, were the most splendid of the Sultan's attendants. They helped to make his weekly procession to a mosque 'one of the finest sights in Europe', in the words of an eighteenth-century traveller.

necessary attribute of royalty'. Splendour made a monarch's task easier since it raised his prestige with his subjects and could dazzle them into obedience. It also impressed foreigners. It was not only their belief in aristocrats' particular reliability, but also their desire for the splendour of ancient aristocratic names, which made monarchs want aristocrats in their guards.[3]

Many other institutions, such as a court, and palaces, as well as a guard, could contribute to the splendour around a monarch. Footmen's livery, and some line regiments' uniforms, could be as magnificent as guards' uniforms. But, in contrast to the often half-despised court, a guard had the prestige of a definite military function, while line regiments usually lacked an intimate royal connection. For most people, no footmen or soldiers of the line could compete with the magic of a perfectly drilled guard, flowing like a river through the streets of a capital or the courtyards of a palace.

The most visible form of guards' splendour was their uniforms. At first uniforms had been a novelty. The first royal guards wore the livery of their monarchs or, in the case of the Pope's guard, the brightest colours available (the uniform of the Swiss Guards is not based on the Medici livery). Thus the entry of the King of France into French and Italian cities in the fifteenth century was made particularly splendid by the *très riche array et estat* of the King's guard, in his livery of red, white and green, covered in gold embroidery and crowns. Often their costumes were decorated with silver spangles, as were those of the Yeomen of the Guard. Their costume was so important that guards were often given, or expected to buy, splendid new uniforms for a royal birthday or funeral, or the entrance of an ambassador.[4] The Ottoman Sultan's guard, from the sixteenth century, was also particularly splendid. The Solaks had 'costumes of extreme cleanliness, of yellow, red and green satin, with large aigrettes'; the Peiks had brocade 'costumes of different colours, axes, quivers and arrows, and bonnets of silver gilt decorated with aigrettes of heron plumes' (see illustration 64).

The guards regiments founded after 1563, larger and less closely connected to the court than the guards already in existence, did not wear, at first, uniform or livery. When the Brandenburg guard began to wear blue uniforms in 1615 they were known as the *blauröcke* or blue coats, because they were such an unusual sight. The Gardes Françaises began to wear uniform only in the 1660s, when the King began to pay for it. Thereafter, in many cases a guard's uniform was so striking, and such an important aspect of its existence, that the colours of its uniform replaced a guard's formal title as its most commonly used name. Hence Maison *Rouge* for the Gendarmes, Chevau-Légers and Mousquetaires de la Garde of the King of France, the *Blues* for the Royal Regiment of Horse Guards of England, the Guardia *Amarilla* of the Habsburg Kings of Spain, the *Blue* Guards of William III and the *Blue* and *Red* Cossacks of the Guard of the Tsars. Less respectfully the English Foot Guards were sometimes called lobsters, the Gardes Françaises blue bottoms, and the Gardes Suisses beetroots.[5]

It is not possible to describe all the varieties of guards uniforms; indeed, words alone are too weak for the task. To choose only some of the most spectacular, however, at the coronation of the first King in Prussia in 1701,

> the hundred Swiss created no small sensation with their officers in brand new uniforms which, like those at the French coronations, were in the old Frankish mode in white satin and silver braidings with split doublets, knee breeches and short cloaks covered with gold and silver lace, pointed silk hats with roses, shoes with buckles, pearl-coloured silk stockings and round Swiss ruffs.

The gold embroidery on the uniform of the Drabants of Charles XII weighed four kilos; their chests were entirely covered in it. The Chevalier-Gardes were, in the opinion of Archdeacon Coxe in 1777, 'a corps perhaps more sumptuously attired than any in Europe...

chains and broad plates of solid silver were braided over their uniforms'. Until the end of the Empire they wore scarlet breast-pieces, high patent-leather boots, elkskin breeches, and double-headed eagle helmets when on duty outside the Tsar's apartments: Marshal Mannerheim remembered that the elkskin breeches were put on 'wet over one's bare skin' so that they should show no creases.[6]

Perhaps the most sumptuous of all guards' uniforms, however, was that of the Hungarian Noble Guard (see illustration VI). 'The most brilliant thing here is the noble Hungarian Guard, a body not numerous of handsome tall men on fine fiery steeds magnificently caparisoned' wrote an American in 1797; the leopard skins hanging from their backs, 'apparently in the very shape in which they came from the animal', and the guards' yellow morocco boots were particularly admired by Mrs Trollope in 1837. The dress of their captain was particularly breathtaking and thought to be worth a million pounds. He wore scarlet cloth embroidered from head to foot in 'four hundred and seventy large pearls and many thousand of inferior size . . . a collar of large diamonds, a very large solitaire in a ring, another on the head of his cane, a plume of diamonds, the hilt and scabbard of his sword set with diamonds, and even on his spurs'. Only someone who had seen the Hungarian Noble Guard, remembered Prince Clary, the last surviving chamberlain of the Emperors of Austria, 'can even begin to picture the splendour of their uniform'.[7]

Clearly, in such a case the splendour of the uniform was almost the entire point of the guard's existence. Who would even think of attacking a monarch surrounded by such a splendid guard? This may indeed have been the main reason for the creation of such exotic units, with extremely expensive uniforms, as the Mamelukes and Tartares de la Garde of Napoleon I, and the Caucasian Escort of the Tsar, the richness and variety of whose uniforms, their arms 'richly decorated with silver and gold and even with precious stones', amazed foreign visitors.

During the nineteenth century there was, if anything, an increase in the splendour of guards' uniforms, one sign of which was a proliferation of breast-plates and helmets. In 1814 the Prussian Garde du Corps, and in 1821 the Household Cavalry, received breast-plates. The Foot Guards wore bearskins from 1830. The Swedish Horse Guards obtained more elaborate helmets in 1825 and 1845, the Arcieren of Austria silver helmets surmounted by a gilded double-headed eagle in 1849, the Hartschieren of Bavaria helmets crowned by a Wittelsbach lion in 1852. Perhaps the increase in the splendour of guards uniforms and head-gear was a royal reaction to the rising tide of democracy.[8]

Under William II the Prussian Guard had particularly elaborate uniforms. The Schloss-garde was given more elaborate and more consciously eighteenth-century uniforms in 1896 and 1909. The Gardes du Corps now had nine different uniforms: the Gala, Guard Gala, Guard, Society, Street, Dancing Gala, Service, Light Service and Court Garden Party uniforms (there is also a special garden-party uniform for the Oman Royal Guard today). At the end of the nineteenth century the Ottoman and Persian guards had uniforms embroidered in silver and gold. The head of the Albanian bodyguard of Prince Ferdinand of Bulgaria in the 1890s was 'so splendidly dressed and moustached' that, in the country, he was often mistaken for the prince himself.[9]

In the United Kingdom the uniforms of the Household Division are still, according to one of the tailors, made to 'exactly the same standards' as before 1914 (in contrast to line regiments, which have abandoned full dress since 1914), although it is proving increasingly difficult to provide doeskin gloves and yak-hair plumes. One of the reasons why service in it is so popular is still, as it always has been, the lure of the uniforms: 'scarlet and gold, not rough khaki like them blokes . . .' For splendid uniforms exist not only to improve a monarchy's image, but also to promote recruitment. They have always been popular with a certain type of soldier. In the memoirs of an officer of the Royal Guard of Louis Bonaparte, his many glorious uniforms, and the effect he had in them, are noted in loving detail. In the recruiting posters for the Garde Royale of France in 1815–16 the beauty of the uniforms is mentioned as prominently and frequently as the rates of pay.[10]

Many other countries maintain as high a standard in uniforms as the United Kingdom. The Carabinieri Guardie of Italy still have six different uniforms. The Guardia Real of Spain have an impressive variety of ceremonial uniforms. The Danish Life Guards, who normally wear blue, still wear special red uniforms for the Queen's Birthday, the presentation of ambassadors' credentials and New Year's Day. The only elements of sartorial splendour in the courts of the Arabian peninsula, where everyone, from the ruler down, wears the same national costume, are provided by the uniforms of the guard. For the guards are intended, in the words of the commander of the Kuwait Emiri Guard, to be 'as beautiful and as splendid as possible'. The uniforms are based on Western, usually British, models in Kuwait, the Emirates and Oman (which prides itself on being one of the smartest royal guards in the world). In Saudi Arabia, however, since the reign of King Abdul Aziz, the traditional Beduin guard has worn, over its national dress, 'full-length capes of red and blue damask embroidered in gold'.[11]

The outward splendour of royal guards was one of physique as well as of dress (in addition big men give more cover). Edward VI wanted 'tall men of personage' in his guard. The future Edward VII revealed a similar royal preoccupation with a guard's height and appearance when, at a review in 1899, he told the soldiers of the Scots Guards, 'You are a fine body of men and I am most impressed with your bearing and physique.' 'Bearing and physique' have always been important in the history of royal guards. The entry of the King of

65.   *The Schlossgarde at a Costume Ball.* 27 February 1897, from Leo von Pfannenberg. *Geschichte der Schlossgarde Kompagnie.*

The Kaiser, in the middle, repeatedly redesigned his guards' uniforms, usually in the direction of greater elaboration and antiquarianism.

France into Troyes in 1468 was impressive not only for the richness of his guards' apparel but also because they *faisoient bonne mine*, and were *haults et courageux et fermes*.

The English Yeomen of the Guard had a particularly vigorous tradition of 'bearing and physique'. In 1520 at the Field of the Cloth of Gold, and a later meeting in 1532, two Yeomen beat two French guards at wrestling; their strength was as much part of the splendour surrounding Henry VIII as were the number of his attendants and the richness of their costume. Elizabeth I's Yeomen were 'the tallest and stoutest men that can be found in all England'. Sir Walter Raleigh, when captain, was especially efficient at maintaining the supply. According to Aubrey, when a tall handsome young man had been sworn in, he was 'ordered to carry up the first dish at dinner, where the Queen beheld him with admiration as if a beautiful young giant had stalked in with the service'. In the eighteenth century, one of the Yeomen, Jack Broughton, a famous boxer and protégé of the Duke of Cumberland, had 'such an extraordinary development of muscle' that he posed to Rysbrack for a statue of Hercules.[12]

Royal guards were, and often still are, chosen for their height as well as their strength. Every royal guard by the eighteenth century had a height requirement: 1m 65cm in the Gardes Françaises from 1691 (the Gardes Suisses were taller); 1m 72 cm in the Danish Life Guards from 1765 to 1817, when it was raised to 1m 75 cm (still the requirement today); 1m 80cm in the British Life Guards from 1788 to 1939 (it is now 1m 75cm).[13]

At times, height and strength were more important in recruitment than social class or reliability. In 1692 a captain of the guard, the Maréchal de Luxembourg, complained to Louis XIV that, 'Only looks and size are considered, which means that men of unknown morals are taken who are not fit to be guards.' The best-known example of the pre-eminence of appearance is the giant guard of Frederick William I of Prussia. Recruited on the basis of physique, not class or race, it was the most international guard in history, composed of 'four thousand giants of all religions and countries' in the words of Count Algarotti. The King was obsessed with his guards. His agents scoured Europe for giants to be recruited, or kidnapped, into his guard. He admitted that 'he who sends them to me can lead where he will', and often received presents of giants from his fellow-monarchs. He knew many of them by name, was godfather to their children and, if they were very tall indeed, hung their portraits in his palaces. This regiment also had lavish uniforms and the first battalion of the First Foot Guards, 'composed of the tallest men in the army', continued its traditions until 1918. The entire regiment 'of magnificent material' had to be over 1m 78cm, the Kaiser Kompagnie over 1m 85cm.[14]

Wraxall called the Prussian Guard 'one of the most imposing sights to be seen anywhere in Europe, except perhaps at Saint Petersburg'. For, in the Russian Guard, size was also extremely important. Unfortunately, it has proved difficult to obtain precise information. But, in 1807, recruits, even if handsome, could be rejected for the guard if their chests were a centimetre too narrow. The Tsar's company in the Preobrazhensky Guards were giants. The Chevaliers-Gardes were 'sixty superb men', for whom their appearance was more important, provided they had powerful protectors, than their social origin. In 1836 the Circassians of the Escort and the Grenadiers of the Guard impressed an English traveller as 'the tallest men I think that I have ever seen ... muscular, broad-shouldered, and deep-chested'. In 1874 an English courtier was forced to tell Queen Victoria, always passionately interested in the appearance of other monarchs' guards, that the Old Guard soldiers were 'magnificent, far finer in height and physique than our Life Guards'. Russian guards continued to be of outstanding physique until the Revolution.[15] In the early nineteenth century, however, some travellers felt that the Swedish Guard was even more impressive and that its soldiers 'should rank among the finest men we have ever seen'.[16]

The splendour of royal guards was a splendour of features as well as of physique and

66. *Colonel the Hon. M. Gifford, Rhodesian Horse, and Captain Ames, Second Life Guards.* 1897. HOUSEHOLD CAVALRY MUSEUM.

Captain Ames was such an impressive sight that he was chosen to lead Queen Victoria's Diamond Jubilee procession. The height of their soldiers has been one way in which royal guards have tried to enhance the majesty surrounding a monarch.

uniform. The Yeomen of the Guard in 1515, according to the Venetian Ambassador, were 'all very handsome men and in excellent array . . . all as big as giants, so that the display was very grand'. To be 'of comely personage' was as important in the Yeomen of the Guard as stature and morals. Cardinal Wolsey's Gentleman Usher, on a visit to the French court in 1526, noticed, as had other observers, that the Gardes Ecossais were 'much comelier persons than all the rest'.[17]

In the nineteenth century, when mass conscription widened the field of choice, royal guards were particularly good-looking. The Prussian Guard was 'recruited among the most handsome men in the kingdom' (line regiments were recruited by region rather than by looks). The Austrian guards were outstanding for their looks, uniform and bearing. Ottoman Guards had been remarkable for their good looks since the sixteenth century. In 1832 an American visitor wrote that 'Among the officers may be found some very handsome men and particularly among those of the Sultan's guard . . . No officers or men of the army of any nation whatsoever dress with more taste or look better than the Sultan's guard.' Thirty years later another American described the Ottoman Guard as 'magnificently uniformed and composed of as handsome a collection of men as could be found anywhere'. Tourists who saw them at the Selamlik were overwhelmed.[18]

But again it was Russia which carried the principle of recruitment by looks further than any other guard. The guard had been outstanding for its looks since the reign of Catherine II. In 1813 Sir Neil Campbell thought them 'the finest-looking and best-dressed men I ever came across', an opinion confirmed by many other observers. By the mid-nineteenth century the principle of dividing up recruits for the different regiments according to type of good looks had been established. Just as the horses of the different guards regiments were of different colours (light bay for the Chevaliers-Gardes, black for the Gardes à Cheval, chestnut for the Dragoons of the Guard), so the soldiers of different guards regiments were of different types of looks: the Preobrazhensky regiment had fair hair, the Semenovsky dark hair and blue eyes, and the Pavlovsky regiment, named after the favourite palace of the snub-nosed Tsar Paul I (see illustration 39), had snub noses.[19] At the division of recruits every year in St Petersburg there would be a furious struggle between the different regiments to get the best-looking recruits and the right sort of faces and hair colour. In 1884 the future William II was deeply impressed by his guard of honour from the Semenovsky Guards: 'The men's faces were remarkably handsome since men are chosen for this regiment just because of their good looks.' That 'Beauty is everything and for a man it means as much as for a woman,' as General Krassnoff wrote, continued to be believed and practised in the Imperial Guard until the end.[20]

Royal guards also derived some of their splendour from movement, or immobility, as well as uniforms, physique and features. Drill was, and is, not only a means to exert discipline and enforce a spirit of obedience but also a way of enhancing the splendour surrounding the monarch's appearances. To see a guard move as one, 'with the regularity and unity of machinery', as one writer describes the Russian Imperial Guard at a May Day parade in the 1830s, was an extraordinarily impressive spectacle, as the Trooping of the Colour in London still is. At court balls during the Second Empire, or at the Selamlik of the Ottoman Sultans, the total immobility of the guards was no less impressive.[21]

Sound or silence was also employed to enhance the splendour of a guard. The Janissaries were probably the first armed force to have organized military bands; they also relied on their perfect discipline to surround the Sultan and his palace with that complete silence which amazed Western visitors. Janissary music was so impressive that it was adopted by many Western armies. At the King of Poland's camp in 1730, his Janissary Guard's 'quite African Musick awakened in the most Incurious all manner of Attention'.[22] The King of Prussia, who had been at this camp, also adopted Janissary music: in 1739 in his giant regiment, 'All the fifes are handsome negroes, very finely dressed with turbans ornamented with plumes of feathers and very elegant chains and earrings of solid silver.' The use of black musicians persisted in the Prussian Guard until 1918, when Staff Sergeant Elo Sambo from the Cameroon, who played the kettle-drums, left the Life Guards Hussars. Black musicians and 'Turkish music' were also used in the French and British guards from the late eighteenth until the mid-nineteenth century.

Royal guards, as machines for splendour, were among the first military units (by the 1760s) to have bands in France and England. The band of the first regiment of grenadiers of the Garde Impériale was the best in the army and often played at court balls during the First Empire. There was a peak of performance and competitiveness among guards bands in the 1850s and 1860s, when they were the leaders of military music in the world. At the 1867 Paris exhibition the band of the Prussian Cuirassier Guards was judged the best.[23]

Thus the full splendour of a guard can be conceived only if its musical accompaniment: drums, bells, fifes, trumpets – or total silence – is remembered. A visitor found the changing of the guard at the royal palace of Madrid in 1835 'altogether most magnificent', not only because of the soldiers' 'martial and inspiring' appearance, their immobility, and their 'noble war-horses with flowing manes', but also because of the drums, the trumpets, the band's 'enchanting strains'. Only in the Arabian peninsula, in Saudi Arabia and until 1962 in the Yemen, has another sense, in addition to sight and sound, been employed to increase the splendour of the guard: guards would precede the monarch with incense burners, 'whose smoke perfumed the air with a suffocatingly sweet odour'.[24]

The splendour of royal guards' appearance, movements and sound effects ensured that monarchs with a splendid royal guard could almost always rely on impressing their subjects and foreign observers. The Janissaries around the Sultan's tent in 1526 looked like fields of lilies and tulips, or 'like the halo around the pavilion of the moon'. A French scholar in 1672, seeing the Sultan leaving Adrianople surrounded by his court and his guards, wrote that it was 'the finest thing I have ever seen in my life, and I can hardly believe that in any court in Europe, except that of France, anything finer could be displayed . . . there is no language strong enough, nor order of words expressive enough, to convey it to the human mind'. Sir George Carew in 1609 described the splendour of the clothes and furnishings of the French: 'but their chiefest splendour is in the things appertaining to the King himself; as in the number of his guards and men of war which attend him (wherein he exceedeth all the other courts in Christendom), in the many pensions which he payeth', and in his palaces and treasure. For centuries the King of France's guards were the wonder of Europe, and the pride and joy of his subjects.[25]

The appearance and composition of the guards of the Electors of the Holy Roman Empire in 1657, and the appearance and music of the guards of the King of Denmark in 1692, were the most impressive aspects of their courts. Sir John Reresby, when he found the English guards sent away from London in early 1689, thought it 'a great alteration', since 'both for their persons and gallantry they were a great ornament to the place'. A visitor to the King of Sweden in 1692 found that 'in his Court . . . there is little regard had to Splendour and Magnificence either in Furniture, Tables or Attendants . . . that which makes the best Appearance is the Foot Guards'. A hundred years later, another visitor to Sweden, impressed by the Drabants, each in a 'superb casque of gilded brass, splendidly plumed and increasted with a lion', wrote: 'The effect of such a guard is regal and becoming a military monarch'.[26] A review of the guard at the Champ de Mars in St Petersburg was 'like a scene from a fairy tale'. Although 'there was not much uniformity of dress and colour' in the Moroccan Guard in 1879, its soldiers blended into 'one harmonious whole which was quite indescribable but upon which the eye never tired or grew wearied of gazing'. Another visitor was particularly impressed by the guards' bows to the ground and cries of '*Allah bark anar Sidna*' ('The blessing of God fill Our Lord'), when the Sultan appeared: 'The effect was really grand . . . The blended clamour of many thousand throats almost persuaded me that the object of so much devotion must be more than mortal. Anything more impressive it would not be easy to find.'[27]

Berlin in the reigns of William I and II was another pinnacle of guards' splendour. The sight of William II in the 'white tunic, dazzling breast-plate and silver helmet surmounted by a Prussian eagle' of the Garde du Corps left on many people 'an impression that has never failed'. Guards uniforms increased the splendour of the capital as well as of the monarch. 'In those days, the military show and splendour in Berlin were really wonderful . . . the streets were always full of officers very well dressed in military uniform and they certainly added greatly to the brightness of the capital,' in the words of a foreign diplomat (similar sentiments were expressed when the British Guards returned in 'full colour' to London after the Second World War). The 'culminating moment' of the day in Berlin was at noon when the soldiers on their way to relieve the old guard marched past the Emperor's palace with the band playing. In Vienna the changing of the guard at 1 p.m. was also enjoyed by large crowds and

67.   *Greetings from the Russian Imperial Guard to their Comrades in the Royal Horse Guards. Easter 1916.*
HOUSEHOLD CAVALRY MUSEUM.

As these illustrations of soldiers of the Cossack Guards, the Escort, the Chevaliers Gardes, and the Cuirassier Guards show, the Russian Imperial Guard maintained its traditions of splendour until the end.

by the Emperor himself.[28]

Thus the history of royal guards reveals not only the greater or lesser extent to which monarchies have relied on, or been manipulated by, military force, but also the importance of splendour as an instrument of government, or at least of propaganda. Indeed, the role of guards as machines of splendour was more extensive than their political role. Royal guards have brightened the palaces and enlivened the capital of every monarchy in Europe and the Middle East. But they have been politically important only in some.

That a splendid guard is an effective way for a government to win popularity is suggested by the fact that the erosion of monarchs' power has by no means led to the erosion of the splendour or popularity of their guards. Today the changing of the guard in London is one of the most popular sights in the world. Just as guards invariably add splendour to state occasions in London, so they invariably appear on posters intended to draw tourists to England. In Sweden, guards also continue to add splendour to state occasions, while 'the changing of the guard is the biggest tourist attraction in the capital' – greater than the royal palace itself. In Canada the changing of the guard ceremony, performed solely for the benefit of the public from June to August, is 'second only to the Niagara Falls in terms of Canadian tourist attractions'. In Rome, the Swiss Guard's uniform and, to a certain extent, its existence, is continued, according to its commander, 'to please the public'. These are solid, and profitable facts, not individual opinions.[29]

The appeal of splendid guards is so strong that they appear in the most unlikely capitals. Nowhere is the full range of guards' splendour – immaculate uniforms, impressive physique and bearing, perfect drill – practised with more dedication that at Lenin's Tomb in Red Square and in the courtyards of the Kremlin.[30]

CONCLUSION

THE HISTORY OF royal guards shows the political importance of the forces of privilege and splendour, and of personal feelings such as fear, loyalty (and disloyalty) and love of pleasure and self-advancement. Personal feelings such as fear and love of splendour made monarchs want to have guards. Love of the uniform, need for money or promotion, and loyalty to the monarch, made men want to join them. In, for example, Stockholm in 1772, Paris in 1789, St Petersburg in 1825 and 1905, and in many other capitals at turning-points in their history, guards' behaviour was determined by the state of their unit, their sense of honour or their relationship with the monarch. The more familiar and plausible explanations of social origin, economic trends or political movements are less convincing. The importance of guards' personal relationship with their monarchs explains why so many monarchs, from such a variety of dynasties, devoted so much time and attention to them.

Another lesson to be drawn from the history of royal guards is the inextricability of the history of the monarchies of Europe and, to a lesser extent, of the Middle East. Monarchs frequently modelled their guards on those of other monarchs, particularly on that of the King of France. The most famous guard of all, the Garde Impériale of Napoleon I, was imitated by opponents such as Alexander I of Russia and Louis XVIII, as well as by his brothers and his nephew Napoleon III. Even today the Garde Grenadiers of the Netherlands and the Escorte Royale of Belgium consider themselves the descendants of the Grenadiers de la Garde of Napoleon I, who also gave the Grenadier Guards of the United Kingdom their name. The Janissaries of the King of Poland, the Mamelukes of Napoleon I, the Caucasian Escort of the Tsars of Russia, the Algerian Guards of Napoleon III and the popularity of Janissary music in Europe in the eighteenth century show how strong was the influence of Middle Eastern guards on European guards. The development of modern royal guards in the Middle East shows the process in reverse.

Another way in which the history of royal guards reveals the openness of the different monarchies of Europe and the Middle East to each other's influence is the fact that royal guards often owed their political role, as well as their organization, composition, uniforms and music, to foreign influences and events. In England in 1688, Spain in 1808, Sweden in 1809, France in 1814–15, Russia in 1917 and Persia in 1906–11 and 1953, it was a foreign war, or ambassadorial intervention, which created the situation in which the guard could play a political role. From the point of view of the history of royal guards, ambassadors were just as often protagonists in the politics of the monarchy to which they were posted, as recorders of guards' appearance and activities.

But perhaps the chief lesson to be drawn from the history of royal guards is that neither in conflicts with the ruling class, nor when faced with revolution, have royal guards, with a few brave exceptions, been wholly reliable. From the point of view of the monarchs they were meant to defend, there is truth in the old saying that the love of the people is the best guard.

NOTES

N.B. There is a complete bibliography immediately following these notes in which works cited here under the authors' surnames can be looked up.

NOTES TO CHAPTER 1
THE RISE OF ROYAL GUARDS, to 1730

1. G. du Fresne de Beaucourt, *Histoire de Charles VII*, 6 vols., 1881–1891, IV, 192, *déposition* of Antoine de Chabannes, 27 September 1446.

2. No royal guard is mentioned in the household ordinances of the King of France of 1388 or 1422, or that of the King of England of 1478. See Bibliothèque Nationale (henceforward referred to as BN), Département des Manuscrits, Nouvelles Acquisitions Françaises (henceforward referred to as NAF) 9740. 437, 443; A.R. Myers, *The Household of Edward IV*, Manchester 1959.

3. Michael Mallett, *Mercenaries and Their Masters*, 1974, p. 110; Edgard Boutaric, *Les Institutions Militaires de la France avant les Armées Permanentes*, 1863, pp. 282-83; R.R. Davies 'Richard II and the Principality of Chester', in F.R. du Boulay and Caroline M. Barren eds. *The Reign of Richard II*, 1971, pp. 267–69.

4. Du Fresne de Beaucourt, op. cit. I, 430; William Forbes-Leith, *The Scots Men-at-Arms and Life-Guards in France*, 2 vols., Edinburgh 1882, II, 205; *ibid*, II, 1–83 reproduces financial accounts for this corps from 1429 to 1500.

5. Bernard Guénée et Françoise Lehoux, *Les Entrées Royales Françaises de 1328 à 1515*, 1968, p. 74; there are no guards in illustrations of the entry of Charles V into Paris in 1364.

6. Forbes-Leith, op. cit. I, 137, II, 73; cf. Yvonne Labande-Mailfert, *Charles VIII et son Milieu (1470–1498)*, 1975, p. 363.

7. Du Fresne de Beaucourt, op. cit. I, 431, IV, 180n; S.L. Lepippre de Noeufville, *Abrégé Chronologique et Historique de l'Origine, des Progrès, et de l'Etat Actuel de la Maison du Roi*, 3 vols., Liege 1734, I, 91.

8. Forbes-Leith, op. cit. I, 65, 68; Labande-Mailfert, op. cit. pp. 149, 307; Eugène Griselle, *Etat de la Maison du Roi Louis XIII*, 2 vols., 1912, II, 42, Règlement général fait par le Roy à Paris le premier jour de janvier 1585 de tous les Etats de sa maison.

9. Rodolphe de Castella de Delley, *Les Cent-Suisses de la Garde du Roi*, 1971, p. 11; François Besson, *Entretien et Examen sur la Création et Information de la Compagnie des Cent Gardes Suisses Ordinaires du Corps du Roi*, 1672, p. 5; Philippe Contamine, *Guerre, Etat et Société à la Fin du Moyen Age*, 1972, p. 294; A-J-G-M. Manca-Amat de Vallombrosa, *Histoire de la Prévôté de l'Hôtel – le-Roi*, 1907, pp. 6, 15, 125.

10. Contamine, op. cit. p. 295; Père Daniel, *Histoire de la Milice Française*, 2 vols., 1721, II, 98; Griselle, II, p. 42.

11. James Grant, *The Constable of France and Other Military Historiettes*, 1866, p. 261.

12. Charles Brusten, 'L'Armée Bourguignonne de 1465 à 1477', *Revue Internationale d'Histoire Militaire*, 1959, pp. 460–61; Oliver de la Marche, *Mémoires*, 4 vols., 1872–1876, IV, 70–76.

13. Ilio Jori, *La 'Casa Militare' alla Corte dei Savoia*, Roma 1928–Anno VI, pp. 7, 9; Henri Lepage, *Sur l'Organisation et les Institutions Militaires de la Lorraine*, 1884, pp. 147, 151.

14. Jakob und Wilhelm Grimm, *Deutsches Wörterbuch*, 15 vols., Leipzig 1854–1960, XI, Abb I, p. 942; O. Bezzel, *Geschichte des Bayerischen Heeres*, 8 vols., München 1901–1931, I, 149n; Leo von Pfannenberg, *Geschichte der Schlossgarde – Kompagnie Seiner Majestät des Kaisers und Königs 1829–1909*, Berlin 1909, pp. 10–12.

15. C.R. Beard 'The Clothing and Arming of the Yeomen of the Guard', *Archaeological Journal*, LXXXII, 1925, pp. 93, 102; James Douglas Alsop, *The Military Functions of Henry VII's Household*, unpublished M.A. thesis, London, Ontario 1974, pp. 5–11, 69.

16. Colonel Sir Reginald Hennell, *The History of the King's Body Guard of the Yeomen of the Guard*, 1904, pp. 60, 94, 59, 127.

17. Harvey Kearsley, *His Majesty's Bodyguard of the Honourable Corps of Gentlemen-at-Arms*, 1937, p. 71; John Glas Sandeman, *The Spears of Honour and the Gentlemen Pensioners*, Hayling Island, 1912, pp. 2–3, 7–10; 21–23; William Tighe, *An Introduction to the Gentlemen Pensioners*, talk given at the Institute of Historical Research, University of London, 23 February 1981.

18. Lieutenant-General F.H. Tyrrell, 'His Holiness the Pope's Military Household', *Journal of the Royal*

United Services Institution, XLVII, July–December 1912, p. 903; Gaston Castella, *La Garde Fidèle du Saint Père*, 1933, p. 102; Hennell, op. cit. p. 69.

19. Castella, op. cit. pp. 130, 149; Judith Hook, *The Sack of Rome*, 1972, pp. 159, 162.

20. (Conde de Clonard) *Memorias para la Historia de las Tropas de la Casa Real de Espana*, Madrid 1828, pp. 30–31, 41; Juan José Lopez, 'Estudio sobre los Monteros de Espinosa', *Guardia Real*, Ano IV, Num. 32, June 1982, p. 32.

21. Clonard, op. cit. p. 42, 71, 73–74; Frederico Navarro y Conrado Mortero, 'Noble Guardia de Arqueros de Corps', *Hidalguia*, 1953, p. 94 Ordonnance of 1545.

22. Clonard, op. cit. pp. 58–59, 61, 65; M. Gachard, *Relations des Ambassadeurs Vénitiens sur Charles Quint et sur Philippe II*, Bruxelles 1856, pp. 44, 256; D.M. Loades, *The Reign of Mary Tudor*, 1979, p. 137; Marquis de Villars, *Mémoires sur la Cour d'Espagne de 1679 à 1681*, 1893, p. 285; Luedin, op. cit. pp. 14–16.

23. Polydore Vergil, *Anglica Historia*, ed. Denys Hay, 1950, p. 7. Jean d'Anton 'Entrevue de Louis XII Roi de France et de Ferdinand Roi d'Aragon, de Naples et de Sicile en 1507', in Cimber et Danjou, *Archives Curieuses de l'Histoire de France*, Série I, tome 2, p. 48; Clonard, op. cit. pp. 58, 61.

24. Djevaad Bey, *Etat Militaire Ottoman*, Constantinople 1882, p. 33; Count Marsigli, *Etat Militaire de l'Empire Othoman*, 2 vols., The Hague 1732. I, 71; anon, *Le Miroir de l'Empire Othoman*, 2 vols., 1678, II 62, 68–69; Barnette Miller, *Beyond the Sublime Porte*, New Haven, 1931, pp. 179–80.

25. Abdulkader Dedeoglu, *Album of the Ottomans*, Istanbul 1982, p. 114; John Fuller, *Narrative of a Tour through Some Parts of the Turkish Empire*, 1829, p. 76; E. Habesci, *The Present State of the Ottoman Empire*, 1784, pp. 152, 220; *Le Miroir de l'Empire Othoman*, II, 11; M. de Mouradja-Ohsson, *Tableau Général de l'Empire Othoman*, 3 vols 1787–1820, III, 292; Arthur Howe Lybyer, *The Government of the Ottoman Empire in the time of Suleiman the Magnificent*, Cambridge 1913, p. 130.

26. Mehmet Zaki Pakalin, *Osmanli Tarih Deyimleri re Terimleri Sozlugu*, 3 vols., Istanbul 1946–56, II, 637; Lybyer, op. cit. p. 159; Ogier Ghislain de Bubescq, *Turkish Letters*, ed. Edward Seymour Foster, Oxford 1927, pp. 59, 61–62, letter of 1 September 1555, p. 150, letter of 1 June 1560; Richard Hellie, *Enserfment and Military Change in Muscovy*, Chicago and London 1971, p. 161; *Sbornik* (Proceedings of the Imperial Russian History Society), XXXIX, 53 Whitworth to Harley, 14/25 March 1705.

27. Jori, op. cit. pp. 11–13; Lepage, op. cit. p. 158; Gilles Veinstein ed. *Mehmet Efendi. Le Paradis des Infidèles*, 1981, p. 99; cf M.A. Shaban, *Islamic History. A New Interpretation*, 2 vols., Cambridge 1974–76, II, 63; C.E. Bosworth, *The Ghaznavids*, Edinburgh 1963, p. 111; Niccolo Giorgetti, *Le Armi Toscani e le Occupazioni Stranieri in Toscana*

(1537–1860), 4 vols., Città di Castello, 1916, I, 52–53.

28. C.E. Jany, *Geschichte der Königlich Preussischen Armee bis zum Ende Jahre 1807*, 5 vols., Berlin 1928–1937, I, 22; Bezzel, op. cit. I, 147–48; 153–56.

29. Noël Lacolle, *Histoire des Gardes Françaises*, 1901, pp. 10-29, 66; Pierre de Vaissière, *De Quelques Assassins*, 1912, pp. 143, 243, 259; Eugène Titeux, *La Maison Militaire du Roi*, 2 vols., 1890, II, 31–33; Jean Robert, 'Les Grande et Petite Ecuries d'Henri III de Navarre', *Bulletin de la Société des Amis du Château de Pau nouvelle série*, LXXXVIII, 1983, 3, pp. 24–27; Jori, op. cit. p. 21.

30. Michel Carmona, *Marie de Médicis*, 1981, p. 317, Henri IV to M. de Beaumont, 28 September 1605; Louis Battifol, *Le Roi Louis XIII à Vingt Ans*, 1923, p. 204.

31. Rodolphe de Castella de Delley, *Le Régiment des Gardes Suisses au Service de France*, Fribourg 1964, pp. 15–16; Titeux, op. cit. II, 34; Battifol, op. cit. pp. 213–14.

32. An. F⁷ 4280, 16 Mémoire sur la Garde de l'Empereur comparativement avec celle de la Garde du Roi, 1806, by L.A. d'Agoult, former Aide-Major-Général des Gardes du Corps; F. Bellanger, *Les Gardes du Corps sous les Anciennes Monarchies*, 1895, p. 25, Règlement de l'Ordre que le Roy veut être tenu par les Capitaines de ses Gardes, p. 31, règlement of 4 August 1623; Major des Gardes du Corps, 'Journal', *Carnets de la Sabretache*, III, 1895, p. 569.

33. Forbes-Leith, op. cit. I, 188–90; James Dunlop, *Papers Relating to the Royal Guard of Scottish Archers in France*, Edinburgh 1835, p. 11, Thomas Edwardes to the Earl of Salisbury, February 1611; BN. Manuscrits Français 21451. 206 Capitulation du Régiment des Gardes Ecossaises, 27 February 1642; Daniel, op. cit. II, 327–28.

34. Pfannenberg, op. cit. p. 17; Carl Herlitz, *Svenska Armens Regementen Regementetstraditioner*, Stockholm 1967, p. 23.

35. O. Schuster und F.A. Francke, *Geschichte der Sächsischen Armee*, 3 vols., Leipzig 1885, I, 45.

36. Lacolle, op. cit. p. 92n; Clonard, op. cit. pp. 85, 94, 100, 111; James Grant, op. cit. pp. 264–65; Michael Foster, 'Sir Troilus Turberville, Captain-Lieutenant of the King's Life Guard', *Royal Stuart Papers*, XVI, 1980, p. 16–17, 19, 22; Major General Sir F. Maurice, *The History of the Scots Guards*, 2 vols., 1934, I, 6, 12; Anthony Fletcher, *The Outbreak of the English Civil War*, 1981, p. 181; Peter Young, *Edgehill 1642: the Campaign and the Battle*, 1967, pp. 87, 90, 192, 225.

37. Pfannenberg, op. cit. pp. 19–20; Crom-Andersen, op. cit. p. 8; Niccolà Brancaccio, *L'Esercito del Vecchio Piemonte*, Roma, 1922, p. 99; Domenico Guerrini, *La Brigata dei Granatieri di Sardegna*, Torino 1905, p. 30n; Jori, op. cit. p. 40.

38. Lieutenant General Sir F.W. Hamilton, *The Origin and History of the First or Grenadier Guards*, 3 vols., 1874–1877, I, 11, 19, 43; Captain Sir George Arthur Bt. *The Story of the Household Cavalry*, 3 vols.,

1909, I, 3, 22, 115–16; Brackenbury, op. cit. pp. 178, 123; Hennell, op. cit. pp. 170, 192; Samuel Pegge, *Curialia*, 5 parts 1791–1806, III, 59 Ordinance of Charles II, 1668.

39. Arthur, op. cit. I, 25, 28; Hamilton, op. cit. I, 43, 48, 74, 97, 110; Maurice, op. cit. I, 17; Captain S.J.L. Roberts 'Faithful Always and Everywhere', *The Guards Magazine*, Spring 1981, p. 177; R. Cannon, *Historical Records of the Life Guards*, second edition, 1840, p. 19.

40. Lois G. Schwoerer, *No Standing Armies!* 1974, pp. 78–83, gives an excellent explanation of the military settlement at the Restoration; Arthur, op. cit. I, 8, 121; Mademoiselle de Montpensier, *Mémoires*, 4 vols., 1857–9, III, 304, 316. I am grateful for this reference to Robert Oresko; Jean Robert, 'Les Gardes Françaises sous Louis XIV', *XVIIe Siècle*, LXVIII, 1965, p. 69; Daniel, op. cit. II, 207, 211, 217–19; Veinstein, p. 96.

41. BN Mss.Fr. 8006. 2 Ordonnance of 30 September 1664, 19vo. décision du Roi; André Corvisier, *L'Armée Française de la Fin du XVIIe Siècle au Ministère de Choiseul*, 2 vols., 1964, II, 777; Titeux, op. cit. II, 113; Daniel, op. cit. II, 113; Louis Hautecoeur, *Histoire des Châteaux du Louvre et des Tuileries*, 1927, p. 94.

42. F.J.G. Ten Raa, *Het Staatsche Leger 1568–1795*, 8 vols., 's Gravenhage 1911–59, V, 437n, VI, 190–94, 204, 230.

43. N. Brancaccio, *L'Esercito del Vecchio Piemonte*, 2 vols., 1922–3, I, 132; Arthur, op. cit. I, 25; Hamilton, op. cit. I, 289, III, 51; Lacolle, op. cit. p. 342.

44. John Childs, *The Army and the Glorious Revolution*, Manchester 1980, pp. 2–3; Earl of Ailesbury, *Memoirs*, 2 vols., 1890, I, 217; Arthur, op.cit. I, 293; Henri and Barbara van der Zee, *William and Mary*, 1973, p. 451; John Cornelius O'Callaghan, *History of the Irish Brigade in the Service of France*, Glasgow 1870, pp. 61–62, 75, 90.

45. Jori, op. cit. pp. 58, 67, 93; Albert Waddington, *Histoire de Prusse*, 2 vols., 1911–21, I, 368; Kurt Wolfgang von Schöning, *Das Regiment Garde du Corps*, Berlin 1854, pp. 1–2; Schuster, op.cit. I, 140–43, 194; May de Romainmotier VII, 492; *Enkyklopedja Staro polska*, Warsaw, 1939, I, 392–93.

46. Pfannenberg, op. cit. pp. 23–26; Zoltan Harsany, *La Cour de Léopold Duc de Lorraine et de Bar*, 1938, pp. 393, 399, 402–03, 414; Lepage, op. cit. pp. 169, 310; Giorgetti op.cit., II, 20; Luedin, op. cit. pp. 44–45.

47. Clonard, op. cit. pp. 122, 131, 136, 138; Colonel Guillaume, *Histoire des Gardes Wallonnes au Service d'Espagne*, 1858, pp. 20–24; Clonard, op. cit. pp. 167, 172, 176.

48. Clonard, op. cit. pp. 147, 150, 159; A. Morel-Fatio, *Etudes sur l'Espagne*, 3 vols., 1888–1904, II, 35; *Guillaume*, pp. 140, 222; Geoffrey Parker, *The Dutch Revolt*, 1977, pp. 258, 260; Joseph Ruwet, *Soldats des Régiments Nationaux au XVIIIe Siècle*, Bruxelles 1962, p. 24.

49. Duc de Saint-Simon, *Mémoires* ed. Cheruel et Regnier, 20 vols., 1873–1879, XVIII, 152; Clonard, op. cit. pp. 185–87; Michelangelo Schipa, *Il Regno di Napoli al Tempo di Carlo di Borbone*, Napoli 1904, pp. 378, 381, 389; May de Romainmotier, op. cit. VIII, 416–17; Henri Bedarida, *Parme dans la Politique Française au XVIIIe Siècle*, 1930, pp. 94–95.

50. Frans G. Bengtsson, *The Life of Charles XII*, 1960, pp. 18, 156; Ragnhild Hatton *Charles XII of Sweden*, 1966, pp. 101, 466; Tor Schreeber von Schreeb, *Carl XII's Drabantkär*, Stockholm 1942, passim.

51. Robert Massie, *Peter the Great: His Life and World*, 1981, p. 68; K. Waliszewski, *Pierre le Grand* 1905, pp. 550–51; J.S. Korb, *The Diary of an Austrian Secretary of Legation at the Court of Czar Peter the Great*, 2 vols., 1863, II, 102, 225, entries for 10 October 1698, 16 January 1700; Pierre le Grand, *Journal . . . depuis l'année 1698 jusqu'à la Conclusion de la Paix de Neustadt*, Berlin 1773, p. 65, entries for 16, 23 September 1699; Hellie, p. 202.

52. John Motley, *The History of the Life of Peter I, Emperor of Russia*, 3 vols., 1739, I 53-54; Peter Henry Bruce, *Memoirs*, 1732, pp. 351–52; Christopher Duffy, *Russia's Military Way to the West*, 1981, p. 43; Général de Manstein, *Mémoires Historiques, Politiques et Militaires sur la Russie*, 2 vols., Lyon 1772, I, 74.

53. Chevalier Chardin, *Voyage en Perse et Autres Lieux de l'Orient*, nouvelle édition, Amsterdam 1735, 4 vols., III, 316–18; M. Sanson, *Voyage ou Relation de l'Etat Présent du Royaume de Perse* 1695, pp. 102–03; Laurence Lockhart, 'The Persian Army in the Safavi Period', *Der Islam*, XXXIV, 1959, pp. 91–94.

54. Léon Godard, *Description et Histoire du Maroc*, 2 vols., 1860, I, 139, II, 515; anon. *La Garde Royale*, Rabat n.d.

NOTES TO CHAPTER 2
ROYAL GUARDS UNDER ATTACK, 1730–89

1. Korb, op. cit. II, 27, 13 July 1698; Lucien Mouillard, *Les Régiments sous Louis XV*, 1882. p. 106–07; Prince de Kaunitz, 'Mémoire sur la Cour de France', *Revue de Paris*, 11e Année, IV, August 1904, pp. 839, 843; Arthur, op. cit. I, 313; Maurice, op. cit. I, 98; Thomas Preston, *The Yeoman of the Guard, their History from 1485 to 1885*, 1885, p. 116; Hamilton, III, 379, 383, 390, 401; Guerrini, op. cit. p. 741, Etat de la Garde par Poste qu'on accoutume de faire à Turin, n.d.; Schipa, op. cit. p. 389; Rev. Edward Clarke, *Letters Concerning the Spanish Nation*, 1764, pp. 126–27.

2. Peggy Miller, *James*, 1971, pp. 72, 257; Hennell, op. cit. p. 299; Captain Mackinnon, *Origin and Services of the Coldstream Guard*, 2 vols., 1833, II, 339; Edward Gregg, *Queen Anne*, 1980, pp. 88, 102;

Archives Nationales (henceforward referred to as AN.) O¹ (papers of the Maison du Roi before 1792) 3673, 1 note of April 28, 1781; General Vansson, 'L'Infanterie Lorraine sous Louis XV', *Carnets de la Sabretache*, I, 1893, p. 270.

3. G.A.H. Guibert, *Journal d'un Voyage en Allemagne fait en 1773*, 2 vols., 1803, II, 8; Louis Battifol, *Autour de Richelieu*, pp. 54, 61–62, May de Romainmotier VII, op. cit. pp. 269, 271–72.

4. Albert Babeau, *La Vie Militaire sous l'Ancien Régime*, 2 vols., 1889, II, 301–07; Clarke, op. cit. pp. 211–14; Schipa, op. cit. pp. 378n, 381; Francis Ley, *Le Maréchal de Münnich et la Russie au XVIIIe Siècle*, 1959, p. 58.

5. Emile Léonard, *L'Armee et ses Problèmes au XVIIIe Siècle*, 1958, p. 45; J. Jaurgain et R. Ritter, *La Maison de Gramont*, 2 vols., Lourdes 1958, II, 401, Louis XV to Duc de Gramont, 422; Kaunitz, op. cit. p. 839.

6. Count Algarotti, *Letters . . . to Lord Hervey and the Marquis Maffei*, 2 vols., 1769, II, 27; anon (Comte de Guibert), *Observations sur la Constitution Militaire et Politique des Armées de sa Majesté Prussienne*, Berlin 1777, p. 135; Comte de Mirabeau, *De la Monarchie Prussienne sous Frédéric le Grand*, 4 vols., London 1788, III, 237; Margrave De Bayreuth, *Mémoires*, 1967, pp. 23, 185.

7. Schöning, op. cit. pp. 3–4; Frédéric le Grand, 'Du Militaire depuis son Institution jusqu'à la Fin du Règne de Frederic-Guillaume', *Oeuvres*, 31 vols., Berlin 1846–1857, I, pp. 182–90; Guibert, op. cit. pp. 76–77; Christopher Duffy, *The Army of Frederick the Great*, 1974, pp. 70, 72, 255.

8. Manstein, op. cit. II, 174; Lacolle, op. cit. p. 402; J.A. Houlding, *Fit for Service. The Training of the British Army 1715–1795*, Oxford 1981, p. 199n; in fact the drill was not entirely based on the Prussian model.

9. Earl of Chesterfield, *Letters . . . to His Son*, Sixth Edition, 4 vols 1775, III, 289; Arthur, op. cit. I, 425–26; Comte de Saint-Germain, *Correspondance Particulière . . . avec M. Paris*, 2 vols., London 1789, I, 41–43.

10. Captain Albert Latreille, *L'Armée et la Nation à la Fin de l'Ancien Régime*, 1914, pp. 75–77.

11. L. Mention, *Le Comte de Saint-Germain et ses Réformes*, 1884, pp. 30–31, 41–42; Léon des Forges de Parny, *Les Gardes du Corps du Roi*, Cannes 1972, p. 149.

12. Marquis de Bombelles, *Journal*, Genève 1978, II, 135, 9 May 1786; Latreille, op. cit. pp. 239–41, 394–97, *Rapport* by Guibert to the Conseil de la Guerre, 28 October 1787, ibid, p. 312; Titeux, op. cit. II, 970 L.R. de Belleval, *Souvenirs d'un Chevau-Léger de la Garde du Roi*, 1866, p. 256, entry for 30 September 1787; *Manca-Amat de Vallombrosa*, p. 194.

13. Giorgetti, op. cit. II, 20, 79; Attilio Simioni, 'L'Esercito Napoletano dalla Minorità di Ferdinando alla Reppublica del 1799', *Archivio Storico per le Provincie Napoletane*, XLV, 1920, pp. 96–97; Arthur, op. cit. I, 406, 480 Duke of York to Earl

Cornwallis, 26 July 1788; J.L. Pimholt, 'The Reform of the Life Guards', *Journal for the Society for Army Historical Research*, LIII, Winter 1975, pp. 194–98, 208.

14. Luedin, op. cit. pp. 62–68, 124; Henry Marczali, *Hungary in the Eighteenth Century*, 1930, p. 19n.

15. Luedin, op. cit. pp. 73–74, 64, 17–18, 85–87; Ivan Ritter von Zolger, *Die Hofstaat des Hauses Habsburg*, Vienna 1917, p. 90n.

16. Emil Paskowitz, *Die Erste Arcieren-Leibgarde Seiner Majestät des Kaisers und Königs*, Wien 1914, pp. 44–45; Oscar Teuber, *Die Österreichische Armee von 1700 bis 1867*, 2 vols., 1895–1904, II, 630; Luedin, op. cit. pp. 34, 83, 87.

17. Boris Mollo, *Uniforms of the Imperial Russian Army*, 1979, p. 123; Pierre Chantreau, *Voyage Philosophique, Politique, et Littéraire fait en Russie pendant les Années 1788 et 1789*, 2 vols., Hamburg 1794 I, 164–66; Philip Longworth, *The Cossacks*, 1969, p. 233; Herlitz, op. cit. pp. 103, 123.

NOTES TO CHAPTER 3
THE GOLDEN AGE OF ROYAL GUARDS, 1789–1830

1. P. Girault de Coursac, 'La Garde du Roi', *Découverte*, XIV, June 1976, p. 16; Titeux, op. cit. I, 291; Caetano Beirao, *Dona Maria I 1777–1792*, Lisbon, 1934, p. 404n: I am grateful to Dr David Higgs for providing this reference.

2. I am grateful to Charles Esdaile, who is preparing a thesis on the Spanish army from 1788 to 1814, for the generosity with which he has shared his knowledge of the Spanish army and guard in this period; Jori, op. cit. p. 132; Herlitz, op. cit. pp. 69, 71, 107, 123.

3. Caetano Beirao, op. cit. p. 404n; J.F. Bourgoing, *Voyage du ci-devant Duc du Châtelet en Portugal*, 2 vols., An VI, II, 10; P. Girault de Coursac, 'La Garde du Roi', *Découverte*, XIV, June 1976, pp. 17–26; XVI, December 1976, pp. 3–4; Comte Mareschal de Bièvre, 'La Garde Constitutionelle de Louis XVI', *Carnets de la Sabretache*, 3e Série, VII, 1924, pp. 352, 375, 381; A.N.O.¹ 3696, 5 Règlement for the Garde Constitutionelle, 11 November 1791.

4. Vicomte de Grouvel, *Les Corps de Troupes de l'Emigration Française*, 3 vols., 1957–1964, III, 49, 59, 61; Jean Pinasseau, *L'Emigration Militaire. Campagne de 1792*, 2 vols., 1957–1964, I, 13–19, II, 147; Paul et Pierrette Girault de Coursac, *Enquête sur le Procès du Roi Louis XVI*, 1982, pp. 160–62; A.N. 101 AP. D4 (Archives de la Maison de Gramont) Comte d'Agoult to Duc de Guiche, 29 January 1792.

5. Marie-Caroline, Reine de Naples et de Sicile, *Correspondance Inédite avec le Marquis de Gallo*, ed. Cdt M-H Weil et le Marquis C. de Somma-Circello, 2 vols., 1911, 1, 329, letter of 10 November 1795; anon, 'Reminiscences of the Court and Times of the Emperor Paul I of Russia up to the Period of his Death', *Fraser's Magazine*, CCCCXXVIIII, August 1865, p. 225; K. Waliszewski, *Le Fils de la Grande*

Cathérine. Paul I, 1912, pp. 123, 267; Boris Mollo, *Uniforms of the Russian Imperial Army*, 1979, pp. 125, 127.

6. Henry Lachouque, *The Anatomy of Glory*, London and Melbourne, 1978, pp. 4, 7, 9–11; Henry Redhead Yorke, *Letters from France*, 2 vols., 1814, I, 281, 286.

7. Jean Savant, *Les Mameloukes de Napoléon*, 1949, pp. 51, 72–74; Roustam, *Mamelouck de Napoléon, Souvenirs*, 1911, pp. 272–73; Lachouque, op. cit. pp. 177, 190, 245, 284.

8. Général Comte François Dumonceau, *Mémoires*, 3 vols., Bruxelles 1958, I, 196, 259; Otto von Pivka, *Spanish Armies of the Napoleonic Wars*, 1975, pp. 28–29; id. *Napoleon's Italian and Neapolitan Troops*, 1979, pp. 5, 6, 20–21; Napoléon I, *Correspondance Générale*, 32 vols., 1858–1869, XV, 235, Napoléon I to Joseph, 4 May 1807, XVIII, 22, id. to Clarke 10 Jan 1809; *Almanach Royal de Westphalie pour l'An MDCCCXIII*, Cassell 1813, pp. 73–78; Nino Cortese, *Memorie di un Generale della Reppublica del'Impero. Francesco Pignatelli, Principe di Stromboli*, 2 vols., Bari 1927, I, pp. ccxvi, ccxxxviii.

9. AAE (Archives du Ministère des Affaires Etrangères, Paris) 604, 72–3, Circular of Senator Dubois-Dubais; F^7 4280, 16 Liste Général des Gardes du Corps du Roy, officiers et jeunes gens de famille qui se sont réunis sous les Auspices de Mr. le Senateur du Bois du Bais pour offrir leurs Services à Sa Majesté l'Empereur et Roy en qualité de ses Gardes du Corps; Mémoire sur . . . la garde de l'Empereur comparativement avec celle de la Garde du Roi, by Louis-Annibal d'Agoult; *Napoléon I*, XII, 423–24, Napoléon I to Joseph 4 May, to Clarke 5 May 1806, XVII, 273, id. to Jerome 5 Jan 1808; Comte d'Espinchal, *Souvenirs*, 2 vols 1901, I, 108, 130, 149.

10. Frédéric Masson, *Napoléon chez Lui*, 1894, pp. 60–61; Dr Lomier, *Histoire des Régiments des Gardes d'Honneur*, Paris-Amiens 1924, pp. 2, 27, 251–52, 262, 265.

11. Lachouque, op. cit. pp. 52, 224, 143; Duke of Wellington, *Supplementary Despatches*, 14 vols., 1858–1872, XIV, 699, Memoir of 1818; W. Zweguintsov, *L'Armée Russe 1801–1825*, 1973, pp. 293–318, 400; Sir Robert Wilson, *Brief Remarks on the Character and Composition of the Russian Army*, 1810, pp. 13–14; J.B.A. Barrès, *Souvenirs d'un Officier de la Grande Armée*, 1923, pp. 101–02.

12. Helen Roeder, *The Ordeal of Captain Roeder*, 1960, p. 163; Otto von Pivka, *Armies of the Napoleonic Era*, 1979, p. 201; William O. Shanahan, *Prussian Military Reform, 1786–1813*, New York 1945, p. 222.

13. Gunther E. Rothenburg, *Napoleon's Great Adversaries*, 1982, p. 188; Comte de Rochechouart, *Souvenirs sur la Revolution, l'Empire et la Restauration*, 1889, pp. 326–28; Luedin, op. cit. p. 92; Boris Uxkull, *Arms and the Woman*, 1966, p. 170, diary for 1 January 1814; Lachouque, op. cit. p. 366.

14. Sir Neil Campbell, *Napoleon at Fontainebleau and Elba*, 1869, p. 222, diary for 9 May 1814; Baron de Bourgoing, *Le Coeur Secret de Marie-Louise*, 2 vols., II, 64; BN.N.A.F. 24062 Procès-Verbaux du Conseil, 1814–15, f.91; AHMG (Archives Historiques du Ministère de la Guerre) XAD 12 Ordonnance of 25 May 1814, XAD 10 Ordonnance of 15 June 1814, Contrôles of the companies of Mousquetaires.

15. AHMG.XAD 10 Contrôles of the companies of Mousquetaires; Vice-Amiral Baron Grivel, *Mémoires*, 1914, p. 326; A.N. 40 A.P. (Beugnot papers), reports of Comte Beugnot to Louis XVIII, 10, 18 September, 29 October, 9, 11 November 1814; *Napoléon I*, XXVIII, 5.

16. Baron Hennet de Goutel, 'Les Derniers Jours de l'Empire raconté par un Cent-Suisse, d'après le journal inédit de M. de Marsilly', *Revue des Etudes Napoléoniennes*, 1908, pp. 273, 5 diary for 11, 13, March 1815; Titeux, op. cit. II, 272; AAE 681.102 Comte Reinhard to Talleyrand, 12 January 1815; J. Nollet, *Histoire de N.C. Oudinot, Maréchal d'Empire*, 1850, p. 209, Berri to Maréchal Oudinot 13 March 1815.

17. Hennet de Goutel, op. cit. p. 278, diary for 19 March 1815; F.J.L. Rilliet, *Souvenirs de 1815*, Geneve 1910, pp. 264–72; Edouard Romberg et Albert Malet, *Louis XVIII et les Cent Jours à Gand*, 2 vols., 1898, II, 112, 113, Artois to Louis XVIII, 21, 27 March 1815.

18. John Keegan, *The Face of Battle*, Penguin 1980, pp. 169, 178; Lachouque, op. cit. pp. 460, 497; A.H. Heriot de Vroil, *Mémoires d'un Officier de la Garde Royale*, 1904, p. 115; Viscount Castlereagh, *Memoirs and Despatches*, 12 vols., 1848–53, X, 329, Orléans to Louis XVIII, 25 April 1815; AHMG XAD3 Projets pour la Maison Militaire du Roi, especially the *projet* of Raguse, 11 July 1815; AAE. 346.4 vo. Note of 8 July 1815.

19. Baron Gay de Vernon, *Vie du Maréchal Gouvion Saint-Cyr*, 1856, pp. 398–99; Chancelier Pasquier, *Mémoires*, 6 vols., 1893–95, III, 409–10, A.N.O^3 533.222 Ordonnance of 25 September 1815.

20 A.N.F^7 9875 Correspondence of Prefets with the Minister of Police, 1815–16; AHMG X AE 7 Rapport au Roi. 30 October 1816; British Museum Add. Mss. 47381.62 diary of Princess Lieven, October 1817; P.G. de Bussy 'Campagnes et Souvenirs d'Espagne' *Revue Hispanique*, XXXII, 1914, p. 554; Mario degli Alberti, *Dieci Anni di Storia Piemontese*, Torino 1908, p. 234, Prince de Carignan to Marquis de la Marmora, 16 November 1823.

21. Otto von Pivka, *Armies of the Napoleonic Era*, 1979, p. 201; anon, *La Cavalerie Allemande*, 189, pp. 310, 321, 328, 359; Gerhard Ritter, *The Sword and the Sceptre*, 4 vols., 1972, I, 103, 171; Peter Paret, *Clusewitz and the State*, Oxford 1976, p. 416n.

22. Uxkull, p. 128, diary for 3 April 1813; Frances Lady Shelley, *Diary*, 1912, entry for July 1815; *Pfannenberg*, p. 32; Walter Scott, *Paul's Letters to His Kinsfolk*, 1816, p. 379.

23. Bezzel, VI, i. 56–67, 64, ii, VII, p. 24; *Mostra delle Arme ed Uniforme Napoletane 1734–1860*, Museo

Principe Gaetano Filangieri, Naples, 1969, p. 21;
General Alessio Chapperon, *L'Organica Militare fra
le due Guerre Mondiali*, Rome 1921, pp. 152, 155,
270; *Brancaccio* II, 15, 62; Captain James Edward
Alexander, *Travels to the Seat of War in the East . . .
in 1829*, 2 vols., 1830, I, 106, II, 236; Comte G. de
Caraman, *Notice sur la Vie Militaire et Privée du
Général Marquis de Caraman*, 1857, p. 183.

24. Herlitz, op. cit. pp. 69, 71, 107; A. Daumont, *Voyage
en Suède*, 2 vols., 1834, II, pp. 124–26; Mackinnon,
op. cit. II, 368; Arthur, op. cit. I, 468, 532, II, 628,
Duke of York to Duke of Wellington, 1 March 1820;
Ian Hay, *The Royal Company of Archers, 1676–
1951*, Edinburgh and London 1951, pp. 23–24.

25. Guillaume, op. cit. pp. 241, 248, 233; J. Pla Dalmau
'La Guardia Real en los tiempos de Ferdinando VII',
Guardia Real, 28, Ano IV, February 1982, pp. 20–21;
Titeux, op. cit. I, 173.

26. Pla Dalmau, op. cit. pp. 21–23; Clonard, op. cit.
p. 195; Eric Christiansen, *The Origins of Military
Power in Spain*, Oxford 1967, pp. 33–34, 43.

27. Avigdor Levy, *The Military Policies of Sultan
Mahmud II, 1808–1839*, unpublished Harvard PhD
thesis, 1968, passim esp. pp. 8, 9, 40, 244–49,
373–81; William Turner, *Journal of a Tour in the
Levant*, 3 vols., 1820, I, 69; S.J. Shaw, *Between Old
and New, The Ottoman Empire under Sultan Selim
III, 1789–1807*, Cambridge Mass. 1971, p. 120, 379.

28. Levy, op. cit. pp. 378–81, 467–68, 564–65; Charles
MacFarlane, *Constantinople in 1828*, Second
Edition 2 vols., 1829, I, 504, II, 163, 171, 174; Captain
Charles Colville Frankland, *Travels to and from
Constantinople in the Years 1827 and 1828*, 2 vols.,
1829, I, 119; Maréchal Marmont, Duc de Raguse,
Voyage . . . en Egypte, 5 vols., 1837–8, II, 63; cf.
Adolphus Slade, *Records of Travels in Turkey,
Greece, etc. in the Years 1829, 1830 and 1831*, 2
vols., 1833, I, 131, II, 208–10.

29. Sir John Malcolm, *The History of Persia*, 2 vols.,
1815, II, 497; James Morier, *A Journey Through
Persia, Armenia, and Asia Minor to Constantinople
in the Years 1808 and 1809*, 1812, pp. 241–43;
Edward Scott Waring, *A Tour to Sheeraz by the
Route of Kazroon and Feerozabad*, Bombay 1804,
p. 87; (C. Dupré) *Voyage en Perse fait dans les
Années 1807, 1808, et 1809*, 2 vols., 1819, II, 294,
298; Sir Harford Jones Brydges, *An Account of the
Transactions of His Majesty's Mission to Persia in
the Years 1807–1811*, 2 vols., 1834, I, 188.

30. Théodore Anne, *Mémoires, Souvenirs et Anecdotes
sur l'Intérieur du Palais de Charles X*, 3 vols., 1831,
II, 315, 353.

NOTES TO CHAPTER 4
THE SURVIVAL OF ROYAL GUARDS, 1830–1984

1. F. Salata ed. *Carlo Alberto Inedito*, Milano 1931,
pp. 76, diary for 12 December 1831, 387
autobiography; Brancaccio, op. cit. II, 131–32, 224,

461; Jori, op cit. pp. 495–96.

2. J. Pla Dalmau, 'Los Reales Guardias Alabarderos en la
Noche Tragica del 7 de octobre de 1841', *Guardia
Real*, IV, 32, June 1982, p. 24; Conde de Clonard,
Historia Organica de las Armas Espanolas, 16 vols.,
Madrid 1851–62, VII, 26.

3. Luedin, op. cit. pp. 95–106; Alan Sked, *The Survival
of the Habsburg Empire*, 1979, p. 176, Philippsburg
to Metternich, 3 April 1847; Zolger, op. cit. p. 100.

4. Capitaine A. Richard, *La Garde (1854–1870)*, 1898,
pp. 2,7,17, 84, 130, 195; Lascelles Wraxall, *The
Armies of the Great Powers*, 1859, pp. 141, 273;
Queen Victoria, *Leaves from a Journal*, 1961, 79, 81,
entry for 19 August 1855; Albert Verly, *L'Escadron
des Cent-Gardes*, 1894, pp. 41, 66, 209, 217;
Sacheverell Sitwell, *Selected Works*, 1955, p. 44.

5. General Alexandre Spiridovitch, *Les Dernières
Années de la Cour de Tsarskoie-Seloe*, 2 vols., 1929,
I, 28–30; Lesley Blanch, *The Sabres of Paradise*,
1960, p. 446; Captain H.M. Hozier, *The Russo–
Turkish War*, 2 vols., 1879, I, 344.

6. Ritter, op. cit. I, 110; anon, *La Cavalerie Allemande*,
pp. 321, 328, 360; Colonel Baron Stoffel, *Rapports
Militaires Ecrits de Berlin*, 1871, pp. 172–73 report
of 24 June 1868; Gordon A. Craig, *The Battle of
Königgratz*, 1966, p. 82, 124, 148; Frederick III, *War
Diary*, ed. A.R. Allinson, 1927, p. 269, entry for 18
January 1871.

7. General Sir Robert Biddulph, *Lord Cardwell at the
War Office*, 1904, p. 19, Memorandum of 3
December 1868; Arthur, op. cit. II, 658.

8. Sir John Ross of Bladenburg, *A History of the
Coldstream Guards from 1815 to 1895*, 1896,
pp. 325–27; Brackenbury, op. cit. p. 199, Hennell, op
cit. pp. 212–16, 298.

9. Jori, op. cit. pp. 242, 295–98, 310; Joaquin de Solto y
Montes, 'Guardias Palacianas y Escoltas Reales de la
Monarquia Espanola', *Revista de Historia Militar*,
1974, pp. 40–47.

10. Robert B.M. Binning, *A Journal of Two Years' Travel
in Persia, Ceylon etc.* 2 vols., 1858, II, 293; Lady
Sheil, *Glimpses of Life and Manners in Persia*, 1856,
p. 385; Robert Grant Watson, *A History of Persia
from the Beginning of the Nineteenth Century to the
Year 1858*, 1866, p. 24; Dr Feuvrier, *Trois Ans à la
Cour de Perse*, seconde édition, 1906, p. 48; Hassan
Arfa, *Under Five Shahs*, 1964, p. 49.

11. Angelo M. Piemontese, 'An Italian Source for the
History of the Qajar Period in Persia: the reports of
Generale Enrico Andrecino (1871–1886)', *East and
West*, New Series, Vol XIX, 1, March–June 1969,
p. 156, report of 28 September 1875; Lord Edward
Gleichen, *A Guardsman's Memoirs*, 1932, p. 66; F.
Kazemzadeh, 'The Origin and Early Development of
the Persian Cossack Brigade', *American Slavic
Review*, XV, 1956, p. 354; C.E. Biddulph, *Four
Months in Persia and a Visit to Transcaspasia*, 1892,
p. 101; Hon. J.M. Balfour, *Recent Happenings in
Persia*, 1922, p. 168; Donald N. Wilber, *Riza Shah
Pahlavi*, Hicksville, 1975, p. 7.

12. Charles MacFarlane, *Turkey and its Destiny*, 2 vols., 1850, II, 324, 59, 595; cf. Lady Hornby *Constantinople During the Crimean War*, 1893, p. 140; Léon Lamouche, *L'Organisation Militaire de l'Empire Ottoman*, 1895, p. 42; Paul de Régla, *La Turquie Officielle*, 1889, p. 51; P. Fesch, *Constantinople aux Derniers Jours d'Abdul Hamid*, 1907, p. 123; H.C. Woods, *Washed by Four Seas*, 1908, p. 24, cf. Anna Bowman Dodds, *In the Palaces of the Sultan*, 1904, pp. 40–42.

13. Spiridovitch, op. cit. I, 28–31, 54, 214; Pfannenberg, op. cit. pp. 37, 80; Albert von Stosch, *Das Königlich Preussische 5 Garde Regiment zu Fuss*, Berlin 1930, p. 1; Kurt Zentner, *Kaiserliche Zeiten*, 1973, p. 40; Wilhelm II, *My Early Life*, 1928, pp. 31, 116, 154, 180.

14. Peter Verney, *The Micks*, 1970, pp. 2–3; F. Loraine Petre, Wilfred Ewart and Major-General Sir Cecil Lowther, *The Scots Guards in the Great War 1914–1918*, 1925, p. 101; Sir Frederick Ponsonby, *The Grenadier Guards in the Great War of 1914–1918*, 3 vols., 1920, I, 201; Robert Haswell Lutz, *The Fall of the German Empire*, 2 vols., Stanford 1932, I, 603; Sir Alfred Knox, *With the Russian Army 1914–1917*, 2 vols., 1921, I, 302, entry for 18 July 1915.

15. General Andolenko, *Histoire de l'Armée Russe*, 1967, pp. 320, 373; *The Letters of the Tsaritsa to the Tsar*, Stanford 1973, pp. 319, 399, letters of 4 September 1915, 15 September 1916; Captain Count M.C. Bennigsen, 'The Preobrajensky Regiment of the Russian Guard', *Journal of the Royal United Service Institution*, LXIX, Feb–Nov 1924, pp. 105–08.

16. Gunther E. Rothenburg, *The Army of Franz Josef*, West Lafayette, 1976, p. 220; W. von Boddien, *Das Regiment der Gardes du Corps im Weltkriege*, Berlin 1928, p. 396; John Retallack, *The Welsh Guards*, 1981, p. 5; information kindly communicated by Professor N. Kurat, Ankara University; General Sir Charles Harington, *Tim Harington Looks Back*, 1940, pp. 125–30.

17. Marvin Zonis, *The Political Elite of Iran*, Princeton 1971, p. 105n; Arfa, op. cit. pp. 122, 189, 235, 405, 410; Dennis Wright, *The English Among the Persians*, 1977, pp. 179, 182.

18. This section is based on interviews with Iranians who have asked not to be identified, 1981–82, with General Oveissi, 24 March 1983; and an annex to a report from the British Military Attaché, 31 October 1978.

19. Herbert Goldhamer, *The Soviet Soldier*, London and New York, 1971, p. 134; Mollo, op. cit. pp. 28–29; *Sovietska Krennaya Enksiklopediya*, Moscow 1976, II, 496–98 (translated by the kindness of Peter Vigor); Herlitz, op. cit. pp. 34–93; interview with Captain V. Hjorth-Anderson, formerly of the Svea Livgarde, 24 June 1981, interview of 22 June 1981 with Captain Gram-Anderson, Danish Life Guards.

20. *The History of His Majesty the King's Guard*, Oslo n.d; *L'Escorte Royale Belge*, Deuxième Edition, Brussels 1973, pp. 13, 16, 22; interview with F.A.T. Smits, Royal Dutch Army Museum, 17 July 1982.

21. Interview with Lt.-Colonel de Meer, Spanish Military Attache, 28 September 1981, with Colonel Luis Fernandez de Mesa y Hoces, Colonel of the Guardia Real, and the officers of the Guardia Real, 9 October 1982; *Guardia Real*, Ano 1, 3, December 1979, p. 22, ano 1, 5, February 1980, p. 60; George Seldes, *The Vatican Yesterday and Today*, New York 1934, p. 68; George Bull, *Inside the Vatican*, 1982, pp. 6, 64; Colonel F. Pfyffer, *Feuille d'Orientation*, Rome 1982, interview, 4 September 1982.

22. Keith Briant, *Fighting with the Guards*, 1958, p. 187; Henry Stanhope, *The Soldiers*, 1979, pp. 168–69, 177; interviews with a Sergeant and an officer of the Blues and Royals, 12, 24 November 1981, 24 October 1982.

23. Peter York, *Style Wars*, 1980, p. 250; Major Nicholas Payan Dawnay, *The Standards, Guidons and Colours of the Household Division, 1660–1973*, 1975, p. xix, foreword by the Duke of Edinburgh; Randolph S. Churchill, *Winston S. Churchill*, vol. I, Youth, 1966, Winston Churchill to Lady Randolph Churchill, 7 January 1897.

24. Interview with Major-General S.M. al-Jaber al Sabah, commander of the Emiri Guard, Kuwait, 19 April 1981; H.V.F. Winstone, *Captain Shakespear*, Second Edition 1978, p. 68; interviews with Sa'ad den Mamilla, commander of the Circassian Honour Guard, Amman, with Major Suleiman Abdul Karim and Captain Ali of the Royal Guard Battalion, Lt.-Colonel Musa S. Lutfi of the Police Training School, Amman, 15 April 1981; with Senator Wasfi Mirza, Amman, 13, 14 April 1981.

25. Tony Geraghty, *Who Dares Wins*, Fontana 1981, pp. 5, 122, 155, 221; interviews with a former officer of the S.A.S., 27 April 1981, with an officer of the Irish Guards, 10 March, 25 May 1981, with a former officer of the Trucial Oman Scouts 17 June, 28 July 1981.

26. Interviews with officers of the Sultan's Armed Forces, 1981, an officer of the Royal Guard Brigade, Oman, 25.41981; a former officer of the Blues and Royals, 25 March 1982.

27. Charles Belgrave, *Personal Column*, 1960, pp. 109–10; Ameen Rihani, *Ibn Sa'oud of Arabia*, 1928, pp. 73, 136; Gerald de Gaury, *Arabia Phoenix*, 1946, pp. 45, 68–70; idem, *Faisal King of Saudi Arabia*, 1966, pp. 93, 100–01; interview with former British Military Attache in Saudi Arabia, 16 March 1981.

28. Interviews with M. Ben Mansour, Historiographe du Royaume, Rabat, 15 April 1983; Colonel Ben Moubaraha, Garde Royale, Rabat, 20 April 1983.

NOTES TO CHAPTER 5
THE COMPOSITION OF ROYAL GUARDS

1. Ibrahim Müteferrika, *Traité de Tactique ou Méthode Artificielle pour l'Ordonnance des Troupes*, Vienne

1769, p. 20; La Trollière, op. cit. p. 41; Samaran, *D'Artagnan, Capitaine des Mousquetaires du Roi,* p. 19; Lacolle, op. cit. p. 93.

2. Louis XIV, *Oeuvres,* 6 vols., 1806, II, p. 185; Louis Tuetey, *Les Officiers sous l'Ancien Régime,* 1908, pp. 107–10, 119–20, 122; Guy Chaussinand-Nogaret, *La Noblesse au XVIIIe Siècle,* 1975, p. 55.

3. Lacolle, op. cit. p. 346; Vanson, op. cit. p. 267; La Trollière, op. cit. pp. 47–49; Belanger, *Les Gardes du Corps sous les Anciennes Monarchies,* pp. 60–67.

4. Chagniot, op. cit. p. 296; A.N.O¹ 3677 Rolle de la Compagnie des deux cens Chevau-Légers de la Garde Ordinaire du Roy; O¹ 3673, 6 Noms et Adresses par Ordre Alphabetique; A. de La Vallette-Montbrun, *Maine de Biran,* 1914, p. 31.

5. William Coxe, *L'Espagne sous les Rois de la Maison de Bourbon,* 6 vols., 1827, I, p. 183, Louis XIV to Comte de Marsin, 1701; A. Morel-Fatio, *Etudes sur l'Espagne,* 3 vols., 1888–1904, II, p. 87; Cortese, op. cit. p. ccxxxii; Simioni, op. cit. p. 104; Zezon, op. cit. p. 391n. Jori, op. cit. p. 391n.

6. N. Lemontey, *Essai sur l'Etablissement Monarchique de Louis XIV,* 1818, p. 343n; Comte de Montbel, *Souvenirs,* 1913, p. 353; Karl Demeter, *The German Officer Corps in Society and State, 1650–1945,* 1965, p. 4; Felix Gilbert ed. *The Historical Essays of Otto Hintze,* New York 1975, p. 54, 'The Hohenzollern and the Nobility'; Jean Meyer, *Noblesses et Pouvoirs dans l'Europe d'Ancien Régime,* 1972, p. 99; Graf Waldersee, op. cit. passim; Schöning, op. cit. passim.

7. Anon., *La Cavalerie Allemande,* 1890, p. 672; Demeter, op. cit., pp. 30–32; Brenda Meehan-Waters, 'Social and Career Characteristics of the Administrative Elite 1689–1761', in Walter McKenzie Pinter and Don Karl Rowney eds., *Russian Officialdom,* 1980, pp. 86–87; *Sbornik,* (Proceedings of the Imperial Russian History Society), 148 vols., St-Petersburg 1867–1916, LXXV, 1891, p. 229, Rondeau to Lord Harrington, 3 September 1730.

8. Voltaire, *Histoire de l'Empire de Russie sous Pierre le Grand,* 2 vols., 1759, I, p. 123; David L. Ransel, *The Politics of Catherinian Russia. The Panin Party,* New Haven and London, 1975, p. 232n, Solms to Frederick II, 27 July 1772.

9. K. Waliszewski, *Le Fils de la Grande Catherine, Paul Ier,* 1912, p. 269; Captain C. Colville Frankland, *Narrative of a Visit to the Courts of Russia and Sweden in the Years 1830 and 1831,* 2 vols., 1832, I, pp., 300–01; Andolenko, op. cit. p. 314; Peter Kenez, 'A Profile of the Pre-revolutionary Officer Corps', in *California Slavic Studies,* 1973, VII, 143; Kozlinianoff, op. cit. p. iii; interview with Colonel Doubentsoff, 5 May 1982.

10. Odelberg, op. cit. pp. 250–53; interview with Captain Hjorth-Andersen, 12 June 1981; Bengtsson, op. cit. pp. 55, 211.

11. C.W. Frearson, *Officers of the Life Guards and Horse Grenadiers 1661–1969,* typescript 1978, passim; idem, *Officers of the Blues, 1661–1969,* typescript 1980, passim; Hamilton, op. cit. III, pp. 426–501;

Mackinnon, op. cit. II, pp. 451–525; Maurice, op. cit. II, pp. 285–373; J.N.P. Watson, *Captain General and Rebel Chief,* 1979, p. 31; Arthur, op. cit. I, pp. 478, 649; Lord Herbert ed. *Pembroke Papers,* 1950, p. 266, Lord Pembroke to Lord Herbert, 16 February 1785.

12. Pimholt, op. cit. p. 196, Yonge to Pitt, 27 December 1787; Elizabeth Longford, *Wellington, The Years of the Sword,* 1969, p. 351n; *The Guards Magazine,* Summer 1980, p. 87; Henry Stanhope, *The Soldiers,* 1979, pp. 182–83; Denis Barker, *Soldiering On,* 1981, p. 30.

13. Jean Pierre Labatut, *Les Noblesses Européennes de la Fin du XVe à la Fin du XVIIIe Siècle,* 1978, p. 85; Brackenbury, op. cit. p. 120; Prince de Ligne, *Mémoires sur le Comte de Bonneval,* 1817, p. 238, Mémoire sur le tactique.

14. John Childs, *Armies and Warfare in Europe 1648–1789,* Manchester 1982, p. 87; Guillaume, op. cit. p. 85; Boutaric, p. 332.

15. S.G.W. Benjamin, *The Turks and the Greeks,* New York 1867, p. 76; Nizam al-Mulk, *The Book of Government, or Rules for Kings,* 1960, p. 104. Other examples of foreign royal guards were the Turkish guards of the Abbasid Caliphs after 800, and the Varangian guard of Scandinavians and (after 1066) Englishmen, which guarded the Byzantine Emperors from the tenth century until 1204, or later.

16. Gaston Zeller, *Les Institutions de la France au XVIe Siècle,* 1948, p. 97; Code, I, pp. 127, 183, instructions to Comte de Marsin, 1701; Raymond O'Shea, *The Sand Kings of Arabia,* 1947, p. 68; interview with Said Salman, Abu Dhabi, 30 April 1981.

NOTES TO CHAPTER 6
INSTRUMENTS OF POWER

1. P.M. Holt, 'The Position and Power of the Mameluke Sultan', *Bulletin of the School of Oriental and African Studies,* 1975, xxxviii, p. 248; Philippe de Commynes, *Mémoires,* 3 vols., 1840–1847, II, p. 268; Childs, *Army and the Glorious Revolution,* p. 30, James II to William of Orange, 19 June 1685, cf. James II, *Memoirs,* 1962, p. 62; Bombelles, op. cit. II, p. 230, diary for 9 September 1788.

2. C.E. Bosworth, 'Recruitment, Muster and Review in Medieval Islamic Armies', in M.E. Yapp and V.H. Parry eds., *War Technology and Society in the Middle East,* 1975, p. 64, cf. M.A. Shaban, *Islamic History: a New Interpretation II 750–1055,* Cambridge 1976, p. 117; R. Levy, op. cit. p. 230.

3. Marcel Durry, *Les Cohortes Prétoriennes,* 1938, pp. 366, 378; A.R. Myers, *Parliaments and Estates in Europe to 1789,* 1975, p. 36; Lachouque, op. cit. p. 124; Joseph Marshall, *Travels Through Holland, Flanders, Germany, Denmark, Sweden, Lapland, Russia, the Ukraine and Poland in the Years 1768, 1769 and 1770,* 3 vols., 1772, III, p. 143, cf. R. Levy, op. cit. p. 229.

4. Busbecq, op. cit. p. 8, letter of 1 September 1555; anon., *An Exact Account of the Late Amazing Revolution in Turkey*, 1730, p. 7.

5. Franz Babinger, *Mehmed the Conqueror and His Times*, 1978, pp. 36, 65; Djevaad, op. cit. pp. 284–85; A.D. Alderson, *The Structure of the Ottoman Dynasty*, Oxford 1956, p. 63.

6. M.A. Damon, *Contribution à l'histoire des Sultans Osman II et Mouctafa*, 1919, pp. 10, 27; A. Pallis, *In the Days of the Janissaries*, 1951, p. 38; Djevaad, op. cit. pp. 300–01.

7. Victor R. Swenson, 'The Military Rising in Istanbul 1909', *Journal of Contemporary History*, 1970, V, 4, p. 174; C.F. Abbott, *Turkey in Transition*, 1909, pp. 172–73, 208.

8. Henry Rosenfeld, 'The Social Composition of the Military in the Process of State Formation in the Arabian Desert', *Journal of the Royal Anthropological Institute of Great Britain and Ireland*, vol. 95, part ii, July 1965, pp. 177, 179 (I am grateful for this reference to William Facey); David Holden, Richard Johns and James Buchan, *The House of Saud*, 1981, pp. 237–39; Robert Lacey, *The Kingdom*, 1981, pp. 313, 319, 350–51; Gerald de Gaury, *Faisal King of Saudi Arabia*, 1966, p. 100.

9. *Sbornik*, XXXIV, La Vie to duc d'Orléans, 28 December 1717; Meehan-Waters, op. cit. p. 85; R. Nisbet Bain, *The Pupils of Peter the Great*, 1897, pp. 73–76; K. Waliszewski, *L'Héritage de Pierre le Grand*, 1900, p. 5; Philip Longworth, *The Three Empresses*, 1972, p. 62.

10. A.I. Turgenev, *La Cour de Russie il y a Cent Ans*, 3rd. ed. Leipzig 1860, pp. 13–14, despatch of Magnan, 31 January 1730, cf. p. 15, despatch of 2 February 1730; Bain, *Pupils*, p. 159; *Sbornik*, LXXV, 1891, p. 136, despatch of Rondeau to Lord Harrington, 16 February 1730.

11. Turgenev, op. cit. p. 33, despatch of Magnan, 26 February/9 March 1730; ibid, p. 37, despatch of 5/16 March 1730; Bain, *Pupils*, pp. 172–74; Longworth, op. cit. pp. 101–10.

12. Longworth, op. cit. pp. 130, 143; Waliszewski, *L'Héritage*, pp. 141–47.

13. Turgenev, op. cit. p. 73, Finch to Lord Harrington, 11 November 1740; ibid. p. 74, La Chétardie to de Valory, 21 November 1740; Waliszewski, *L'Héritage*, pp. 296, 300, 305–06; *Sbornik*, 1893, LXXXV, p. 384, Edward Finch to Lord Harrington, 18 November 1740.

14. Albert Vandal, *Louis XV et Elizabeth de Russie*, 1884, pp. 155–60, La Chétardie to Louis XV, 7 December 1741; Waliszewski, *L'Héritage*, pp. 359–363; idem, *La Dernière des Romanov*, 1902, p. 26, Mardefeld to Frederick II, 12, 19 December 1741.

15. Sir Robert Murray Keith, *Memoirs and Correspondence*, 2 vols., 1849, I, p. 55, despatch of 2/13 July 1762; R. Nisbet Bain, *Peter III, Emperor of Russia*, 1902, pp. 106, 156; Princess Dashkov, *Memoirs*, ed. Kyril Fitzlyon, 1958, pp. 57, 68, 73–74; Catherine the Great, *Memoirs*, ed. Dominique

Maroyer, 1955, pp. 341–45, Catherine to Stanislas Augustus Poniatowski, 2 August 1762.

16. Kozlianinoff, op. cit. p. vii; *Sbornik*, 1878, xxii, pp. 75, 84, 95, Solms to Frederick II, 7/18 June, 1/12 July, 22 July/2 August 1763; L. Ransel, op. cit. p. 232n, Solms to Frederick II, 27 July 1772; Isabel de Madariaga, *Russia in the Age of Catherine the Great*, 1981, pp. 258–59.

17. Feld-Maréchal Comte de Stedingk, *Mémoires Posthumes*, 3 vols., 1844–5, II, p. 11; Bennigsen, *Mémoires*, 3 vols. 1907–08, III, p. 407, letter by Bennigsen, March 1801; Waliszewski, *Le Fils de la Grande Cathérine. Paul 1er*, 1912, pp. 560, 615.

18. Bennigsen, op. cit. III, pp. 403–08; Waliszewski, *Paul 1er*, pp. 605–30; anon., 'Reminiscences of the Court and Times of the Emperor Paul I of Russia up to the Period of His Death', *Fraser's Magazine*, September 1865, CCCXXIX, p. 313.

19. Waliszewski, *Paul 1er*, p. 641; Glynn Barratt, *The Rebel on the Bridge. A Life of the Decembrist Baron Andrey Rosen*, 1975, pp. 36–37; idem, *Voices in Exile*, 1974, pp. 36, 146.

20. Comte Korff, *Avènement au Trône de l'Empereur Nicolas 1er*, 1857, p. 187; Barratt, *Voices*, p. 72; Anatole G. Mazour, *The First Russian Revolution, 1825. The Decembrist Movement*, Berkeley California 1937, pp. 166, 169.

21. Korff, op. cit. pp. 190, 280, 232–35; Barratt, *Voices*, pp. 74–76; Constantin de Grunwald, *La Vie de Nicolas 1er*, 1946, p. 14, Lebzeltern to Metternich, 6 January 1826; C.A.A. Disbrowe, *Original Letters from Russia*, 1878, p. 67, Mrs Disbrowe to Hon Robert Kennedy, 16/28 December 1825; ibid, p. 78, anon., Memorandum, 10/22 January 1826.

22. John Sheldon Curtiss, *The Russian Army Under Nicholas I*, Durham N.C., 1965, pp. 17, 51; Korff, op. cit. p. 208n; Barratt, *Voices*, p. 73.

23. W. Bruce Lincoln, *The Romanovs*, New York 1981, p. 702; Colonel Paul Rodzianko, *Tattered Banners*, n.d. p. 218; Maurice Paléologue, *An Ambassador's Memoirs*, 1973, pp. 740–41, 763, diary for 5 January, 13 January 1917; Alexandre Bloch, *Les Derniers Jours du Régime Impérial*, 1931, pp. 64–65, police reports for 28 January, 10 February 1917.

24. Christopher Duffy, *The Army of Maria Theresa*, 1977, p. 68; Felix Gilbert, op. cit. pp. 35, 44–45, 51, 60; Sir Charles Webster, *The Foreign Policy of Castlereagh 1812–1815*, 1950, p. 467, Castlereagh to Liverpool, 24 August 1815; Gerhard Ritter, *The Sword and the Scepter*, 4 vols., 1972–1973, I, p. 106.

25. Prince Frederick Charles, 'The Origins and Development of the Spirit of the Prussian Officer, its Manifestation and its Effect', 3 January 1860 in *Demeter*, p. 259; Alan Palmer, *Bismarck*, 1975, p. 236, Prince William to Count Eulenburg, 8 January 1887.

26. M. Reverdil, *Mémoires*, 1858, pp. 94, 183–34, 301–15; Falkenskjold, *Authentic Elucidation of the History of Counts Struensee and Brandt*, 1789, pp. 97, 141–48.

27. Keith, op. cit. I, p. 225, despatch of 6 October 1771; Reverdil, op. cit. pp. 330–39; Falkenskjold, op. cit. pp. 159–72; M. de Falkenskjold, *Mémoires*, 1826, p. 187.

28. M. Drevon, *A Journey through Sweden . . . with some particulars relating to the History of Denmark*, Dublin 1790, p. 170.

29. I.A.A. Thompson, *War and Government in Habsburg Spain*, 1976, p. 155; Clonard, op. cit. pp. 113, 117; M. Gachard, *Don Carlos et Philippe II*, Deuxième Edition, 1867, pp. 362, 365; Yves Bottineau, *L'Art de Cour dans l'Espagne de Philippe V*, Bordeaux 1960, pp. 183, 185–90.

30. De Marcillac, *Nouveau Voyage en Espagne*, 1805, p. 109; Dalrymple, op. cit. p. 51; Corona Baratech, *Revolucion y Reaccion en el Reinado de Carlos IV*, 1957, pp. 369, 374; information kindly communicated by Charles Esdaile; J. Garcia Mercadal, *Palafox*, Madrid 1948, pp. 24–35.

31. Andreas von Schepeler, *Histoire de la Révolution d'Espagne et du Portugal*, 3 vols., Liège 1829, I, pp. 22–25; Madrid Servicio Historico Militar, Documentos della Guerra d'Independenza, Legajo 4, Copeta 32, Marques de Lezan, 'Resumen Historico'; E. Marti Gilabert, *El Motin de Aranjuez*, Pamplona 1972, pp. 124, 207, 115–16, 130–35; Antonio Alcala Galiano, *Memorias*, 1886, p. 146; Charles Esdaile, 'The Spanish Army 1788–1814', manuscript, Chapter III.

32. Comte Murat, *Murat, Lieutenant de l'Empereur en Espagne*, 1897, pp. 253, 267, Maria Luisa to Murat, 6 April, 12 April 1808.

33. Paul Le Brethon ed., *Lettres et Documents pour servir à l'Histoire de Joachim Murat*, 8 vols., 1908–10, V, p. 446, Murat to Napoleon, 9 April 1808; ibid, V, p. 473, Murat to Bessières, 16 April 1808; Guillaume, op. cit. pp. 238–44.

34. Christiansen, op. cit. p. 22; PRO FO 72/234 Henry Wellesley to Lord Castlereagh, 7 March 1820; *Representacion dirigada al Congreso Naccional por el Capitan de Cuartel del Cuerpo de Guardias*, 1821; *El Cuerpo de Guardias de la Persona del Rey, Representaccion*, 7 April 1821, p. 3.

35. Un Espagnol témoin oculaire, *Histoire de la Revolution d'Espagne de 1820 à 1823*, 2 vols., 1824, II, pp. 136, 295; Guillaume, op. cit. pp. 249–55; G.G.D.V., *Letters on the Internal Political State of Spain During the Years 1821, 1822 and 1823*, 2 vols., 1824, passim, esp. I, p. 196, letter of 29 June 1822, p. 218, letters of 29 June, 1 July, 1 August 1822; Mercadal, op. cit. pp. 246, 262–64.

36. Christiansen, op. cit. p. 45; Baron de Los Valles, *The Career of Don Carlos Since the Death of Ferdinand the Seventh*, 1835, pp. 42–45; Christiansen, op. cit. pp. 159–60, account by Sergeant Gomez, 1840; Sir Herbert Maxwell, *The Life and Letters of George William Frederick Fourth Earl of Clarendon*, 2 vols., 1913, I, p. 114, George to Edward Villiers, 31 August 1836; Baron Charles Dembowski, *Deux Ans en Espagne et en Portugal pendant la Guerre Civile 1838–1840*, pp. 116–24, entry for 20 June 1839.

37. Captain S.E. Widdington, *Spain and the Spaniards in 1843*, 2 vols., 1844, I, pp. 59–66 (based on information from Madame Mina, the Queen's Governess); J. Pla Dalmau, 'Los Reales Guardias Alabarderos en la Noche Tragica del 7 de Octobre de 1841', *Guardia Real*, Ano IV, Num. 33, Julio-Agosto 1982, pp. 19–24; PRO FO 72/579 Aston to Aberdeen, 9 October 1841.

38. Du Fresne de Beaucourt, op. cit. VI, p. 27; V, 86; Pierre de Vaissière, *De Quelques Assassins*, 1912, p. 143; Lacolle, op. cit. pp. 41–46.

39. Vaissière, op. cit. pp. 226, 261, 275, 285–87, 295, 298.

40. Vaissière, op. cit. p. 362; Michel Carmona, *Marie de Médicis*, 1981, pp. 158, 222; James II, op. cit. p. 62.

41. Maréchal de Bassompierre, *Mémoires*, 4 vols., 1870–1877, II, pp. 85–88; Battifol, *Le Roi Louis XIII*, pp. 50, 62–63, 79; Héroard, op. cit. II, pp. 298, 304, 13 August 1624, 13 June 1626; Claude Dulong, *Anne d'Autriche*, 1980, pp. 189, 242, 283.

42. Jaurgain et Ritter, op. cit. II, pp. 334–35; E.J.F. Barbier, *Journal Historique*, 4 vols., 1847–1906, I, pp. 40–42, 21 July 1720.

43. Narbonne, op. cit. p. 146; Major des Gardes du Corps, op. cit. p. 361; Bombelles, op. cit. II, p. 182, entry for 3 September 1787; Jean Egret, *La Prérévolution Française*, 1962, pp. 252–53.

44. Major des Gardes du Corps, op. cit. p. 349; A.N.O.[1]3679 Décisions, Baron de Breteuil to Louis XVI, 1786; F[7]4280, 16 Agoult to Napoleon I, 1806.

45. Lachouque, op. cit. pp. 44, 124, 409–10; Frédéric Masson, *La Vie et les Conspirations du Général Malet*, n.d. pp. 101, 175; Général de Caulaincourt, *Mémoires*, 3 vols., 1933, III, pp. 178, 192, 235, 252.

46. Jean Thiry, *La Première Abdication*, 1939, pp. 190–91; C.F. Palmstierna ed. *Marie-Louise et Napoléon. Lettres Inédites*, 1955, p. 201, Marie-Louise to Napoleon I, 8 April 1814, cf. p. 216; Emile Marco de Sainte-Hilaire, *Histoire Politique, Militaire et Anecdotique de la Garde Impériale*, 1847, p. 542, account of Lieutenant-Général Laborde.

47. Neil Campbell, op. cit. pp. 126, 188, 249; Lieutenant-Général Comte Beker, *Relation de la Mission . . . auprès de l'Empereur Napoléon*, Clermont-Ferrand 1841, pp. 20, 39, 65; Jean Thiry, *La Seconde Abdication de Napoléon Ier*, 1945, p. 37; Lachouque, op. cit. p. 503; A. Debidour, *Le Général Fabvier*, 1904, pp. 157, 238.

48. AHMG X AE 7, Maréchal de Raguse to Duc de Feltre, 23 May 1817; Philip Mansel, *Louis XVIII*, 1981, p. 349; Ernest Daudet, *Louis XVIII et le Duc Decazes*, 1899, pp. 425, 429, Louis XVIII to Decazes, 17 February 1820.

49. General Carascosa, *Mémoires Historiques, Politiques et Militaires sur la Révolution du Royaume de Naples en 1820 et 1821*, London 1823, pp. 203, 269, 331; General Guillaume Pepe, *Mémoires*, 1906, p. 354; George T. Romani, *The Neapolitan Revolution of 1820–1821*, Evanston 1950, passim.

50. Brancaccio, op. cit. II, p. 16; Mario degli Alberti, *Dieci Anni di Storia Piemontese (1814–1824)*, Torino 1908, pp. 160, 164, 168; Carlo Torta, *La Rivoluzione Piemontese nel 1821*, Roma-Milano 1908, pp. 110–01, 147.

51. Robert Lacey, *Robert Earl of Essex*, 1971, pp. 281–89; idem, *Sir Walter Raleigh*, 1973, p. 263; Loades, op. cit. p. 95; Brackenbury, op. cit. p. 110.

52. Samuel Pepys, *Diary*, ed. Lord Braybrooke, 2 vols., 1906, II, p. 431, entry for 20 January 1668; Schwoerer, op. cit. pp. 106, 121, 133; R.J.T. Hills, *The Life Guards*, 1971, p. 9.

53. John Childs, 'The Army and the Oxford Parliament of 1681', *English Historical Review*, July 1979, CCCLXXII, pp. 581–82; Arthur, op. cit. I, p. 147; J.N.P. Watson, op. cit. pp. 153, 201.

54. Ibid, p. 71, 95; Hamilton, op. cit. I, p. 197, Duke of York to Colonel Legge, 7 June 1679, 302; Maurice, op. cit. I, p. 50; Arthur, op. cit. I, p. 215.

55. Marquess of Cambridge, 'The March of William of Orange from Torbay to London 1688', *Journal of Society for Army Historical Research*, 1966, XLIV, p. 153; Arthur, op. cit. I, p. 218; Childs, op. cit. 1980, pp. 185–86; Bishop Burnet, *History of His Own Time*, 4 vols., 1753, II, p. 533.

56. Arthur, op. cit. I, p. 217n, Thomas Philips to Lord Dartmouth, 16 November 1688; Earl of Ailesbury, *Memoirs*, 2 vols., 1890, I, p. 193.

57. Arthur, op. cit. I, pp. 226–28; Ailsbury, op. cit. I, pp. 213–14.

58. Mackinnon, op. cit. I, pp. 193–95, William to Craven, 15 December 1688, Arthur, op. cit. I, p. 230; Ailesbury, op. cit. I, p. 217.

59. Mackinnon, op. cit. I, p. 197; Hamilton, op. cit. I, p. 316; Clarke, op. cit. II, p. 265–69.

60. Arthur, op. cit. I, pp. 301–03; Hamilton, op. cit. I, pp. 333, 414n, 339; Brackenbury, op. cit. p. 149; Burnet, op. cit. II, pp. 556–57.

61. Arthur, op. cit. I, p. 318; Mary Countess Cowper, *Diary*, 1864, p. 5; W.A. Speck, *The Butcher*, Oxford 1981, p. 88; Lord Hervey, *Memoirs*, 3 vols., 1931, I, pp. 257, 450; McCordell, op. cit. pp. 43, 93; Maurice, op. cit. I, p. 142; Lytton Strachey and Roger Fulford, eds. *The Grenville Memoirs*, 8 vols., 1938, I, p. 23, entry for August 1830.

62. Claude Nordmann, *Grandeur et Liberté de la Suède*, 1971, pp. 230, 263; O–G. de Heidenstam, *Louise-Ulrique Reine de Suède*, 1897, pp. 175–77; Comte de Hordt, *Mémoires*, 2 vols., 1793, I, pp. 272–73; Odelberg, op. cit. pp. 255, 258, 261.

63. Ibid, pp. 262–65; Heidenstam, op. cit. p. 375, Gustavus III to Louise-Ulrique, 20 August 1772; Louis Bonneville de Marsangy, *Le Comte de Vergennes. Son Ambassade en Suède*, 1898, p. 224; Charles Francis Sheridan, *A History of the Late Revolution in Sweden*, 1778, pp. 294–96.

64. Odelberg, op. cit. pp. 266, 268, 273; H. Arnold Barton, 'Late Gustavian Autocracy in Sweden', *Scandinavian Studies*, Summer 1974, vol. 46, p. 268; Sten Carlsson, *Gustav IV Adolf's Fall*, Lund 1944, p. 223.

65. Anon., *An Historical Sketch of the Last Years of the Reign of Gustavus the Fourth Adolphus, late King of Sweden*, 1812, pp. 217, 221–22; Colonel Gustafsson, *La Journée du 13 Mai, 1809*, St-Gall 1835, pp. 19–20.

66. H. Arnold Barton, *Count Hans Axel von Fersen*, Boston 1975, pp. 369, 375–77; Odelberg, op. cit. pp. 276–78.

67. F.B. Bradley-Birt, *Through Persia from the Gulf to the Caspian*, 1907, p. 296; Edward G. Browne, *The Persian Revolution of 1905–1909*, Cambridge 1910, pp. 120, 161, 166, 196, 202, 209, 321; W. Morgan Shuster, *The Strangling of Persia*, 1912, p. 189.

68. H.I.M. Mohammed Reza Shah, *Mission for My Country*, 1961, pp. 102–03; Richard W. Cottam, *Nationalism in Iran*, Pittsburgh 1964, pp. 155, 226; E. Abrahamian, 'The Crowd in Iranian Politics 1908–1953', *Past and Present*, xli, 1968, pp. 199; Peter Avery, *Modern Iran*, 1964, p. 439; interviews with officers of the Imperial Guard, 1981–1983.

NOTES TO CHAPTER 7
GUARDS AND REVOLUTIONS

1. Bellanger, op. cit. règlement, 1598, p. 46; John George Keysler, *Travels through Germany, Bohemia, Hungary, Switzerland and Lorraine*, 4 vols., 1757, II, p. 10, writes of the Swiss Guard of the Pope 'their chief employment is to keep off the crowds at public solemnities'; Hennell, op. cit. p. 186; Baron de Tott, *Mémoires sur les Turcs et les Tartares*, 4 vols., Amsterdam 1784, III, p. 157; interview with a former Gentleman at Arms, 1982.

2. Gregg, op. cit. p. 150; Ibrahim, op. cit. p. 17, cf. p. 47; Sir George Carew, *A Relation of the State of France*, 1749, p. 461; Barratt, *Voices in Exile*, p. 36.

3. Gregg, op. cit. p. 306; Maurice, op. cit. I, pp. 104, 173; Arthur, op. cit. II, p. 473, Horace Walpole to Lord Hertford, 20 May 1765; Christopher Hibbert, *King Mob*, 1958, pp. 41, 70–93.

4. Bombelles, op. cit. II, p. 104, entry for 11 January 1786; Jean Chagniot, *Paris et l'Armée au XVIIIe Siècle*, Thèse pour le Doctorat d'Etat, Université de Paris–IV, 1983, pp. 206, 234, 686, 867.

5. Lacolle, op. cit. p. 310–15; Samuel F. Scott, *The Response of the Royal Army to the French Revolution*, 1978, pp. 52–56.

6. Scott, op. cit. p. 67; Louis Gottschalk and Margaret Maddox, *La Fayette*, I, pp. 187, 206, ibid, II, p. 194; *Mémoire des Maréchaux de Camp, Brigadiers, et Gardes du Corps du Roi à l'Assemblée Nationale*, 19 August 1789; *Journal des Amis de la Constitution*, 1 July 1789 (reference kindly communicated by P. Girault de Coursac).

7. Lucien de Chilly, *La Tour du Pin*, 1909, pp. 66, 69–70, 76; *Procédure Criminelle Instruite au Châtelet de Paris*, 3 vols., 1790, I, pp. 75, 249, *déposition* of Comte de Sainte-Aulaire, officer of Gardes du Corps; ibid, II, p. 144, *déposition* of J.

Schmid, Cent-Suisse; Comte Fleury, *Fantômes et Silhouettes*, 1902, p. 200, relation du Duc de Guiche.

8. *Procédure*, op. cit. I, p. 26, *déposition* of Du Repaire, Garde du Corps; ibid, p. 39, *déposition* of de Miomandre, Garde du Corps; ibid, p. 250, *déposition* of Comte de Sainte-Aulaire; A.N.O.[1]3673 Etat du Guet, January 1787–October 1789, and letters passim e.g. from Boursaut, 27 September 1789.

9. *Procédure*, op. cit. II, p. 42, *déposition* du Duc d'Ayen; ibid, III, p. 62–63, *déposition* of Saint-Virieu, Garde du Corps; ibid, II, p. 147, *déposition* of Chavannes, Garde du Corps.

10. Capitaine de Vallière, *Histoire du Regiment des Gardes Suisses en France*, Lausanne et Paris 1912, pp. 149, 151, Capitaine d'Erlauben to Avoyer de Mülinen, 1 August 1792; P. Girault de Coursac, *Enquête sur le Procès du Roi Louis XVI*, 1982, pp. 496–97, 549; Rodolphe de Castella de Delley, *Le Régiment des Gardes Suisses au Service de France*, Fribourg 1964, pp. 148, 162.

11. Castella de Delley, op. cit. pp. 165–70.

12. Lt-Colonel Ross of Bladensburg, *A History of the Coldstream Guards from 1815 to 1895*, 1896, pp. 73, 79–81; T.A.D. Burnett, *The Rise and Fall of a Regency Dandy*, 1981, p. 187; Arthur, op. cit. p. 631; Duke of Wellington, *Supplementary Despatches (New Series)*, I, p. 127, Wellington to Liverpool, 'Memorandum respecting the state of the Guards', June 1820; ibid, p. 145, Herbert Taylor to Wellington, 19 September 1820; *Letters of Harriet, Countess Granville, 1810–1845*, 2 vols., 1894, I, p. 155, Letter of 17 August 1820.

13. Ross, op. cit. pp. 76, 87, 313; Maurice, op. cit. II, p. 128; Higginson, op. cit. p. 37; Hamilton, op. cit. III, p. 109; Edward M. Spiers, *The Army and Society*, 1980, p. 219.

13. AHMG. XAE 7 Raguse to La Tour-Maubourg, 19 December 1819; XAE 6 Clermont-Tonnerre to Major-Général de service, 28 April 1825; Douglas Porch, *Army and Revolution*, 1974, pp. 32–33; AN. CC 551 1026–1029 Papers of the Chambre des Pairs, trial of the Ministers of Charles X; Bermond, *La Garde Royale en 1830*, 1830, p. 5.

15. Bermond, op. cit. pp. 5, 24–25, 79, 85, 95.

16. Capitaine de Courcy, 'La Garde Royale', *Carnets de la Sabretache*, 1927, p. 349; Bermond, op. cit. pp. 46, 95, 109, 125; AN 101 AP Archives de la Maison de Gramont D 2 10.6 Ordre du Jour, 3 August 1830; E35 Journal du Duc de Guiche, p. 11.

17. David H. Pinkney, *The French Revolution of 1830*, Princeton 1972, pp. 166, 176; Elisée Coutan, *Rapport sur les Evènements de Paris pendant la Dernière Semaine de Juillet 1830*, Genève 1830, pp. 5, 29.

18. Alfred von Besser, *Geschichte des Garde-Schützen-Bataillons*, Berlin 1889, pp. 29, 32; Jacques Droz, *Les Révolutions Allemandes de 1848*, 1957, pp. 200, 204, 222, 343, 389; R. John Rath, *The Vienna Revolution of 1848*, Austin 1957, p. 196.

19. Sidney Harcave, *First Blood. The Russian Revolution of 1905*, 1964, pp. 86–89, 93–96; Walter Sablinsky, *The Road to Bloody Sunday*, Princeton 1976, pp. 246–50, 267.

20. Nicholas II, *Journal*, p. 232, entry for 6 August 1905, pp. 245–50; *idem, Correspondence with Wilhelm II*, n.d. p. 228, Wilhelm II to Nicholas II, 14 June 1906.

21. Allan K. Wildman, *The End of the Russian Imperial Army*, Princeton 1980, pp. 63, 125–26, 158; Spiridovitch, op. cit. II, p. 78; Tsuyoshi Hasegawa, *The February Revolution. Petrograd 1917*, Seattle and London 1981, pp. 163–64; Maklakov, op. cit. p. 524, letter of General Doubenski, 12/15 January 1917; Bloch, op. cit. p. 62, Okhrana report of 5 February 1917.

22. Hasegawa, op. cit. p. 166–67; Maklakov, op. cit. p. 388, interrogatoire du Général Khabalov; ibid, p. 211, interrogatoire de A.D. Protopopov.

23. Wildman, op. cit. pp. 133, 139; Hasegawa, op. cit. pp. 278–85, 292; PRO. FO 371/2995. 297, report of 11 March 1917.

24. George Katkov, *Russia 1917. The February Revolution*, 1967, p. 290n; Wildman, pp. 151, 245; Hasegawa, op. cit. pp. 294–95, 445; cf. Katkov, op. cit. p. 245, diary of a Pavlovsky officer, 'Between us and them is an impassable gulf'.

25. Wildman, op. cit. p. 151; Hasegawa, op. cit. pp. 300–07.

26. Maklakov, op. cit. p. 397, interrogatoire du Général Voieikov; ibid, pp. 500–01, interrogatoire du Général Ivanov; ibid, p. 524, interrogatoire du Général Doubenski; Nicholas II, *Letters to the Tsarina*, pp. 317–18, letters of 27 February 1917.

27. Count Paul Benckendorff, *Last Days at Tsarskoe Seloe*, 1927, pp. 6–11, 37–38; Tatiana Botkine, *Au Temps des Tsars*, 1980, pp. 237, 243, 248, 254; Wildman, op. cit. p. 198; General P.A. Polovtsoff, *Glory and Downfall. Reminiscences of a Russian General Staff Officer*, 1935, p. 186; Alexander Rabinovitch, *Prelude to Revolution*, Bloomington 1968, pp. 179, 221–22; idem, *The Bolsheviks Come to Power*, 1979, pp. 262–74; David R. Jones, 'The Officers and the October Revolution', *Soviet Studies*, April, 1976, xxviii, no 2, p. 222.

28. Luedin, op. cit. p. 175; Gordon Brook-Shepherd, *The Last Habsburg*, 1968, pp. 201–06, 243; Viktoria Luise, Duchess of Brunswick, *Memoirs*, 1977, p. 135.

29. Maurice Baumont, *The Fall of the Kaiser*, 1931, pp. 112, 128, 158, William II to Crown Prince, 9 November 1918, p. 235.

30. Ibid, p. 187; Count Harry Kessler, *The Diaries of a Cosmopolitan*, 1971, pp. 9, 12, entries for 9, 14 November 1918; Prince Max of Baden, *Memoirs*, 2 vols., 1928, II, pp. 315, 350, 356.

31. Kessler, op. cit. p. 13, entry for 14 November 1918; ibid, p. 43, entry for 26 December 1918; Craig, op. cit. p. 356; Albrecht von Stosch, *Das Königlich Preussische 5 Garde Regiment zu Fuss 1897–1918*, Berlin 1930, p. 517; W. von Boddien, *Das Regiment der Garde du Corps im Weltkrieg*, Berlin 1928, p. 409; Robert G.L. Waite, *Vanguard of Nazism. The Freecorps Movement in Postwar Germany*, Cambridge Mass. 1952, p. 61–62.

32. Waite, op. cit. p. 73; Kessler, op. cit. pp. 41, 45, 58,

63, entries for 24 December 1918, 28 December 1918, 15 January 1919, 22 February 1919.

33. *Das Erste Garderegiment zu Fuss im Weltkrieg 1914–1918*, Berlin 1934, pp. 280–81 and forewords; Harold J. Gordon, *The Reichswehr and the German Republic 1919–1926*, Princeton 1957, pp. 201, 223, 310, 313; Craig, op. cit. p. 456.

34. Interview with General Oveissi, 24 March 1983; interviews with an officer of the Iranian Imperial Guard, 11 September, 27 December 1981; David Wheeler, 'The Fall of the Shah', BBC Radio, 23 March 1982.

35. Interview with a former adviser of the Shah, 21 December 1981; 'TV Eye', February 1979; John D. Stempel, *Inside the Iranian Revolution*, Bloomington 1981, pp. 151, 171.

NOTES TO CHAPTER 8
LIFE IN THE GUARDS

1. Pegge, op. cit. III, p. 76, Order of 16 May 1692; Osbert Sitwell, *Great Morning*, 1948, p. 201.

2. Interview with Peter Clayton 28 June 1981; interview with former officers of the Sultan's Armed Forces, 26 April 1981, 23 June 1981; interview with an officer of the Irish Guards on loan to the Dubai Defence Force, 10 March 1981; O'Shea, op. cit. p. 68; Al Qalqashandi on the Khāssikiya guards of the Mameluke Sultans of Egypt, in David Ayalon, *Studies in the Structure of the Mameluke Army*, 1977, p. 214.

3. L.S. Mercier, *Tableau de Paris* (nouv. ed. corr. et aug.), 12 vols., Amsterdam 1783–8, X, p. 159; Walter Scott, *Paul's Letters to His Kinsfolk*, 1816, p. 359; Chevalier de Villebresme (a Mousquetaire), *Souvenirs*, 1897, p. 9; Gaspard Richard de Soultrait, 'Lettres', *Carnets de la Sabretache*, 3e Série, 1923, VI, p. 430, to father, 20 September 1814; Edouard Dechy, *Souvenirs d'un Ancien Militaire*, 1860, pp. 316–17; AHMG XAE 11, 9, Marquis de Choiseul to Général Bordessoule, 27 January 1827, Comte de Virieu to Général Partouneau, 12, 20 January 1827; Verly, op. cit. p. 123.

4. J.B.A. Barrès, *Souvenirs d'un Officier de la Grande Armée*, n.d. p. 6; Colonel de Suckow, *Fragments de ma Vie*, 1901, p. 35; Baroness von Bunsen, *A Winter in Berlin*, 1883 pp. 32, 52; Princess Friedrich Leopold, op. cit. p. 41.

5. Ransel, op. cit. p. 232; Stedingk, *Choix de Dépêches Diplomatiques, Rapports Secrets et Lettres Particulières de 1790 à 1796*, 2 vols. Stockholm 1919, I, p. 209, Jennings to Franc, October 1791; David Magarshack, *Pushkin*, 1967, p. 48; Lawrence Kelly, *Lermontov. Tragedy in the Caucasus*, 1977, p. 108, Lermontov to Marya, late 1838.

6. Countess Kleinmichel, *Memories of a Shipwrecked World*, 1923, p. 133; Mannerheim, op. cit. p. 7; Krassnoff, op. cit. I, pp. 147, 198; Polovtsoff, op. cit. p. 38.

7. Ailesbury, op. cit. I, p. 129; Willard Connelly, *Sir*

Richard Steele, 1934, p. 53; James Boswell, *London Journal*, ed. Frederick A. Pottle 1953, p. 131, entry for 9 January 1763, p. 201, entry for 25 February 1763, p. 219, entry for 15 March 1763; H.W. Studd, *Notes for Parents who Desire to Obtain Commissions for Their Sons*, 1921, pp. 12–13.

8. Captain Gronow, *Reminiscences and Recollections*, 2 vols., 1892, II, p. 268; Higginson, op. cit. pp. 33, 343; Lord Ormathwaite, *When I was at Court*, 1937, pp. 39, 46.

9. Mary King Waddington, *Letters of a Diplomat's Wife*, 1903, p. 201, letter of 24 February 1885; Nigel Nicolson, *Alex*, 1973, p. 27, Alex to Countess of Caledon, 8 May 1912, 16 January 1913; cf. for guards' performance on the dance-floor, Sonia Keppel, *Edwardian Daughter*, 1958, p. 181; Humphrey Lyttelton, *I Play as I Please*, 1954, p. 100; interview with a former officer of the Grenadier Guards, 8 March 1982; interview with a former officer of H.M. the Queen's Guard, 3 February 1982.

10. *Times Literary Supplement*, 25 December 1981, p. 1495, letter from Oswyn Murray; Arthur, op. cit. I, pp. 89, 346–47; Gronow, op. cit. II, p. 209; Firbank, op. cit. p. 67; Keegan, op. cit. p. 182; *The Guards Magazine*, Spring 1983, p. 17.

11. Chagniot, op. cit. p. 784; Gleichen, op. cit. pp. 50, 87; John Bushnell, 'The Tsarist Officer Corps 1881–1914; Custom, Duties, Inefficiency', *American Historical Review*, 4 Oct 1981, vol. 86, pp. 756, 763; M.D. Calvocoressi, *Mussorgsky*, 1946, pp. 5–7; Lt.-Gen. A.A. Ignatyev, *A Subaltern in Old Russia*, 1944, pp. 92–93.

12. Wilber, op. cit. p. 9; Cecil Roth, *The House of Nasi. The Dukes of Naxos*, Philadelphia 1948, p. 36; J.E. Alexander, *Travels to the Seat of War in the East in 1829*, 2 vols., 1830, II, p. 302; Pardoe, op. cit. II, p. 312; Richard Davey, *The Sultan and His Subjects*, 2 vols., 1897, I, p. 53.

13. See e.g. AHMG XAE7 Rapport of 29 February 1816 for fears that life in Paris will 'entirely corrupt the morale and ruin the health' of soldiers of the Garde Royale; M. de Marville, *Lettres . . . au Ministre Maurepas*, 3 vols., 1896–1905, III, p. 179, letter of 8 March 1747;0 Vallière, op. cit. p. 110; A. Janvier, *MM les Gardes du Corps de la Compagnie de Luxembourg. Episodes de l'Histoire d'Amiens*, Amiens 1887, p. 111; Prince de Ligne, *Fragments de l'Histoire de Ma Vie*, 2 vols., 1928, I, p. 79; Chagniot, op. cit. pp. 301, 605, 774.

14. F-F Billon, *Souvenirs d'un Vélite de la Gade*, 1905, p. 46; Musée Carnavalet 35[14] Moeurs, Vie Militaire; Lieut. Chevalier, *Souvenirs*, 1970, pp. 131–32, 154, 174.

15. Winston S. Churchill, *Marlborough. His Life and Times*, 4 vols., I, p. 61; E.S. Turner, *Gallant Gentleman*, 1956, p. 61; Alan Roland, *Guardsman*, 1955, p. 10; G. Cornwallis-West, *Edwardian Hey-Days*, 1930, p. 48; Ferenc Molnar, *The Plays*, New York 1926, p. 151.

16. Dalrymple, op. cit. p. 45, letter of 29 July 1774; A Resident Officer, *Madrid in 1835. Sketches of the*

Capital of Spain, 2 vols., 1836, I, p. 149; Rudolphe de Steiger, *Lettres à sa Famille*, Genève 1916, p. 194, letter of 12 July 1813; Polovtsoff, op. cit. pp. 17, 36; Krassnoff, op. cit. I, pp. 21, 245.

17. Interview with a former soldier in the Coldstream Guards, 21 June 1981; A.D. Harvey, 'Prosecutions for Sodomy in England at the Beginning of the Nineteenth Century', *Historical Journal*, 21 April 1978, p. 943; H.M. Hyde, *The Other Love*, 1972, pp. 90, 99, 110, 140, 227, 300; Ian Harvey, *To Fall Like Lucifer*, 1971, p. 102; Roland, op. cit. pp. 107–08.

18. AN. ABXIX 14 Prefet de Police to Comte de Fezensac, an officer in the Garde Royale, 31 May 1820, cf. O³225.12 Note de Police, 15 January 1823; Anon., 'Idée de la Personne . . . et de la Cour du Roi de Prusse', 1753, B.M. Stowe 307 f. 62vo; Duffy, *Army of Frederick the Great*, p. 60.

19. Marczali, op. cit. pp. 19n, 237n; Marc Raeff, *The Origins of the Russian Intelligentsia*, 1966, p. 71; Jesse V. Clardy, *G.R. Dezhavin*, The Hague 1967, pp. 11, 26, 34.

20. Magarshack, op. cit. pp. 15, 47, 65; Kelly, op. cit. p. 38; Alfred de Vigny, *Servitude et Grandeur Militaires*, ed. Nelson, n.d. pp. 95, 165; Eliane Maingot, *Le Baron Taylor*, 1963, p. 105.

21. Gilbert, op. cit. III, pp. 578, 581; Thomas Wright, *The Life of Colonel Fred Burnaby*, 1908, pp. 34, 47, 61; Anthony Powell, *Messengers of Day*, 1978, p. 38.

22. Colonel F.I. Maxse, *Seymour Vandeleur. The Story of a British Officer*, 1905, p. 25, 288; Studd, op. cit. p. 5; Lacolle, op. cit. p. 395; Arthur, op. cit. I, p. 470; Sir John Fortescue, *A History of the British Army*, 13 vols, 1899–1930, XI, pp. 28–29; Forrest A. Miller, *Dmitri Miliutin and the Reform Era in Russia*, Charlotte 1968, pp. 91–95.

23. Duc de La Force, *Lauzun*, 1919, pp. 43, 144, 201, 216; Saint-Priest, op. cit. I, pp. 40, 99, cf. M. de La Roche, *Souvenirs d'un Officier de la Gendarmerie*, 2ᵉ ed. 1914, pp. 30–32; de Vigny, op. cit. p. 147.

24. Comte de Villeneuve-Bargemont, 'Les Honneurs de la Cour', *Carnets de la Sabretache*, 3e Série, 1920, iii, p. 258; Sir Frederick Charles Stephenson, *At Home and on the Battlefield*, 1915, p. 91, letter of 17 July 1854; Harold Macmillan, *Winds of Change*, 1966, p. 98; Sitwell, op. cit. p. 193; Windsor, op. cit. p. 189.

25. Sked, op. cit. p. 13; Wraxall, op. cit. p. 66; Kenez, op. cit. p. 137; Bruce, op. cit. p. 51; M. de Falckenskiold, *Mémoires*, 1826, p. 18; Levy, op. cit. p. 432.

26. Baron N. Wrangel, *Memoirs*, 1927, p. 114; Polovtsoff, op. cit. p. 16; Krassnoff, op. cit. passim; Falckenskiold, *Mémoires*, p. 395.

27. Princess Friedrich Leopold, op. cit. p. 30; Walter Görlitz, *Die Junker*, Limburg an der Lahn 1964, p. 354; Corti, op. cit. p. 253, Alexander of Hesse-Darmstadt to Tsarina of Russia, 27 November 1865; Janvier, op. cit. p. 32 and passim; Guillaume, op. cit. pp. 82–83, officers to Philip V, February 1716.

28. McCordell, op. cit. p. 92; interview with a former officer of the Grenadier Guards, 8 March 1982;

interview with Colonel Jefe de la Guardia Real, *Guardia Real*, Ano 1, Dec 1979, No. 3, p. 22.

29. Guillaume, op. cit. pp. 82–83; Lachouque, op. cit. p. 7; Maurice, op. cit. I, p. 368; Higginson, op. cit. p. 230, letter of 26 January 1855.

30. *The Letters of Lord and Lady Wolesley*, 1922, pp. 75, 77, Lord to Lady Wolesley, 31 August 1882, 10 September 1882.

31. Arthur Chuquet, *Etudes d'Histoire*, 8 vols., 1905–20, V, pp. 230–34, based on German accounts; cf. Roeder, pp. 87, 174; J.E. Guitaud, *Souvenirs Militaires du Premier Empire*, 1934, for the Emperor's inability to control the looting by his guard.

32. Longford, op. cit. p. 464; Michael Howard, *The Franco-Prussian War*, University Paperbacks, 1981, p. 175; Krassnoff, op. cit. I, pp. 118, 121; interview with General Oveissi, 24 March 1983.

NOTES TO CHAPTER 9
SPLENDOUR

1. Hennell, op. cit. p. 140, AN.R⁵56 Observations sur le Service des Gardes du Corps de Mgr. le Comte de Provence relativement à celui des Gardes du Corps du Roy.

2. Chester V. Easum, *Prince Henry of Prussia*, Madison 1942, p. 224; Gustave III, *Ecrits Politiques, Littéraires et Dramatiques*, 5 vols., Stockholm 1805, V, frontispiece, Gustave III to Prince Charles, 7 October 1790; Luedin, op. cit. p. 16; cf. Jori, op. cit. p. 34.

3. U.H.R. Broughton, *The Dress of the First Regiment of Life Guards in Three Centuries*, 1925, pp. 6–7; Patricia Crone, *Slaves on Horse-Back*, 1981, p. 263; Madame de Staël, *Considérations sur la Révolution Française*, 3 vols., London 1818, 111, p. 2.

4. Colonel Répond, *Le Costume de la Garde Suisse Pontificale et la Renaissance Italienne*, Rome 1917, p. 35; Guénée et Lehoux, op. cit. p. 191 and passim; Forbes-Leith, op. cit. I, pp. 58–59, 143–44; Preton, op. cit. p. 60.

5. Francesco Sansovino, *Delle Historia Universale dell' Origine et Imperio de Turchi*, 3 vols., Venezia, 1560, I, p. 47; Antoine Galland, *Journal*, 2 vols., 1881, I, p. 97, 9 April 1672; ibid, p. 137, 7 May 1672; Pfannenberg, op. cit. pp. 17–18; Paul Martin, *European Military Uniforms*, 1967, p. 92; McCordell, op. cit. p. 74.

6. C.A. McCartney, *The Habsburg and Hohenzollern Dynasties in the Seventeenth and Eighteenth Centuries*, 1970, p. 281, quoting J. von Besser, *Preussische Kronungsgeschichte*, 1712; after their final disbandment in 1815, a Mousquetaire proclaimed to his commander, '*je suis rouge de race, de coeur et d'âme*'; A.N.341 AP 25 anon to Marquis de la Grange, n.d.; Schreber von Schreeb, op. cit. p. 8; Coxe, op. cit. I, p. 487; Mannerheim, op. cit. p. 8.

7. E. Jared Sparkes, *The Life of Gouverneur Morris*, 3

vols., Boston 1832, I, p. 450, diary for 1 January
1797; Lady Shelley, op. cit. p. 304, November 1816;
Mrs. F. Trollope, *Vienna and the Austrians*, 2 vols.,
1838, II, p. 58; Prince Clary, *A European Past*, 1978,
p. 152.

8. John Mollo, *Military Fashion*, 1972, pp. 142, 154;
Luedin, op. cit. p. 134; Bismarck, op. cit. p. 74.

9. Pfannenberg, op. cit. p. 58; D.S.V. Fosten, *Cuirassiers
and Heavy Cavalry*, 1972, pp. 2, 27, 31; Capitaine Le
Brun-Renaud, *La Perse Politique et Militaire au XIXe
Siècle*, 1894, p. 23; Stephen Constant, *Foxy
Ferdinand, Tsar of Bulgaria*, 1979, p. 96.

10. Interview with Peter Davy, tailor, 17 March 1983;
Roland, op. cit. p. 10; interview with a former soldier
of the Coldstream Guards, 21 June 1981; interview
with a former officer of the Grenadier Guards, 8
March 1982; Dumonceau, op. cit. I, pp. 50, 60n, 345;
AN F⁷ 9875 Correspondence of Prefects with
Minister of Police, 1815–1816; Proclamation of
Prefect of Creuse, 15 November 1815.

11. Interview with Major General Salim Mahmoud
Al-Jaber Al-Sabah, Kuwait, 19 April 1981; interview
with Major Suleimen al-Adwani, Muscat, 25 April
1981; Arnold, op. cit. pp. 20, 22.

12. Maurice, op. cit. II, p. 151; Edward VI, *Chronicle
and Political Papers*, 1966, p. 63, diary for 14 May
1551; Guenée et Lehoux, op. cit. p. 275; Jocelyne G.
Russell, *The Field of the Cloth of Gold*, 1969, p. 212;
Paul Hentzer, *Travels in England*, 1797, p. 37; Lacey,
Raleigh, p. 102; Preston, op. cit. p. 106.

13. Lacolle, op. cit. pp. 342, 365; Gram-Andersen, op.
cit. p. 14; Hills, op. cit. p. 41.

14 Tuetey, op. cit. p. 112, Luxembourg to Louis XIV, 19
September 1692; Algarotti, op. cit. II, pp. 23–25,
letter of 13/30 September 1739; anon., *Observations
on the Military Establishment and Discipline of His
Majesty the King of Prussia*, p. 61; Gleichen, op. cit.
p. 83.

15. Wraxall, op. cit. p. 68; H.M. Hyde, ed., *The Journals
of Martha and Catherine Wilmot*, 1934, p. 155, entry
for 14 November 1807; R.B. Paul, *Journal of a Tour to
Moscow in the Summer of 1836*, 1836, p. 44;
Chantreau, op. cit. I, p. 165; Mary Howard
McClintock, *The Queen Thanks Sir Howard*, 1945,
p. 171, Sir Howard Elphinstone to Queen Victoria,
15 January 1874.

16. Alexandre Daumont, *Voyage en Suède*, 2 vols.,
1834, II, p. 121; Robert Bremner, *Excursions in
Denmark, Norway and Sweden*, 2 vols., 1840, II,
p. 407.

17. Hennell, op. cit. p. 69; George Cavendish, *The Life of
Cardinal Wolsey*, ed. Roger Lockyer, 1962, p. 82.

18. Haillot, op. cit. I, p. 198; Edmond Favre, *L'Autriche
et ses Institutions Militaires*, 1866, p. 113; Pakalin,
op. cit. III, p. 255; David Porter, *Constantinople and
its Environs in a Series of Letters*, 2 vols., New York
1835, I, p. 194, letter of 15 May 1832; S.C.W.
Benjamin, *The Turks and the Greeks*, New York
1867, p. 76; Georges Dorys, *Abdul-Hamid Intime*,
Sixième Edition, 1903, p. 196.

19. Neil Campbell, op. cit. p. 69; cf. Sir Archibald

Alison, *Travels in France*, 2 vols., 1816, I, p. 47;
Bismarck, op. cit. p. 23; Londonderry, op. cit. II,
p. 199.

20. Wilhelm II, *My Early Life*, p. 246, 314, ketter to
Wilhelm I, 18 May 1884; Volkov, op. cit. p. 14;
Krassnoff, op. cit. I, p. 168; Robert R. McCormick,
With the Russian Army, 1915, p. 202, interview with
Colonel Doubenstkoff, 8 April 1982.

21. Maxwell, op. cit. p. 161; Verly, op. cit. p. 70; Anna
Bowman Dodds, *In the Palaces of the Sultan*, 1904,
p. 40.

22. Babinger, op. cit. p. 418; Ali Bey, *Travels in
Morocco, Tripoli, Cyprus, Egypt, Arabia, Syria, and
Turkey between the Years 1803 and 1807*, 2 vols.,
1816, II, p. 333; Henry George Farmer, *Military
Music*, 1950, pp. 21, 35; anon., *A Short Journal of
His Polish Majesty's Camp of Radewitz in Saxony in
the Year 1730*, 1733, p. 24.

23. Baron Bielfeld, *Letters*, 3 vols., 1770, III, p. 65, letter
of 16 October 1739; D.G.H. Hagger, *Hussars and
Mounted Rifles*, 1974, p. 69; Maurice, op. cit. II,
p. 264; Farmer, op. cit. pp. 46–47, 56.

24. Slidell Mackenzie, *Spain Revisited*, 2 vols., 1836, I,
pp. 186–87; Arnold, op. cit. p. 24; D. Van der
Meulen, *Faces in Shem*, 1961, p. 135.

25. Kemal Pacha Zadeh, *Histoire de la Campagne de
Mohacz*, 1859, pp. 45–46; Galland, op. cit. I, pp. 123,
diary for 7 April 1672; Carew, op. cit. p. 435;
Mercier, op. cit. IV, p. 147; Kaunitz, op. cit. p. 839.

26. Maréchal de Gramont, *Mémoires*, 2 vols., 1716, II,
p. 45; Molesworth, *An Account of Denmark as it was
in the Year 1692*, 3rd ed., 1694, p. 146; Arthur, op.
cit. I, p. 81n; Mackinnon, op. cit. I, p. 197; Robinson,
An Account of Sweden, 1694, pp. 81–83; Sir Robert
Ker Porter, *Travelling Sketches in Russia and
Sweden during the Years 1805, 1806, 1807, 1808*, 2
vols., 1809, II, p. 138.

27. Rodzianko, op. cit. p. 91; Philip Durham Trotter,
Our Mission to the Court of Morocco in 1880,
Edinburgh 1881, p. 115; Arthur Leared, *A Visit to the
Court of Morocco*, 1879, p. 33.

28. John C.G. Röhl, 'The Emperor's New Clothes', in
Röhl ed. *Kaiser Wilhelm II. New Interpretations*,
1982, p. 122; cf. Daisy, Princess of Pless, *The Private
Diaries*, 1950, p. 35, entry for 7 September 1896;
Lord Hardinge of Penshurst, *Old Diplomacy*, 1947,
p. 23; Jules Laforgue, *Berlin, la Cour et la Ville*, 1922,
pp. 15–16; Thomas Browne, op. cit. p. 16; A.S.
Levetus, *Imperial Vienna*, 1905, p. 89.

29. Ralph Herrmann and Hans Hammerskiold, *The
Royal Palace of Stockholm*, Stockholm 1978, pp. 8,
10, 133; letter from Lieutenant-Colonel commanding
the Governor General's Foot Guards, 8 February
1983; interview with Commander of Pontifical Swiss
Guard, 4 September 1982.

30. Known as 'the principal guard-post of the country –
post no. 1', Lenin's Tomb is guarded by the
uniformed branch of the KGB, which has guarded
the Kremlin since 1935. See A. Abramov, *At the
Kremlin Wall*, Moscow 1980, pp. 28–32.

SOURCES

I. MANUSCRIPTS

1. ARCHIVES NATIONALES

   O^1 3672 – 9 Garde Ancien Régime
   O^1 3696 – 9 Garde Louis XVI
   O^3 2558   Garde Louis XVI
      2562   Garde Louis XVI

   CC551 Chambre des Pairs. Trial of Ministers of Charles X, 1831

   F^{7}4280, 16 Mémoire sur la Garde de l'Empereur comparativement avec celle de la Garde du Roi, L-A d'Agoult, 1806

   F^{7}9875   Correspondance of Prefects with Ministers of Police, 1815–16

   101 AP D2, D4, E35 Archives de la Maison de Gramont

2. ARCHIVES HISTORIQUES DU MINISTÈRE DE LA GUERRE
X AD 1–15, 24	Maison Militaire	1814–1830
X AE 1–11	Garde Royale	1815–1830

3. BIBLIOTHÈQUE NATIONALE. DÉPARTMENT DES MANUSCRITS
Mss. Français	21451.206	Capitulation du Régiment des Gardes Ecossaises, 1642
	8006	Ordonnances of Kings of France
Nouvelles Acquisitions Françaises	9740	Ordonnances of Kings of France

4. MUSÉE CARNIVALET
   35^{14} Moeurs. Vie Militaire

5. BRITISH MUSEUM. DEPARTMENT OF MANUSCRIPTS
   Stowe Mss 307 Idée de la Personne, de la Manière de Vivre et de la Cour du Roi de Prusse, juin 1753

6. PUBLIC RECORD OFFICE
   Foreign Office 22/6 Despatches from the British Ambassador to Denmark, 1784
   27/224 Despatches from the British Ambassador to France, 1820
   72/160, 234, 286, 579 Despatches from the British Ambassador to Spain, 1814, 1820, 1824, 1841
   371/2994, 2995 Despatches from the British Ambassador, and other diplomatic agents, in Russia, 1917

II. BIBLIOGRAPHY

Unless otherwise stated books in French are published in Paris and books in English in London.

1. BOOKS SPECIFICALLY ABOUT ROYAL GUARDS

Alsop, James Douglas, *The Military Functions of Henry VII's Household*, unpublished M.A. Thesis, London Ontario 1974.
Anon., *Considérations sur les Gardes du Corps et sur leur Mode de Recrutement*, 1821.
— *Garde-Jäger-Battaillon*, Oldenburg 1934.

— *Garde-Schützen Bataillon*, Berlin 1928.
— *Garde – und Leibtruppen im Reichsheer bis 1918 – Feldzeichin des Königlich Preussischen Gardekorps*, Rastatt, Wehrgeschichtliches Museum, 1983.
— *Governor-General's Foot Guards. Centennial*, Ottawa 1972.
— *Gut und Blut für Unsern Kaiser. Zur Erinnerung an den 100 Jährigen Gedenktag der Errichtung der K.u.K. Leibgarde Infanterie Compagnie*, Vienna 1902.
— *Die Leibhusaren, Ihre Geschichte im Weltkriege*, Berlin 1929.
— *La Garde Royale*, Rabat n.d.
— *L'Escorte Royale Belge*, Second Edition, Brussels, 1973.
— *The History of His Majesty the King's Guard*, Oslo n.d.
— *The Royal Guard Regiment*, Muscat n.d.
Arthur, Captain Sir George, *The Story of the Household Cavalry*, 3 vols., 1909.
Averton, M. d', *Notice Historique sur la Garde Constitutionelle*, 1814.
Beard, C.R., 'The Clothing and Arming of the Yeoman of the Guard', *Archaeological Journal*, 1925, LXXXII, pp. 91–148.
Bellanger, F., *Les Gardes du Corps sous les Anciennes Monarchies*, 1895.
Bennigsen, Captain Count M.C., 'The Preobrajhensky Regiment of the Russian Guard', *Journal of the Royal United Services Institution*, LXIX, 1924, 2–11, pp. 99–108.
Bergensträhle, Gillis, *Historiska Anteckningor om Kungl. Göta Livgarde*, Stockholm 1907.
Bermond, F., *La Garde Royale pendant les Evènements du 26 Juillet au 5 Aout, 1830*, 1830.
Besser, Alfred von, *Geschichte der Garde-Schützen–Bataillons*, Berlin 1889.
Besson, François, *Entretien et Examen sur la Création et Information de la Compagnie des Cent Gardes Suisses Ordinaires du Corps du Roy*, 1672.
Beutner, Major, *Die Königlich Preussische Garde-Artillerie*, 2 vols., Berlin 1889–1894.
Boddien, W. von, *Das Regiment der Garde du Corps im Weltkriege*, Berlin 1928.
Boullier, M., *Histoire des Divers Corps de la Maison Militaire des Rois de France*, 1818.
Brackenbury, Major Henry, *The History of His Majesty's Body Guard of the Honourable Corps of Gentlemen at Arms. The Nearest Guard*, 1905.
Briant, Keith, *Fighting with the Guards*, 1958.
Broughton, U.H.R., *The Dress of the First Regiment of Life Guards in Three Centuries*, 1925.
Bruehl, Ferdinand von, *Übersicht der Geschichte des Königlichen Regiments der Garde du Corps von 1740 bis 1890*, Berlin 1890.
Cannon, R., *Historical Records of the Life Guards*, Second Edition, 1840.
Capitan de Cuartel del Cuerpo de Guardias de la Persona del Rey, *Representacion Dirigida al Congreso Nacional*, 1821.
Carlsson, Sten, 'Gardesdegradiring', *Historisk Tidskrift*, 1943, pp. 369–97.
Cart, J., 'Le Dix-Aout et le Régiment des Gardes Suisses', *Revue des Etudes Historiques*, 1909, pp. 481–519, 647–67.
Castella, Gaston, *La Garde Fidèle du Saint Père*, 1935.
Castella de Delley, Rodolphe de, *Le Régiment des Gardes Suisses au Service de France*, Fribourg 1964.
— *Les Cent Suisses de la Garde du Roi*, 1971.
[Cionard, Conde de], *Memorias para la Historia de las Tropas de la Casa Real de Espana*, Madrid 1828.
Capitaine de Courcy, 'La Garde Royale, 1815–1830', *Carnets de la Sabretache*, 3e Série, 1927, pp. 326–49, 414–39, 486–510, 530–56, 4e Série, 1928, I, pp. 44–61.
Cuerpo de Guardias de la Persona del Rey, *Representacion*, 7 April 1821.
Curling, James Bunce, *Some Account of the Ancient Corps of Gentlemen at Arms*, 1850.
Dawnay, Major Nicholas Payan, *The Standards, Guidons and Colours of the Household Division 1660–1973*, 1975.
Dunlop, James, *Papers Relating to the Royal Guard of Scottish Archers in France*, Edinburgh 1835.
Durieux, Joseph, *Gardes Françaises du 14 Juillet*, 1933.
Ferrara, Generale de Divisione Arnualdo, *I Carabinieri-Guardie del Presidente della Reppublica*, Rome 1973.
Fitzgerald, Major D.J.L., *History of the Irish Guards in the Second World War*, Aldershot 1949.
Flammermont, J., 'Les Gardes Françaises en Juillet 1789', *La Revolution Française*, XXXVI, January 1899, pp. 12–24.
Fonjalez, J.G., 'Journal d'un Garde Suisse', *Revue de Paris*, 15 September 1908, pp. 305–421, 1 October 1908, pp. 607–23.
Forbes-Leith, William, *The Scots Men-at-Arms and Life Guards in France*, 2 vols., Edinburgh 1882.
Forges de Parny, Léon des, *Les Gardes du Corps du Roi*, Cannes 1972.
Foster, Michael, *Sir Troilus Turberville, Captain of the King's Life Guard*, Royal Stuart Papers 1980.
Frearson, C.W., *Officers of the Life Guards and Horse Grenadiers 1661–1969*, Typescript Windsor 1978.
— *Officers of the Blues 1661–1969*, Typescript Windsor 1978.
Gamez, Pedro Jose, *Exposicion que Hace a las Cortes Generales y Extraordinarias el Real Cuerpo de Guardias de Corps*, Cadiz 1811.

Girault de Coursac, P., 'La Garde du Roi', *Découverte*, XIV, June 1976, pp. 3–20, XV, September 1976, pp. 16–31, XVI, December 1976, pp. 3–20.

Goodinge, Anthony, *The Scots Guards*, 1969.

Gow, Lt-Gen Sir Michael, *A History of the Sovereign's Birthday Parade by the Household Troops*, c. 1978.

Gram-Andersen, Captain J., *The Royal Danish Life Guards*, Odense 1980.

Grenadier Guards, The, *A Tercentenary Exhibition*, 1956.

Guerrini, Domenico, *La Brigata dei Granatieri di Sardegna*, Turin 1905.

Guillaume, Colonel, *Histoires des Gardes Wallonnes au Service d'Espagne*, Brussels 1858.

Haering, Oscar, *Geschichte der Preussischen Garde*, Berlin 1891.

Hall, Colonel Sir John Bt., *The Coldstream Guards 1885–1914*, Oxford 1924.

Hamilton, Lt-Gen Sir F.W., *The Origins and History of the First or Grenadier Guards*, 3 vols., 1874–1877.

Hay, Ian, *The Royal Company of Archers 1676–1951*, Edinburgh and London 1951.

Headlam, Cuthbert, *History of the Guards Division in the Great War 1915–1918*, 2 vols., 1924.

Hennell, Colonel Sir Reginald, *The History of the King's Body Guard of the Yeomen of the Guards*, 1904.

Hennet, Leon, 'L'Escadron Sacré', *Carnets de la Sabretache*, 2e Série, VIII, 1909, pp 691–704, 759–60.

Hills, Colonel R.J.T., *The Life Guards*, 1971
— *The Royal Horse Guards (The Blues)*, 1970

Howard, Michael and John Sparrow, *The Coldstream Guards 1920–1946*, 1951.

Janvier, A.M., *Les Gardes du Corps de la Compagnie de Luxembourg. Episodes de l'Histoire d'Amiens*, 1887.

Jones, David R., 'The Imperial Russian Life Guards Grenadier Regiment 1906–1917: The Disintegration of an Elite Unit', *Military Affairs*, October 1969, pp. 289–302.

Jori, Ilio., *La 'Casa Militare' alla Corte dei Savoia*, Rome 1928, Anno VI.

Kaehne, Hermann, *Geschichte des Königlich Preussischen Garde-Train-Bataillons*, Berlin 1903.

Kathen, H. von, *Das 3 Garde Regiment zu Fuss 1860 bis 1890*, Berlin 1890.

Kearsley, Harvey, *His Majesty's Bodyguard of the Honourable Corps of Gentlemen-at-Arms*, 1937.

Kozlianinoff, Colonel W., *Manuel Commémoratif de la Garde à Cheval 1739–1930*, 1931.

Krieg, Paul M., *Die Schweizergarde in Rom*, Lucerne 1960.

Krogh, C.C. von, *Meddelser om den Kongelige Livgarde till Hast*, Copenhagen 1886.

Kunz, Major H., *Zur Geschichte der Kaiserlich Französischen Garde von 1854–1870*, Berlin 1898.

Lachouque, Henry, *The Anatomy of Glory*, London and Melbourne, 1978.

Lacolle, Noel, *Histoire des Gardes Françaises*, 1901.

Lancaster, Osbert, 'Bodyguards of Europe', *The Geographical Magazine*, VIII, December 1938, 2, pp. 105–20.

Lang, Giovanni, *Dalle Guardie del Corpo allo Squadrone Carabinieri – Guardie del Re*, Genoa 1914.

La Tour, M., *Maison Militaire du Roi*, 1790.

La Trollière, J. de et R. de Montmarie, *Les Chevau-Légers de la Garde du Roy*, 1953.

Leasor, James, *The Sergeant Major*, 1955.

La Pippre de Noeufville, Simon Lamoral, *Abrégé Chronologique et Historique de l'Origine, des Progrès et de l'Etat Actuel de la Maison du Roi*, 3 vols., Liège 1734.

Le Senne, Emile, *La Garde Suisse des Champs-Elysées au XVIIIe Siècle*, 1914.

Le Thueux, *Essais Historiques sur les Deux Compagnies des Mousquetaires du Roi de France*, 2 vols., La Haye 1778.

Lomier, Docteur, *Histoire des Regiments des Gardes d'Honneur*, Paris Amiens 1924.

Lopez, Juan Jose, 'Estudio sobre los Monteros de Espinosa', *Guardia Real*, Ano IV, Num. 32, June 1982, pp. 29–35.

Loqueyssie, M. de, *Essai sur la Maison Militaire Equestre du Roi*, 1815.

Lüdinghausen, Otto Freiherr von, *Geschichte der Königlich Preussischen 2 Garde Regiment zu Fuss 1813–1892*, Berlin 1892.

Luedin, Maja, *Die Liebgarden am Wiener Hof*, unpublished dissertation, Vienna 1965.

Mackinnon, Captain, *Origins and Services of the Coldstream Guards*, 2 vols., 1833.

Major des Gardes du Corps, 'Journal', *Carnets de la Sabretache*, II, 1894, pp. 219–224, 349–365, 548–557, III, 1895, pp. 177–87, 377–81, 569–82.

Manca-Amat de Vallombrosa, André-Joseph-Gabriel-Marie, *Histoire de la Prévôté de l'Hôtel-le-Roi*, 1907.

Marco de Saint-Hilaire, Emile, *Histoire Anecdotique, Politique, et Militaire de la Garde Impériale*, 1847.

Mareschal de Bièvre, Comte, 'La Garde Constitutionelle de Louis XVI', *Carnets de la Sabretache*, 3e Serie, VII, 1924, pp. 331–402, 428–502.

Marker, Colonel R.J. and Major A.G.C. Dawnay, *The Record of the Coldstream Guards*, 1923.

Maurice, Major-General Sir F., *The History of the Scots Guards*, 2 vols., 1934.

Mathieu, Robert, 'La Garde du Roi de Rome', *Revue des Etudes Napoléoniennes*, XXXVI, January–June 1933, pp. 22–27.

Matt, Leonard von, *Die Päpstliche Schweizergarde*, Zürich 1948.

Mignonneau, M., *Maison Militaire des Rois de France depuis Louis XIV. Aperçu des Avantages Immenses dont la France est redevable aux Monarques de la Maison de Bourbon*, 1815.

Minkiewicz, Colonel, *Notes on Polish Guards Units*, typescript, London 1983.

Moussoir, G., 'Les Gardes Françaises à Versailles', *Revue de l'Histoire de Versailles*, 17e Annee, 1915, pp. 5–24.

Navarro, Frederico y Conrado Morterero, 'Noble Guardia de Arqueros de Corps', *Hidalguia*, 1953, pp. 93–106.

Odelberg, Wilhelm, 'Gardet och Kungamakten', in C. Barkman and Sven Lundkvist, *Kungl. Svea Livgardes Historia 1719–1976*, Stockholm 1976.

Orde, Roden, *Second Household Cavalry Regiment*, Aldershot 1953.

Packe, Edmund, *An Historical Record of the Royal Regiment of Horse Guards or Oxford Blues*, 1847.

Paskowitz, Emil, *Die Erste Arcieren–Leibgarde Seiner Majestät des Kaisers und Königs*, Vienna 1914.

Paul, James Balfour, *The History of the Royal Company of Archers*, Edinburgh and London 1875.

Petre, F. Loraine, Wilfred Ewart and Major General Sir Cecil Lowther, *The Scots Guards in the Great War 1914–1918*, 1925.

Petri, Gustaf, *Kungl. Första Livgrenadjarregementets Historia*, 5 vols., Stockholm 1926–1930.

Pfannenberg, Leo von, *Geschichte der Schlossgarde Kompagnie Seiner Majestät des Kaisers und Königs*, Berlin 1909.

Pfyffer, Colonel F., *Feuille d'Orientation*, Rome 1982.

Pimholt, J.L., 'The Reform of the Life Guards 1788', *Journal of the Society for Army Historical Research*, Winter 1975, LIII, 216, pp. 194–209.

Pla Dalmau J., 'La Guardia Real en los Tiempos de Ferdinando VII', *Guardia Real*, Ano IV, 28, Feb. 1982, pp. 16–22.

— 'Los Reales Guardias Alabarderos en la Noche Tragica del 7 de Octobre de 1841', *Guardia Real*, Ano IV, 32, June 1982, pp. 21–27.

Ponsonby, Right Hon. Sir Frederick, *The Grenadier Guards in the Great War of 1914–1918*, 3 vols., 1920.

— *Notes on the Duties of the Field-Officer in Brigade Waiting*, 1908.

Pontoppidan, Axel, *Kongelige Livgarde*, 2 vols., Copenhagen 1941–2.

Preston, Thomas, *The Yeomen of the Guard, their History to 1885*, 1885.

Puell Bau, Fernando, 'El Real Cuerpo de Guardias Alabarderos', *Guardia Real*, Ano I, no. 6, March 1980, pp. 40–3.

Rembowski, Alexandre, *Sources Documentaires concernant le Régiment des Chevau-Légers de la Garde de Napoléon I*, 4 vols., Warsaw 1899–1903.

Repond, Colonel, *Le Costume de la Garde Suisse Pontificale et la Renaissance Italienne*, Rome 1917.

Retallack, John, *The Welsh Guards*, 1981.

Richard, Capitaine A., *La Garde 1854–1980*, 1898.

Robert, Jean, 'Les Gardes Françaises sous Louis XVI', *XVIIe Siècle*, LXVIII, 1965, pp. 3–36.

Roberts, Captain S.J.L., 'Faithful Always and Everwhere', *The Guards Magazine*, Spring 1981, pp. 177–180.

Ross-of-Bladensburg, Lt-Col. Sir John, *A History of the Coldstream Guards from 1815 to 1895*, 1896.

— *The Coldstream Guards 1914–1918*, 2 vols., 1928.

St. Jorre, John de, *The Guards*, 1981.

Sandeman, John Olas, *The Spears of Honour and the Gentlemen Pensioners*, Hayling Island 1912.

— *Facsimiles of the Ordinances and Statutes of the Gentlemen Pensioners*, Hayling Island 1909.

Savant, Jean, *Les Mameloukes de Napoléon*, 1949.

Schöning, Kurt Wolfgang von, *Das Regiment Garde du Corps*, Berlin 1854.

Schreeber von Schreeb, Tor, *Carl XII:s Drabantkär*, Stockholm 1942.

Smith, Thomas, *Some Account of the Royal Body-Guard entitled the Ancient Corps of the Yeomen of the Guard*, 1852.

Sotto de Montes, Joaquin de, 'Guardias Palacianas y Escoltas Reales de la Monarquia Espanola', *Revista de Historia Militar*, 1974, pp. 7–47.

Stosch, Albrecht von, *Das Königlich Preussische 5 Garde Regiment zu Fuss 1897–1918*, Berlin 1930.

Stud, H.W., *The Coldstream Guards. Notes for Parents who Try to Obtain Commissions for their Sons*, 1921.

Tighe, William, *An Introduction to the Gentlemen Pensioners*, talk given at the Institute of Historical Research, 23 February 1981.

Titeux, Eugene, *La Maison Militaire du Roi*, 2 vols., 1890.

Tyrrell, Lt-Gen F.H., 'His Holiness the Pope's Military Household', *Journal of the Royal United Services Institution*, January–December 1903, pp. 901–19.

Uzuncarsali, Professor Ismail Hakki, *Osmanli Devleti Ieskilatinden Kapukala Klari*, 2 vols., Ankara 1943–4.

Vallière, Capitaine de, *Histoire du Régiment des Gardes Suisses de France*, Lausanne and Paris 1912.

Verly, Albert, *L'Escadron des Cent-Gardes*, 1894.

Verney, Peter, *The Micks*, 1970.

Waldersee, Graf, *Das Erste Garde-Regiment zu Fuss*, Berlin 1854.

Whitworth, Major-General R.H., *The Grenadier Guards*, 1974.

Wilkinson, Major Sir Nevile, *The Guards Chapel*, 1938.

II. OTHER WORKS (those marked with an asterisk are by or about officers and soldiers who have served in royal guards).

Abbott, C.F., *Turkey in Transition*, 1909.

Aberg, Alf, 'The Swedish Army from Lützen to Narva', in Michael Roberts ed., *Sweden's Age of Greatness 1632–1718*, 1973, pp. 265–87.

Abrahamian, A.E., 'The Crowd in Iranian Politics', *Past and Present*, 1968, 41, pp. 184–210.

Abramov, A., *At the Kremlin Wall*, Moscow 1980.

Ailesbury, Earl of, *Memoirs*, 2 vols., 1890.

Alderson, A.D., *The Structure of the Ottoman Dynasty*, Oxford 1956.

Alexander, Captain James Edward, *Travels to the Seat of War in the East in 1829*, 2 vols., 1830.

*Alexander, Grand Duke, *Once a Grand Duke*, 1934.

*Alexander, Michael, *The True Blue*, 1957.

Alexandra Feodorovna, Tsaritsa, *Letters to the Tsar*, Stamford 1973.

Algarotti, Count, *Letters to Lord Hervey and the Marquis Maffei*, 2 vols., 1769.

Alonso, José Ramon, *Historia Politica del Ejercito Espanol* Madrid, 1974.

Andolenko, General, *Histoire de l'Armée Russe*, 1967.

Anne, Théodore, *Mémoires, Souvenirs et Anecdotes sur l'Intérieur du Palais de Charles X*, 3 vols., 1831.

Anon., *A Short Journel of His Polish Majesty's Camp of Radewitz in Saxony in the Year 1730*, 1733.

— *A Succinct Account of the Person, the Way of Living and the Court of the King of Prussia*, 1759.

— *An Exact Account of the Late Amazing Revolution in Turkey*, 1730.

— *An Historical Sketch of the Last Years of the Reign of Gustavus the Fourth Adolphus, late King of Sweden*, 1812.

— 'Reminiscences of the Court and Times of the Emperor Paul I of Russia up to the Period of His Death', *Fraser's Magazine*, August 1865, CCCXXVIII, pp. 222–241, September 1865, CCCXXIX, pp. 302–327.

— *La Cavalerie Allemande*, Paris-Nancy 1891.

— *Le Miroir de l'Empire Othoman*, 2 vols., 1678.

— *Mostra delle Arme ed Uniformi Napoletane 1734–1860*, Naples, Museo Principe Gaetano Filangieri 1969.

— *Observations sur la Constitution Militaire et Politique des Armées de Sa Majesté Prussienne*, Berlin 1777.

— *Procédure Criminelle Instruite au Châtelet de Paris*, 3 vols., 1790.

Arnold, Jose, *Golden Pots and Swords and Pans*, 1964.

Ashton, Major-General Sir George, *His Royal Highness the Duke of Connaught and Strathearn*, 1929.

Avery, Peter, *Modern Iran*, 1964.

Ayalon, David, *Studies on the Mamelukes of Egypt (1250–1517)*, 1977.

— *The Mameluke Military Society*, 1979.

Babeau, Albert, *La Vie Militaire sous l'Ancien Regime*, 2 vols., 1889.

Babinger, Franz, *Mehmed the Conqueror and His Times*, Princeton 1978.

Bailleu, Paul ed., *Briefwechsel König Friedrich Wilhelm III und der Königin Luise mit Kaiser Alexander I*, Leipzig 1900.

Bain, R. Nisbet, *Peter III Emperor of Russia*, 1902.

— *The Pupils of Peter the Great*, 1897.

Balfour, Hon. J.M., *Recent Happenings in Persia*, 1922.

Baratech, G., *Revolucion y Reaccion en el Reinado de Carlos IV*, Madrid 1957.

Barbier, E.J.F., *Journal Historique*, 4 vols., 1847–1906.

Barker, Dennis, *Soldiering On*, 1981.

Barnett, Correlli, *Britain and Her Army 1509–1970*, 1970.

*Barratt, Glyn, *The Rebel on the Bridge. A Life of the Decembrist Baron Andrez Rozen*, 1975.

— *Voices in Exile*, Montreal and London 1974.

*Barrès, J.B.A., *Souvenirs d'un Officier de la Grande Armée*, 1923.

*Barton, H. Arnold, *Count Hans Axel von Fersen*, Boston 1975.

Basseches, Nicholas, *The Unknown Army. The Nature and History of the Russian Military Forces*, 1943.

*Bassompierre, Maréchal de, *Mémoires*, 4 vols.

Battifol, Louis, *Autour de Richelieu*, 1937.

— *Le Roi Louis XIII à Vingt Ans*, 1923.

Baumont, Maurice, *The Fall of the Kaiser*, 1931.

Bedarida, Henri, *Parme dans la Politique Française au XVIIIe Siècle*, 1930.

Beker, Lt-Gen Comte, *Relation de sa Mission Auprès de l'Empereur Napoléon*, Clermont-Ferrand 1841.

Belgrave, Charles, *Personal Column*, 1960.

*Belleval, L.R. de, *Souvenirs d'un Chevau-Léger de la Garde du Roi*, 1866.

Benckendorff, Count Paul, *Last Days at Tsarskoe Seloe*, 1927.

Bengtsson, Frans G., *The Life of Charles XII King of Sweden 1697–1718*, 1960.

Benjamin, S.C.W., *The Turks and the Greeks*, New York 1867.

Bennigsen, General, *Mémoires*, 3 vols., 1907–1908.

Best, Geoffrey, *War and Society in Revolutionary Europe*, 1982.

Bezzel, O., *Geschichte des Bayerischen Heeres*, 8 vols., Munich 1901–1931.

Biddulph, General Sir Robert, *Lord Cardwell at the War Office*, 1904.

Bielfeld, Baron, *Letters*, 3 vols., 1770.

Bien, David, 'La Réaction Aristocratique avant 1789: l'Exemple de l'Armée', *Annales E.S.C.*, 29e Année, 1 January 1974, pp. 232–48; 2 March 1974, pp. 505–34.

*Billon, F.F., *Souvenirs d'un Vélite de la Garde*, 1905.

Bimbinet, Eugène, *Fuite de Louis XVI à Varennes*, 1868.

Bismarck, Lt-Gen Comte de, *Des Forces Militaries de l'Empire Russe en l'Année 1835*, 1836.

Blaxland, Gregory, *The Regiments Depart*, 1971.

Bloch, Alexandre, *Les derniers Jours du Regime Impérial*, 1931.

Blondel, Sigfus, *The Varangians of Byzantium*, Cambridge 1978.

Bombelles, Marquis de, *Journal*, Geneva 1978.

Bonneville de Marsangy, Louis, *Le Comte de Vergennes. Son Ambassade en Suède*, 1898.

Bosworth, C.E., 'Recruitment, Muster and Review in Medieval Islamic Armies', in V.J. Parry and M.E. Yapp, *War, Technology and Society in the Middle East*, 1975.

Bottineau, Yves, *L'Art de Cour dans l'Espagne de Philippe V*, Bordeaux 1960.

Bourke, Richard Southwell, *Saint Petersburg and Moscow: a Visit to the Court of the Czar*, 2 vols., 1846.

Bradley-Birt, F.B., *Through Persia from the Gulf to the Caspian*, 1907.

Brancaccio, Niccola, *L'Esercito del Vecchio Piemonte*, Rome 1922.

Braun, Frank H. 'Morocco: Anatomy of a Palace Revolution that failed', *International Journal of Middle East Studies*, 1978, ICXIX, pp. 63–72.

Brook-Shepherd, Gordon, *The Last Habsburg*, 1968.

Browne, Edward G., *The Persian Revolution*, Cambridge 1910.

*Browne, Thomas, *A Guardsman's Cup of Tea*, 1955.

Bruce, Anthony, *The Purchase System in the British Army 1660–1871*, 1980.

Bruce, Peter Henry, *Memoirs*, 1732.

Brusten, Charles, 'L'Armée Bourguignonne de 1465 à 1477', *Revue Internationale d'Histoire Militaire*, 1959.

Brydges, Sir Harford Jones, *An Account of His Majesty's Mission to Persia in the Years 1807–1811*, 2 vols., 1834.

Bull, George, *Inside the Vatican*, 1982.

Bunsen, Baroness von, *A Winter in Berlin*, n.d.

*Burnaby, Fred, Captain Royal Horse Guards, *A Ride to Khiva. Travels and Adventures in Central Asia*, Second Edition, 1876.

Busbecq, Ogier Ghislain de, *Turkish Letters*, ed. Edward Seymour Foster, Oxford 1927.

Bushnell, John, 'The Tsarist Officer Corps 1881–1914: Customs, Duties, Inefficiency', *American Historical Review*, vol. 86, October 1981, 4, pp. 753–80.

Buxhoevden, Baroness Sophie, *The Life and Tragedy of Alexandra Feodorovna, Empress of Russia*, 1928.

*Calvocoressi, M.D., *Mussorgsky*, 1946.

Cambridge, Marquess of, 'The March of William of Orange from Torbay to London 1688', *Journal of the Society for Army Historical Research*, XLIV, 1966, pp. 152–74.

Campbell, Sir Neil, *Napoleon at Fontainebleau and Elba*, 1869.

Caraman, Comte G. de, *Notice sur la Vie Militaire et Privée du Général Marquis de Caraman*, 1857.

Carascosa, General, *Mémoires Historiques, Politiques et Militaires sur la Révolution du Royaume de Naples en 1820 et 1821*, London 1823.

Carew, Sir George, *A Relation of the State of France*, 1749.

Carlsson, Sten, *Gustav IV Adolf's Fall*, Lund 1944.

Carmona, Michel, *Marie de Médicis*, 1981.

Carr, Raymond, *Spain 1808–1939*, Oxford 1966.

Catherine the Great, *Memoirs*, ed. Dominique Mazour, 1955.

Chagniot, Jean, *Paris et l'Armée au XVIIIe Siècle*. Thèse pour le Doctorat d'Etat. Université de Paris IV. 1983.

Chantreau, Pierre, *Voyage Philosophique, Politique et Littéraire fait en Russie pendant les Années 1788 et 1789*, 2 vols., Hamburg 1794.

Chapman, Hester, *Queen Anne's Son*, 1954.

Chardin, Chevalier, *Voyage en Perse et Autres Lieux de l'Orient*, New Edition, 4 vols., Amsterdam 1735.

Chaussinand-Nogaret, Guy, *La Noblesse au XVIIIe Siècle*, 1975.

Chelminski, Jean U. et A. Malibran, *L'Armée du Duché de Varsovie*, 1913.

Chénier, M. de, *Recherches Historiques sur les Maures et Histoire de l'Empire du Maroc*, 3 vols., 1787.

*Chevalier, Lieutenant, *Souvenirs*, 1970.

Chevket Pasha, Mahmoud, *L'Organisation et les Uniformes de l'Armée Ottomane depuis sa Création jusqu'à Nos Jours*, Constantinople 1907.

Childs, John, *The Army of Charles II*, London, Toronto and Buffalo 1976.

— 'The Army and the Oxford Parliament of 1681', *English Historical Review*, CCCLXXII, July 1979, pp. 580–87.

— *The Army and the Glorious Revolution*, Manchester 1980.

— *Armies and Warfare in Eurpe 1648–1789*, Manchester 1982.

Chilly, Lucien de, *La Tour du Pin*, 1909.

Christiansen, E., *The Origins of Military Power in Spain*, Oxford 1967.

*Churchill, Randolph S., *Winston S. Churchill*, 1966, Vol I, Youth.

*Clardy, Jesse, *V.G.R. Derzhavin*, The Hague 1967.

Clarke, Reverend Edward, *Letters concerning the Spanish Nation*, 1764.

Clarke, Rev. J.S., *Life of James II*, 2 vols., 1816.

*Combermere, Mary Viscountess, and Captain W.W. Knollys, *Memoirs and Correspondence of Field-Marshal Viscount Combermere*, 2 vols., 1866.

Commynes, Philippe de, *Mémoires*, 3 vols., 1840–1847.

*Connelly, Willard, *Sir Richard Steele*, 1934.

*Contamine, Philippe, *Guerre, Etat et Société à la Fin du Moyen Age*, 1972.

Cook, M.A. ed., *A History of the Ottoman Empire to 1730*, Cambridge 1976.

Cornéty, Jules, *Le Czar et le Roi*, 1884.

*Cornwallis-West, G., *Edwardian Hey-Days*, 1930.

Cortese, Nino, *Memorie di un Generale della Reppublica e del'Impero. Francesco Pignatelli, Principe di Strongoli*, 2 vols., Bari 1927.

*Corti, Count Egon, *The Downfall of Three Dynasties*, 1934.

Corvisier, Andre, *L'Armée Française de la Fin du XVIIe Siècle au Ministère de Choiseul*, 2 vols., 1964.

Cottam, Richard W., *Nationalism in Iran*, Pittsburgh 1964.

*Coutan, Elisée, *Rapport sur les Evènements de Paris pendant la dernière semaine de Juillet 1830*, Geneve 1830.

Cowper, Mary Countess, *Diary*, 1864.

Coxe, William, *Travels into Poland, Russia, Sweden, and Denmark*, 3 vols., 1784–1790.

Craig, Gordon A., *The Battle of Königgratz*, 1966.

— *The Politics of the Prussian Army*, 1962.

Crone, Patricia, *Slaves on Horses. The Evolution of the Islamic Polity*, Cambridge 1980.

*Cross, A.G., *N.M. Karamzin*, Carbondale and Edwardsville 1971.

Curtiss, Johns Shelton, *The Russian Army under Nicholas I*, Durham N.C. 1965.

*Cust, Lady Elizabeth, *Some Account of the Stuarts of Aubigny in France*, 1891.

*Cyril, H.I.H. Grand Duke, *My Life in Russia's Service Then and Now*, 1939.

Dally, A. *L'Armée Russe*, n.d.

Dalrymple, Major William, *Travels Through Spain and Portugal in 1774*, 1777.

Daniel, Père, *Histoire de la Milice Française*, 2 vols., 1721.

Danon, M.A., *Contribution à l'Histoire des Sultans Osman II et Moustafa*, 1919.

Darnton, Robert ed., 'The Memoirs of Lenoir, Lieutenant de Police de Paris', *English Historical Review*, CCLXXXV, July 1970, pp. 532–59.

Dashkov, Princess, *Memoirs*, ed. Kyril Fitzlyon, 1958.

Daumont, Alexandre, *Voyage en Suède*, 2 vols., 1834.

Davies, R.R., 'Richard II and the Principality of Chester 1397–1399', in F.R.D. Du Boulay and Caroline M. Brown eds., *The Reign of Richard II*, 1971, pp. 256–77.

*Debidour, A., *Le General Fabvier*, 1904.

*Dechy, Edouard, *Souvenirs d'un Ancien Militaire*, 1860.

De Gaury, Gerald, *Arabia Phoenix*, 1946.

— *Faisal, King of Saudi Arabia*, 1964.

Degli Alberti, Marco, *Dieci Anni di Storia Piemontese (1814–1824)*, Turin 1908.

De Grunwald, Constantin, *La Vie de Nicolas Ier*, 1946.

Dehn, Lilli, *The Real Tsaritsa*, 1922.

De Madariaga, Isabel, *Russia in the Age of Catherine the Great*, 1981.

Dembowski, Baron Charles de, *Deux Ans en Espagne et en Portugal pendant la Guerre Civile 1838–1840*, 1841.

Demeter, Karl, *The German Officer Corps in Society and State 1650–1945*, 1965.

Derossi di Santa Rosa, Comte, *De la Révolution Piémontaise*, Third Edition, 1822.

Disbrowe, C.A.A., *Original Letters from Russia*, 1878.

*Djevaad Bey, *Etat Militaire Ottoman*, Constantinople 1882.

Dodds, Anna Bowman, *In the Palaces of the Sultan*, 1904.

*Donaldson, Frances, *Edward VIII*, 1974.

*Dorpalen, Andreas, *Hindenburg and the Weimar Republic*, Princeton 1964.

Droz, Jacques, *Les Révolutions Allemandes de 1848*, 1957.

Duffy, Christopher, *The Army of Frederick the Great*, 1974.

— *The Army of Maria Theresa*, 1977.

— *Russia's Military Way to the West*, 1981.

Duffy, Michael ed., *The Military Revolution and the State 1500–1800*, Exeter 1980.

Du Fresne de Beaucourt, G., *Histoire de Charles VII*, 6 vols., 1881–1891.

Dulong, Claude, *Anne d'Autriche*, 1980.

Du Mans, P. Raphael, *Etat de la Perse*, 1890.

*Dumonceau, Général Comte François, *Mémoires*, 3 vols., Brussels 1958.

*Dundonald, Lt-Gen the Earl of, *My Army Life*, 1934.

Dupré, C., *Voyage en Perse fait dans les Années 1807, 1808, et 1809*, 2 vols., 1819.

Durrieux, Joseph, *Les Vainqueurs de la Bastille*, 1933.

Durry, Marcel, *Les Cohortes Prétoriennes*, 1938.

El-Edroos, Brigadier Syed Ali, *The Hashemite Arab Army 1908–1979*, Amman 1980.

Engelhart, Gustav, *Svenska Armens och Flottans Officers Militars och Civil Uniformes*, Stockholm 1888.

Ergang, Robert, *The Potsdam Führer*, New York 1941.

Esad, Mehmed, *Précis Historique de la Destruction du Corps des Janissaires*, 1833.

Esdaile, Charles, *The Spanish Army 1788–1814*, Unsubmitted PhD Thesis. Lancaster.

*Espinchal, Comte d', *Souvenirs*, 2 vols.

Evrard, Fernand, *Versailles, Ville du Roi*, 1935.

Fairholme, Captain W.E. and Captain Count Gleichen, *Handbook of the Armies of Bulgaria, Greece, Montenegro, Roumania, and Servia*, 1895.

Falckenskiold, M. de, *Mémoires*, 1826.

— *Authentic Elucidations of the History of Counts Struensee and Brandt*, 1789

Farmer, Henry George, *Military Music*, 1950.

Favre, Edmond, *L'Autriche et ses Institutions Militaires*, 1866.

Feuvrier, Dr, *Trois Ans à la Cour de Perse*, Second Edition, 1906.

*Firbank, Thomas, *I Bought a Star*, 1953.

Fletcher, Anthony, *The Outbreak of the English Civil War*, 1981.

*Fleury, Comte, *Fantômes et Silhouettes*, 1902.

Fortescue, Sir John, *A History of the British Army*, 13 vols., 1899–1930.

Fosten, D.S.V., *Cuirassiers and Heavy Cavalry*, 1972.

Frankland, Captain Charles Colville, *Travels to and from Constantinople in the Years 1827 and 1828*, 2 vols., 1829.

— *Narrative of a Visit to the Courts of Russia and Sweden in the Years 1830 and 1831*, 2 vols., 1832.

Fraser, David, *Persia and Turkey in Revolt*, 1910.

Frederick III, *The War Diary of the Emperor, 1870–1871*, ed. A.R. Allinson, 1927.

Friedrich Leopold of Prussia, H.R.H. Princess, *Behind the Scenes at the Prussian Court*, 1939.

Gachard, M., *Relations des Ambassadeurs Vénétiens sur Charles Quint et sur Philippe II*, Bruxelles 1856.

Galiano, Alberto Alcala, *Memorias*, 1886.

Galland, Antoine, *Journal*, 2 vols., 1881.

Gayda, M., *L'Armée Russe sous Alexandre 1er*, 1955.

Gay de Vernon, Baron, *Vie du Maréchal Gouvion Saint-Cyr*, 1856.

Gembarzewski, Bronislaw, *Zolnceriz Polski*, 5 vols., Warsaw 1962.

Geufroy, F. Antoine, *Brieve Description de la Court du Grand Turc*, 1543.

Gibb, Sir Hamilton and Harold Bowen, *Islamic Society and the West*, 2 vols., 1956–1957.

Gilabert, E. Marti, *El Motin de Aranjuez*, Pamplona 1972.

Gilbert, Felix ed., *The Historical Essays of Otto Hintze*, New York 1975.

Giorgetti, Niccolo, *Le Armi Toscane e le Occupazioni Stranieri in Toscana (1537–1860)*, 4 vols., Città di Castello 1916.

Girault de Coursac, P., 'Les Cinquante Jours du Roi', Découverte, III, October 1973, pp. 18–34, V, April 1974, pp. 25–40.

— 'Un Conseiller Mal Ecouté', Découverte, XVIII, June 1977, pp. 41–48.

— *Enquête sur le Procès du Roi Louis XVI*, 1982.

*Gleichen, Lord Edward, *A Guardsman's Memoirs*, 1932.

Godard, Léon, *Description et Histoire du Maroc*, 2 vols., 1860.

Gordon, Harold J., *The Reichswehr and the German Republic 1919–1926*, Princeton 1957.

Gottschalk, Louis and Margaret Maddox, *Lafayette in the French Revolution through the October Days*, 1973.

Gourko, General Basil, *Memories and Impressions of War and Revolution in Russia 1914–1917*, 1918.

Grand Ducs, *Lettres à Nicholas II*, 1926.

Grant, James, *The Constable of France and Other Military Historiettes*, 1866.

— Colville of the Guards, 3 vols., 1885.

Gregg, Edward, Queen Anne, 1980.

*Grinstead, Roger, Some Talk of Alexander, 1943.

Griselle, Eugène, Etat de la Maison du Roi Louis XIII, 2 vols., 1912.

*Grivel, Vice-Amiral Baron, Mémoires, 1914.

*Gronow, Captain, Reminiscences and Recollections, 2 vols., 1892.

Grouvel, Vicomte de, Les Corps de Troupes de l'Emigration Française, 3 vols., 1957–1964.

Guénée, Bernard et Francoise Lehoux, Les Entrées Royales Françaises de 1328 à 1515, 1968.

Guibert, G.A.H., Journal d'un Voyage en Allemagne fait en 1773, 2 vols., 1803.

Guigues de Champvans, Marquis F., Histoire et Législation des Ordres de Chevalerie, Marques d'Honner et
  Medailles du Saint-Siège, 2 vols., 1932–33.

*Guitaud, J.E., Souvenirs Militaires du Premier Empire, 1934.

Gustafsson, Colonel, La Journée du Treize Mars 1809, Saint Gall 1835.

Gustavus III, Ecrits Politiques, Littéraires et Dramatiques, 5 vols., Stockholm 1805.

Habesci, E., The Present State of the Ottoman Empire, 1784.

Haddad, George M., Revolution and Military Rule in the Middle East. The Northern Tier, New York 1965.

Hagger, D.H., Hussars and Mounted Rifles, 1974.

Haillot, C.A. et Giustiniani, Henri de, Statistique Militaire et Recherches sur l'Organisation et les Institutions
  Militaires des Armées Etrangères, 2 vols., 1846, 1851.

Hammer-Purgstall, J de, Histoire de l'Empire Ottoman, 18 vols., 1835–1843.

Harcave, Sydney, First Blood. The Russian Revolution of 1905, 1964.

Hardinge of Penhurst, Lord, Old Diplomacy, 1947.

*Harewood, Lord, The Tongs and the Bones, 1981.

Harsany, Zoltan, La Cour de Léopold, Duc de Lorraine et de Bar (1698–1729), Nancy 1938.

*Hartmann, Cyril Hughes, The King's Friend, 1951.

Hasegawa, Tsuyoshi, The February Revolution. Petrograd 1917, Seattle and London 1981.

Hassan II, The Challenge, 1978.

Hatton, R.M., Charles XII of Sweden, 1968.

Hautecoeur, Louis, Histoire des Châteaux du Louvre et des Tuileries, 1927.

Hauthal, F., Geschichte der Sächsischen Armee von ihrer Reorganisation nach dem Siebenjährigen Kriege bis auf
  unsere Zeit, Leipzig 1858.

Hayter, Tony, The Army and the Crowd in Mid-Georgian England, 1978.

Heidenstam, O-G de, Louise-Ulrique Reine de Suède, 1897.

Helldorf, J.M. Baron de, An Historical Account of the Prussian Army, 1783.

Hellie, Richard, Enserfment and Military Change in Moscow, Chicago and London, 1971.

*Hennet de Goutel, Baron, 'Les Derniers Jours de l'Empire racontés par un Cent-Suisse d'après le Journal Inédit de
  M. de Marsilly', Revue des Etudes Napoléoniennes, 1908, pp. 175–200, 271–95.

*Heriot de Vroil, M.H., Mémoires d'un Officier de la Garde Royale, 1904.

Herlitz, Carl, Svenska Armens Regementen Regementetstraditioner, Stockholm 1967.

Hermans, Ralph and Hammerskiold, Hans, The Royal Palace of Stockholm, Stockholm 1978.

Héroard, Jean, Journal, 2 vols., 1868.

Hervey, Lord, Memoirs, 3 vols., 1931.

Hibbert, Christopher, King Mob, 1958.

Hirzel, Werner, Tanta est Fiducia Gentis. Les Régiments Suisses au Service des Pays Bas, Coppet 1972.

*Higginson, General Sir George, Seventy-One Years of a Guardsman's Life, 1916.

Holt, P. M., Studies in the History of the Near East, 1973.

— 'The Position and Power of the Mameluke Sultan', Bulletin of the School of Oriental and African Studies, 1975,
  XXXVIII.

*Hordt, Comte de, Mémoires, 2 vols., 1793.

Hornby, Lady, Constantinople during the Crimean War, 1893.

Houlding, J.A., Fit for Service. The Training of the British Army 1715–1795, Oxford 1981.

Howard, Michael, The Franco-Prussian War, University Paperbacks 1981.

— War in European History, 1976.

Hozier, Captain H.N., The Russo-Turkish War, 2 vols., 1879.

Hull, Isabel V., The Entourage of Kaiser Wilhelm II, 1888–1918, Cambridge 1982.

*Ibrahim Efendi, Officier Müteferrika de la Porte Ottomane, Traité de Tactique ou Méthode Artificielle pour
  l'Ordonnance des Troupes, Vienna 1769.

*Ignatyer, Lt-Gen A.A., A Subaltern in Old Russia, 1914.

James II, Memoirs, 1962.

Jany, C.E., Geschichte der Königlich Preussischen Armee bis zum Ende Jahre 1851, 5 vols., Berlin 1928–1937.

*Jaurgain, Jean de, *Troisvilles, d'Artagnan et les Trois Mousquetaires*, 1910.

*Jenkins, Michael, *Arakcheev*, 1969.

*Jonas, Klaus W., *The Life of the Crown Prince Wilhelm*, 1961.

Jones, David R., 'The Officers and the October Revolution', *Soviet Studies*, XXVIII, April 1976, no 2, pp. 207–23.

Juchereau de Saint-Denys, Baron, *Histoire de l'Empire Ottoman depuis 1792 jusqu'en 1844*, 4 vols., 1844.

Katkov, George, *Russia 1917. The February Revolution*, 1967.

Kaunitz, Prince de, 'Mémoire sur la Cour de France', *Revue de Paris*, lle année, IV, August 1904, pp. 836–43.

Keegan, John, *The Face of Battle*, Penguin 1978.

Keep, John L.H., 'The Secret Chancellery, the Guards and the Dynastic Crisis of 1740–1741', *Forschungen zur Ost-europäischen Geschichte*, XXV, 1978, pp. 169–93.

*Keith, Field-Marshal James, *A Fragment of a Memoir*, Edinburgh 1843.

Keith, Sir Robert Murray, *Memoirs and Correspondence*, 2 vols., 1849.

*Kelly, Laurence, *Lermontov, Tragedy in the Caucasus*, 1977.

Kenez, Peter, 'A Profile of the Prerevolutionary Officer Corps', *California Slavic Studies*, VI, 1973, pp. 121–58.

*Kessler, Count Harry, *The Diaries of a Cosmopolitan*, 1971.

Kitowicz, Jedrzej, *Opis Obyczajow zu Panowannia Augustus III*, Wroclaw 1950.

Knox, Sir Alfred, *With the Russian Army. 1914–1917*, 2 vols., 1921.

Korb, J.S., *Diary of an Austrian Secretary of Legation at the Court of Czar Peter the Great*, 2 vols., 1862.

Korf, Comte, *Avènement au Trône de l'Empereur Nicolas I*, 1857.

*Krassnoff, General P.N., *From the Two-Headed Eagle to the Red Flag*, 4 vols., 1925.

Labande-Mailfert, Yvonne, *Charles VIII et son Milieu. 1470–1498*, 1975.

Labatut, Jean-Pierre, *Les Noblesses Européennes de la Fin du XVe Siècle à la Fin du XVIIIe Siècle*, 1978.

Lacey, Robert, *Robert, Earl of Essex*, 1971.

— *Sir Walter Raleigh*, 1973.

— *Majesty*, Sphere 1978.

— *The Kingdom*, 1981.

*La Force, Duc de, *Lauzun*, 1919.

Laforgue, Jules, *Berlin, la Cour et la Ville*, 1922.

La Marche, Olivier de, *Mémoires*, 4 vols., 1872–1876.

La Martinière, H.M.P. de, *Morocco*, 1889.

*Lamon, S., *Souvenirs d'un Chasseur de la Vieille Garde*, Geneva 1916.

Lamouche, Léon, *L'Organisation Militaire de l'Empire Ottoman*, 1895.

Lange, G., *Das Deutsche Reichsheer*, Berlin 1888–9.

Latrielle, Capitaine Albert, *L'Armée et la Nation à la Fin de l'Ancien Régime*, 1914.

La Vallette-Monbrun, A. de., *Maine de Biran*, 1914.

Leared, Arthur, *A Visit to the Court of Morocco*, 1879.

Le Brethon, Paul ed., *Lettres et Documents pour Servir à l'Histoire de Joachim Murat*, 8 vols., 1908–1910.

Léonard, Emile, *L'Armée et ses Problèmes au XVIIIe Siècle*, 1953.

Lepage, Henri, *Sur l'Organisation et les Institutions Militaires de la Lorraine*, 1884.

*Lever, Charles, *Jack Hinton the Guardsman*, 1857.

Levi, Arrigo, *The Military Policy of Sultan Mahmud II*, unpublished Ph.D. thesis, Harvard 1968.

— 'The Officer Corps in Sultan Mahmud II's new Ottoman Army. 1826–1839', *International Journal of Middle East Studies*, II, 1971, pp. 21–39.

Levy, Reuben ed., *The Qabus Nama by Kai Ka'us Ibn Iskander, Prince of Gurgan*, 1951.

Lewis, Jenkin, *Queen Anne's Son*, 1881.

*Ley, Francis, *Le Maréchal de Münnich et la Russie au XVIIIe Siècle*, 1959.

*Ligne, Prince de, *Fragments de l'Histoire de ma Vie*, 2 vols., 1928.

— *Mémoires sur le Comte de Bonneval*, 1817.

*Lignières, Comte de, *Souvenirs de la Grande Armée et de la Vieille Garde Impériale*, 1933.

Lincoln, W. Bruce, *The Romanovs*, New York 1981.

*Lloyd, R.A., *A Trooper in the Tins*, 1938.

Loades, D.M., *The Reign of Mary Tudor*, 1979.

Lockhart, Laurence, 'The Persian Army in the Safavi Period', *Der Islam*, XXXIV, 1959, pp. 89–98.

*Londonderry, Marquess of, *Recollections of a Tour in the North of Europe in 1836–1837*, 2 vols., 1838.

*Longford, Elizabeth, *Wellington. The Years of the Sword*, 1969.

Longworth, Philip, *The Three Empresses*, 1972.

Louis XIV, *Oeuvres*, 6 vols., 1806.

Lybyer, Arthur Howe, *The Government of the Ottoman Empire in the Time of Suleiman the Magnificent*, Cambridge 1913.

Lyons, Marvin, *The Russian Imperial Army*, Stanford 1968.

— *Russia in Original Photographs. 1860–1920*, 1977.

— *Nicholas II. The Last Tsar*, 1974.

*Lyttelton, Humphrey, *I Play as I Please*, 1954.

Macdiarmid, D.S., *The Life of Lieutenant-General Sir James Moncrieff Grierson*, 1923.

Macdonald, Robert, *Personal Narrative of Military Travel and Adventures in Turkey and Persia*, Edinburgh 1859.

MacFarlane, Charles, *Constantinople in 1828*, Second Edition, 2 vols., 1829.

Mackenzie, Slidell, *Spain Revisited*, 2 vols., 1836.

*Macmillan, Harold, *Winds of Change*, 1966.

Magarschack, David, *Pushkin*, 1967.

Magnus, Philip, *King Edward the Seventh*, 1964.

*Maingot, Eliane, *Le Baron Taylor*, 1963.

Maklakoff, B. ed., *Interrogatoires des Ministres, Conseillers, Généraux, Haut Fonctionnaires de la Cour Impériale Russe par la Commission Extraordinaire du Gouvernment Provisoire de 1917*, 1927.

Malcolm, Sir John, *The History of Persia*, 2 vols., 1815.

Malcolm, Joyce L., 'A King in Search of Soldiers. Charles I in 1642', *Historical Journal*, 21, February 1978, pp. 251–73.

Mallett, Michael, *Mercenaries and Their Masters*, 1974.

Mangin, Lt-Col., *La Force Noire*, 1910.

*Mannerheim, Marshal, *Memoirs*, 1953.

Manstein, Général de, *Mémoires Historiques, Politiques et Militaires de la Russie*, 2 vols., Lyon, 1772.

Marcillac, M. De, *Nouveau Voyage en Espagne*, 1805.

Marczali, Henry, *Hungary in the Eighteenth Century*, Cambridge 1910.

Marie Theresa and Joseph II, *Ihre Correspondenz*, 3 vols., 1867.

Marie-Caroline, Reine de Naples et de Sicile, *Correspondance Inédite avec le Marquis de Gallo*, ed. Cdt. M-H. Weil et Marquis C. de Somma-Riva, 2 vols., 1911.

Marshall, Joseph, *Travels Through Holland, Flanders, Germany, Denmark, Sweden, Lapland, Russia, the Ukraine and Poland in the Years 1768, 1769, and 1770*, 3 vols., 1772.

Marsigli, Comte, *Etat Militaire de l'Empire Ottoman*, 2 vols., The Hague 1732.

Martin, Paul, *European Military Uniforms*, 1967.

*Masson, Frédéric, *La Vie et les Conspirations du Général Malet*, Second Edition, n.d.

— *Napoléon Chez Lui*, 1894.

Max of Baden, Prince, *Memoirs*, 2 vols., 1928.

*Maxse, Colonel, F.I., *Seymour Vandeleur. The Story of a British Officer*, 1905.

Maxwell, John S., *The Czar, His Court and His People*, New York 1848.

May de Romainmotier, M., *Histoire Militaire des Suisses et celle des Suisses dans les Différents Services de l'Europe*, 8 vols., Lausanne 1788.

Mazour, Anatole G., *The First Russian Revolution 1825. The Decembrist Movement*, Berkeley California 1937.

*McCardell, Leon, *Ill-Starred General. Braddock of the Coldstream Guards*, Pittsburgh 1958.

McCormick, Robert R., *With the Russian Army*, 1915.

*McGrigor, Sir James, *Autobiography*, 1861.

McNeill, William H., *The Pursuit of Power. Technology, Armed Force and Society since A.D. 1000*, Oxford 1983.

Meehan-Waters, Brenda, 'Social and Career Characteristics of the Administrative Elite, 1689–1761', in Walter McKenzie Pintner and Don Karl Rowney eds., *Russian Officialdom*, 1980, pp. 76–105.

Mellor, Captain F.H., *The Papal Forces*, 1983.

Mention, L., *Le Comte de Saint-Germain et ses Réformes*, 1884.

*Mercadal, J. Garcia, *Palafox*, 1948.

Meyer, Jean, *Noblesses et Pouvoirs dans l'Europe de l'Ancien Regime*, 1972.

Miller, Barnette, *Beyond the Sublime Porte*, New Haven 1931.

Miller, John, *James II. A Study in Kingship*, 1978.

Miller, Peggy, *James*, 1971.

Mirabeau, Comte de, *De la Monarchie Prusienne sous Frédéric le Grand*, 4 vols., London 1788.

Mohamed Reza Shah, *Mission for My Country*, 1961.

Molesworth, Mr, *An Account of Denmark as it was in the Year 1692*, Third Edition, 1694.

Mollo, Boris, *Uniforms of the Russian Imperial Army*, 1979.

Mollo, John, *Military Fashion*, 1972.

Molnar, Ferenc, *The Plays of*, New York, 1929.

Montpensier, Mlle de, *Mémoires*, 4 vols., 1857–1859.

Morier, James, *A Journey Through Persia, Armenia, and Asia Minor to Constantinople in the Years 1808 and 1809*, 1812.

Mossolov, A.A., *At the Court of the Last Tsar*, 1935.

Motley, John, *The History of the Life of Peter I, Emperor of Russia*, 3 vols., 1739.

Mouillard, Lucien, *Les Régiments sous Louis XV*, 1882.

Murat, Comte, *Murat, Lieutenant de l'Empereur en Espagne*, 1897.

Myers, A.R., *The Household of Edward IV*, Manchester 1959.

— *Parliaments and Estates in Europe to 1789*, 1975.

Napoléon I, *Correspondance Générale*, 32 vols., 1858–1869.

Narbonne, Pierre, *Journal des Règnes de Louis XIV et de Louis XV*, 1866.

Nash, David, *The Prussian Army 1808–1815*, 1972.

Nicholas II, *Letters to the Tsaritsa 1914–1917*, 1929.

— *Letters of . . . and Empress Marie*, 1937.

— *Journal Intime*, 1925.

*Nicolson, Nigel, *Alex*, 1973.

Nizam al Mulk, *The Book of Government or Rules for Kings*, 1960.

Nordmann, Claude, *Grandeur et Liberté de la Suède (1660–1792)*, 1971.

O'Callaghan, John Cornelius, *History of the Irish Brigade in the Service of France*, Glasgow 1870.

Ohsson, M. de M****, *Tableau Général de l'Empire Othoman*, 3 vols., 1787–1820.

*Ormathwaite, Lord, *When I Was at Court*, 1937.

O'Shea, Raymond, *The Sand Kings of Arabia*, 1947.

Pakalin, Mehment Zaki, *Osmanli Tarih Deyimleri ve Terimleri Sozlugin*, 3 vols., Istanbul 1939–1946.

Palaéologue, Maurice, *An Ambassador's Memoirs*, 1973.

Pallis, A., *In the Days of the Janissaries*, 1951.

Palmstierna, C.F. ed., *Marie-Louise et Napoléon. Lettres Inédites 1813–1814*, 1955.

Pardoe, Juliet, *The City of the Sultan and Domestic Manners of the Turks in 1836*, 2 vols., 1837.

Parry, V.H. and M.E. Yapp, *War, Technology and Society in the Middle East*, 1975.

Pegge, Samuel, *Curialia*, 5 parts, 1791–1806.

Pepe, General Guillaume, *Memoirs*, 1906.

— *A Narrative of the Political and Military Events which Took Place at Naples in 1820 and 1821*, 1821.

Perrero, Domenico, *Gli Ultimi Reali di Savoia del Ramo Primogeito ed il Principe Carlo-Alberto di Carignano*, Turin 1889.

Petersen, E. Ladewig, *The Crisis of the Danish Nobility 1550–1660*, Odense 1967.

Pierre le Grand, *Journal . . . depuis l'Année 1698 jusqu'à la Conclusion de la Paix de Neustadt*, Berlin 1773.

Pietsch, Paul, *Die Formations und Uniformierungs Geschichte des Preussischen Heeres 1808–1914*, 2 vols., Hamburg 1963.

Pinasseau, Jean, *L'Emigration Militaire. Campagne de 1792*, 2 vols., 1957–1964.

Pinkney, David H., *The French Revolution of 1830*, Princeton 1972.

Pollnitz, Charles-Louis Baron de, *Memoirs*, Third Edition, 5 vols., 1745.

Polovtsoff General P.A., *Glory and Downfall. Reminiscences of a Russian General Staff Officer*, 1935.

Pope-Hennessy, Una, *A Czarina's Story*, 1948.

Porch, Douglas, *Army and Revolution. France 1815–1848*, 1974.

Porter, David, *Constantinople and its Environs in a Series of Letters*, 2 vols., New York 1835.

Potocki, Jean, *Voyage dans l'Empire du Maroc fait en l'Année 1791*, Varsovie 1792.

Pushkin, Alexander, *The Captain's Daughter and Other Stories*, New York n.d.

Quin, Michael J., *A Visit to Spain in the latter part of 1822 and the First Four Months of 1823*, 1823.

Rabinovich, Alexander, *The Bolsheviks Come to Power*, New York 1979.

— *Prelude to Revolution*, Bloomington 1968.

Ransel, David L., *The Politics of Catherinian Russia. The Panin Party*, New Haven and London 1975.

Rath, R. John, *The Vienna Revolution of 1848*, Austin 1957.

Régla, Paul de, *La Turquie Officielle*, 1889.

Reresby, Sir John, *Memoirs*, 1858.

Resident Officer, A., *Madrid in 1835. Sketches of the Metropolis of Spain*, 2 vols., 1836.

Reverdil, M., *Mémoires*, 1858.

Rihani, Ameen, *Ibn Sa'oud of Arabia*, 1928.

*Rilliet, F.J.L., *Souvenirs de 1815*, Genève 1910.

Ringoir, H., *Afstammelingen en Voorleitzettingen der Infanterie*, 's Gravenhage 1977.

Ristell, A.F., *Characters and Anecdotes of the Court of Sweden*, 2 vols., 1790.

Ritter, Gerhard, *The Sword and the Sceptre*, 4 vols., 1972–1973.

Ritter, Raymond et Jean Jaurgain, *La Maison de Gramont*, 2 vols., Lourdes 1968.

Robert, Jean, 'Les Grande et Petite Ecuries d'Henri III de Navarre', *Bulletin de la Société des Amis du Château de Pau*, Nouvelle Série LXXXVIII, 1982, 3, pp. 3–39.

Robinson, Mr., *An Account of Sweden*, 1694.

*Rochechouart, Général Comte de, *Souvenirs sur la Révolution, l'Empire, et la Restauration*, 1889.

*Rodzianko, Colonel Paul, *Tattered Banners*, n.d.

*— *Mannerheim*, 1940.

*Roeder, Helen ed., *The Ordeal of Captain Roeder*, 1960.

*Roland, Alan, *Guardsman*, 1955.

Romani, George T., *The Neapolitan Revolution of 1820–1821*, Evanston 1950.

Rosenfeld, Henry, 'The Social Composition of the Military in the Process of State Formation in the Arabian Desert', *Journal of the Royal Anthropological Institute of Great Britain and Ireland*, Vol 95, January 1965, I, pp. 75–86, July 1965, II, pp. 174–94.

*Roth, Cecil, *The House of Nasi. The Duke of Naxos*, Philadelphia 1948.

Rothenburg, Gunther E., *The Art of Warfare in the Age of Napoleon*, 1970.

— *The Army of Franz Josef*, West Lafayette 1976.

*Roustam, Mamelouck de Napoléon 1er., *Souvenirs*, 1911.

Rustow, Dankert A., 'The Army and the Founding of the Turkish Republic', *World Politics*, July 1959, pp. 513–52.

Ruwet, Joseph, *Soldats des Regiments Nationaux au XVIIIe Siècle*, Brussels 1962.

S., J.F., *Memoires pour Servir à l'Histoire de l'Armée Prussienne*, Amsterdam 1759.

Sablinsky, Walter, *The Road to Bloody Sunday*, Princeton 1976.

*St. Aubyn, Giles, *The Royal George*, 1963.

*Saint-Chamans, Comte de, *Mémoires*, 1896.

Saint-Germain, Jacques, *Louis XIV Secret*, 1970.

*Saint-Priest, Comte de, *Mémoires*, 2 vols., 1929.

*Saint-Simon, Duc de, *Mémoires*, ed. Cheruel et Regnier, 20 vols., 1873–1879.

Salata, Fred, *Carlo Alberto Inedito*, Milan 1931.

*Samaran, Charles, *D'Artagnan, Capitaine des Mousquetaires du Roi*, 1912.

Sanson, M., *Voyage ou Relation de l'Etat Présent du Royaume de Perse*, 1695.

Sansovino, Francesco, *Dell'Historia Universale dell'Origine et Imperio de'Turchi*, 3 vols., Venice 1560.

Savant, Jean, *Les Mameloucks de Napoléon*, 1949.

[Sbornik], *Proceedings of the Imperial Russian History Society*, 148 vols., St-Petersburg 1867–1916.

Schepeler, Andreas von, *Histoire de la Revolution d'Espagne et du Portugal*, 3 vols., Liège 1829.

Schipa, Michelangelo, *Il Regno di Napoli al Tempo di Carlo di Borbone*, Naples 1904.

Schneider, Louis, *L'Empereur Guillaume*, 3 vols., 1888.

Schuster, O. and F.A. Francke, *Geschichte der Sächsischen Armee*, 3 vols., Leipzig 1885.

Schwoerer, Lois G., *No Standing Armies!*, 1974.

Scott, Samuel F., *The Response of the Royal Army to the French Revolution*, 1978.

Said, Mustapha, *Diatribe . . . sur l'Etat Actuel de l'Art Militaire du Génie et des Sciences à Constantinople*, 1810.

Shanahan, William O., *Prussian Military Reforms. 1786–1813*, New York 1945.

Shaw, Stanford J., 'The Origins of Ottoman Military Reform: the Nizam-i-Cedid Army of Sultan Selim III', *Journal of Modern History*, XXXVII, September 1965, pp. 291–305.

Shelley, Frances Lady, *Diary*, 1913.

Sheridan, Charles Francis, *A History of the Late Revolution in Sweden*, 1778.

Shuster, W. Morgan, *The Strangling of Persia*, 1912.

Simioni, Attilio, 'L'Esercito Napoletano dalla Minorità di Ferdinando alla Repubblica dell'1799', *Archivio Storico per le Provincie Napoletane*, XLV, 1920, pp. 88–109, 295–324.

*Sitwell, Sacheverell, *Truffle Hunt*, 1953.

Sked, Alan, *The Survival of the Habsburg Empire*, 1979.

*Soultrait, Gaspard-Richard de, 'Lettres', *Carnets de la Sabretache*, Série V, VI, 1923, pp. 406–34.

Speck, W.A., *The Butcher*, Oxford 1981.

Spiers, Edward M., *The Army and Society*, 1980.

Spiridovitch, General Alexandre, *Les Dernières Années de la Cour de Tzarskoie-Selo*, 2 vols., 1929.

Squires, P.S., *The Third Department*, Cambridge 1968.

Stahlberg, G.G., *A History of the Late Revolution in Sweden*, Edinburgh 1776.

Stanhope, Henry, *The Soldiers*, 1979.

Stedingk, Comte de, *Choix de Dépêches Diplomatiques, Rapports Secrets et Lettres Particulières de 1790 à 1796*, 2 vols., Stockholm 1919.

Stempel, John D., *Inside the Iranian Revolution*, Bloomington 1981.

*Stephenson, Sir F.C., *At Home and on the Battle-field*, 1915.

Stoffel, Colonel Baron, *Rapports Militaires Ecrits de Berlin. 1866–1870*, 1871.

Stone, Norman, *The Eastern Front*, 1975.

Strachey, Lytton and Roger Fulford eds., *The Greville Memoirs*, 8 vols., 1938.

*Sturler, Rudolph de., *Lettres à sa Famille*, Geneve 1916.

*Suckow, Colonel de, *Fragments de l'Histoire de ma Vie*, 1901.

Swenson, Victor R., 'The Military Rising in Istanbul 1909', *Journal of Contemporary History*, V, 4, 1970, pp. 171–84.

Talbot Rice, Tamara, *Elizabeth, Empress of Russia*, 1970.

Ten Raa, F.J.G., *Het Staatsche Leger. 1568–1795*, 8 vols., 'S Gravenhage, 1911–1959.

Teuber, Oscar, *Die Osterreichische Armee von 1700 bis 1867*, 2 vols., Vienna 1895–1904.

Thiry, Jean, *La Première Abdication*, 1939.

— *La Seconde Abdication*, 1945.

Thompson, I.A.A., *War and Government in Habsburg Spain*, 1976.

Thornton, Thomas, *The Present State of Turkey*, Second Edition, 2 vols., 1809.

Torta, Carlo, *La Rivoluzione Piemontese nel 1821*, Rome Milan 1908.

Trotter, Philip Durham, *Our Mission to the Court of Morocco in 1880*, Edinburgh 1881.

Tuetey, Louis, *Les Officiers sous l'Ancien Régime*, 1908.

Turgenev, A.I., *La Russie il y a Cent Ans*, Third Edition, Leipzig 1860.

Un Espagnol Témoin Oculaire, *Histoire de la Révolution d'Espagne de 1820 à 1823*, 2 vols., 1824.

V, G.G.D., *Letters on the Internal Political State of Spain During the Years 1821, 1822, and 1823*, 2 vols., 1824.

Vaissière, Pierre de, *De Quelques Assassins*, 1912.

Vallière, P. de, *Honneur et Fidelité. Histoire des Suisses au Service Etranger*, Lausanne n.d.

Vandal, Albert, *Louis XV et Elizabeth de Russie*, 1884.

Vanson, General, 'L'Infanterie Lorraine sous Louis XV', *Carnets de la Sabretache*, 1893, I, pp. 265–78, 369–86, 1894, II, pp. 40–48, 128–40, 193–202, 445–55, 530–44, 575–90.

Vassili, Paul, *La Sainte Russie*, 1890.

Veinstein, Gilles ed., *Mehmet Efendi. Le Paradis des Infidèles*, 1981.

Verbruggen, K.J.F., *The Art of Warfare in Western Europe during the Middle Ages*, Amsterdam 1972.

Victoria, Queen, *Leaves from a Journal*, 1961.

*Vigny, Alfred de, *Servitude et Grandeur Militaires*, n.d.

Viktoria Luise, Duchess of Brunswick, *Memoirs*, 1977.

Villars, Marquis de, *Mémoires sur la Cour d'Espagne de 1679 à 1681*, 1893.

*Villebresme, Chevalier de, *Souvenirs*, 1897.

*Volkov, Alexis, *Souvenirs*, 1928.

Voltaire, M. de, *Histoire de l'Empire de Russie sous Pierre le Grand*, 2 vols., 1759.

Vorres, Ian, *The Last Grand Duchess*, 1964.

Waite, Robert, G.L., *Vanguard of Nazism. The Freikorps Movement in Postwar Germany*, Cambridge Mass, 1952.

Waliszewski, K., *La Dernière des Romanov*, 1902.

— *Le Fils de la Grande Cathérine. Paul 1er*, 1912.

— *L'Héritage de Pierre le Grand*, 1900.

— *Pierre le Grand*, 1905.

Walton, W., *The Revolutions of Spain from 1808 to the End of 1836*, 2 vols., 1837.

*Wantage, Harriet S., *Lord Wantage V.C. A Memoir*, 1907.

*Watson, J.N.P., *Captain-General and Rebel Chief*, 1979.

Watson, Robert Grant, *A History of Persia from the Beginning of the Nineteenth Century to the Year 1858*, 1866.

Weissman, Nahoum, *Les Janissaires*, 1938.

Wellington, Duke of, *Supplementary Despatches*, 15 vols., 1858–1872.

— *Supplementary Despatches. New Series*, 8 vols., 1867–1883.

*Whitworth, Rex, *Field Marshal Lord Ligonier*, Oxford 1958.

Widdington, Captain, S.E., *Spain and the Spanish in 1843*, 2 vols., 1844.

Wilber, Donald, N., *Riza Shah Pahlavi*, Hicksville 1975.

Wildman, Allan K., *The End of the Russian Imperial Army*, Princeton 1980.

*Wilhelm II, *Letters to the Tsar*, ed. N.F. Grant, n.d.

*Wilhelm, Crown Prince of Germany, *Memoirs*, 1922.

Wilson, Sir Robert, *Brief Remarks on the Character and Composition of the Russian Army*, 1810.

*Windsor, Duke of, *A King's Story*, 1951.

*Woods, H.C., *Washed by Four Seas*, 1908.

*Wrangel, Baron N., *Memoirs*, 1927.

Wraxall, Lascelles, *The Armies of the Great Powers*, 1859.

Wright, Denis, *The English Among the Persians*, 1977.

Young, Peter, *Edgehill 1642. The Campaign and the Battle*, 1967.

Zadeh, Kemal Pacha, *Histoire de la Campagne de Mohacz*, 1859.

Zezon, Antonio, *Tippi Militari dei Differenti Corpi che Compangono il Reale Esercito e l'Armata di Mare di S.M. il Re del Regno delle due Sicilie*, Naples 1850.

Zolger, Ivan von, *Die Hofstaat des Hauses Habsburg*, Vienna 1917.
Zweguintsov, W., *L'Armée Russe*, 5 vols., 1964–1979.

III. INTERVIEWS

Abdul Karim, Major Suleiman, Jordan Royal Guard, 15 April 1981.
Adams-Cairns, Ruarailh, 3 February 1982.
Al-Adwani, Major Suleiman, Royal Guard Brigade, Oman, 25 April 1981.
Ali, Captain, Jordan Royal Guard, 15 April 1981.
Al-Sabah, Major-General Salim Mahmoud Al Jaber, Kuwait, 19 April 1981.
Amirsadeghi, Hossein, 21 December 1981.
Baddeley, Colonel, former British Defence Attache in Iran, 9 September 1981.
Ben Moubaraha, Colonel, Garde Royale, Morocco, 20 April 1983.
Ben Mansour, M. Historiographe du Royaume, Morocco, 15 April 1983.
Boggis-Rolfe, Richard, Coldstream Guards, 13 December 1981.
Briggs, Captain Jack, Dubai Police, 28 April 1981.
Caldwell David, Coldstream Guards, 21 June 1981.
Clayton, Peter, 17 June, 28 July 1981.
Chicano, Ortega, Guardia Real, Spain, 9 October 1981.
Courage, Major A., 21 August 1982.
Courtney, Colonel R., former British Defence Attache in Iran, 23 June 1981.
Cram-Andersen, Captain, Danish Life Guards, 20 June 1981.
Davy, Peter, tailor, 17 March 1983.
De Gaury, Gerald, 2 June 1982, 21 June 1983.
De Meer, Lt-Colonel, former officer of the Guard of His Excellency the Head of State, Spain, 28 September 1981.
Den Mamilla, Sa'ad, Jordan Honour Guard, 15 April 1981.
Dixon, Violet, 18 April 1981.
Doubentsoff, Colonel, former officer in the Cossack Guards of His Majesty, 8 May 1982, 24 March 1983.
El-Edroos, Brigadier, 12 April 1981.
Ellery, James, Sultan of Oman's Armed Forces, 4 January 1982.
Elwell, Charles, Grenadier Guards, 8 March 1982.
Fernandez de Mesa y Hoces, Commander, Guardia Real, Spain, 9 October 1981.
Gomez Guttierez Bueno, Lieutenant, Guardia Real, Spain, 9 October 1981.
Graham, Robert, 8 October 1981.
Herbert, Lance-Corporal, Welsh Guards, 6, 7 October 1981.
Herd, Frauke, 2 May 1981.
Hjorth-Anderson, U, Svea Livgarde, 24 June 1981.
Imperial Iranian Guard, a former officer of the, 20 March, 11 September, 27 December 1981.
Langley, Major-General Desmond, 2 March 1981, 2 February 1983.
Leese, Colonel Brian, former British Defence Attache in Saudi Arabia, 16 March 1981.
Lutfi, Lt-Colonel Musa S., Police Training School, Jordan, 15 April 1981.
McEvoy, Sergeant, Blues and Royals, 24 October 1982.
Mackie, James, former officer of the Blues and Royals and the Sultan's Armed Forces, 25 March 1982, 24 April 1983.
Manasir, Major Suleiman A., Royal Guard, Jordan, 15 April 1981.
Mirza Senator Wasfi, 13, 14 April 1981.
Oveissi, General, former Commander of the Imperial Iranian Guard, 24 March 1983.
Pfyffer d'Altishofen, Colonel F., Commander of the Pontifical Swiss Guard, 4 September 1982.
Salmain, Sayid, 30 April 1981.
S.A.S., a former officer in, Dubai, 27 April 1981.
Smiley, Colonel David, former officer of the Sultan's Armed Forced and Gentleman at Arms, 18 April 1982.
Smits, F.A.T., Royal Dutch Army Museum, 17 July 1982.
Shojai, Mr., 7 June 1981.
Shakerley, Major G. Irish Guards and Dubai Defence Force, 10 March, 25 May 1981.
Sultan's Armed Forces, an officer of the, 26 April 1981.
Thwaites, Brigadier Peter, Grenadier Guards and the Sultan's Armed Forces, 15, 23 June 1981.
Whyte-Spunner, Captain B., The Blues and Royals, 12, 24 November 1981.

INDEX

DATE DUE
